NATIONALITY AND STATELESSNESS IN EUROPE

"I wish there was a treaty we could sign..."
– Leonard Cohen, Treaty (2016)

Human Rights Research Series, Volume 97.

The titles published in this series are listed at the end of this volume.

Nationality and Statelessness in Europe

European Law on Preventing and Solving Statelessness

Caia Vlieks

INTERSENTIA
Antwerpen – Gent – Cambridge

Intersentia Ltd
8 Wellington Mews | Wellington Street
Cambridge | CB1 1HW | United Kingdom
Tel.: +44 1223 736 170
Email: mail@intersentia.co.uk
www.intersentia.com | www.intersentia.co.uk

Distribution for the UK and the rest of the world (incl. Eastern Europe):
NBN International
1 Deltic Avenue, Rooksley
Milton Keynes MK13 8LD
United Kingdom
Tel.: +44 1752 202 301 | Fax: +44 1752 202 331
Email: orders@nbninternational.com

Distribution for Europe:
Lefebvre Sarrut Belgium NV
Hoogstraat 139/6
1000 Brussels
Belgium
Tel.: +32 3 680 15 50 | Fax: +32 3 658 71 21
Email: mail@intersentia.be

Distribution for the USA and Canada:
Independent Publishers Group
Order Department
814 North Franklin Street
Chicago, IL60610
USA
Tel.: +1 800 888 4741 (toll free) | Fax: +1312 337 5985
Email: orders@ipgbook.com

Nationality and Statelessness in Europe. European Law on Preventing and Solving Statelessness

Cover design by Danny Juchtmans / www.dsigngraphics.be
Photo by Hal Gatewood on Unsplash

ISBN 978-1-83970-261-7 (paperback)
ISBN 978-1-83970-262-4 (PDF)
D/2022/7849/68

British Library Cataloguing in Publication Data. A catalogue record for this book is available from the British Library.

LIST OF ABBREVIATIONS AND ACRONYMS

1930 Hague Convention	Convention on Certain Questions relating to the Conflict of Nationality Laws
1933 Montevideo Convention	Montevideo Convention on Rights and Duties of States
1951 Convention	Convention relating to the Status of Refugees
1954 Convention	Convention relating to the Status of Stateless Persons
1957 Convention	Convention on the Nationality of Married Women
1961 Convention	Convention on the Reduction of Statelessness
ACERWC	African Committee of Experts on the Rights and Welfare of the Child
ACFC	Advisory Committee on the Framework Convention for the Protection of National Minorities (CoE)
ACHPR	African Charter on Human and Peoples' Rights
ACHR	American Convention on Human Rights
ACmHPR	African Commission on Human and Peoples' Rights
ACRWC	African Charter on the Rights and Welfare of the Child
ACtHPR	African Court on Human and Peoples' Rights
ArCHR	Arab Charter on Human Rights
ASEAN	Association of Southeast Asian Nations
AU	African Union
Banjul Charter	*See ACHPR*
BRP	Basisregistratie Personen (Dutch Basic Registration of Persons)
CCPR	UN Human Rights Committee
CDCJ	European Committee on Legal Co-operation
CDL	European Commission for Democracy through Law, *see also VC*
CEAS	Common European Asylum System
CEDAW	Convention on the Elimination of All Forms of Discrimination against Women
CETS	Council of Europe Treaty Series
CIS	Commonwealth of Independent States
CJ-DAM	Committee of Experts on Administrative Detention of Migrants (CoE)

CJ-NA	Committee of Experts on Nationality (CoE)
CJ-NA GT	Committee of Experts on Nationality Working Party (CoE)
CJ-PL	Committee of Experts on Multiple Nationality (CoE)
CJ-S-NAT	Group of Specialists on Nationality (CoE)
CJEU	Court of Justice of the European Union
CM	Committee of Ministers of the Council of Europe
CoE	Council of Europe
CRC	Convention on the Rights of the Child
CRCI	Covenant on the Rights of the Child in Islam
CRPD	Convention on the Rights of Persons with Disabilities
EC	European Commission (EU)
ECHR	European Convention on Human Rights / European Convention for the Protection of Human Rights and Fundamental Freedoms
ECN	European Convention on Nationality
ECOSOC	Economic and Social Council
ECRE	European Council on Refugees and Exiles
ECRI	European Commission against Racism and Intolerance (CoE)
ECSC	European Coal and Steel Community
ECSS	Council of Europe Convention on the Avoidance of Statelessness in relation to State Succession
ECtHR	European Court of Human Rights
EEC	European Economic Community
EMN	European Migration Network
ENS	European Network on Statelessness
EP	European Parliament (EU)
ERRC	European Roma Rights Centre
ERT	Equal Rights Trust
EU	European Union
EU Charter	Charter of Fundamental Rights of the European Union
Euratom	European Atomic Energy Community
FCNM	Framework Convention for the Protection of National Minorities
FRA	European Union Agency for Fundamental Rights
HO	Home Office (UK)
IACtHR	Inter-American Court of Human Rights
ICCPR	International Covenant on Civil and Political Rights
ICERD	International Convention on the Elimination of All Forms of Racial Discrimination
ICESCR	International Covenant on Economic, Social and Cultural Rights

ICJ	International Court of Justice
ICMW	International Convention on the Protection of the Rights of All Migrant Workers and Members of their Families
IGCR	Intergovernmental Committee on Refugees
ILC	International Law Commission
ILEC	Involuntary Loss of European Citizenship
IPU	Inter-Parliamentary Union
IRO	International Refugee Organisation
ISI	Institute on Statelessness and Inclusion
LAS	League of Arab States
LoN	League of Nations
MEP	Member of European Parliament (EU)
NGO	Non-governmental organization
OAS	Organization of American States
OAU	Organisation of African Unity
OIC	Organisation of Islamic Cooperation
OSCE	Organization for Security and Co-operation in Europe
PACE	Parliamentary Assembly of the Council of Europe
PCIJ	Permanent Court of International Justice
Refugee Convention	*See 1951 Convention*
SDG	Sustainable Development Goal
SFRY	Socialist Federal Republic of Yugoslavia
Statelessness Conventions	*See 1954 Convention and 1961 Convention*
TCN	Third-country national (EU)
TEU	Treaty on European Union
TFEU	Treaty on the Functioning of the European Union
UDHR	Universal Declaration of Human Rights
UK	United Kingdom
UN	United Nations
UNGA	United Nations General Assembly
UNHCR	(Office of the) United Nations High Commissioner for Refugees
UNRWA	United Nations Relief and Works Agency for Palestine Refugees in the Near East
UPR	Universal Periodic Review
USSR	Union of Soviet Socialist Republics
VC	Venice Commission, *see also CDL*

ACKNOWLEDGEMENTS

Writing a dissertation is a transformative process, which – for me – could not have resulted in this book without the help and support of many people. Given the length of my PhD trajectory, a lot of inspiring people have crossed my path, and the list below may therefore be incomplete. To all of those who are not mentioned explicitly: I am very much obliged to you for any kind words or feedback, and genuine interest in me and my project!

First and foremost, I want to thank my supervisors: Professor Ernst Hirsch Ballin and Dr Laura van Waas. Ernst, I have always very much enjoyed our collaboration, whether that was in the context of my dissertation, or with regard to education and other research. Assisting you with some of your research has been an eye-opening experience, and provided an important background to further developing my thoughts on nationality and statelessness. I am really grateful for your encouragement, insightful comments and for our in-depth discussions on these topics!

Laura, honestly, I am not even sure where to start. It has been more than ten years since we started to work together on the topic of statelessness, which has allowed me to understand statelessness as a phenomenon in ways that I could not have imagined when I first heard about it as a law student. Throughout it all, I have really appreciated your positive spirit, guidance and eye for opportunities. I am so thankful for your practical, clear and critical comments on my work, and our continued fantastic cooperation.

During my time at Tilburg University, I have met amazing colleagues, who have been supportive in many ways. I remember the lovely chats over tea – still reminded of Karin's words about my tea: "Caia, dat is geen thee.. Dat is water met een kleurtje!" – or helpful conversations about course development, teaching, research, that article deadline, and so on. My thanks go to Anna, Anne, Annelieke, Conny, Eva, Gerhard, Giel, Han, Helen, Hervé, Jurgen, Karin, Loet, Maria, Maurice, Michiel, Paul, Philip, Tjebbe, amongst others. Teaching different courses through the years and supervising various research conducted by students, I have also drawn insights from the discussions with them. I am appreciative of the work of Eline and Simone in particular, whose research as part of their Top Class-program was directly relevant to this project.

I am indebted to my colleagues at the Institute on Statelessness and Inclusion for their constant support as well. Dear Amal, Alena, Deneisha, Georgia, Mark, Natalie, Stefania and Vera, you are an absolute inspiration and star team. I cannot wait to see to what new and exciting level we will be able to take our work together next!

The field of statelessness research has been growing in the past years, and during that time, I have met many wonderful people and experts in the field. I am so pleased that a number of them are part of my PhD committee and thankful for the time they have invested in this. I also want to express my gratitude to Chris, Katja, Marlotte and Tamás for the terrific collaboration over the years and I look forward to new opportunities to work together in the future.

Special words of thanks go out to my paranymphs: Alice and Sangita. Alice, you and I have had some great adventures, starting already when we were students in the Top Class! And Sangita, you and I worked together on the first bit of in-depth research I did on statelessness in the Netherlands and it has been great having you as a roommate at the office. You both have been part of my PhD journey since the beginning and I have been able to lean on you both for discussions about my research and the overall trajectory, as well as for fun distraction from it all. Thank you so much!

Many other friends have also been an incredibly supportive and have offered a sometimes much-needed break from the research and work. A big shout-out especially to Lotte, all the ladies of 'het Tilburgs vriendinnenclubje', Joeri (and JAM as a whole of course!), Ilona and Roderick. I anticipate many more spectacular dinners, lunches, walks in the park, music quizzes, weekend trips, board games, ballet and theater visits, cat showdowns, boat rides, shopping sessions, barbecues and high wines in the future.

My deep and sincere gratitude go to my family for their continuous love, help and support. It has been through them that I was first introduced to nationality questions, inspiring me to pursue this further. I have always enjoyed and continue to look forward to spending a day at 'de berg' in Sjlennich with all of you!

Finally, there are no words that can describe how much I have depended on my two guys while writing this dissertation. Kees and Loki, I continue to depend on you – you're simply the best!

Caia Vlieks, 3 January 2022

CONTENTS

List of Abbreviations and Acronyms v
Acknowledgements ix

PART I.
INTRODUCTION AND CONTEXT 1

Chapter 1. Introduction 3

1.1. Research questions and approach 5
1.2. Research methods and sources 7
1.3. Relevance 8
1.4. Conceptual framework 10
 1.4.1. Statelessness 10
 1.4.2. Nationality and citizenship 15
 1.4.3. Nationality, statelessness and administration 21
 1.4.4. European lawmaking and European law 25
1.5. Analytical framework: first steps 27
 1.5.1. International law on nationality and the reduction of statelessness 27
  The 1930 Hague Convention and the UDHR (1948) 27
  Refugees and the stateless (1951–1961) 30
  UN human rights treaties (1965–2006) 34
  State succession 42
 1.5.2. Other regional instruments (1969–2018) 43
 1.5.3. Analytical framework 47
1.6. Concluding remarks 49

Chapter 2. Europe and Statelessness 51

2.1. Introduction 52
2.2. 19th-century Europe 55
2.3. World War I and its aftermath 60
2.4. World War II 70
2.5. (Re)building Europe and nationality matters 76
2.6. The end of the Cold War: a new Europe? 77
2.7. Statelessness in Europe today 82
2.8. Conclusion 89

PART II.
EUROPEAN LAW ON NATIONALITY AND STATELESSNESS 93

Chapter 3. The Council of Europe 95

3.1. Introduction 95
3.2. The Council of Europe and nationality matters: instruments, actors and trends 97
3.2.1. Introduction 97
3.2.2. Nationality and statelessness 101
1963 Convention on the Reduction of Cases of Multiple Nationality and on Military Obligations in Cases of Multiple Nationality 101
European Convention on Nationality 104
Convention on the Avoidance of Statelessness in Relation to State Succession 109
Other instruments on nationality and statelessness 112
3.2.3. Human rights and minority protection 118
European Convention on Human Rights 119
Framework Convention for the Protection of National Minorities. 121
Other relevant instruments on human rights and minority protection 123
3.2.4. Concluding remarks 126
3.3. Preventing and solving statelessness 126
3.3.1. Childhood statelessness 127
3.3.2. Conflicts of nationality law, loss and deprivation of nationality 134
3.3.3. State succession 144
3.3.4. Acquisition of nationality 150
3.3.5. Non-discrimination 155
3.3.6. Concluding remarks 160
3.4. Conclusion: the Council of Europe's contribution to the legal conception of nationality 163

Chapter 4. The European Union 167

4.1. Introduction 167
4.2. The EU and nationality matters: instruments, actors and trends 168
4.2.1. Introduction 168
4.2.2. European citizenship 173
4.2.3. Migration and asylum policy 182
4.2.4. Fundamental rights 189
4.2.5. Other legal instruments 193
4.2.6. Concluding remarks 194
4.3. Preventing and solving statelessness 194

4.3.1. Childhood statelessness 195
4.3.2. Conflicts of nationality law, loss and deprivation of nationality 202
4.3.3. State succession 205
4.3.4. Acquisition of nationality 207
4.3.5. Non-discrimination 211
4.3.6. Concluding remarks 216
4.4. Conclusion: the EU's contribution to the legal conception of nationality 218

PART III.
CONCLUSIONS AND REFLECTIONS 221

Chapter 5. Comparison and Analysis 223

5.1. Introduction 223
5.2. Human rights analysis and norms: findings 224
5.3. Frameworks: findings 228
5.4. Conclusion 230

Chapter 6. Discussion and Conclusions 231

6.1. Introduction 231
6.2. Discussion: the concept of nationality 231
6.3. Conclusion 235
6.4. Final reflections and recommendations 237

Annexes 239

Annex I. Schematic overview of relevant provisions from international and other regional instruments in different substantive categories on preventing and solving statelessness 241
Annex II. Schematic overview of legal instruments of the Council of Europe and the European Union in different substantive categories on preventing and solving statelessness 243

Summary 245
Samenvatting (Nederlands) 251
Bibliography 257

PART I
INTRODUCTION AND CONTEXT

CHAPTER 1
INTRODUCTION

"To be without documents and a nationality is as if you never existed in this world."
– Isa, a stateless person from Former Yugoslavia and currently living in Serbia[1]

The world today is divided into (nation-)states, making belonging to – and being able to enter, reside in, and leave – a state important. To prove and legally qualify the bond between a person and a state, the legal concept of nationality, legal rules on acquiring and losing nationality, and the passport were introduced.[2] Nationality has become an instrument for states to build nations, and to exercise power and control over their citizens, and also (by default) over non-citizens and questions of migration. Nationality, in this regard, could be a compelling reward for loyalty to the state. Nationality or citizenship is also a way for citizens to be part of society and co-decide on matters that concern them – in democratic states at least. At the same time, some people have been excluded from nationality, left out, or forgotten by this system. They remain disenfranchised, without any nationality, stateless.

Statelessness is a fascinating legal anomaly. It is an entirely manmade problem, which is created by the law. Statelessness is, however, not only a legal problem. It is also a human (rights) problem.[3] As the above quote from a stateless person illustrates, to be stateless means having no nationality whatsoever and often possessing no documents to prove your identity. It can make a person feel as if he or she is invisible. Statelessness can indeed have grave consequences for the person involved, including problems with accessing some of the most basic human rights. Many stateless people are unable to access health care and education, to get married, to find work, to travel or to vote, or experience difficulties in this regard. This makes it very hard for most stateless people to fully participate in society.

This human (rights) problem should be enough to compel states to acknowledge that statelessness is an issue that deserves their attention, but a state perspective on the matter also brings up other considerations. Large numbers of stateless people can be

---

1 European Network on Statelessness (ENS), 'Still Stateless, Still Suffering. Why Europe Must Act Now to Protect Stateless Persons' (ENS 2014) <www.statelessness.eu/sites/www.statelessness.eu/files/ENS_Still_Stateless_Still_Suffering_online%20version_2.pdf> accessed 22 August 2021.

2 Cf John Torpey, *The Invention of the Passport. Surveillance, Citizenship and the State* (Cambridge Studies in Law and Society, Cambridge University Press 2000).

3 Carol A Batchelor, 'Statelessness and the Problem of Resolving Nationality Status' (1998) 10 International Journal of Refugee Law 156, 159.

considered as undesirable, because it could potentially destabilize the system of states and societies of citizens that has been built: it may create or worsen "international tensions and disorder" and could challenge states' "ability to control and order their subject populations".[4] Indeed, Dutch parliamentarians, for instance, recognized back in 1953 that "nationality provisions are not only important for the order of our society and our state, but also are important to the order of the society of peoples".[5]

From a (formalistic) legal perspective, it would seem that statelessness is entirely preventable and solvable if proper laws were enacted to address it. The Office of the United Nations High Commissioner for Refugees (UNHCR) reports a global number of 4.2 million stateless people, but recognizes that the actual number is much higher, because "UNHCR does not have any information on stateless populations for most of the world's countries".[6] It is estimated that more than 10[7] to 15[8] million people worldwide are stateless today. The statistics that have currently been collected with regard to statelessness grapple with methodological difficulties in mapping the issue, as well as gaps in data. With still millions of people stateless around the globe today, but without a clear picture of the magnitude of the problem, it seems evident that statelessness is not as easily prevented or solved as one might think. At the same time, the human (rights) side of the issue highlights the need and importance of ensuring the human rights of stateless people, as well as finding solutions to the issue.

Important to finding solutions to statelessness is nationality: to be stateless means to be without any nationality. Statelessness and nationality are thus closely related – they are opposites by definition and represent two sides of the same coin. Statelessness is therefore a lens to better understand the concept of nationality, or citizenship. Nationality, or citizenship, is a concept with many dimensions, which has different forms and perspectives to it.[9] These are often interconnected with what nationality means to people and to the state. It is therefore likely that statelessness cannot be solved using only legal norms. As such, this study tries to provide a comprehensive picture of nationality and preventing and solving statelessness, also

---

4 Matthew J Gibney, 'Statelessness and Citizenship in Ethical and Political Perspective' in Alice Edwards and Laura van Waas (eds), *Nationality and Statelessness under International Law* (Cambridge University Press 2014) 44–63, 49–52.

5 Translated from: "nationaliteitsvoorzieningen niet alleen van betekenis zijn voor het bestel van onze maatschappij en van onze staat, maar ook betekenis hebben voor de orde van de samenleving der volkeren" (transl CV). This statement was made in the context of a discussion on provisions to address statelessness in Dutch Parliament, *Handelingen II* 1952/53, 17 April 1953, 2251.

6 UNHCR, 'Global Trends. Forced Displacement in 2020' (UNHCR 2021) 50 <https://www.unhcr.org/60b638e37/unhcr-global-trends-2020> accessed 22 August 2021.

7 Eg UNHCR, 'UNHCR Statistical Reporting on Statelessness' (UNHCR Statistics Technical Series 2019/1) <https://www.unhcr.org/statistics/unhcrstats/5d9e182e7/unhcr-statistical-reporting-statelessness.html> accessed 22 August 2021.

8 Institute on Statelessness and Inclusion (ISI), *The World's Stateless* (Wolf Legal Publishers 2014) <https://www.institutesi.org/worldsstateless.pdf> accessed 22 August 2021.

9 Cf Ayelet Shachar, Rainer Bauböck, Irene Bloemraad & Maarten Vink (eds), *The Oxford Handbook of Citizenship* (Oxford University Press 2017).

moving beyond the law.[10] It does so by focusing on the region that constitutes the cradle of modern conceptions of nationality: Europe. It sketches the background and context, before providing a deeper analysis of legal norms that have been enacted at a regional level to address statelessness, aiming to understand what is truly needed to prevent and solve statelessness. In doing so, this research adds a statelessness perspective to the broader discussions on nationality and citizenship, which contributes to understanding these concepts.

1.1. RESEARCH QUESTIONS AND APPROACH

In light of the above, this research explores and attempts to understand the legal and political approaches that states have taken together, at the regional level – in Europe, to address statelessness. In particular, this study considers the role that European law[11] can play in preventing and solving statelessness in Europe. This means that this study of statelessness is narrowed down in two ways: in the geographical sense, focusing on Europe; and as regards the topic or aspects of statelessness that it concerns – preventing and solving statelessness. The European context, as we will see, provides an interesting and specific context to study nationality and statelessness questions, given its historical development and its political and legal cooperation. The issue of statelessness is not new to the continent and questions around protection of stateless people and statelessness determination have been researched already. At the same time, there has – to date – not been a comprehensive mapping of European legal instruments that address preventing and solving statelessness, and thereby, nationality matters, through a statelessness lens. This dissertation therefore also aims to make a contribution to better understanding the concept of nationality, or citizenship, by examining what the current approaches to preventing and solving statelessness in European law tell us about (the content of) the current conception of nationality. Hence, the main research question of this project is as follows:

> *How does European law contribute to preventing and solving statelessness in Europe and what does this contribution add to the understanding of nationality today?*

This research question defines this research's approach, which is to first identify and analyze how European laws address the prevention of and solutions to statelessness. After having gained an understanding of Europe's legal instruments for addressing statelessness, which includes any good practices or new developments as well as gaps in the legal framework, an examination of these norms, to better understand what

---

10 Please note that this research was completed 3 January 2022.

11 The notion of 'European law' in the context of this research is considered further in para 1.4.4 of this chapter.

nationality means, follows. In order to answer the aforementioned main question, the following sub questions are considered:

A. What is the distinctive (European) context in which European law concerning the prevention of and solutions to statelessness operates?
B. How does European law made by the Council of Europe (CoE) contribute to preventing and solving statelessness in Europe?
C. How does European law made by the European Union (EU) contribute to preventing and solving statelessness in Europe?
D. What does European law on preventing and solving statelessness contribute to the broader understanding of nationality in Europe?

In this first chapter, the research design is further outlined. In particular, attention is paid to the research questions, research methods and sources, definitions of key concepts, relevance of the research, and the analytical framework for this study. The latter includes the international legal context in which the European legal instruments need to be understood. Chapter 2 of this dissertation aims to gain a better understanding of the 'real-world' European context in which European law on preventing and solving statelessness is operating. It does so by exploring the causes and responses to statelessness in European history, starting from some decades before World War I – given the developments that led to large-scale emergence of statelessness in that period – until now, in order to understand the current situation with regard to this issue in Europe. Chapter 2, together with section 1.5 of this chapter, provides an answer to sub question A.

Chapters 1 and 2 make up Part I of this book: introduction and context. Together, these two chapters demonstrate the involvement of European states in the development of both international and European norms relating to statelessness and nationality matters. Chapter 1 highlights – as part of this book's analytical framework – how the right to a nationality is legally interpreted at the international level and in other regions of the world. In chapter 2, we zoom in on context and the historical and factual reasons for the development of legal standards on statelessness at the European level. The question here is which factors – in addition to the legal ones, i.e. the right to a nationality as laid down in international and human rights law and the way in which this is given substance – are relevant to preventing and solving statelessness. Chapter 2 thus considers the differences between the problems that exist(ed) 'on the ground' with regard to statelessness and nationality and the legal responses, in which politics of course play an important role.

Part II then continues from that and examines the legal interpretation of the right to a nationality by the two important European cooperation mechanisms: the CoE and the EU. Chapter 3 consists of identifying and analyzing the legal norms on preventing and solving statelessness of the CoE, thus answering sub question B. Chapter 4 considers the legal instruments of the EU that could contribute to preventing and solving statelessness, which answers sub question C. The conclusions of the two chapters in Part II also draw on the analysis in those chapters to indicate what the respective organizations' legal instruments offer to understanding the concept of nationality. Hence, sub question D is to some extent included here as well.

Part III of this book presents comparisons, reflections, conclusions and recommendations. Chapter 5 concentrates on identifying how European law contributes to preventing and solving statelessness in Europe (part of main question) by comparing the efforts of the CoE and the EU while also considering international (human rights) law. Chapter 6 concludes with final observations on how all of this furthers our understanding of the concept of nationality (sub question D and main question) and some recommendations and reflections on preventing and solving statelessness in Europe.

1.2. RESEARCH METHODS AND SOURCES

The method and approach applied primarily in this project is that of doctrinal and critical legal research, because this study aims to research the way in which the position of individuals in the (nation-)state system has been legally categorized and defined using nationality and statelessness. It therefore considers the tensions between practice and law. Law is an expression of power relations, and this study critiques these power relations. This means that relevant legal instruments, case law, and other legal sources are systematized and analyzed while considering legal theory. However, the historical background and today's reality in which these legal instruments operate is taken into account where possible and relevant. Furthermore, and therefore, this research involves literature study of secondary sources from academic authors, which are assessed critically for their relevance and "precise and accurate fit" with the research question.[12] As a complementary source, (policy) reports of organizations such as UNHCR[13], as well as of non-governmental organizations (NGOs) are used.

Throughout this book, national laws of certain countries are sometimes used to demonstrate the implementation of certain treaty obligations, or to otherwise illustrate practice in nationality matters and the development thereof at the national level. These should be treated as examples and illustrations based on national legal practice, which aim to contribute to a better understanding of the issues and legal instruments discussed, looking beyond legal constructs and considering impacts to some extent.[14]

---

12 Marnix Snel, *Meester(s) over bronnen. Een empirische studie naar kwaliteitseisen, gevaren en onderzoekstechnieken die betrekking hebben op het brongebruik in academisch juridisch-dogmatisch onderzoek [Master(s on) resources]* (Boom juridisch 2016) 190–191.

13 UNHCR is of particular relevance to this research, because it has an official mandate with regard to the issue. This is explored further in para 1.5.1 (under the header 'Refugees and the stateless').

14 The importance of doing this in human rights related research is highlighted in Siobhán McInerney-Lankford, Legal Methodologies and Human Rights Research: Challenges and Opportunities' in Bård

They do not present a systematic comparative study of national laws, which would go beyond the scope of this project.

In this chapter, and partly in chapter 2, an analytical framework is established to consider the different norms in European law for preventing and solving statelessness. This framework is established by exploring the right to a nationality and other norms addressing statelessness in international (human rights) law. Relevant (human rights) standards of other regional frameworks and mechanisms for intergovernmental cooperation are also included. From this, some lines or broader categories for considering the prevention of and solutions to statelessness are drawn. These serve as a way to systematize and categorize the legal norms in European law, and also increase the comparability of the findings in chapter 3 on the CoE and chapter 4 on the EU. Chapter 2 provides the necessary context and gives an insight into the (historical) background to statelessness in the region and the context in which the European cooperation mechanisms and the norms addressing statelessness and nationality were enacted and currently still operate. This helps to further delineate and confirm the analytical framework established for analyzing and systematizing European law in the following chapters. It is also key in working towards the conclusions in chapters 5 and 6, because it adds to the critical dimension if this research, as well as to its explorative nature – "[r]elating legal research to the ongoing nature of [processes in which existing rules are reinterpreted and new rules formulated], and asking which interpretations, additions and changes may become part of these processes".[15] As such, this research systematizes the relevant law, but also critically analyzes and compares it, placing it in a social-historical perspective and exploring strengths and weaknesses.

1.3. RELEVANCE

Statelessness is considered an 'issue' or 'problem' from different perspectives, as could be seen at the start of this chapter, not least from a societal perspective. Stateless people often lack the rights and ability to truly be part of society. This dissertation, aimed at studying prevention of and solutions to statelessness, can therefore be of relevance in addressing the position of stateless people in society and help to identify ways for ensuring their full participation. Furthermore, the issues surrounding nationality – who is included in society and is given the status, i.e. nationality, to prove it and who is not – are today constantly visible in public debate. An example is the matter of stripping jihadists of citizenship, to which some states in Europe have (re)turned as a national security measure discussed throughout Europe to prevent terrorism.[16] The

A Andreassen, Hans-Otto Sano & Siobhán McInerney-Lankford (eds), *Research Methods in Human Rights. A Handbook* (Handbooks of Research Methods in Law, Edward Elgar Publishing 2018) 48–50.

15 Ernst Hirsch Ballin, *Advanced Introduction to Legal Research Methods* (Elgar Advanced Introductions, Edward Elgar 2020) 87.

16 Eg Sangita Jaghai & Laura van Waas, 'Stripped of Citizenship, Stripped of Dignity? A Critical Exploration of Nationality Deprivation as a Counter-Terrorism Measure' in Christophe Paulussen &

contribution that this study intends to make on the concept of nationality or citizenship from a human rights perspective on preventing and solving statelessness in Europe can therefore be of interest to this more general societal debate on nationality and its contemporary meaning and limits.

In academic (legal) debate and on the human rights agenda, statelessness is no longer a novelty or 'forgotten' issue.[17] However, it is at the same time not as established and well-researched as, for instance, the plight of refugees. As such, this dissertation adds to the state of the art on the issue of statelessness. In particular, it makes a new contribution by specifically focusing on European law on preventing and solving statelessness. No such comprehensive analysis has so far been conducted on this specific topic, even if we have seen different publications focusing on statelessness in Europe.[18] Furthermore, this study aims to contribute to theories on and conceptions of nationality and citizenship – concepts that remain under discussion in academic circles from different perspectives.[19] With the specific focus on preventing and solving

---

Martin Scheinin (eds), *Human Dignity and Human Security in Times of Terrorism* (T.M.C. Asser Press 2020) Ch 8; Gerard-René de Groot & Olivier Vonk, 'Jihad en ontneming van nationaliteit. Nederlandse plannen in vergelijkend perspectief' in Pauline Kruiniger (ed), Recht van de Islam 30: 'Jihad, islam en recht: jihadisme en reacties vanuit het Nederlandse en Belgische recht' (Boom juridische uitgevers 2017); Patrick Wautelet, 'Deprivation of citizenship for 'jihadists'. Analysis of Belgian and French practice and policy in light of the principle of equal treatment' in Pauline Kruiniger (ed), Recht van de Islam 30: 'Jihad, islam en recht: jihadisme en reacties vanuit het Nederlandse en Belgische recht' (Boom juridische uitgevers 2017).

17 Cf Laura van Waas, "Are We There Yet?' Emergence of Statelessness on the International Human Rights Agenda' (2014) 32 Netherlands Quarterly of Human Rights 342; Tamás Molnár, 'Remembering the Forgotten: International Legal Regime on Protecting the Stateless Persons – Stocktaking and New Tendencies' (2014) 11 US-China Law Review 822.

18 Many commentaries focus either on protection of stateless people, on specific issues relating to statelessness (discrimination, minorities) or stateless groups, or focus for instance on (the) EU (law) solely. eg Laura van Waas, 'Statelessness: A 21st Century Challenge for Europe' (2009) 20 Security and Human Rights 133; Caroline Sawyer & Brad K Blitz, *Statelessness in the European Union. Displaced, Undocumented, Unwanted* (Cambridge University Press 2011); Jessica Parra, 'Stateless Roma in the European Union: Reconciling the Doctrine of Sovereignty concerning Nationality Laws with International Agreements to Reduce and Avoid Statelessness' (2011) 34 Fordham International Law Journal 1666; Claude Cahn, 'Minorities, Statelessness and Citizenship in Europe' (2012) 14 European Journal of Migration and Law 297; Gábor Gyulai, 'Statelessness in the EU Framework for International Protection' (2012) 14 European Journal of Migration and Law 279; Laura van Waas, 'Fighting Statelessness and Discriminatory Nationality Laws in Europe' (2012) 14 European Journal on Migration and Law 243; Olivier Vonk, Maarten Vink & Gerard-René de Groot, 'Protection Against Statelessness: Trends and Regulations in Europe' (GLOBALCIT, EUDO Citizenship Observatory, Country Reports, 2013/01) <http://cadmus.eui.eu//handle/1814/30201> accessed 22 August 2021; Katja Swider & Maarten den Heijer, ' Why Union Law Can and Should Protect Stateless Persons' (2017) 19 European Journal of Migration and Law 101.

19 Eg T Alexander Aleinikoff & Douglas Klusmeyer (eds), *Citizenship Today. Global Perspectives and Practices* (Carnegie Endowment for International Peace 2001); Christian Joppke, 'Transformation of Citizenship: Status, Rights, Identity' (2007) 11 Citizenship Studies 37; Ernst Hirsch Ballin, *Citizens' Rights and the Right to Be a Citizen* (Developments in International Law Vol 66, Brill Nijhoff 2014); Audrey Macklin, 'Sticky Citizenship' in Rhoda E Howard-Hassmann & Margaret Walton-Roberts (eds) *The Human Right to Citizenship. A Slippery Concept* (University of Pennsylvania Press 2015); Rainer Bauböck (ed), *Debating Transformations of National Citizenship* (IMISCOE Research Series, SpringerOpen 2018).

statelessness, this research provides another, not yet elaborately explored view on the concept of nationality or citizenship that adds to the existing body of knowledge, as its main focus is addressing the lack of nationality from a European perspective. With Europe being the cradle of modern conceptions of nationality, it also where statelessness originates from. At the same time, Europe has no explicit right to a nationality in its legal instruments, which makes for an interesting case study of how the issue has been addressed.

1.4. CONCEPTUAL FRAMEWORK

In the above research questions and throughout this book, a number of central concepts are used. The below exploration offers a first look at these key concepts, explaining and defining them.

1.4.1. STATELESSNESS

A stateless person has been defined in international law as "a person who is not considered as a national by any state under the operation of its law".[20] This definition is also considered to be part of international customary law.[21] As this is a legal study of statelessness, this definition is also used in this research. The definition is not without its ambiguities. The phrase 'not considered as a national … under the operation of its law' could mean the factual refusal of recognizing a person as a national or a legal situation that denies a person recognition as a citizen.[22] Further guidance on how to interpret the definition of statelessness in the Convention relating to the Status of Stateless Persons (1954 Convention) has been provided by UNHCR[23], which has a global mandate on statelessness.[24] This Handbook provides interpretation of the terms 'by any state' and 'not considered as a national … under the operation of its law', and

20 Art 1(1) Convention relating to the Status of Stateless Persons (adopted 28 September 1954, entered into force 6 June 1960) 360 UNTS 117 (1954 Convention).

21 International Law Commission (ILC), 'Draft Articles on Diplomatic Protection (with Commentaries)' in UNGA, Supplement No. 10: Report of the International Law Commission, 58th Session (2006) A/61/10, 49.

22 Cf ISI, *The World's Stateless* (Wolf Legal Publishers 2014) 40–41 <https://www.institutesi.org/worldsstateless.pdf> accessed 22 August 2021.

23 UNHCR, 'Handbook on the Protection of Stateless Persons under the 1954 Convention relating to the Status of Stateless Persons' (Geneva, 2014) <www.unhcr.org/protection/statelessness/53b698ab9/handbook-protection-stateless-persons.html> accessed 2 August 2021.

24 UNHCR was given a specific mandate on stateless by the United Nations General Assembly (UNGA). See UNGA Res 428 (Fifth Session, 14 December 1950) 46, UNGA Res 50/152 (1995) A/RES/50/152, UNGA Res 61/137 (2006) A/RES/61/137. See also Mark Manly, 'UNHCR's Mandate and Activities to Address Statelessness' in Alice Edwards & Laura van Waas (eds), *Nationality and Statelessness under International Law* (Cambridge University Press 2014) 88–115. See also para 1.5.1 (under the header 'Refugees and the stateless') of this chapter.

considers statelessness determination and procedures to that end in more depth. What is also important to note, is that an individual is stateless according to the definition in international law "from the moment that the conditions in Article 1(1) of the 1954 Convention are met".[25] Finding that an individual is stateless is hence a declaratory (and not a constitutive) act.

Statelessness around the world has different causes, which can manifest themselves at birth or later in the life of an individual or of entire groups of people. These causes can be generally considered to fit within one (or more) of the following categories: conflicts of nationality laws, state succession, the legacy of colonization, arbitrary and discriminatory deprivation of nationality, administrative barriers and lack of documentation, and inheritance of statelessness.[26] In light of the focus of this study on Europe, the causes of statelessness are more elaborately discussed for Europe in chapter 2.

The definition of statelessness used in this research follows the definition in the 1954 Convention and thus in principle only refers to persons who are *de jure* statelessness. This means that this research focuses on those who are legally stateless – without a legal bond to any state (and therefore without protection of a state). *De jure* statelessness can be distinguished from *de facto* statelessness, which refers to the situation of persons that are factually *(de facto)* without legal protection by a state, but do, legally speaking, have a nationality, i.e. a legal bond with a state. In a way, their nationality is thus not effective. A group that is often referred to as being *de facto* stateless are refugees. A specific international legal regime is applicable to them: refugee law. However, there is no international legal instrument that defines *de facto* statelessness nor is there an instrument that protects this category of persons or grants them a specific status.[27] At the same time, the Final Act of the Convention on the Reduction of Statelessness (1961 Convention)[28] contains a recommendation for states to treat persons who are *de facto* stateless as far as possible as de jure stateless so that they may acquire an effective nationality.[29] The distinction between *de jure* and *de facto* statelessness has been – and still is – a topic of discussion in literature.[30] It is therefore good to be aware of this

25 UNHCR, 'Handbook on the Protection of Stateless Persons under the 1954 Convention relating to the Status of Stateless Persons' (Geneva, 2014) para 16 <www.unhcr.org/protection/statelessness/53b698ab9/handbook-protection-stateless-persons.html> accessed 22 August 2021.

26 ISI, *The World's Stateless* (Wolf Legal Publishers 2014) 23–27 <https://www.institutesi.org/worldsstateless.pdf> accessed 22 August 2021.

27 UNHCR, 'Handbook on the Protection of Stateless Persons Under the 1954 Convention Relating to the Status of Stateless Persons' (UNHCR 2014) para 7, <www.unhcr.org/protection/statelessness/53b698ab9/handbook-protection-stateless-persons.html> accessed 22 August 2021.

28 Convention on the Reduction of Statelessness (with Final Act of the United Nations Conference on the Elimination or Reduction of Future Statelessness held at Geneva from 24 March to 18 April 1959, and Resolutions I, II, III and IV of the Conference) (adopted 30 August 1961, entered into force 13 December 1975) 989 UNTS 175 (1961 Convention).

29 1961 Convention and Final Act (ibid), Resolution I.

30 Laura van Waas, *Nationality Matters. Statelessness under International Law* (School of Human Rights Research Series vol 29, Intersentia 2008) 19–27; Jason Tucker, 'Questioning *de facto* Statelessness by Looking at *de facto* Citizenship' (2014) 19 *Tilburg Law Review* 276; Peter Rodrigues, '*De facto*

distinction, also because some European norms use these terms.[31] Even if this study is primarily focused on *de jure* statelessness, and as such on the norms that address this situation, it is aware that the line between *de jure* and *de facto* is not always easily drawn, for instance when we think of situations where someone is at risk of statelessness. Some of the norms on *de facto* statelessness may therefore also be relevant to fully understanding the concept of nationality. Conversely, some of the findings of this research may be relevant for those who remain factually without protection of a state or rights that are generally associated with nationality.

In academic literature as well as in reports on statelessness, a distinction is sometimes made between statelessness *in situ* (i.e. in the original place) and statelessness in a migratory context.[32] These terms are used to indicate a difference in the situation and context in which statelessness occurs, and also say something about the level of attachment of a stateless person to the country where he or she resides.[33] This is evident when attempting to provide definitions for the two concepts. Statelessness *in situ* concerns persons who remain stateless in their 'own country', often since birth and thus (usually) in a non-migratory context. Their situation is characterized by the fact that they are long-standing residents or were residents at the time of state succession and they have (personal and/or family) ties to the country, which they have with no other country. Persons who are stateless in a migratory context are migrants or have a migratory background with no or no significant ties to the country they live in (yet).[34] It has furthermore been held that the response to the two contexts of statelessness should differ in view of the (stronger) level of attachment to the country of residence. Persons who are stateless in a migratory context should be identified as such (through statelessness determination procedures) and be afforded protection as a stateless person.

Staatloosheid of de Uitdaging van Onuitzetbaren' [*De facto* Statelessness or the Challenge of Undeportable Persons] (2013) 5/6 *Asiel & Migrantenrecht* 281; Katja Swider, 'A Rights-Based Approach to Statelessness' (PhD, University of Amsterdam 2018); Alison Harvey, 'Statelessness: the "de facto" Statelessness Debate' (2010) 24 Journal of Immigration Asylum and Nationality Law 257; UNHCR (Hugh Massey), 'UNHCR and de facto Statelessness' (April 2010) LPPR/2010/01 <www.refworld.org/docid/4bbf387d2.html> accessed 22 August 2021; Equal Rights Trust (ERT), 'Unravelling Anomaly. Detention, Discrimination and the Protection Needs of Stateless Persons' (July 2010) chapter 2 <www.equalrightstrust.org/ertdocumentbank/UNRAVELLING%20ANOMALY%20small%20file.pdf> accessed 22 August 2021.

31 Eg Recommendation CM/Rec (2009) 13 of the Committee of Ministers to member states on the nationality of children (adopted by the Committee of Ministers on 9 December 2009 at the 1073rd meeting of the Ministers' Deputies) and Explanatory Memorandum, which mentions *de facto* statelessness.

32 Eg Laura van Waas, 'Stateless Children' in Jacqueline Bhabha, Jyothi Kanics & Daniel Senovila Hernández, *Research Handbook on Child Migration* (Edward Elgar Publishing 2018) 213–228, 213; Gábor Gyulai, 'Statelessness in the EU Framework for International Protection' (2012) 14 European Journal of Migration and Law 279, 279–280; Mark Manly, 'UNHCR's Mandate and Activities to Address Statelessness in Europe' (2012) 14 *European Journal of Migration and Law* 261.

33 Caia Vlieks, 'Contexts of Statelessness. The Concepts 'Statelessness in situ' and 'Statelessness in the Migratory Context' in Tendayi Bloom, Katherine Tonkiss & Phillip Cole, *Understanding Statelessness* (Routledge 2017) 35–52, 36.

34 Ibid 35–52, 50.

For stateless populations *in situ*, however, targeted nationality campaigns or nationality verification efforts would be more appropriate.[35] But no matter in what context statelessness occurs, nationality (eventually) would be seen as the solution.

The focus in this book is on preventing and solving statelessness. These terms are often encountered in law, literature and reports on statelessness and can be distinguished from the notions of 'reduction' of statelessness and 'protection' and 'identification' of stateless people, which are also used in this context.[36] The 1961 Convention is on the reduction of statelessness and includes both norms that aim to prevent and solve statelessness in different contexts. However, the 1954 Convention also includes a norm on solving statelessness: Article 32, which concerns facilitated naturalization of stateless people. At the same time, UNHCR uses prevention and reduction of statelessness, as well as the protection and identification of stateless people to delineate their mandate. It is therefore important to define here how preventing and solving statelessness are used in this study. The goal of this research is to analyze European law on preventing and solving statelessness. This can include any legal norm that helps us to ensure that less persons become or remain stateless. From this perspective, the notion of 'reducing statelessness' can therefore include both the prevention of and the solutions to statelessness.[37] As a general rule, the specific rights that stateless people can enjoy after being identified as stateless (protection as a stateless person) and ways to ensure this identification (identification of stateless people) are not the primary object of study. However, it is acknowledged that these lines cannot be easily drawn and they are therefore not applied too strictly. Throughout this research preventing and solving statelessness are the focus. In some contexts, identification also is a prerequisite for preventing and solving statelessness; if you do not know about (possible) statelessness, how can you hope to prevent or solve it? As also explained in paragraph 1.4.3 of this chapter, identification has a link with both nationality and statelessness and therefore has relevance to this research. All four UNHCR 'pillars' on statelessness – identification, prevention, reduction and protection – are thus covered in some way in this study, but only to the extent that they contribute to reducing statelessness in Europe as defined above.

In addition to these four 'pillars', it is also important to be reminded of the impact of statelessness and of the powerlessness in the democratic and political sense. Without

---

35 UNHCR, 'Handbook on the Protection of Stateless Persons under the 1954 Convention relating to the Status of Stateless Persons' (Geneva, 2014) para 58–61 <www.unhcr.org/protection/statelessness/53b698ab9/handbook-protection-stateless-persons.html> accessed 22 August 2021.

36 Eg UNHCR, 'Statelessness: An Analytical Framework for Prevention, Reduction and Protection' (2008) <www.refworld.org/docid/49a28afb2.html> accessed 22 August 2021. Note that UNHCR's mandate on statelessness includes four 'categories' of activities: identification, prevention, reduction and protection, see UNHCR ExCom, 'Conclusion on Identification, Prevention and Reduction of Statelessness and Protection of Stateless Persons', No. 106 (LVII) (6 October 2006); UNGA Res 61/137 (2006) A/RES/61/137.

37 This deviates to some extent from the use of these words in the UNHCR mandate, in which 'reduction' is used to refer to solving existing situations of statelessness. Here, the term 'reducing' or 'reduction' is used in a broader sense, more in line with what the 1961 Convention seems to suggest.

a nationality, stateless people are deprived of a right to vote and more generally of a status that is essential and indispensable because of the civil rights that are attached to it. This question of participatory rights attached to nationality more generally also comes back in this research, in particular where a closer look is taken at the EU and in the reflections in Part III.

A final note on the concept of 'statelessness' concerns terminology used in this research. First of all, it should be acknowledged that 'statelessness' or 'stateless person' as a legal label may be useful from a legal perspective, but may equally be very problematic in specific situations. Indeed, some people who are usually 'labelled' as stateless, reject this label:

> "Some Rohingya have argued that the term 'stateless' influenced popular discourses that negatively impacted their identity claims, had very little strategic value in terms of social action or claiming rights, and profoundly impacted international policy discussions about repatriations and their possible futures in Myanmar. In rejecting the label, participants demand that the international human rights community recognise the arbitrary deprivation of their citizenship as an extreme violation of their rights for which the state is culpable. Further, the label of 'stateless' in the countries with the largest Rohingya populations is yet to be endowed with access to protections, rights, and services."[38]

This shows how the label 'statelessness' may not always lead to rights and may even have an adverse effect on a population claiming their rights (as citizens) in a country. In legal research, nonetheless, it is common to refer to those affected by it as 'stateless persons' – following one of the key legal instruments on the matter, the 1954 Convention on the Status of *Stateless Persons* (emphasis added). This research certainly is a legal study of statelessness and therefore the choice of using 'stateless persons' throughout would seem straightforward. However, this research does also look 'outside' of the legal sphere, by considering the context and history of norms for instance, and the author would also hope that it can be used beyond the legal discipline and can be part of a progressive and multidisciplinary field of statelessness research. Moreover, this study wants to recognize the very real *people* that hide behind legal conceptions and norms. Where possible, those who are affected are therefore referred to as 'stateless people', while recognizing that the label as such may be problematic in some circumstances, but also aware that there is no real alternative that can be used in a study like this that is of a legal nature and does not focus on one community exclusively. Only where necessary, for instance because it concerns strict legal terminology, 'stateless persons' is retained.

---

38 Natalie Brinham, '"We Are Not Stateless! You Can Call Us What You Like, But We Are Citizens of Myanmar!": Rohingya resistance and the Stateless Label' in Tendayi Bloom & Lindsey N Kingston (eds), *Statelessness, Governance, and the Problem of Citizenship* (Manchester University Press 2021) 339–352, 348.

1.4.2. NATIONALITY AND CITIZENSHIP

From the above paragraph, it is evident that to be stateless means to be without any nationality. In other words: stateless people lack the legal bond of nationality with a state. However, nationality[39] and citizenship are, as mentioned above as well, concepts with many dimensions: legal, socio-political and associated not only with legal status, but also with rights and obligations, membership and (national) identity.[40] Here, however, the concepts of nationality and citizenship are explored in view of this research's aim and its connection with (the prevention of and solutions to) the issue of statelessness. The (legal) absence of nationality and/or citizenship, which defines statelessness, is exactly what connects statelessness with these concepts. The lack of nationality can have serious consequences in terms of access to human rights and participation in society for the person involved. But nationality can also solve statelessness. After all, when a stateless person acquires a nationality, (s)he is no longer stateless – from a legal perspective at least. Furthermore, nationality can prevent statelessness, for instance where the nationality of a state is granted to a child born in that country who would otherwise be stateless. Below is considered first what nationality is and what citizenship is from a legal perspective – how can nationality and citizenship be defined? Are these concepts two words to describe the same thing? And how do you (legally) acquire or lose nationality and citizenship?

According to a modern English dictionary, nationality is the status of belonging to a particular state.[41] From a legal perspective, one of the often-used definitions of nationality is that of the International Court of Justice (ICJ):

---

39 The (human) right to nationality and nationality in international law have been the subject of many commentaries over the years, but none of them had a specific focus on preventing and solving statelessness. See for instance WR Bisschop, 'Nationality in International Law' (1943) 37 American Journal of International Law 320; Haro Frederik van Panhuys, *The Role of Nationality in International Law. An Outline* (PhD Thesis Leiden University, AW Sijthoff's Uitgeversmaatschappij 1959); Ian Brownlie, 'The Relations of Nationality in Public International Law' (1963) 39 British Yearbook of International Law 284; Paul Weis, *Nationality and Statelessness in International Law* (2nd ed, Sijthoff & Noordhoff 1979); Johannes M M Chan, 'The Right to a Nationality as a Human Right. The Current Trend Towards Recognition' (1980) 12 Human Rights Law Journal 1; Ruth Donner, *The Regulation of Nationality in International Law* (2nd ed, Transnational Publishers, Inc 1994); Kay Hailbronner, 'Nationality in Public International Law and European Law', in Rainer Bauböck, Eva Ersbøll, Kees Groenendijk & Harald Waldrauch (eds), *Acquisition and Loss of Nationality. Policies and Trends in 15 European States. Vol. 1: Comparative Analyses* (Amsterdam University Press 2006) 35–104; Peter J Spiro, 'A New International Law of Citizenship' (2011) 105 American Journal of International Law 694; Serena Forlati & Alessandra Annoni, *The Changing Role of Nationality in International Law* (Routledge 2013); Alice Edwards & Laura van Waas (eds), *Nationality and Statelessness under International Law* (Cambridge University Press 2014); Ernst MH Hirsch Ballin, *Citizen's Rights and the Right to Be a Citizen* (Developments in International Law Series Vol 66, Brill Nijhoff 2014); Mónika Ganczer, 'The Right to a Nationality as a Human Right?' in Marcel Szabó, Petra Lea Láncos, Réka Varga & Tamás Molnár (eds), *Hungarian Yearbook of International Law 2014* (Eleven International Publishing 2015) 15–33; Rhoda E Howard-Hassmann & Margaret Walton-Roberts, *The Human Right to Citizenship. A Slippery Concept* (University of Pennsylvania Press 2015).

40 Eg Linda Bosniak, *The Citizen and the Alien. Dilemmas of Contemporary Membership* (Princeton University Press 2006).

41 Eg Lexico – powered by Oxford University Press <https://www.lexico.com/definition/nationality> accessed 22 August 2021.

> "[N]ationality is a legal bond having as its basis a social fact of attachment, a genuine connection of existence, interests and sentiments, together with the existence of reciprocal rights and duties. It may be said to constitute the juridical expression of the fact that the individual upon whom it is conferred, either directly by the law or as the result of an act of the authorities, is in fact more closely connected with the population of the [s]tate conferring nationality than with that of any other [s]tate."[42]

Turning to the European level, the European Convention on Nationality (ECN)[43] defines nationality in Article 2: "[N]ationality means the legal bond between a person and a [s]tate and does not indicate a person's ethnic origin (...)."

Citizenship, on the other hand, has not been defined separately in a legal document or instrument. Whereas nationality really stresses the international, legal side to being a member of a state – belonging to a particular country, citizenship sometimes emphasizes the meaning of this membership at the national level. A definition that demonstrates that the two concepts are the same, but indeed highlights different aspects of nationality or citizenship is the following: "Conceptually and linguistically, the terms 'nationality' and 'citizenship' emphasize two different aspects of the same notion: [s]tate membership. 'Nationality' stresses the international, 'citizenship' the national, municipal, aspect."[44]

In this research, the concepts 'nationality' and 'citizenship' are used interchangeably. This choice has been made in light of the close link between the two concepts and because of the fact that this research looks for ways to prevent and solve statelessness. As such, the 'label' used is secondary to addressing statelessness. Indeed, it has been held that "[f]rom a rights perspective, the label is less important than the ability to exercise rights".[45] Therefore, nationality and citizenship are today considered to be concepts that are interchangeable from a legal perspective by different scholars[46], even though it has been held that they articulate different things: nationality represents the legal bond between a person and a state, whereas citizenship stresses the reciprocal relationship between state and citizen – to be a member of a polity.[47] Nonetheless, in essence, they are two sides of the same coin.

42 *Nottebohm Case (Liechtenstein v Guatemala)* [1955] ICJ Rep 4.

43 European Convention on Nationality (Strasbourg, 1997, CETS No. 166) (ECN).

44 Paul Weis, *Nationality and Statelessness in International Law* (2nd ed, Sijthoff & Noordhoff International Publishers 1979) 4–5.

45 Alice Edwards, 'The Meaning of Nationality in International Law in an Era of Human Rights: Procedural and Substantive Aspects' in Alice Edwards & Laura van Waas (eds), *Nationality and Statelessness under International Law* (Cambridge University Press 2014) 14.

46 Peter Spiro, 'A New International Law of Citizenship' (2011) 105 The American Journal of International Law 694; Alice Edwards, 'The Meaning of Nationality in International Law in an Era of Human Rights: Procedural and Substantive Aspects' in Alice Edwards & Laura van Waas (eds), *Nationality and Statelessness under International Law* (Cambridge University Press 2014).

47 Cf Ernst Hirsch Ballin, *Citizens' Rights and the Right to be a Citizen* (Developments in International Law vol 66, Brill Nijhoff 2014).

A closer look is taken next at how someone becomes a citizen of a country: the acquisition of nationality.[48] The two main principles based on which nationality is attributed are *jus sanguinis* and *jus soli. Jus sanguinis* means 'law of the blood', which articulates that nationality is acquired by descent: the nationality of a country is attributed to a child when one or both parents are a national of the state concerned. *Jus soli* can be translated as 'law of the soil', meaning that the nationality that is acquired at birth is based upon the place – country – of birth.

Most laws and policies on the attribution of nationality at birth can be linked to either or both of these principles. In Europe, there is a tendency towards using the *jus sanguinis*-principle as the main principle for nationality attribution.[49] Nationality is often viewed as something that is passed from parent(s) to child(ren). It has been held that this has a historical background, influenced by Christianity even, as

> "the family, instead of the individual, seems to have been the unit, and that the aggregation of such units formed the group or society which we may, for present purposes, call the state; and that the family, as well as the groups of families forming the society, status, or state, was one of blood relationship".[50]

The *jus sanguinis*-principle is visible in a number of European legal instruments, as well as in national laws. For children of stateless people in Europe, that would however mean that they could remain stateless if (a) parent(s) is unable to pass nationality on to the child(ren). Yet, also *jus soli*-elements can be found in current nationality laws in Europe. It thus appears that European states are indeed aware of the need for using both principles for attributing nationality. However, and as can be seen in chapter 2, the large number of stateless people in Europe demonstrates that this has not really solved the problem. At the same time, there remains a factor of coincidence in relation to acquisition of nationality, as an individual cannot decide about his or her place of birth, nor choose his or her parents – important facts in relation to the possibility to acquire a nationality. Hence, the acquisition of citizenship, and thereby political membership, has been termed the 'birthright lottery'.[51]

A last principle, important to the acquisition of nationality at a later point in life through naturalization, is that of *jus domicilii*. It means 'law of residence' and is the

---

48 See also Laura van Waas, *Nationality Matters. Statelessness under International Law* (School of Human Rights Research Series vol 29, Intersentia 2008) 32–33 and Alice Edwards, 'The Meaning of Nationality in International Law in an Era of Human Rights: Procedural and Substantive Aspects' in Alice Edwards & Laura van Waas (eds), *Nationality and Statelessness under International Law* (Cambridge University Press 2014) 16–21.

49 Cf Caia Vlieks and Katja Swider, 'The *Jus Sanguinis* Bias of Europe and What It Means for Childhood Statelessness' (*ENS Blog*, 17 June 2015) < www.statelessness.eu/blog/jus-sanguinis-bias-europe-and-what-it-means-childhood-statelessness> accessed 22 August 2021.

50 James Brown Scott, 'Nationality: Jus Soli or Jus Sanguinis' (1930) 24 The American Journal of International Law 58, 60.

51 Ayelet Shachar, *The Birthright Lottery. Citizenship and Global Inequality* (Harvard University Press 2009).

principle of the basis of which nationality may be granted to the applicant based on legal residence for a certain number of years by the competent authorities. Very often, additional conditions are attached to the acquisition of nationality through naturalization, such as integration requirements.[52] Furthermore, nationality can be acquired later in life through marriage, adoption[53] or investment.[54]

In academic discussions, the concept of *jus nexi* (or *jus nexus*[55]) has been contrasted with the existing 'modes' for acquiring nationality. Shachar has convincingly argued that the application of what she calls *ius nexi*, citizenship based on rootedness, "offers a path for earned citizenship arising from the existence of already established, real, and genuine ties toward the political community".[56] This could offer solutions to those who are unable to claim 'membership' based on the prevailing principles of *jus sanguinis* and *jus soli*. This approach to citizenship has been endorsed by for instance Hirsch Ballin[57] and by some experts in a debate on 'bloodlines and belonging'.[58]

As was indicated already above, the bond of nationality can also cease to exist at some point.[59] This happens when nationality is voluntarily renounced, or when nationality is involuntarily lost (by operation of the law) or when a person is deprived of nationality (through an administrative act). This can – under circumstances – result in statelessness, for instance when the person involved has no other (second) nationality or does not acquire a new nationality, and can happen in individual cases but also on a large-scale basis.

The concept of nationality was traditionally "intended to regulate relationships among sovereign states".[60] Nationality was indeed the connection between a person and

---

52 On integration requirements see for instance Tamar de Waal, 'Conditional Belonging: A Legal-Philosophical Inquiry into Integration Requirements for Immigrants in Europe' (PhD, University of Amsterdam 2017).

53 See also Laura van Waas, *Nationality Matters. Statelessness under International Law* (School of Human Rights Research Series vol 29, Intersentia 2008) 34.

54 Rainer Bauböck (ed), *Debating Transformations of National Citizenship* (IMISCOE Research Series, SpringerOpen 2018), Part I: Should Citizenship Be for Sale?, 2–70.

55 Ernst Hirsch Ballin, *Citizens' Rights and the Right to Be a Citizen* (Developments in International Law Vol 66, Brill Nijhoff 2014) 83.

56 Ayelet Shachar, 'Earned Citizenship: Property Lessons for Immigration Reform' (2011) 23 Yale Journal of Law & the Humanities 110, 113. See also Ayelet Shachar, *The Birthright Lottery. Citizenship and Global Inequality* (Harvard University Press 2009).

57 Ernst Hirsch Ballin, *Citizens' Rights and the Right to Be a Citizen* (Developments in International Law Vol 66, Brill Nijhoff 2014).

58 Rainer Bauböck (ed), *Debating Transformations of National Citizenship* (IMISCOE Research Series, SpringerOpen 2018), Part II: Bloodlines and Belonging, 71–160.

59 Laura van Waas, *Nationality Matters. Statelessness under International Law* (School of Human Rights Research Series vol 29, Intersentia 2008) 34, Alice Edwards, 'The Meaning of Nationality in International Law in an Era of Human Rights: Procedural and Substantive Aspects' in Alice Edwards & Laura van Waas (eds), *Nationality and Statelessness under International Law* (Cambridge University Press 2014) 21–23. On loss of nationality in Europe see also Maarten Vink & Gerard-René de Groot, 'Loss of Citizenship: Trends and Regulations in Europe' (EUDO Citizenship Report 2010) RSCAS/EUDO-CIT-Comp. 2010/4 <https://cadmus.eui.eu/handle/1814/19575> accessed 22 August 2021.

60 Johannes M M Chan, 'The Right to a Nationality as a Human Right. The Current Trend Towards Recognition' (1980) 12 Human Rights Law Journal 1.

a state and an expression of membership of a state, which was the only way through which an individual could benefit from international law[61], through diplomatic protection for instance. This has changed with the growth of the international human rights framework after World War II, through which individuals can now claim their rights and nationality being proclaimed as a human right.[62] This implies that individuals should be able to claim the right to a nationality, but at the same time the question remains to which nationality an individual has a right. Also, states remain the important actors: they decide who is granted nationality and who is not. In determining who is a citizen, a one-sidedness still exists and the notion of reciprocity is not yet commonplace in this regard. It is no accident that nationality law has been called "the last bastion in the citadel of sovereignty".[63] As such, there is a clear dichotomy between the conception of nationality and a right thereto in (international) law.

It was already noted that the lack of a nationality could have serious consequences for stateless people due to problems with accessing basic rights. Indeed, it has often been held that the right to a nationality is the right to have rights[64] – nationality and the right thereto provide the gateway to the enjoyment of other (human) rights. This would seem to mean that having a nationality comes with a set of rights. There is no legal document at universal or European regional level that lists the rights that are associated with a status as a national. Nonetheless, Alice Edwards, drawing on international (human rights) norms, has indicated a number of rights that are generally connected to holding a nationality:

- "the right to leave one's 'own country' and to re-enter and reside permanently in the territory of the state of one's nationality;
- the right to consular assistance (…);
- the right to vote and participate in public life (…)[65];
- rights to economic, social and cultural advancement."[66]

These are rights that a state should provide to its citizens. Still, in the event that the state is unable or unwilling to take action and ensure these rights for its nationals, the legal status of citizen is not altered; one remains a national. Conversely, a citizen does not only have certain rights, (s)he also has duties, such as paying taxes, military service or another form of participation in the community.

61 L Oppenheim, *International Law. A Treatise* (Vol 1: Peace; Longmans, Green and Co. 1905) 344–346; WR Bisschop, 'Nationality in International Law' (1943) 37 American Journal of International Law 320, 321.

62 Universal Declaration of Human Rights (adopted 10 December 1948 UNGA Res 217 A(III) (UDHR) Art 15.

63 Peter Spiro, 'A New International Law of Citizenship' (2011) 105 *The American Journal of International Law* 694, 746.

64 Eg Chief Justice Earl Warren in *Trop v Dulles* 356 US 86 (1958).

65 Including the right to be elected.

66 Alice Edwards, 'The Meaning of Nationality in International Law in an Era of Human Rights: Procedural and Substantive Aspects' in Alice Edwards & Laura van Waas (eds), *Nationality and Statelessness under International Law* (Cambridge University Press 2014) 40.

From a human rights perspective, however, it has been held that a nationality that results in no rights is undesirable: nationality cannot be just a status or 'label'. An article on solving statelessness in relation to the right to a nationality, which draws on international (human rights) law, as well as scholarship and reports on these matters, demonstrates this aptly:

> "[T]he right to a nationality, and therefore solutions to statelessness, are about so much more than just 'a' nationality. They are about giving people rights, dignity, identity, inclusion, equality, and a home. (...) other solutions may fail to achieve the function of nationality as the heart of democratic legitimacy of States, disregard the individual's valid interests, and fail to address the deeper issues attached to statelessness. In order to solve statelessness, it is necessary to recognise but also move beyond a State-centric understanding of the right to nationality toward an understanding of nationality as the content of a human right to citizenship. What is necessary is a nationality that represents a meaningful connection between a person and a State that enables the person involved to actively enjoy the full array of rights and to take part in society as a citizen."[67]

The above considerations show that nationality (or citizenship) is a concept of a versatile and variable nature. For the purpose of this research, the definition of this notion is approached from a legal perspective, i.e. nationality is the legal bond between a person and a state, the nature of which can vary depending on the (municipal, national, European, international) 'level' on which it is studied, the content of which can differ from one situation to another, and the parameters of which keep changing.[68] At the same time, it is a legal status that implies certain rights and duties. In this way, the approach to nationality in this research wants to acknowledge the different dimensions to this concept. In light of the focus on Europe – i.e. the 47 member states of the CoE[69] – the conception of nationality used in this study presumes citizenship in a state that is (aspiring to be) a democratic state and acknowledges existing territorial borders. With the former explication of this research's definition of nationality, the democratic dimension to nationality, meaning membership in a political community[70], is explicitly included. This research thus concerns itself with forms of 'full' nationality or citizenship that lead to the aforementioned rights and duties between the individual and state. As such, certain types of, for instance, British nationality[71], are in principle excluded from this study. Furthermore, even though questions around unrecognized or partially

---

67 Caia Vlieks, Ernst Hirsch Ballin & María José Recalde Vela, 'Solving Statelessness: Interpreting the Right to Nationality' (2017) 35 Netherlands Quarterly of Human Rights 158, 175.

68 See also Kristin Henard, 'The Shifting Parameters of Nationality' (2018) 65 Netherlands International Law Review 269.

69 See also para 1.4.4.

70 Cf Rainer Bauböck, 'Political Membership and Democratic Boundaries' in Ayelet Shachar, Rainer Bauböck, Irene Bloemraad & Maarten Vink (eds), *The Oxford Handbook of Citizenship* (Oxford University Press 2017) 60–82.

71 See Gov.uk, 'Types of British nationality' <https://www.gov.uk/types-of-british-nationality/british-citizenship> accessed 22 August 2021.

recognized states also exist in Europe, e.g. in the context of Cyprus and Kosovo, this is not considered further in this research.

1.4.3. NATIONALITY, STATELESSNESS AND ADMINISTRATION

An important observation that should be made after discussing both statelessness and nationality, is the undeniable link that exists between these concepts and the state, and that identification, administration and registration also play a role in shaping states' approaches to nationality and statelessness. This has a background in the history of the modern state. The 17th century witnessed, according to many, the birth of the modern state, in particular through the Westphalian peace treaties of 1648 that "introduced the idea of sovereign equality among the states of Europe".[72] A clear and agreed upon definition of what a state is, is hard to find. However, for the purpose of international law, a well-known definition is found in the 1933 Montevideo Convention on Rights and Duties of States.[73] According to this definition, a state is characterized by a permanent population, a defined territory, government and capacity to enter into relations with other states.[74] States thus need a population, which would primarily be made up of its citizens – those who 'belong' to the state and have a particular connection with the state. However, the "Westphalian Europe was a long way from the modern international order in which the citizenship law we recognize today emerged" because it was about sovereignty of monarchs and the "territorial scope of the sovereign's realm".[75] Revolutionary thinking[76] made the replacement of the sovereign with 'the people' possible: "Only when the idea took hold that the sovereignty of states was (if only rhetorically) based on the consent or authority of their people, did it become important to identify the members of particular states as against each other".[77] In particular after the First World War and with the process of democratization, a closer connection between the citizen and the state was evident –

72 Randall Lesaffer, 'The Westphalia Peace Treaties and the Development of the Tradition of Great European Peace Settlements prior to 1648' (1997) 18 Grotiana 71, 72.

73 Montevideo Convention on the Rights and Duties of States (Inter-American) (adopted 26 December 1933, entered into force 26 December 1934) 165 LNTS 19 (1933 Montevideo Convention). See also Karen Knop, 'Statehood: territory, people, government' in James Crawford & Martti Koskenniemi (eds), *The Cambridge Companion to International Law* (Cambridge University Press 2012) 95.

74 Art 1 1933 Montevideo Convention.

75 Helen Irving, *Citizenship, Alienage, and the Modern Constitutional State. A Gendered History* (Cambridge University Press 2017) 32.

76 Cf the French and American revolutions of the 18th century.

77 Helen Irving, *Citizenship, Alienage, and the Modern Constitutional State. A Gendered History* (Cambridge University Press 2017) 32. That is not to say that identification of individuals was something exclusive to more recent history: already in Late Medieval and Renaissance Europe we saw official, written systems of registration, see for instance Valentin Groebner, 'Describing the Person, Reading the Signs in Late Medieval and Renaissance Europe: Identity Papers, Vested Figures and the Limits of Identification, 1400–1600' in Jane Caplan & John Torpey (eds), *Documenting Individual Identity. The Development of State Practices in the Modern World* (Princeton University Press 2001) 15–27.

making it important to distinguish between those who were to enjoy the political and economic benefits of a state.[78] To make this identification possible, it was necessary to introduce systems of registration, administration and identity documentation. These systems simplified practice and were "devoted to rationalizing and standardizing" in order to make societies governable and legible.[79]

> "Passports became essential to the bureaucratic administration of modern mass migration, just as identity cards have become something like the 'currency' of domestic administration, marking out eligibles from ineligibles in the areas of voting, social services and much more besides."[80]

This "administrative ordering of nature and society" has been held to "undergird the concept of citizenship".[81] Systems for the registration of identity "have been crucial practical tools which have facilitated the endowing of all individuals with legal personhood, which is defined as the entity to which rights and duties are ascribed by law".[82] At the same time, not only individuals benefit from, for instance, birth registration. For a modern state, benefits "include the effective functioning, planning and monitoring efforts"[83] of such a state. As such, the existence of and possibility to distinguish between legal conceptions of nationality and statelessness are logically related to systems of administration, registration and identification of people.

Even though there is evidence that registration of people and households already existed during the Han Dynasty in China (2nd century BC)[84], Europe has had a tradition of registration of people, probably already in ancient times.[85] Evidence of registration of

---

78 John Torpey, *The Invention of the Passport. Surveillance, Citizenship and the State* (Cambridge University Press 2000) 121.

79 James C Scott, *Seeing Like a State. How Certain Schemes to Improve the Human Condition Have Failed* (Yale University Press 1998) 2–4; Christiane Reinecke, 'Staatliche Macht im Aufbau: Infrastrukturen der Kontrolle und die Ordnung der Migrationsverhältnisse im Kaiserreich' in Jochen Oltmer (ed), *Handbuch Staat und Migration in Deutschland seit dem 17. Jahrhundert* (De Gruyter 2015) 342.

80 John Torpey, *The Invention of the Passport. Surveillance, Citizenship and the State* (Cambridge University Press 2000) 121.

81 James C Scott, *Seeing Like a State. How Certain Schemes to Improve the Human Condition Have Failed* (Yale University Press 1998) 4.

82 Simon Szreter and Keith Breckenridge, 'Editor's Introduction. Recognition and Registration: The Infrastructure of Personhood in World History' in Simon Szreter & Keith Breckenridge, *Registration and Recognition. Documenting the Person in World History* (Oxford University Press/British Academy 2012) 22.

83 Wendy Hunter, *Undocumented Nationals* (Cambridge Elements in the Politics of Development, Cambridge University Press 2019) 2.

84 Michel Poulain & Anne Herm, 'Central Population Registers as a Source of Demographic Statistics in Europe' (2013) 68 Population 183.

85 See for instance the Bible, Luk. 2:1–3, which says that the Roman emperor had ordered a registration or census, causing Joseph and Mary to travel to Bethlehem to register themselves. The Roman Empire also encompassed large parts of what we call 'Europe' for the purposes of this study (i.e. the member states of the CoE). See also Etienne van de Walle, 'Historical Development of Civil Registration Systems: A European Perspective' (2018) UN Department of Economic and Social Affairs Population Division Technical Paper No. 2018/1, 2 <https://www.un.org/en/development/desa/population/

people can be found more steadily from the 16th century onwards in parishes keeping track of members. Indeed, "the success of civil registration in Europe" has been held to be "the outcome of a long history of recording events in parish registers".[86] These registers could include information on affiliation to particular denominations, marriages, births and deaths.

Legal instruments and states today often operate from a presumption that these systems of registration and identification – more advanced than the abovementioned parish registers of course – exist and in practice, (stateless) individuals are confronted with their importance. To start with, the dominant principles in attributing nationality already demand that the parents or place of birth is known (and officially recorded) in order for a newborn to be considered as a national. And in practice, we see that registration and identification present difficulties for stateless people. In the Netherlands, for instance, the main avenue for recognition as a stateless person is – as it stands January 2022 – to be registered in the Dutch Basic Registration of Persons (Basisregistratie Personen, BRP) by the municipal authorities as such. In order to be registered as stateless, a person should, however, be able to identify as being stateless using official legal documentation certifying that (s)he is stateless. This has proven to be very hard, which has likely led to stateless people – including children – being registered as of 'unknown nationality' – a practice common in more European states.[87] Furthermore, it has proven to be near impossible to change a designation in the BRP as of 'unknown nationality' to 'stateless'.[88] As such, the importance of being recorded properly in the official registration system is even bigger, as is – in turn – having proper documentation to that end to 'prove' your (lack of any) nationality.

At the same time, registration of the (lack of any) nationality of an individual is important to (practically) 'implementing' nationality matters at a national level: "states create and interrogate individual's evidence of citizenship"[89], which is often particularly important when potential benefits of nationality (or of being recognized as stateless) are at stake. Here, think for instance about the possibility of a national to participate in public life and democratic processes. As such, the registration and administration of people as belonging to a certain state or not is often considered an important part of our understanding of nationality today. This might also be a reason for the inclusion

---

publications/pdf/technical/TP2018-1.pdf> accessed 22 August 2021, who mentions that "[t]here may have been attempts at registration of births and deaths in Antiquity, but these have left no traces in the statistical record".

86 Etienne van de Walle, 'Historial Development of Civil Registration Systems: A European Perspective' (2018) UN Department of Economic and Social Affairs Population Division Technical Paper No. 2018/1, 2 <https://www.un.org/en/development/desa/population/publications/pdf/technical/TP2018-1.pdf> accessed 22 August 2021.

87 ENS, 'No Child Should Be Stateless' (ENS 2015) <https://www.statelessness.eu/sites/www.statelessness.eu/files/ENS_NoChildStateless_final.pdf> accessed 22 August 2021.

88 Karel Hendriks, Jelle Klaas & Marlotte van Dael, 'Juridische spoken verdwijnen nog niet' [Legal ghosts are not disappearing yet] (2017) 2 Asiel & Migrantenrecht 75, 77.

89 Benjamin N Lawrance & Jacqueline Stevens (eds), *Citizenship in Question. Evidentiary Birthright and Statelessness* (Duke University Press 2017) 2.

of legal identity – including birth registration – in the Sustainable Development Goals (SDGs).[90]

Furthermore, testimonies from the daily lives of stateless people all over Europe confirm how important documentation and registration are to the enjoyment of rights and protection.

> "Not having documentation causes problems on many areas of my life. Namely, I cannot find a job... because I cannot be registered as employee if I do not have ID... There is no way out for me unless I receive documents... Since I do not have documents, I cannot prove who am I, and often have to spend night in prison and not being guilty for anything... If I want to have a telephone number I must register my number by using personal ID also, and now for me it is not possible ... Everybody thinks of me as different... I have no reputation or status. And I have no way to explain to my children why this is happening to us."
> – Romani man, Montenegro[91]

Indeed, the Roma in Europe – a group that is often (at risk of) stateless(ness) – face a "radical (...) citizenship deficit, that presents in tandem with (...) pervasive exclusion. A dramatic dearth of Roma documentary evidence underpins this deficit (...)."[92] But not only Roma face issues with documentation and registration – this is a widespread concern for stateless people (or people at risk of statelessness).

> "Okeke has always lived in the United Kingdom (UK) and was probably born in the UK although he has no birth certificate. He believes that his parents are British but he lost contact with them as a teenager after fleeing many years of domestic abuse. He is in his thirties. Okeke has faced a life of destitution and isolation in the UK due to the lack of documents and the abuse he suffered as a child. After serving a criminal conviction for theft, his immigration detention started in April 2016 as the Home Office (HO) sought to deport him. Despite being classified by the HO as a person of 'unknown nationality', they attempted to deport him to Nigeria on the basis that he has a Nigerian name. Okeke was released in August 2016 on the grounds that his detention was not reasonable anymore. His solicitor intends to make a statelessness application on his behalf."[93]

To present a proper legal perspective on nationality and preventing and solving statelessness in Europe, it is thus important to be sensitive towards the administrative side of these issues and concepts. As such, the consideration that the different European

---

90 See also para 1.5.1 (under the header 'UN human rights treaties') of this chapter.

91 European Roma Rights Centre (ERRC), 'Roma Belong – Discrimination, Statelessness and Marginalisation of Roma in the Western Balkans and Ukraine' (*errc.org*, 26 October 2017) 32 <www.errc.org/uploads/upload_en/file/roma-belong.pdf> accessed 22 August 2021.

92 Jacqueline Bhabha, 'The Politics of Evidence. Roma Citizenship Deficits in Europe' in Benjamin N Lawrance & Jacqueline Stevens (eds), *Citizenship in Question. Evidentiary Birthright and Statelessness* (Duke University Press 2017) 43–59, 47.

93 ENS, 'Protecting Stateless Persons from Arbitrary Detention in the United Kingdom' (ENS 2016) 8 <https://www.statelessness.eu/sites/www.statelessness.eu/files/ENS_Detention_Reports_UK.pdf> accessed 22 August 2021.

legal instruments give to administration, registration and identification in nationality matters is contemplated on throughout this book.

1.4.4. EUROPEAN LAWMAKING AND EUROPEAN LAW

In this study, the term 'European law' is used to refer to legal instruments of the CoE and the EU. This may seem surprising, as the CoE and the EU engage in lawmaking in two different contexts and differ in legal character. The CoE is a European intergovernmental organization and forum of inter-state cooperation. The CoE's main legal(ly binding) instruments consist of treaties, but also include other (more political and non-legally binding) forms of standard setting, as is considered also below. The CoE treaties, however, should be ratified by the CoE member states before they have legal effect for the state concerned. As such, the power of this organization to create binding laws is limited. The EU is also an international organization that allows for state cooperation, but has grown into a supranational entity. Not only the EU treaties are relevant legal instruments of this organization, but also its regulations and directives are, for instance, important legislative acts that are generally immediately legally binding on the member states: states do not need to accede to such instruments. The EU has produced a legal order in the treaties and further case law, which is an extension of national legal orders of its member states. As such the influence of the EU on national law is very direct, whereas the (legal) impact of the CoE is more indirect.

In view of this, the two frameworks of the CoE and the EU may therefore not be easily compared. Both organizations engage in European lawmaking though – they create and adopt legal instruments (of a legally binding and non-binding nature) that have an effect beyond the individual state, at a European regional level. Furthermore, the CoE and the EU provide an important source of law in Europe, both drawing on a range of European legal traditions and thereby having a unifying effect on law in the region.[94] Moreover, they both legislate on fundamental rights, which is the key analytical perspective taken in this research, which can help to overcome these differences and is explained further in paragraph 1.5.3.

European law is often used to refer to EU law only. However, European law has on different occasions been defined more broadly. The CoE itself, for instance, has defined European law as follows:

> "The law governing the structure, organs and functioning of the Council of Europe and other European organizations or institutions; further the law contained in the conventions and agreements of the Council of Europe and instruments of other European organizations or institutions".[95]

---

94 Paolo Carozza, 'European Law' in *Encyclopedia Britannica* <https://www.britannica.com/topic/European-law#ref992078> accessed 22 August 2021.

95 Quoted in Frits Hondius, 'The New Architecture of Europe and Ius Commune Europeum' in Bruno de Witte & Caroline Forder (eds), *The Common Law of Europe and the Future of Legal Education* (Metro/

These instruments of European organizations or institutions can of course include EU law[96], making European law a suitable term to refer to lawmaking by both the CoE and the EU.

Under the definition of European law, and also of law as used in this research more generally, hard law – meaning legally binding legal instruments such as treaties – and soft law – or quasi-legal instruments – are included. This definition also includes custom, general legal principles, jurisprudence and doctrine. For a legal study like this, the importance of studying legally binding European law instruments is self-evident. However, soft law or non-legally binding instruments are also examined. Soft law can encompass a wide range of instruments, and it has been held that it can "influence the course or content of international law".[97] Importantly, they can also encompass more political instruments and/or commitment. Within the CoE, for instance, it has been acknowledged that soft law-instruments have gained importance and it is even noted that their capacity to modify state behavior is sometimes "not much inferior to that of hard law instruments".[98] As such, it is possible that soft law plays a relevant role in addressing statelessness in Europe, making it important to include this in this research.

Several organizations have been founded in Europe to further cooperation between states. One cooperation mechanism not explored in depth in this study is the Organization for Security and Co-operation in Europe (OSCE). Its aims also include for instance the promotion of human rights, tolerance and non-discrimination. Even though this organization is concerned with Europe, it has 57 member states, which include states that really are beyond the scope of Europe as defined for the purpose of this research, such as states from Central Asia and North America. Furthermore, the decisions of this organization are taken by consensus and are politically, but not legally binding. As it is this research's main objective to study legal instruments – and not political ones – the OSCE nor its instruments are studied further in this book.[99]

Pursuant to the usage of 'European law' in this research, please also note that whenever the term 'Europe' is used in this study, it refers in principle to the geographical area consisting of the 47 member states of the CoE – thus also including the EU member states.

Kluwer 1992) 213–222, 215.

96 Ernst-Joachim Mestmäcker, 'On the Legitimacy of European Law' (1994) 58 Rabels Zeitschrift für ausländisches und internationales Privatrecht 615.

97 James Crawford & Martti Koskenniemi 'Introduction' in James Crawford & Martti Koskenniemi (eds), *The Cambridge Companion to International Law* (Cambridge University Press 2012) 11.

98 Recommendations of the CoE Commitee of Ministers are mentioned as an example. See Jörg Polakiewicz, 'Alternatives to Treaty-Making and Law-Making by Treaty and Expert Bodies in the Council of Europe' in Rüdiger Wolfrum & Volker Röbin (eds), *Developments of International Law in Treaty Making* (Springer 2005) 245–290, 287.

99 For a short overview of the OSCE see Philippe Sands & Pierre Klein, *Bowett's Law of International Institutions* (6th ed, Sweet & Maxwell 2009) 202–204. See also <www.osce.org/> accessed 3 January 2022. Some of the work done within the OSCE does relate to nationality and statelessness matters, see for instance Arie Bloed, 'Citizenship Issues and the OSCE High Commissioner on National Minorities' in Síofra O'Leary & Teija Tiilikainen (eds), *Citizenship and Nationality Status in the New Europe* (Sweet & Maxwell 1998) 39–52.

1.5. ANALYTICAL FRAMEWORK: FIRST STEPS

Norms on preventing and solving statelessness are not exclusive to European law. Legal standards on statelessness and nationality have been adopted at the international level, as well as in other regions of the world. To fully understand the norms on preventing and solving statelessness at the European regional level, and to recognize what these add to the conception of nationality, it is therefore necessary to consider how they fit within the bigger system of international and regional legal instruments addressing nationality and statelessness. Hence, as a first step in creating an analytical framework for this research, these legal instruments are analyzed further. Below, the international and other regional standards relating to preventing and solving statelessness are therefore briefly studied in order to help establish this framework. Building an analytical framework, it is important to explore the content of these norms and see whether a pattern or possible categories of norms based on this content can be distilled. The focus throughout this section is on norms that relate to the prevention of and solutions to statelessness. The next paragraph below considers international norms relating to the regulation of nationality and the reduction of statelessness. Paragraph 1.5.2 turns to other regional instruments dealing with these matters, meaning that the standards enacted in regional cooperation mechanisms outside of Europe are studied. A concluding paragraph is dedicated to the different 'categories' of norms that can be drawn from the analysis in this section.

1.5.1. INTERNATIONAL LAW ON NATIONALITY AND THE REDUCTION OF STATELESSNESS

This section considers the relevant international legal instruments relating to the prevention of and solutions to statelessness in chronological order. It is divided up into different parts, focusing on the key early instruments on nationality first, and turning next to the instruments that were enacted after World War II to address the situation of refugees and stateless people. UN human rights treaties that contain provisions that are relevant to preventing and solving statelessness are included below under the header 'UN human rights treaties'.

The 1930 Hague Convention and the UDHR (1948)

The Convention on Certain Questions relating to the Conflict of Nationality Laws, which was adopted in 1930 (1930 Hague Convention) in the context of the League of Nations (LoN)[100], is one of the first international instruments aimed at establishing

[100] Convention on Certain Questions relating to the Conflict of Nationality Laws (adopted 12 April 1930, entered into force 1 July 1937) 179 LTS 89 (1930 Hague Convention).

rules relating to nationality[101] and can be viewed as a turning point with regard to nationality and statelessness matters. Indeed, Laura van Waas has called the adoption of this treaty "a watershed moment in the international community's dealings with nationality issues".[102] Because conflicts of nationality laws can cause statelessness when persons remain without any nationality of any state involved in a particular situation – are "left 'unclaimed' by any state as its national"[103] – the 1930 Hague Convention remains relevant to the topic of this chapter, even if its pertinence today is limited in light of the number of states parties to the Convention and the number of reservations that were made to this treaty.[104] The 1930 Hague Convention was a "first international attempt to provide everyone with a nationality"[105], and attempted to prevent statelessness among the following groups: married women (whose nationality was often, and sometimes still is, dependent on their husband)[106] and children (including foundlings and adopted children).[107] The 1930 Hague Convention clearly aims to solve conflicts of nationality laws[108] and avoid loss of nationality without the acquisition of a new one[109], but is also concerned specifically with preventing and solving childhood statelessness. The 1930 Hague Convention was accompanied by protocols, of which two concerned statelessness.[110] The Protocol relating to a Certain Case of Statelessness[111] "only directs states to grant their nationality to children born in their territory who would otherwise be stateless but are nevertheless born to a mother who possesses the nationality of the country of birth".[112] The Special Protocol concerning Statelessness[113] only entered into force in 2004 and concerns the specific situation where a person, after entering a foreign country, loses his nationality without acquiring a new one. In such

---

101 On other attempts at formulating principles relating to nationality before the 1930 Hague Convention see Ruth Donner, *The Regulation of Nationality in International Law* (2nd ed, Transnational Publishers, Inc 1994) 43–45.

102 Laura van Waas, 'A 100-year (Hi)Story of Statelessness' (*Peace Palace Library Blog*, 25 August 2016) <https://peacepalacelibrary.nl/blog/2016/100-year-history-statelessness> accessed 4 September 2021.

103 Laura van Waas, *Nationality Matters. Statelessness under International Law* (School of Human Rights Research Series, Vol 29; Intersentia 2008) 32.

104 The 1930 Hague Convention attracted a number of signatures not followed by ratification. For the current status of the 1930 Hague Convention, see the overview provided by the online United Nations Treaty Collection <https://treaties.un.org/pages/LONViewDetails.aspx?src=LON&id=516&chapter=30&clang=_en> (accessed 4 September 2021).

105 Carol A Batchelor, 'Stateless Persons: Some Gaps in International Protection' (1995) 7 International Journal of Refugee Law 232, 249.

106 Arts 8–11 1930 Hague Convention.

107 Arts 12–17 1930 Hague Convention.

108 Preamble to 1930 Hague Convention.

109 See also Art 7 1930 Hague Convention.

110 The other one was the Protocol relating to Military Obligations in Certain Cases of Double Nationality adopted 12 April 1930, entered into force 25 May 1937) 178 LTS 227.

111 Protocol relating to a Certain Case of Statelessness (adopted 12 April 1930, entered into force 1 July 1937) 179 LTS 115.

112 Gerard-René de Groot & Olivier Willem Vonk, *International Standards on Nationality Law. Text, Cases and Materials* (Wolf Legal Publishers 2015) 98.

113 Special Protocol concerning Statelessness (adopted 12 April 1930, entered into force 15 March 2004) 2252 UNTS 435.

a case, the state whose nationality he last possessed is bound to admit this person, at the request of said foreign state if he is permanently indigent or has been sentenced to imprisonment.[114] Both Protocols are, therefore, quite limited in scope and relevance to preventing and solving statelessness – in particular in light of the range of legal instruments on human rights, nationality and statelessness existing today.

The Universal Declaration of Human Rights (UDHR), adopted by the United Nations General Assembly (UNGA) in 1948, contains – for the first time – a human right to a nationality and the prohibition of arbitrary deprivation of nationality in Article 15. Furthermore, Article 2 contains a non-discrimination clause. This entails that everyone is entitled to all the rights and freedoms set forth in the UDHR, without distinction of any kind, such as race, color, sex, language, religion, political or other opinion, national or social origin, property, birth or other status. This means that no one should be discriminated in claiming their right to a nationality, which helps to prevent statelessness. The UDHR is a non-binding legal instrument, but has been very influential. Also, many of its provisions are now binding international law because they are currently part of international customary law or have been included in treaties.[115] The inclusion of the right to a nationality in the UDHR was not uncontroversial. Nonetheless, the entire article was eventually adopted, indicating that many states accepted that there are certain human rights aspects to nationality.[116] By proclaiming that every individual has the right to a nationality, the individual was introduced "as an actor in relation to matters traditionally decided exclusively by states".[117] The right to a nationality as provided for in the UDHR was not transposed into other UN treaties, but aspects of it can be found in many legal instruments. These are discussed in more depth below.

In 1957, a treaty relating to both the 1930 Convention and the UDHR was adopted: the Convention on the Nationality of Married Women (1957 Convention).[118] Where the 1930 Convention still accepted inequality between men and women in nationality matters and included provisions to mitigate the risk of statelessness resulting from this inequality, the 1957 Convention explicitly recognizes in its preamble everyone's right to a nationality pursuant to the UDHR. Even if this treaty does not prescribe complete equality between men and women in nationality matters, it does go a step further than the 1930 Convention by providing that the nationality of the wife is not automatically affected in certain circumstances, thus rendering Articles 8 and 9 of the 1930 Convention obsolete.[119] As such, the 1957 Convention is a relevant document

114 Art 1 Special Protocol Concerning Statelessness.

115 Cf John Dugard, 'The Influence of the Universal Declaration as Law' (2009) 24 Maryland Journal of International Law 85.

116 Ineta Ziemele & Gunnar G Schram, 'Article 15' in Gudmundur Alfredsson & Asbjørn Eide, *The Universal Declaration of Human Rights. A Common Standard of Achievement* (Martinus Nijhoff Publishers 1999) 297–323, 300–302.

117 Ibid 297–323, 297–298.

118 Convention on the Nationality of Married Women (adopted 20 February 1957, entered into force 11 August 1958) 309 UNTS 65 (1957 Convention).

119 Gerard-René de Groot & Olivier Willem Vonk, *International Standards on Nationality Law. Text, Cases and Materials* (Wolf Legal Publishers 2015) 151. Art 8 and 9 1930 Convention assumed that

with regard to the conflict of nationality laws and preventing statelessness for married women. At the same time, however, some of its provisions conflict with complete equality between men and women as prescribed by CEDAW.[120] Some states have therefore since denounced this treaty.[121]

Refugees and the stateless (1951–1961)

Because the international community was concerned about the status of people who remained without proper protection after World War II, particularly in Europe, a number of legal instruments were adopted in the context of the United Nations (UN) to address the issues that refugees and stateless people face(d).[122] The 1951 Convention Relating to the Status of Refugees (1951 Convention)[123] was the first to be adopted and concerns the protection of refugees as defined in this treaty. Not only does the 1951 Convention set forth a definition of a refugee, it also includes basic minimum standards for the treatment of refugees and contains important principles: non-discrimination[124], non-penalization (for illegal entry or stay) and *non-refoulement*.[125] As the 1951 Convention created binding obligations for states, states were able to share the burden of responsibility of refugees among them.[126] It is thus an instrument of protection, but also of burden-sharing between states. According to the definition of Article 1(A)(2) of the 1951 Convention[127] a refugee is any person

> "owing to well-founded fear of being persecuted for reasons of race, religion, nationality, membership of a particular social group or political opinion, is outside the country of his nationality and is unable or, owing to such fear, is unwilling to avail himself of the protection

---

states still provided in their national laws for the loss of nationality of a married women and made this conditional on the acquisition of the nationality of the husband. Art 1 1957 Convention provides that states agree that marriage, dissolution thereof or the change of nationality by the husband during marriage, shall not automatically affect the nationality of the wife.

120 See para 1.5.1 (under the header 'UN human rights treaties').

121 Eg Luxembourg, the Netherlands and United Kingdom. See also Gerard-René de Groot & Olivier Willem Vonk, *International Standards on Nationality Law. Text, Cases and Materials* (Wolf Legal Publishers 2015) 151 and the UN Treaty Collection <https://treaties.un.org/Pages/ViewDetailsIII.aspx?src=TREATY&mtdsg_no=XVI-2&chapter=16&Temp=mtdsg3&clang=_en> accessed 4 September 2021.

122 See also chapter 2 of this book.

123 Convention relating to the Status of Refugees (adopted 28 July 1951, entered into force 22 April 1954) 189 UNTS 137 (1951 Convention/Refugee Convention).

124 Art 3 1951 Convention.

125 See more elaborately for instance Guy S Goodwin-Gill & Jane McAdam, *The Refugee in International Law* (3rd ed, Oxford University Press 2007), which gives a broad overview of the international laws relating to refugees and includes chapters like '*Non-Refoulement* in the 1951 Refugee Convention'.

126 Terje Einarsen, 'Drafting History of the 1951 Convention and the 1967 Protocol' in Andreas Zimmerman (ed), *The 1951 Convention Relating to the Status of Refugees and Its 1967 Protocol. A Commentary* (Oxford University Press 2011) 37–73, 40; preamble to the 1951 Convention.

127 Read in line with the 1967 Protocol relating to the Status of Refugees (adopted 31 January 1967, entered into force 4 October 1967) 606 UNTS 267, which mainly concerns the universality of the refugee definition.

> of that country; or who, not having a nationality and being outside the country of his former habitual residence, is unable or, owing to such fear, is unwilling to return to it. In the case of a person who has more than one nationality, the term "the country of his nationality" shall mean each of the countries of which he is a national, and a person shall not be deemed to be lacking the protection of the country of his nationality if, without any valid reason based on well-founded fear, he has not availed himself of the protection of one of the countries of which he is a national."

This definition demonstrates that the 1951 Convention applies to both refugees with a nationality, as well as to refugees without a nationality. Hence, some stateless people – i.e. those who are refugees – are eligible for protection and solutions to their predicament under this instrument. Important for solving statelessness is Article 34 of the 1951 Convention, obliging states parties to facilitate the naturalization of refugees, which means that stateless refugees should be able to acquire a nationality at some point.

Two treaties specifically dealing with statelessness were adopted in the context of the UN after World War II: the Convention Relating to the Status of Stateless Persons in 1954 (1954 Convention) and the Convention on the Reduction of Statelessness in 1961 (1961 Convention), which were both briefly mentioned above already. These treaties contain provisions regarding the prevention of and solutions to statelessness, even if the 1961 Convention at first glance seems more focused on this.

The 1954 Convention is "devoted to the improvement of the status of stateless persons by setting out a minimum standard of treatment for the stateless to enjoy, without discrimination".[128] The Convention was modelled after the 1951 Convention[129] and mimics this treaty in terms of topics, even though the way in which a stateless person should be treated may vary per right as compared to refugees. Also, the entitlements following from the provisions of the 1954 Convention are extended based on the degree of attachment between a person and the country (s)he finds him- or herself in.[130] Even if the protection of stateless people is in principle outside of this study's scope, the 1954 Convention does provide provisions to relevant to the prevention of and solutions to statelessness. Importantly, the 1954 Convention contains the definition of a stateless person in Article 1 – the only place where international law defines 'statelessness'. Using the definition, we can identify who is (at risk of) stateless(ness) and thus see where statelessness can be prevented or solved. Identifying persons as being (at risk of) stateless is thus in any case an important first step in trying to provide a person with a solution to their situation or preventing them from becoming statelessness. This is also evidenced when looking at a durable solution to statelessness

---

128 Laura van Waas, *Nationality Matters. Statelessness under International Law* (School of Human Rights Research Series, Vol 29; Intersentia 2008) 229.

129 Convention Relating to the Status of Refugees (adopted 28 July 1951, entered into force 22 April 1954) 189 UNTS 137 (1951 Convention/Refugee Convention).

130 Laura van Waas, 'The UN Statelessness Conventions' in Alice Edwards & Laura van Waas (eds), *Nationality and Statelessness under International Law* (Cambridge University Press 2014) 64–87, 73–74.

in the 1954 Convention, which is provided by Article 32 in the form of facilitated acquisition of nationality through naturalization.

The 1961 Convention – the other treaty on statelessness – aims to reduce statelessness and is important in its consolidation of different principles relating to nationality, such as non-discrimination[131], the rights of children and the avoidance of statelessness. Even though this treaty's influence has been limited because of a rather low number of ratifications for years, the number of states parties to this convention has been increasing in the 21st century.[132] The 1961 Convention is only applicable when there is a risk of statelessness[133], even though there is no clarification anywhere in the text of the convention as to what that means. Nonetheless, the definition of statelessness in the 1954 Convention is presumed by the 1961 Convention.[134] Substantively, the 1961 Convention contains a number of provisions concerning the prevention of statelessness in different circumstances: at birth – where a child fails to acquire the nationality of any state; later in life – when a person loses, renounces or is deprived of his or her nationality; in the context of state succession.[135] To be more specific: Articles 1–4 of the 1961 Convention are clearly focused on preventing and solving childhood statelessness[136], whereas Articles 5–9 are concerned with preventing statelessness in cases of loss and deprivation of nationality, with Article 9 specifically containing the principle of non-discrimination.[137] Moreover, Article 10 of the 1961 Convention deals with preventing statelessness in the context of state succession.

There is no judicial body that oversees the implementation of the three UN treaties that were discussed above – the 1951 Convention, the 1954 Convention and the 1961 Convention.[138] However, the Office of the United Nations High Commissioner for Refugees (UNCHR) has a role with regard to refugees and stateless people under these treaties. According to its 1950 Statute, UNHCR originally only had a mandate to address the situation of stateless refugees.[139] Indeed, "UNHCR's supervisory responsibility is [considered] an integral and inherent part of its international refugee protection

131 Art 9 1961 Convention.

132 Cf Mark Manly & Santhosh Persaud, 'UNHCR and Responses to Statelessness' (2009) 32 Forced Migration Review 7.

133 With the exception of Art 9 of the 1961 Convention, which is a general norm, and reads as follows: "A Contracting State may not deprive any person or group of persons of their nationality on racial, ethnic, religious or political grounds".

134 Carol A Batchelor, 'Stateless Persons: Some Gaps in International Protection' (1995) 7 International Journal of Refugee Law 232.

135 Laura van Waas, *Nationality Matters. Statelessness under International Law* (School of Human Rights Research Series, Vol 29; Intersentia 2008) 44.

136 Cf UNHCR, 'Guidelines on Statelessness No. 4: Ensuring Every Child's Right to Acquire a Nationality through Articles 1–4 of the 1961 Convention on the Reduction of Statelessness' (2012) HCR/GS/12/04.

137 See also UNCHR, 'Expert Meeting: Interpreting the 1961 Statelessness Convention and Avoiding Statelessness resulting from Loss and Deprivation of Nationality ("Tunis Conclusions")' (2014) <https://www.refworld.org/docid/533a754b4.html> accessed 4 September 2021.

138 The 1954 Convention and the 1961 Convention together are also referred to as 'Statelessness Conventions'.

139 UNGA Res 428 (Fifth Session, 14 December 1950) 46.

function".[140] In 1995, the UNGA included statelessness in a resolution regarding UNHCR.[141] More specifically, the UNGA asked UNHCR to promote accession to the 1954 Convention and the 1961 Convention as well as to provide relevant technical and advisory services pertaining to the preparation and implementation of nationality legislation to interested states.[142] This provided UNHCR with a "broad global mandate" to address statelessness.[143] A "turning point" can be seen in 2006, when UNHCR was provided with more guidance on the implementation of their mandate by UNHCR's Executive Committee[144], which was later endorsed by the UNGA.[145] Furthermore, UNHCR has a specific role under Article 11 of the 1961 Convention as a body to which a person claiming the benefit of the 1961 Convention may apply for the examination of his or her claim and for assistance in presenting it to the appropriate authority.[146] Also, UNHCR has in practice fulfilled the role of the Secretary-General in Article 33 of the 1954 Convention and advises states parties on the implementation of the 1954 Convention.[147]

With regard to the 1954 Convention, UNHCR has also provided further interpretative guidance in its Handbook on the Protection of Stateless Persons, focusing on determining statelessness, procedures for statelessness determination and the status of stateless people at the national level.[148] On the 1961 Convention, UNHCR has issued Guidelines on Statelessness No. 4 and No. 5 on ensuring every child's right to acquire a nationality and on loss and deprivation of nationality.[149]

---

140 Volker Turk, 'UNHCR's Supervisory Responsibility' (2002) UNHCR New Issues in Refugee Research: Working Paper No. 67, 4 <https://www.refworld.org/docid/4fe405ef2.html> accessed 4 September 2021.

141 UNGA Res 50/152 (1995) A/RES/50/152.

142 Ibid, para 15.

143 About the origins of UNHCR's global mandate on statelessness and why it was only conferred decades after the adoption of the Statelessness Conventions see Matthew Seet, 'The Origins of UNHCR's Global Mandate on Statelessness' (2016) 28 International Journal of Refugee Law 7.

144 Mark Manly, 'UNHCR's Mandate and Activities to Address Statelessness' in Alice Edwards & Laura van Waas (eds), *Nationality and Statelessness under International Law* (Cambridge University Press 2014) 88–115, 90.

145 UNGA Res 61/137 (2006) A/RES/61/137.

146 The UNGA already entrusted UNHCR with this specific task in relation to statelessness after the entry into force of the 1961 Convention, see UNGA Res 3274 (XXIX) (1974) A/RES/3274(XXIX) & UNGA Res 31/36 (1976) A/RES/31/36.

147 Art 33 1954 Convention reads as follows: The Contracting States shall communicate to the Secretary-General of the United Nations the laws and regulations which they may adopt to ensure the application of this Convention. See also Mark Manly, 'UNHCR's Mandate and Activities to Address Statelessness' in Alice Edwards & Laura van Waas (eds), *Nationality and Statelessness under International Law* (Cambridge University Press 2014) 90–91.

148 UNHCR, 'Handbook on the Protection of Stateless Persons under the 1954 Convention relating to the Status of Stateless Persons' (Geneva, 2014) <www.unhcr.org/protection/statelessness/53b698ab9/handbook-protection-stateless-persons.html> accessed 4 September 2021.

149 UNHCR, 'Guidelines on Statelessness No. 4: Ensuring Every Child's Right to Acquire a Nationality through Articles 1–4 of the 1961 Convention on the Reduction of Statelessness' (2012) HCR/GS/12/04; UNHCR, 'Guidelines on Statelessness No. 5: Loss and Deprivation of Nationality under Articles 5–9 of the 1961 Convention on the Reduction of Statelessness' (2020) HCR/GS/20/05.

In light of UNHCR's global mandate to address statelessness, its work regarding the Statelessness Conventions[150] and its #IBELONG Campaign to end statelessness by 2024[151], this organization and its output continue to be relevant to preventing and solving statelessness globally.

With regard to the question of the stateless and refugees, it should furthermore be noted that in 1949, a separate agency was founded to implement relief and works programs for Palestinian refugees[152]: UN Relief and Works Agency for Palestine Refugees in the Near East (UNRWA).[153] Palestinians, one of the large groups of stateless people in the world, are excluded from the international protection regime for refugees and the stateless as described above and in chapter 2. This because Palestinians fall under the mandate of UNRWA and are therefore separately receiving protection and assistance from the UN as described in Article 1(2)(i) of the 1954 Convention.

UN human rights treaties (1965–2006)

At UN level, a number of human rights treaties have been adopted that contain provisions of relevance to preventing and solving statelessness. All of the UN human rights treaties considered here, have dedicated 'treaty bodies' (Committees), in which experts monitor the implementation of the standards from the treaties by the states parties. These treaty bodies can make general recommendations or comments and/or concluding observations and recommendations to states – a form of 'soft law' – and can sometimes, under certain conditions, consider individual complaints or communications from individuals.[154] As some examples below demonstrate, treaty bodies have also made relevant contributions to guiding standard-setting at the international level on preventing and solving statelessness.[155]

In 1965, the International Convention on the Elimination of All Forms of Racial Discrimination (ICERD) was adopted.[156] In the spirit of every human being's equal dignity and rights, this treaty obliges states to enact policies to eliminate racial discrimination, which includes discrimination based on descent, race, national or

150 Ie the 1954 Convention and the 1961 Convention.

151 UNHCR, '#IBelong Campaign', <https://www.unhcr.org/ibelong/> accessed 4 September 2021. See also UNHCR, 'Global Action Plan to End Statelessness' (4 November 2014) <www.unhcr.org/statelesscampaign2014/Global-Action-Plan-eng.pdf> accessed 4 September 2021.

152 On the Palestinians see also Michal Baer, 'The Palestinian People: Ambiguities of Citizenship' in Rhoda E Howard-Hassmann & Margaret Walton-Roberts (eds) *The Human Right to Citizenship. A Slippery Concept* (University of Pennsylvania Press 2015) 45–61.

153 UNGA Res 302 (IV) (8 December 1949) UN Doc A/RES/302 (IV).

154 See also Helen Keller & Geir Ulfstein, *UN Human Rights Treaty Bodies. Law and Legitimacy* (Cambridge University Press 2012).

155 Recommendations made by UN treaty bodies and monitoring mechanisms that are relevant to statelessness and nationality can be explored easily using the ISI Database on Statelessness & Human Rights <https://database.institutesi.org> accessed 4 September 2021.

156 International Convention on the Elimination of All Forms of Racial Discrimination (adopted 21 December 1965, entered into force 4 January 1969) 660 UNTS 195 (ICERD).

ethnic origin.[157] In particular, states should guarantee everyone's right to equality before the law in the enjoyment of the right to nationality.[158] At the same time, however, Article 1(3) of the ICERD explicitly mentions that nothing in the convention may be interpreted as affecting in any way the legal provisions of states concerning nationality, citizenship or naturalization, provided that such provisions do not discriminate against any particular nationality. Implementation of ICERD is monitored by the Committee on the Elimination of Racial Discrimination. The Committee's General Comment 30 pays particular attention to access to citizenship, i.e. the acquisition of nationality by non-citizens, including stateless people, as well as to the reduction of (childhood) statelessness.[159] Furthermore, the Committee has made reference to the right to a nationality in concluding observations and communications it received.[160]

The International Covenant on Civil and Political Rights (ICCPR), which was adopted in 1966[161], contains a right for every child to acquire a nationality.[162] Also, it obliges states to register a child immediately after birth, which can help to prevent statelessness from occurring.[163] Even though the (legally binding) ICCPR contains a number of rights also included in the UDHR, a right to a nationality for everyone is missing. *Travaux préparatoires* reveal that this was not included because of the complexity of the issue as well as the belief that this was already addressed by the 1961 Convention.[164] As such, the ICCPR has a clear focus on preventing and solving childhood statelessness. Of relevance to preventing and solving statelessness is furthermore that the ICCPR contains the principle of non-discrimination, which is important to ensuring non-discriminatory nationality laws for instance.[165]

The implementation of the ICCPR by the states parties is monitored by the UN Human Rights Committee (CCPR). In its General Comment on Article 24 of the ICCPR (rights of the child), the CCPR explicitly notes that the purpose of Article 24(3) is to prevent a child from being afforded less protection by society and the state because

---

157 Art 1(1) and 2(1) ICERD.

158 Art 5(d)(iii) ICERD.

159 CERD, 'General Recommendation 30: Discrimination Against Non-Citizens' (2004) CERD/C/64/Misc.11/rev.3.

160 Michiel Hoornick, 'Addressing Statelessness through the International Convention on the Elimination of All Forms of Racial Discrimination (ICERD)' (2020) 2 Statelessness and Citizenship Review 222.

161 International Covenant on Civil and Political Rights (adopted 16 December 1966, entered into force 23 March 1976) 999 UNTS 171 (ICCPR).

162 Art 24(3) ICCPR.

163 Cf Maureen Lynch & Melanie Teff, 'Childhood Statelessness' (2009) 32 Forced Migration Review 31; UNHCR, 'Good Practices Paper – Action 7: Ensuring Birth Registration for the Prevention of Statelessness' (2017) <https://www.refworld.org/docid/5a0ac8f94.html> accessed 4 September 2021.

164 Draft International Covenants on Human Rights, Report of the Third Committee, 17th Session, 10 December 1961, A/5655, see also more elaborately Johannes M M Chan, 'The Right to a Nationality as a Human Right. The Current Trend Towards Recognition' (1980) 12 Human Rights Law Journal 1, 4–5; María José Recalde Vela, 'How Far has the Protection of the Right to Nationality under International Human Rights Law Progressed from 1923 until the Present Day?' (Master, Tilburg University 2014) 80–83.

165 Art 2(1), 26 and specifically for children in Art 24(1) ICCPR.

(s)he is stateless.[166] Dependent on the ratification of the First Optional Protocol to the ICCPR, the CCPR can also examine individual complaints on possible violations of the ICCPR by states. The CCPR has for instance dealt with a case on the refusal to grant nationality through naturalization: *Q v. Denmark*.[167] Another unprecedented case involving statelessness and Article 24(3) of the ICCPR is that of DZ against the Netherlands.[168] The Netherlands refuses to register DZ, who was born in the Netherlands in 2010, as being stateless, which prevents him from accessing the rights of the 1954 Convention and, eventually, acquisition of a nationality. According to the Human Rights Committee, this violated the ICCPR and the Netherlands was "to review its decision on the author's application to be registered as stateless in the civil registry [...] as well as its decision on the author's application to be recognized as a Dutch citizen, taking into account the Committee's findings".[169] In addition, the Netherlands needed to adapt its laws and policies in this regard "to avoid similar violations in the future".[170] This shows a real impact at national level, which goes beyond the individual case.

In 1979, a document specifically on the elimination of discrimination against women was adopted: the Convention on the Elimination of All Forms of Discrimination against Women (CEDAW).[171] This treaty contains a provision[172] on the equality – i.e. non-discrimination – of women and men as regards nationality matters, which could be helpful in preventing statelessness because it is aimed at preventing conflict of nationality laws and loss of nationality of women. This instrument is also useful to preventing childhood statelessness, because it allows a mother – like a father – to pass on nationality to the child.[173] The CEDAW Committee has addressed equal nationality rights for women in two General Recommendations: No. 21 (equality in marriage and family relations)[174] and No. 32[175] on the gender-related dimensions of refugee status, asylum, nationality and statelessness of women. Furthermore, the CEDAW Committee

---

166 CCPR, 'General Comment No. 17: Article 24 (Rights of the Child)' (1989) 35th Session, para 8.

167 *Q v Denmark* Com No 2001/2010 (CCPR, 19 May 2015) UN Doc CCPR/C/113/D/2001/2010 (2015).

168 Open Society Foundations, 'Litigation: Zhao v Netherlands' (2017) <https://www.opensocietyfoundations.org/litigation/zhao-v-netherlands> accessed 3 January 2022. Full communication to CCPR in this case is available <https://pilpnjcm.nl/wp-content/uploads/2016/11/ECD-1507-Zhao-5-Communication-As-Sent-SB-11.23.16.pdf> accessed 3 January 2022.

169 *DZ v the Netherlands* Com No 2918/2016 (CCPR, 20 January 2021) UN Doc CCPR/C/130/D/2918/2016 (2020), para 10.

170 Ibid, para 10.

171 Convention on the Elimination of All Forms of Discrimination against Women (adopted 18 December 1979, entered into force 3 September 1981) 1249 UNTS 13 (CEDAW).

172 Art 9 CEDAW.

173 See also ISI, 'Statelessness & Human Rights: The Convention on the Elimination of All Forms of Discrimination against Women' (2018) Statelessness Essentials No. 7 <www.institutesi.org/statelessness_and_CEDAW.pdf> accessed 4 September 2021.

174 CEDAW Committee, 'General Recommendation No. 21: Equality in Marriage and Family Relations' (1994) 13th Session.

175 CEDAW Committee, 'General Recommendation No. 32 on on the Gender-related Dimensions of Refugee Status, Asylum, Nationality and Statelessness of Women' (2014) CEDAW/C/GC/32.

has made recommendations to states in its concluding observations in order to ensure gender equal nationality laws.[176]

The almost universally ratified Convention on the Rights of the Child (CRC)[177] of 1989 includes, similar to the ICCPR, a right for every child to acquire a nationality[178], but also explicitly mentions preventing statelessness.[179] Furthermore, the CRC obliges states to ensure that children are registered immediately after birth[180] and includes a non-discrimination provision specific to children.[181] Furthermore, states are obliged to respect the right of the child to preserve his or her identity, including nationality, as recognized by law without unlawful interference. Where a child is illegally deprived of some or all of the elements of his or her identity, states are to provide assistance and protection.[182] As such, the CRC is definitely relevant to addressing childhood statelessness.[183] The CRC Committee monitors the CRC, but has not yet addressed the children's right to a nationality in a General Comment.[184] Nonetheless, Article 7 CRC has been the subject of concluding observations and recommendations by the CRC Committee.[185]

In 1990, another human rights treaty was adopted in the context of the UN: the International Convention on the Protection of the Rights of All Migrant Workers and Members of their Families (ICMW).[186] The relevant provisions here are similar to those already included in the other human rights treaties above, but are specific to (children of) migrant workers: the principle of non-discrimination[187], the right to registration

176 ISI, 'Statelessness & Human Rights: The Convention on the Elimination of All Forms of Discrimination against Women' (2018) Statelessness Essentials No. 7 <www.institutesi.org/statelessness_and_CEDAW.pdf> accessed 4 September 2021.

177 Convention on the Rights of the Child (adopted 20 November 1989, entered into force 2 September 1990) 1577 UNTS 3 (CRC).

178 Art 7(1) CRC.

179 Art 7(2) CRC: "States Parties shall ensure the implementation of these rights in accordance with their national law and their obligations under the relevant international instruments in this field, in particular where the child would otherwise be stateless."

180 Art 7(1) CRC.

181 Art 2 CRC.

182 Art 8 CRC.

183 See also ISI, 'Statelessness & Human Rights: The Convention on the Rights of the Child' (2018) Statelessness Essentials No. 6 <https://files.institutesi.org/statelessness-and-CRC.pdf> accessed 4 September 2021.

184 Some useful language can, however, be found in the Joint General Comments of the CRC and the CMW: CMW & CRC, 'Joint General Comment No. 3/22 on the General Principles regarding the Human Rights of Children in the Context of International Migration' (2017) CMW/C/GC/3-CRC/C/GC/22; CMW & CRC, 'Joint General Comment No. 4/No. 23 on State Obligations regarding the Human Rights of Children in the Context of International Migration in Countries of Origin, Transit, Destination and Return' (2017) CMW/C/GC/4-CRC/C/GC/23.

185 ISI, 'Nationality and Statelessness under the CRC' (2017) <www.statelessnessandhumanrights.org/crc/nationality-statelessness-under-the-crc> accessed 4 September 2021.

186 International Convention on the Protection of the Rights of All Migrant Workers and Members of their Families (adopted 18 December 1990, entered into force 1 July 2003) 2220 UNTS 3 (ICMW). The Committee on Migrant Workers (CMW) monitors implementation of the ICMW.

187 Art 1 & 7 ICMW.

of birth and the right to a nationality.[188] The ICMW's contribution on preventing and solving statelessness is hence focused on non-discrimination of migrant workers and preventing and solving childhood statelessness among children of migrant workers in particular.

Likewise, the Convention on the Rights of Persons with Disabilities (CRPD)[189] of 2006 protects the rights of disabled persons specifically. The treaty obliges states to guarantee on an equal basis with others a right to liberty of movement and nationality for disabled persons.[190] In particular, persons with disabilities have the right to acquire and change a nationality and are not to be deprived of their nationality arbitrarily or on the basis of disability.[191] Special reference is made to documentation of nationality and identification in the CRPD[192], as well as to the right of every disabled child to be registered immediately after birth and to acquire a nationality.[193] The CRPD thus seems to protect quite some aspects of (the right to a) nationality for persons with disabilities, which is helpful to reducing statelessness: it is concerned with childhood statelessness, acquisition of a nationality, arbitrary deprivation of nationality and non-discrimination in nationality matters.

States can also be held accountable through review of their efforts to fulfil their human rights obligations under the UDHR and the UN human rights treaties in the Universal Periodic Review (UPR). Also in this context, statelessness is increasingly being raised. Research of the Institute on Statelessness and Inclusion (ISI) shows that 84% of UN member states has received one or more recommendations from other states relevant to statelessness and/or nationality matters during UPR Cycles 1 and 2.[194]

Furthermore, the Special Procedures[195] of the Human Rights Council[196] are relevant to statelessness. These Special Procedures are divided into country-specific and thematic mandates. Up until 2022 there has been no separate thematic mandate with regard to statelessness and there is no country-specific mandate with regard to any of the European states that are the focus of this research. However, recommendations to governments to amend nationality laws are encountered in

188 Art 29 ICMW.

189 Convention on the Rights of Persons with Disabilities (adopted 13 December 2006, entered into force 3 May 2008) 2515 UNTS 3 (CRPD). The Committee on the Rights of Persons with Disabilities (CRPD Committee) monitors implementation of the CRPD.

190 Art 18 CRPD.

191 Art 18(1)(a) CRPD.

192 Art 18(1)(b) CRPD.

193 Art 18(2) CRPD.

194 ISI, 'Nationality and Statelessness in the UPR' (2017) <www.statelessnessandhumanrights.org/upr-universal-periodic-review/nationality-statelessness-in-the-upr> accessed 4 September 2021.

195 See <https://www.ohchr.org/EN/HRBodies/SP/Pages/Welcomepage.aspx> accessed 4 September 2021. UN Special Procedures are in fact appointed independent experts, also referred to as Special Rapporteurs, who offer guidance and recommendations on human rights.

196 The Human Rights Council is a UN inter-governmental body tasked with the promotion and protection of human rights globally.

reports of country-specific Special Procedures.[197] Also, the different thematic Special Procedures hold relevance to statelessness. For instance, the Special Rapporteur on minority issues has identified statelessness as a minority issue, and recommends – *inter alia* – that states do "not arbitrarily or discriminatorily deny or deprive minorities of citizenship".[198] A number of Special Rapporteurs have furthermore made reference to statelessness specifically in their reports and some of them endorsed the Principles on Deprivation of Nationality as a National Security Measure, which pay attention to arbitrary deprivation of nationality, ensuring everyone's right to a nationality and the avoidance of statelessness in the specific context of national security and counter-terrorism measures.[199]

More broadly, the Human Rights Council has proven to be a relevant forum considering preventing and solving statelessness, issuing resolutions relating to the right to a nationality and statelessness, for example calling upon states "to adopt and implement nationality legislation consistent with their obligations under international law with a view to prevent and reduce statelessness among women and children"[200] or "to refrain from (..) enacting or maintaining legislation that would arbitrarily deprive persons of their nationality".[201]

Another UN instrument of relevance is the 2030 Agenda for Sustainable Development, which includes the SDGs.[202] Even if these are not legally binding, they are influential and attempt to address the global challenges we face today, including poverty, inequality and climate change. Indeed, "the SDGs have the potential to leverage considerable interest and investment, which go far beyond what human rights players generally have access to".[203] There is, however, no specific SDG or Target that focuses on statelessness as such. Nonetheless, a number of SDGs are relevant to preventing and solving statelessness. In particular, Target 5.1 of SDG 5 on ending all

---

197 Cf Rachel Brett, 'Using the UN Human Rights Special Procedures to address statelessness' (*ENS Blog*, 1 October 2015) <https://www.statelessness.eu/blog/using-un-human-rights-special-procedures-address-statelessness> accessed 4 September 2021.

198 UNGA, 'Report of the Special Rapporteur on minority issues. Statelessness: a minority issue' (20 July 2018) UN Doc A/73/205.

199 The Principles on Deprivation of Nationality as a National Security Measure (2020) < https://www.refworld.org/pdfid/5f3bf26d4.pdf> accessed 4 September 2021, have been endorsed by *inter alia* the UN Special Rapporteur on contemporary forms of racism, racial discrimination, xenophobia and related intolerance; the UN Special Rapporteur on Minority Issues; the UN Special Rapporteur on the promotion and protection of human rights and fundamental freedoms while countering terrorism; UN Special Rapporteur on the promotion of truth, justice, reparation, and guarantees of non-recurrence. See also <https://www.institutesi.org/pages/principles-endorsements> accessed 4 September 2021.

200 UNGA, 'Resolution adopted by the Human Rights Council. The right to a nationality: women and children' (16 July 2012) UN Doc A/HRC/RES/20/4.

201 UNGA, 'Resolution Adopted by the Human Rights Council. Human rights and arbitrary deprivation of nationality' (15 July 2016) UN Doc A/HRC/RES/32/5.

202 There are 17 SDGs and 169 associated Targets, which are part of the 2030 Agenda for Sustainable Development, UNGA Res 70/1 (25 September 2015) A/RES/70/1.

203 ISI, 'Statelessness, Human Rights and the Sustainable Development Agenda. A Working Paper' (2017) 42 <www.institutesi.org/SDG_working-paper2017.pdf> accessed 4 September 2021.

forms of discrimination against all women and girls everywhere in relevant in battling inequality between men and women in nationality laws and preventing statelessness arising as a consequence of that.[204] SDG 10 and Target 10.3 furthermore aim to ensure equal opportunity and reduce inequalities of outcome, including by eliminating discriminatory laws, policies and practices and by promoting appropriate legislation, policies and action in this regard. As statelessness is often the result of exclusion and discrimination, this target is pertinent to preventing and solving statelessness.[205] Also useful to preventing and solving statelessness is SDG 16 and Target 16.9[206], which aim to achieve legal identity for all, including birth registration, by 2030. Birth registration is often the first step in realizing every child's right to a nationality. Furthermore, nationality documentation – proof of legal identity – is important for claiming nationality and the benefits attached thereto.[207] Indeed, SDG Target 16.9 can be an opportunity for people at risk of statelessness or who are stateless. "The opportunity is the belated emphasis on the importance of official recognition and registration as a means for an individual to assert rights as a member of society."[208] At the same time, one should also be aware of the threats that "short cuts and interim solutions" pose: "a utilitarian commitment to the majority or to the priorities of the state rather than the individual, mean those of 'doubtful' status are – despite the SDG commitment – left behind".[209]

Moreover, SDG Target 16.7 aims to ensure responsive, inclusive, participatory and representative decision-making at all levels, hinting in particular at the rights that stateless people notoriously lack: electoral and participatory rights, which are reserved for citizens. At the same time, "[g]enuine democratic elections expressing the will of the people are essential to securing the legitimate authority of governments and the promotion and protection of human rights".[210] The participatory rights for stateless people have been identified as an issue pertaining to international (human rights) law in this context[211], for which citizenship often remains a precondition. Addressing the participatory rights of stateless persons may therefore also demand further consideration of solutions – i.e. granting of nationality.

---

204 UNHCR, 'The Sustainable Development Goals and Addressing Statelessness. Briefing Note' (2017) 3 <https://www.refworld.org/pdfid/58b6e3364.pdf> accessed 5 September 2021.

205 Ibid.

206 See also ISI, 'Sustainable Development Goal 16.9. Legal Identity, Nationality & Statelessness' (2018) Statelessness Essentials No. 9 <https://files.institutesi.org/Legal-identity.pdf> accessed 5 September 2021.

207 Ibid, 4. See also para 1.4.3 of this chapter on the relation between registration, documentation, legal identity, nationality and statelessness.

208 Bronwen Manby, '"Legal Identity for All" and Statelessness: Opportunity and Threat at the Junction of Public and Private International Law' (2020) 2 Statelessness and Citizenship Review 248, 271.

209 Bronwen Manby, '"Legal Identity for All" and Statelessness: Opportunity and Threat at the Junction of Public and Private International Law' (2020) 2 Statelessness and Citizenship Review 248, 271.

210 The Carter Center & OHCHR, 'Human Rights and Election Standards: A Plan of Action' (December 2017) 4 <https://www.ohchr.org/Documents/Issues/Democracy/Elections/POA_EN.pdf> accessed 5 September 2021.

211 Ibid, 7.

Finally, in the past years, Global Compacts on migration[212] and on refugees[213] have been adopted, which "promise to respect the human rights of people on the move, to provide the conditions for them to live in safety and with dignity, and to empower them to enrich the societies in which they live", but also "to build consensus on principles and practices to improve international cooperation on and management of human mobility".[214] These Global Compacts are not treaties and are not legally binding, but do provide a "roadmap" for cooperation and coordination on these matters.[215] They also pay specific attention to preventing and solving statelessness. The Global Compact for Migration, for instance, recognizes the need to

> "[s]trengthen measures to reduce statelessness, including by registering migrants' births, ensuring that women and men can equally confer their nationality on their children, and providing nationality to children born in another State's territory, especially in situations where a child would otherwise be stateless, fully respecting the human right to a nationality and in accordance with national legislation".[216]

The Global Compact on Refugees furthermore highlights the importance of identification of stateless people or those who are at risk of statelessness[217], considers the relevance of birth registration to preventing statelessness[218], and refers to other standards, good practices and initiatives on preventing and reducing statelessness, such as UNHCR's #IBELONG campaign.[219] Commentary on, in particular, the Global Compact for Migration, however, shows that there is certainly still room for improvement with regard to the people who are non-citizens everywhere. For instance, it "needs to be strengthened by an enhanced commitment to eliminating discrimination between citizens and migrants, and between different categories of migrants"[220] and needs "future advocacy efforts [to] make explicit the relevance of statelessness to all

---

212 Global Compact for Safe, Orderly and Regular Migration (2018) UN Doc A/CONF/231/3 <https://refugeesmigrants.un.org/sites/default/files/180713_agreed_outcome_global_compact_for_migration.pdf> accessed 5 September 2021.

213 Global Compact on Refugees (2018) UN Doc A/73/12 (Part II) <https://www.unhcr.org/gcr/GCR_English.pdf> accessed 5 September 2021.

214 Jane McAdam, 'The Global Compacts on Refugees and Migration: A New Era for International Protection' (2018) 30 International Journal of Refugee Law 571, 572.

215 Cf António Guterres, 'Secretary-General's Remarks at Intergovernmental Conference to Adopt the Global Compact for Migration' (10 December 2018) <https://www.un.org/sg/en/content/sg/statement/2018-12-10/secretary-generals-remarks-intergovernmental-conference-adopt-the-global-compact-for-migration-delivered> accessed 5 September 2021.

216 Global Compact for Safe, Orderly and Regular Migration (2018) UN Doc A/CONF/231/3, para 20 (e) <https://refugeesmigrants.un.org/sites/default/files/180713_agreed_outcome_global_compact_for_migration.pdf> accessed 5 September 2021.

217 Global Compact on Refugees (2018) UN Doc A/73/12 (Part II) para 60 <https://www.unhcr.org/gcr/GCR_English.pdf> accessed 5 September 2021.

218 Ibid, para 82.

219 Ibid, para 83.

220 Elspeth Guild, 'The UN Compact for Safe, Orderly and Regular Migration: What Place for Human Rights' (2018) 30 International Journal of Refugee Law 661, 663.

dimensions of global migration governance".[221] These UN instruments thus take into account statelessness, showing how this has become an issue that is more commonly associated with any questions that concern migration and refugees.

State succession

State succession[222] refers to the situation where one state replaces the other in the responsibility for the international relations of territory.[223] It has been held that state succession is "[a] particular context in which the risk of a conflict of nationality laws is high, and where a large number of persons may simultaneously be affected".[224] State succession can occur in different forms, which are listed conveniently in Part II of the Draft Articles on Nationality of Natural Person in relation to the Succession of State by the International Law Commission (ILC)[225]: transfer of part of the territory; unification of states; dissolution of a state; and separation of part(s) of the territory. Thus, state succession could lead to statelessness, for instance where a person is not considered a national of the successor state(s) nor the predecessor state(s). Also, and particularly, it can create statelessness on a large scale – a result of (new) states using mass denationalization as a tool to establish power of a territory and the people populating it.[226] As such, legal instruments concerning state succession would be helpful in preventing statelessness from occurring.

As was considered above, the 1961 Convention pays only limited attention to state succession, and no comprehensive international (UN level) treaty on state succession currently exists. Nonetheless, the ILC Draft Articles on Nationality of Natural Persons in relation to the Succession of States[227] aim to address nationality matters in the context of state succession. Of particular interest is Article 4 on the prevention of

221 Tendayi Bloom, 'Statelessness and the Global Compact for Safe, Orderly and Regular Migration. Policy Brief' (ENS/OU 2018) 4 <https://www.statelessness.eu/sites/default/files/2020-09/ENS_Statelessness_Global_Compact_Migration_policy-brief.pdf> accessed 5 September 2021.

222 For an overview of state succession and issues of nationality and statelessness see Ineta Ziemele, 'State Succession and Issues of Nationality and Statelessness' in Alice Edwards & Laura van Waas (eds), *Nationality and Statelessness under International Law* (Cambridge University Press 2014) 217–246.

223 Cf Art 2(1)b Vienna Convention on the Succession of States in respect of treaties (adopted 23 August 1978, entered into force 6 November 1996) 1946 UNTS 3.

224 ISI, *The World's Stateless* (Wolf Legal Publishers 2014) 24.

225 ILC, 'Draft Articles on Nationality of Natural Persons in relation to the Succession of States with Commentaries' (1999) 2 Yearbook of the International Law Commission (part two) 19; annex to UNGA Res 55/153 (12 December 2000) UN Doc A/RES/55/153. The ILC is a permanent UN organ, established by the UNGA and tasked with making recommendations for the development of international law and the codification thereof. See also Art 13 (1) UN Charter and Gerard-René de Groot & Olivier Willem Vonk, *International Standards on Nationality Law. Text, Cases and Materials* (Wolf Legal Publishers 2015) 324.

226 Francesco Costamagna, 'Statelessness in the Context of State Succession. An Appraisal under International Law' in Alessandra Annoni & Serena Forlati, *The Changing Role of Nationality in International Law* (Routledge 2013) 37–53, 38.

227 ILC, 'Draft Articles on Nationality of Persons in relation to the Succession of States' (1999) 2 *Yearbook of the International Law Commission* 23 (1999 ILC Draft Articles).

statelessness, which obliges states to "take all appropriate measures to prevent persons who, on the date of the succession of states, had the nationality of the predecessor state from becoming stateless as a result of such succession". Also, relevant is that "states shall not deny persons concerned the right to retain or acquire a nationality or the right of option upon the succession of states by discriminating on any ground".[228] It has been held that these Draft Articles very much rely on the principle of "effective nationality"[229] to determine obligations on states in nationality matters and "utilize a mix of criteria for states to use in determining effective nationality, emphasizing domicile as the predominant criterion (...)".[230] As such, they aim not only to ensure that every person who had a nationality before state succession has a nationality after occurrence of this event, but also has a nationality that corresponds with the factual ties between a person and a state. The Draft Articles are not legally binding on states, but with regard to state succession they "provide the most authoritative guidance on the accepted norms of international law in this area".[231]

1.5.2. OTHER REGIONAL INSTRUMENTS (1969–2018)

A number of other regional cooperation mechanisms, similar to those in Europe that are considered in more depth in this study, have introduced legal norms on (the right to a) nationality and the reduction of statelessness. This paragraph looks at the norms that relate to the prevention of and solutions to statelessness of these regional organizations. Below, the legal instruments introduced on these matters in the African and American regions are considered in particular, due to their similarity to the European region in terms of (the status of) legal instruments and supervisory mechanisms.

In the context of the Organization of American States (OAS), the American Convention of Human Rights (ACHR)[232] was adopted in 1969. Unlike its European 'sister', the ACHR includes a right to a nationality in quite an extensive form. According to Article 20 of this treaty:

> (1) Every person has the right to a nationality.
> (2) Every person has the right to the nationality of the state in whose territory he was born if he does not have the right to any other nationality.
> (3) No one shall be arbitrarily deprived of his nationality or the right to change it.

---

228 Art 15 1999 ILC Draft Articles.

229 This refers to the principle of effective nationality as enunciated in the *Nottebohm* case, in which the ICJ considered whether the legal status of national was in line with existing factual ties between an individual and the state. See also para 1.4.2 above.

230 Jeffrey L Blackman, 'State Succession and Statelessness: The Emerging Right to an Effective Nationality Under International Law' (1998) 19 Michigan Journal of International Law 1141, 1170.

231 Bronwen Manby, *Citizenship in Africa. The Law of Belonging* (Wolf Legal Publishers 2015) 38.

232 American Convention on Human Rights – 'Pact of San José' (adopted 22 November 1969, entered into force 18 July 1978) OAS Treaty Series No 36 (ACHR).

In its (legally binding) judgments, the Inter-American Court of Human Rights (IACtHR) has shed more light on nationality and statelessness by interpreting this human right, as well as the relations of these issues with other rights guaranteed by the ACHR.[233] These cases have also highlighted childhood statelessness and the importance of non-discrimination in nationality matters.[234] As such, the ACHR can address a wide range of issues relating to preventing and solving statelessness: reducing childhood statelessness, preventing (arbitrary) deprivation of nationality, the right to acquire a nationality, and non-discrimination in nationality matters. The OAS has furthermore passed some resolutions on statelessness, which for instance call upon member states to ratify the Statelessness Conventions and to ensure training of member state officials.[235] In December 2014, the Latin American and Caribbean governments, gathered to commemorate the 30th anniversary of the 1984 Cartagena Declaration on Refugees[236], have furthermore adopted the Brazil Declaration and Plan of Action.[237] This Declaration aims to implement cooperation on protection and solutions for refugees, displaced people and stateless people. It includes different instances in which preventing and solving statelessness are considered, highlighting for instance non-discrimination, facilitated naturalization, but also promoting accession to the Statelessness Conventions, facilitating birth registration and statelessness determination procedures.

On the African continent, the Organisation of African Unity (OAU), since 2002 replaced by the African Union (AU), adopted the African Charter on Human and Peoples' Rights (ACHPR)[238] in 1981. The ACHPR does not include a right to a nationality, but in its communications on (alleged) violations of the ACHPR by states, the African Commission on Human and Peoples' Rights (ACmHPR)[239] has considered

---

233 Eg *Ivcher-Bronstein v Peru* Series C No 74 (IACtHR, 6 February 2001); *Case of the Girls Yean and Bosico v Dominican Republic* Series C No 130 (IACtHR, 8 September 2005); *Gelman v Uruguay* Series C No. 221 (IACtHR, 24 February 2011); *Case of the Expelled Dominicans and Haitians v Dominican Republic* Series C No. 282 (IACtHR, 28 August 2014).

234 Eg *Case of the Girls Yean and Bosico v Dominican Republic* Series C No 130 (IACtHR, 8 September 2005).

235 AG/RES. 2826 (XLIV-O/14) *Prevention and Reduction of Statelessness and Protection of Stateless Persons in the Americas* (adopted at 2nd plenary session, 4 June 2014); Kristy A Belton, *Statelessness in the Caribbean. The Paradox of Belonging in a Postnational World* (University of Pennsylvania Press 2017) 49–51.

236 About the 1984 Cartagena Declaration and ensuing process, also see Carlos Maldonado Castillo, 'The Cartagena Process: 30 Years of Innovation and Solidarity' (2015) 49 Forced Migration Review 89.

237 Brazil Declaration, 'A Framework for Cooperation and Regional Solidarity to Strengthen the International Protection of Refugees, Displaced and Stateless Persons in Latin America and the Caribbean', Brasilia, 3 December 2014 <https://www.refworld.org/docid/5487065b4.html> accessed 5 September 2021.

238 African (Banjul) Charter on Human and Peoples' Rights (adopted 27 June 1981, entered into force 21 October 1986) OAU Doc. CAB/LEG/67/3 rev. 5, 21 I.L.M. 58 (1982) (ACHPR).

239 The ACmHPR is tasked with oversight and interpretation of the ACHPR. However, with a protocol to the ACHPR, the African Court on Human and Peoples' Rights (ACtHPR) was created. This Court complements the quasi-judicial mandate of the Commission and can issue legally binding decisions.

issues of nationality and statelessness.[240] Moreover, in March 2018 for instance, the African Court on Human and Peoples' Rights (ACtHPR) decided that Tanzania had arbitrarily deprived the applicant of his nationality, which constituted a violation of Article 15(2) of the UDHR.[241] When considering the different cases under the ACHPR, it appears that a number of rights are relevant to nationality and statelessness, such as the principle of non-discrimination[242], the right to equal treatment before the law[243], the right to respect of the dignity inherent in a human being and to the recognition of his legal status[244] and certain rights relating to freedom of movement and non-nationals and expulsion.[245] Specific to women, the Protocol to the African Charter on Human and Peoples' Rights on the Rights of Women in Africa includes some strong language on non-discrimination.[246] Yet, it is meager as regards the nationality rights of women.[247]

In the African context, a specific instrument on the rights of children has been enacted too: the African Charter on the Rights and Welfare of the Child (ACRWC).[248] In particular, its Article 6 contains the right of every child to be registered immediately after birth and the right to acquire a nationality. Furthermore, states parties to the ACRWC should ensure that their constitutional legislation recognizes the principles according to which a child shall acquire the nationality of the state in the territory of which he has been born if, at the time of the child's birth, he is not granted nationality by any other state in accordance with its laws.[249] The fulfilment of children's rights in Africa under this instrument is monitored by the African Committee of Experts on the Rights and Welfare of the Child (ACERWC). This body has adopted a General Comment on the aforementioned Article 6 of the ACRWC[250] and has, for instance, issued a decision in which nationality and stateless play a (significant) role, and which held that "being stateless as a child is generally antithesis to the best interests of children".[251] The ACERWC's General Comment on Article 6 of the ACRWC provides

---

240 Eg *Amnesty International v Zambia* Comm No 212/98 (ACmHPR, 5 May 1999); *John K Modise v Botswana* Comm No 97/93 (ACmHPR, 6 November 2000); *Open Society Justice Initiative v Côte d'Ivoire* Comm No 318/06 (ACmHPR, 28 February 2015).

241 *Anudo Ochieng Anudo v United Republic of Tanzania* App No 012/2015 (ACtHPR, 22 March 2018).

242 Art 2 ACHPR.

243 Art 3 ACHPR.

244 Art 5 ACHPR.

245 Art 12 ACHPR.

246 Eg calling for the "elimination of discrimination against women" in Art 2 and the "elimination of harmful practices" in Art 5.

247 See Bronwen Manby, *Citizenship and Statelessness in Africa: The Law and Politics of Belonging* (Wolf Legal Publishers 2015) 50–51.

248 African Charter on the Rights and Welfare of the Child (adopted 11 July 1990, entered into force 29 November 1999) OAU Doc. CAB/LEG/24.9/49 (1990) (ACRWC).

249 Art 6(4) ACRWC.

250 ACERWC, General Comment No 2 on Article 6 of the African Charter on the Rights and Welfare of the Child, ACERWC/GC/02 (2014).

251 *Institute for Human Rights and Development in Africa (IHRDA) and Open Society Justice Initiative on Behalf of Children of Nubian Descent in Kenya v the Government of Kenya* Com No Com/002/2009 (ACERWC, 22 March 2011), para 46.

further explanation to the guarantees in this Article has been considered "the most comprehensive interpretation to date of a state's obligations under international law in relation to the grant of nationality to children born in that state".[252]

Together, the ACHPR and the ACRWC show that there are certainly substantive provisions and interpretations thereof that contribute to preventing and solving statelessness: in the context of children, with provisions on non-discrimination, but also by giving effect to the human right to a nationality and taking a strong stance on arbitrary deprivation of nationality and childhood statelessness. Efforts are furthermore being made within the AU to adopt a Protocol to the African Charter on Human and Peoples Rights on the Specific Aspects on the Right to a Nationality and the Eradication of Statelessness in Africa. An expert meeting took place to discuss a draft of this Protocol 7–11 May 2018.[253] The available draft contains not only some general principles on nationality and statelessness, but also specific provisions on non-discrimination, attribution of nationality at birth, acquisition, loss deprivation, renunciation and recovery of nationality, habitual residence, marriage, nomadic and cross-border populations, children's rights, multiple nationality, evidence and documentation of nationality, state succession, and the protection of stateless people.[254]

Some legal instruments from other regions of the world also consider the right to a nationality, prevention of arbitrary deprivation of nationality, and the prevention of and solutions to childhood statelessness. The League of Arab States (LAS) has adopted the Arab Charter on Human Rights (ArCHR)[255], which contains provisions on the right to a nationality in Article 29. In the context of the Organisation of Islamic Cooperation (OIC) a legal document specifically addressing the rights of children was agreed upon: the Covenant on the Rights of the Child in Islam (CRCI).[256] Article 7 of this Covenant concerns 'identity' and includes reference to the importance of birth registration and obliges states parties to safeguard the elements of the child's identity, including nationality. Also, states are to make every effort to resolve the issue of statelessness for any child born in their territories or to any of their citizens outside their territory.[257] In Asia, cooperation within the Association of Southeast

---

252 Bronwen Manby, *Citizenship and Statelessness in Africa: The Law and Politics of Belonging* (Wolf Legal Publishers 2015) 52.

253 'Member States Experts Meeting on the Draft Protocol to the African Charter on Human and Peoples Rights on the Specific Aspects on the Right to a Nationality and the Eradication of Statelessness in Africa' (*African Union*, 7–11 May 2018) <https://au.int/en/newsevents/20180507/member-states-experts-meeting-draft-protocol-african-charter-human-and-peoples> accessed 5 September 2021.

254 The draft text of the Protocol to the ACHPR on the Specific Aspects of the Right to a Nationality and the Eradication of Statelessness in Africa can be found here: <https://www.achpr.org/public/Document/file/English/draft_citizenship_protocol_en_may2017.pdf> accessed 5 September 2021.

255 Arab Charter on Human Rights (adopted 22 May 2004, entered into force 15 March 2008) reprinted in (2005) 12 Int'l Hum Rts Rep 893 (ArCHR). Note that this is the updated and amended version of the ArCHR, which was originally issued in 1994.

256 Covenant on the Rights of the Child in Islam (adopted June 2005) OIC/9-IGGE/HRI/2004/Rep.Final (CRCI). The Covenant has not yet been ratified by a sufficient number of states to enter into force and is therefore of limited relevance.

257 Art 7(2) CRCI.

Asian Nations (ASEAN) has led to the (unanimous) adoption of the ASEAN Human Rights Declaration.[258] In paragraph 18 of this Declaration, the right of every person to a nationality as prescribed by law is included, which also provides that no person shall be arbitrarily deprived of such nationality nor of the right to change that nationality. Finally, the Commonwealth of Independent States (CIS)[259] Convention on Human Rights and Fundamental Freedoms[260] provides that everyone shall have the right to citizenship and that no one shall be arbitrarily deprived of his citizenship or the right to change it.[261]

1.5.3. ANALYTICAL FRAMEWORK

Based on the examination of international and 'other' regional instruments in this section, conclusions can be drawn for an analytical framework that helps to understand and categorize norms on preventing and solving statelessness from a human rights perspective, and that can be applied to the analysis of European law. The findings in this regard should, however, be regarded as preliminary, as the European context that is studied in chapter 2 may give rise to further delineation and refinement of the categories presented below given the presence of certain issues in Europe in particular. Paragraph 2.8 contains further reflections on this.

Substantively, a number of provisions or norms on certain topics return repeatedly in the (human rights) instruments discussed. For instance, there are clearly a number of instruments dealing with preventing and solving childhood statelessness specifically. Every child's right to acquire a nationality is also more firmly enshrined in legal instruments than a general right to a nationality for all. The principle of non-discrimination in nationality matters is encountered numerous times in human rights instruments as well. Furthermore, there are norms dealing with preventing loss and (arbitrary) deprivation (including the denial) of nationality, sometimes attempting to provide solutions to conflicts of nationality laws, sometimes specifically focused on (married) women, and sometimes concerning the context of state succession in particular. With state succession, however, we see that there is more than just conflict of nationality

258 ASEAN Human Rights Declaration (adopted 19 November 2012).

259 The CIS was created in 1991 and unites the following countries: Azerbaijan, Armenia, Belarus, Georgia, Kazakhstan, Kyrgyzstan, Moldova, Russia, Tajikistan, Turkmenistan, Uzbekistan and Ukraine.

260 Commonwealth of Independent States Convention on Human Rights and Fundamental Freedoms (adopted 26 May 1996, entered into force 11 August 1998) reprinted in (1996) 3 Int'l Hum Rts Rep 1, 212 (CIS Convention on Human Rights and Fundamental Freedoms). Note that the CoE has been rather skeptical about this document as it offers less protection than the ECHR. The Parliamentary Assembly of the CoE has therefore recommend to those CoE member or applicant states which are also members of the CIS not to sign or ratify the CIS Convention and to those states that have already ratified the CIS Convention to recognize the supremacy of the ECHR. See PACE Res 1249 (2001) Co-existence of the Convention on Human Rights and Fundamental Freedoms of the Commonwealth of Independent States and the European Convention on Human Rights.

261 Art 24 CIS Convention on Human Rights and Fundamental Freedoms.

laws that plays a role: it is clearly about preventing statelessness, but also about rules on acquisition of nationality and non-discrimination in a very specific situation that has a big impact on nationality matters. Moreover, there are of course legal standards that proclaim the right to a nationality or that deal with the acquisition of nationality by stateless people through facilitated naturalization.

Based on the above exploration, at least five categories of substantive legal norms on preventing and solving statelessness can be distinguished, which articulate different aspects of the human right to a nationality[262]:

- legal norms aimed at preventing and solving *childhood statelessness*;
- legal norms concerning solutions to *conflicts of nationality law* and preventing *loss / (arbitrary) deprivation / denial of nationality* (later in life – in order to prevent statelessness);
- nationality matters and reduction of statelessness in the context of *state succession*;
- legal norms aimed at the *right to a nationality* and *acquisition of a nationality for people who became stateless in the past and remain stateless today and/or who arrive to a country stateless* (in order to solve statelessness);
- legal norms ensuring *non-discrimination* and *equality before the law* in nationality matters (acquisition and loss and (arbitrary) deprivation of nationality – in order to prevent and solve statelessness).

Legal norms addressing the nationality of (married) women were not given a separate category, similar to preventing and solving childhood statelessness, because they were simply less prominent. These legal norms fit, however, within the categories on non-discrimination and on preventing conflicts of nationality laws and loss of nationality.

It is acknowledged that, even with this preliminary categorization, it might be hard to distinguish one category from the other. That is no surprise and is also not problematic, because all types of norms concern the prevention of and solutions to statelessness in the end, which makes it only logical that they are interrelated to some extent. For instance, there are norms specifically for children that also fit in the other categories – where it concerns non-discrimination of children in nationality matters for instance. However, because they focus on children, such norms can most appropriately be considered under the heading of childhood statelessness.

Moreover, it should be noted that it is difficult to separate the substantive norms on preventing and solving from the more procedural ones. For instance, in order to be able to prevent statelessness or solve statelessness, it is necessary to know what this entails and to be able to identify it. As such, the definition of statelessness and adequate procedures for determining statelessness, but also fair procedures for acquisition of nationality are important to all categories of legal norms identified above. This presupposes that the rights to due process and an effective remedy[263] are also adequately ensured.

---

[262] For a schematic overview, please refer to annex I.

[263] On the rights to due process and an effective remedy, see for instance Arts 2(3) & 14 ICCPR.

1.6. CONCLUDING REMARKS

In this study, the main question is how European law contributes to preventing and solving statelessness in Europe and what this adds to our understanding of nationality today, including the consideration that is given to administrative issues in nationality matters. This chapter introduced the issue of statelessness, the relevance of this research, and the methods and sources used. It also showed how statelessness and nationality or citizenship can be understood from a legal perspective, and how the strength of connections between a person and a state, as well as administration, registration and identification play an important role in this.

From this chapter can be drawn that there is an undeniable link between nationality and (human) rights and protection thereof: persons without nationality remain among the most vulnerable in the world. In legal norms on these matters at the international level and in regions outside Europe, obligations for states have been created in relation to nationality matters and the reduction of statelessness. There is also clear 'rights language' visible in international and regional law on this topic: individuals, and in particular children, have been given a right to a nationality to claim. Furthermore, another human rights dimension to preventing and solving statelessness has been created with the principle of non-discrimination, which applies to nationality laws and can be helpful in addressing, for example, gender discrimination in such laws or laws that discriminate against minorities. Indeed, all 'categories' of substantive legal norms on preventing and solving statelessness identified in the analytical framework[264] contain human rights aspects: the human right of children to birth registration and to acquire a nationality, the prohibition of arbitrary deprivation of nationality, everyone's right to a nationality and the principle of non-discrimination. Inescapably, this research thus takes a human rights perspective in order to understand properly European legal norms on preventing and solving statelessness, as well as the legal categorizations of reality through concepts like nationality and statelessness.

In the next Chapter, the European context in which European legal instruments operate is studied. Chapter 2 also aims to delineate the analytical framework further, before looking in more depth at European law on preventing and solving statelessness in Part II.

264 See para 1.5.3.

CHAPTER 2
EUROPE AND STATELESSNESS

Und ich mußte immer an das Wort denken, das mir vor Jahren ein exilierter Russe gesagt: "Früher hatte der Mensch nur einen Körper und eine Seele. Heute braucht er noch einen Paß dazu, sonst wird er nicht wie ein Mensch behandelt".
– Stefan Zweig, from Die Welt von Gestern. Erinnerungen eines Europäers[265]

~

Monday 7 November 1938. Herschel Grynszpan shoots Ernst vom Rath, a diplomat at the German embassy in Paris. Vom Rath dies shortly after, which purportedly provided the National Socialists with an immediate reason for 'retaliation': the Reichskristallnacht on 9–10 November 1938.[266]

Herschel Grynszpan was the son of Sendel and Riva Grynszpan. They were Polish Jews who had been working and living in Germany. Herschel had moved to France in 1936, fleeing Nazi persecution. His family remained in Germany. At the end of October 1938, they and 12.000–17.000 Polish Jews were taken from their homes and brought to the Polish border by train.[267] *The situation at the border between Neu-Bentschen (Germany)*[268] *and Zbaszyn (Poland), where the Grynszpan family was taken, was one of "panic and chaos"*[269]*, with people stuck in very primitive conditions and suffering greatly.*[270] *Sendel Grynszpan recalled the following when he testified at the Eichmann trial in 1961:*

> *"They took us to a village of about six thousand people, and we were twelve thousand. The rain was driving hard, people were fainting – on all sides one saw old men and women. Our suffering was great. There was no food, since Thursday we had not eaten…". They were taken to a military camp and put into "stables, as there was no room elsewhere… I think it was*

[265] Stefan Zweig, *Die Welt von Gestern. Erinnerungen eines Europäers* (Deutscher Bücherbund 1981) <https://www.projekt-gutenberg.org/zweig/weltgest/titlepage.html> accessed 12 September 2021.

[266] Das Bundesarchiv, *Memorial Book: Victims of the Persecution of Jews under the National Socialist Tyranny in Germany 1933 – 1945*, The Expulsion of Polish Jews from the German Reich 1938/1939 and their records <https://www.bundesarchiv.de/gedenkbuch/zwangsausweisung.html.en?page=1> accessed 12 September 2021.

[267] Ibid. See also Laurence Rees, *The Holocaust: A New History* (Viking / Penguin 2017).

[268] Currently Zbąszynek in Poland.

[269] Sybil Milton, 'The Expulsion of the Polish Jews from Germany October 1938 to July 1939 (1984) 29 Leo Baeck Institute Yearbook 169, 171.

[270] Joseph Marcus, *Social and Political History of the Jews in Poland 1919–1939* (De Gruyter Mouton 1983) 380.

> *our second day [in Poland]. On the first day, a lorry with bread came from Poznan, that was on Sunday. And then I wrote a letter to France... to my son: 'Don't write any more letters to Germany. We are now in Zbaszyn.'"*[271]

When Herschel Grynszpan learned of the expulsion and suffering of his family, he revenged them by shooting Vom Rath.

Behind these events lies a story relating to statelessness. The expulsion of the Polish Jews by the German authorities was caused by the Polish government announcing in March 1938 that the passports of Polish citizens residing abroad for more than five years would need to be revalidated, which had the "avowed aim of withdrawing such documents from Jews living abroad".[272] *The German government felt that these passport regulations were directed towards Polish Jews living in Germany (and annexed Austria), who would then remain stateless in the country.*[273] *In the beginning of October 1938, the Polish authorities communicated "that the decree would take effect on 30th October, the deadline for passport revalidation".*[274] *In light thereof, the German Foreign Office decided that the Polish Jews should be deported just before the new measures entered into force. This, however, did not prevent a situation of chaos and statelessness between the German and Polish border. Indeed, the Polish Jews were not considered to be citizens of Poland, and were (largely) not admitted, but at the same time, the German authorities did not consider them their problem and wanted them out of the country. They were without the protection of a state – the sad results thereof were described above.*

~

2.1. INTRODUCTION

Today, states are a self-evident part of our everyday lives and the order of the world around us. In chapter 1, we saw that, even though often unnoticed, an individual depends on states – and usually one state in particular – for undertaking straightforward activities such as travelling for instance, that are often taken for granted. However, the modern system of states of today remains imperfect, evidenced by the hundred thousands of people who are stateless in Europe. The situation described above, dating back to 1938, is therefore not exclusive for that time – many stateless people today are also stuck in limbo. There is a significant gap in time between the beginning of the 20th century and today of course, and this chapter provides a bridge between the two,

---

271 Hannah Arendt, *Eichmann in Jerusalem. A Report on the Banality of Evil* (revised and enlarged edn, The Viking Press 1964) 227–230. Here, he is referred to as Zindel.

272 Joseph Marcus, *Social and Political History of the Jews in Poland 1919–1939* (De Gruyter Mouton 1983) 380.

273 Sybil Milton, 'The Expulsion of the Polish Jews from Germany October 1938 to July 1939 (1984) 29 Leo Baeck Institute Yearbook 169.

274 Ibid.

aiming to demonstrate the reasons for statelessness occurring in Europe in such a way that states felt it necessary to respond to it through law-making.

Europe has a unique history, which reveals its particularities, also as regards statelessness. Today, statelessness remains a significant problem in Europe and this chapter demonstrates the link between nationality questions, statelessness and Europe's history. Europe, in this sense, should be understood as not only a continent in the geographical sense; there appears to be a common basis of culture and understanding of the world. As the famous adage by Umberto Eco – "the language of Europe is translation"[275] – demonstrates, Europe has found a specific way of connecting between cultures, states and even people or citizens despite the differences between them.

> "Europe is not merely a geographical expression. It implies not only a definite area on the earth's surface, but also a certain type of civilisation. The conceptions of European states concerning social life and government, concerning religion and art and science, have, underneath all their differences, a certain resemblance which may be difficult to define, but which appears unquestionable when they are compared with the ideas of the old civilisations of Asia or the conditions in Africa or the New World. This basis of common ideas and practices is not the result of a common nationality, for the peoples of Europe are many, and some are widely removed from others; it is the result of the historical development of the European lands".[276]

The above quote shows that some historians confirm the image of Europe's peculiarities. This image has been shaped by the history of the continent, filled with great wars and states dissolving, (re)appearing, or otherwise transforming or ceasing to exist, and being succeeded by new states.[277] Given the changes of borders throughout Europe's history, the nationals or citizens of a state needed to be defined repeatedly, which would – often deliberately – result in people being left out and (sometimes) becoming stateless. Such actions which left people out or whereby people became stateless were frequently targeted, driven by totalitarianism and discrimination in Europe, and leading to direct rights deprivation.

The 'birth' of statelessness coincides with the start of the period of time until today in which modern citizenship – or nationality[278] – became a scheme for distinguishing between 'us' – nationals or citizens of a country – and 'them' – non-citizens, foreigners or stateless people. It also relates to the moment when states came to be in charge of decisions regarding nationality – when they "came to possess the sole legal authority to confer, withdraw or withhold nationality from any natural person under

275 Umberto Eco, 'The language of Europe is translation', lecture given at the Dixièmes Assises de la traduction littéraire (Arles 1993).

276 AJ Grant & Harold Temperley, revised and edited by Lillian M Penson, *Europe in the Nineteenth and Twentieth Centuries (1789–1950)* (Longmans, Green and Co Ltd 1961) 1.

277 Eg Andreas Dorpalen, *Europe in the 20th Century. A History* (Macmillan 1968) 157–160 on the break-up of Austria-Hungaria in 1918 with Austria, Hungary and Czechoslovakia succeeding this state.

278 On the use of nationality and citizenship in this book, please refer to para 1.4.2.

its control".[279] The exact start of this period is hard to pinpoint. Some events and acts, however, demonstrate more clearly than others how citizenship is a sovereign decision of a state and can be a demarcation between those who belong to a state and are *included*, and those who do not belong to that state (but possibly to another) and are *excluded*. In this context, stateless people are those excluded from any state, belonging nowhere. The exclusion of people through denying citizenship is not a new phenomenon and traces back through history to ancient times.[280] Here, however, the focus is on when statelessness – a form of exclusion (or perhaps the ultimate form of exclusion) by means of a bureaucratic designation to which rights and duties are attached: nationality – became a phenomenon that was in need of a legal response by European states, requiring them to work together to address it. In short: the matters of in- and exclusion have a longer history, but the particular (legal) status of nationality, and thereby statelessness, are of a later date and are the focus of this chapter.

In attempting to understand statelessness and its emergence in Europe, the focus is essentially on why, how and when nationality became a mechanism for in- and exclusion because, and as was mentioned above, statelessness is the ultimate form of exclusion based on nationality. For the purposes of the study in this chapter, the definition of statelessness currently used in international law[281] serves as a point of reference. However, it is not always easy to apply this definition throughout history, since there was not always a clear distinction between refugees and stateless people for instance, nor was there always a reason for distinguishing between the two. In fact, the current definition was shaped by developments in Europe in particular that are now considered history.[282] The chapter adheres to the current definition of statelessness as much as possible, attempting to uncover or deduce from the usage of the term whether sources indeed use 'stateless' or 'statelessness' to describe people who are not recognized as a national by any state under the operation of its law.

For statelessness to become a concern of states, it was first necessary that modern states were formed in such a way that it led to exclusion of people from any other state. In history, in particular in the run-up to World War I, there are certainly such developments visible that can help in gaining a better understanding of the emergence of statelessness. The nineteenth century and the beginning of the twentieth century were times of rapid developments and change. Even though the different developments are interrelated, there are unquestionably developments that are relevant to making a clearer distinction between people, which led to exclusion, and which eventually led to statelessness. The next paragraph highlights some of the important developments in this regard.

---

279 William E Conklin, *Statelessness. The Enigma of the International Community* (Hart Publishing 2014) 6.

280 Ibid 5. See also Ernst Hirsch Ballin, *Citizen's Rights and the Right to Be a Citizen* (Brill Nijhoff 2014) 1–16.

281 In international law, a stateless person is defined as "a person who is not considered as a national by any State under the operation of its law". See also Art 1(1) 1954 Convention.

282 Eg Mira L Siegelberg, *Statelessness. A Modern History* (Harvard University Press 2020).

From 19th-century Europe, the chapter takes us through history to where we are today. This chapter thus chronologically explores relevant events, forms of cooperation and ways in which statelessness was dealt with. In this chapter, the different causes of statelessness and stateless groups in Europe are discussed as well. The main sources used in this chapter are secondary sources that relate to history, causes and responses to statelessness. However, also general accounts of the history of Europe from (just before) World War I until now are used in view of the limited amount of literature that concerns statelessness specifically. Given the significance of regional cooperation mechanisms for this chapter, sources relating to (the history of) such cooperation mechanisms in particular are used too. Where available or appropriate, primary sources are consulted. Even though this chapter is of historical nature, the research relies on legal research methods in this section: academic sources and other literature are examined for relevance and reliability, and their contents are analyzed and systematized. This chapter therefore is of a descriptive nature and does not present an exhaustive historical overview of statelessness in Europe. It provides background to this research's priority of uncovering how European legal instruments can contribute to preventing and solving statelessness in Europe. Methodological choices, such as the period of history that is studied, the emphasis on certain topics and the literature considered, are therefore made with this focal point in mind.

As the title of this book demonstrates, the present study is concerned with laws, including treaties, which address statelessness at the regional, European level. The European regional cooperation mechanisms of the CoE and the EU are studied in particular. This chapter aims to demonstrate the reasons for conducting this research, as well as its context, relevance and importance. It therefore asks how and why statelessness and related matters came to be addressed in legal instruments in a European context. This question entails a study of how statelessness has occurred in this region and how states responded from a legal perspective. This chapter does so by discussing developments since the 19th century (paragraph 2.2), but also during the two World Wars (paragraphs 2.3 and 2.4). It moves on to discuss the (re)building of Europe (paragraph 2.5) and highlights further developments including the end of the Cold War (paragraph 2.6). The chapter moves closer to current times in paragraph 2.7. A summary and remarks on the meaning of the background provided by this chapter to this research are included in paragraph 2.8. In doing so, the chapter shows that statelessness has been considered as an issue or problem that that was in need of a (legal) response, and that different responses would vary depending on the context in which they were initiated.

2.2. 19TH-CENTURY EUROPE

This section briefly considers different developments in the 19th century that were relevant to paving the way to statelessness becoming a widespread and serious problem in the beginning of the 20th century. It demonstrates how nationality and the registration of people became more important, which in turn enabled the possibility of exclusion.

In the decades before World War I, Europe saw a time sometimes characterized as an "age of security".[283] Europe was relatively secure because war was not tearing up the continent as it had before the Congress of Vienna in 1815. At the same time, however, the continent saw rapid developments and growing tensions, which culminated into 'the roaring twenties' in the beginning of the 20th century. This included major economic growth and significant changes to daily life by widespread use of, for instance, phones and automobiles. Also, Wall Street crash in 1929 and the ensuing Great Depression caused great hardship and new tensions between groups of people within states and beyond borders.

But what had happened before the first World War? The nineteenth century in Europe was an age of industrial development. Important to this development were the "burgeoning fortunes of economic liberalism" which "made free circulation appear an unavoidable necessity".[284] The possibilities of investment and trade made freedom of movement imperative; a more welcoming atmosphere towards foreigners by states, which included the relaxation of passport controls, recognized the important role of them in this.[285] Against this background, freedom of movement of people also increased, in particular for the lower classes of society. Nonetheless, "the expansion of legal and bureaucratic mechanisms to control migration developed in tandem with the liberal argument that progress depended on the capacity of individuals and capital to flow freely around the world".[286]

Nineteenth-century Europe also saw changes in ways of governing people. Political authority was no longer that of kings or other authoritarian leaders, but of parliaments.[287] These parliaments, however, did usually not represent everyone – only (some) men – as suffrage was often subject to further criteria, such as gender, age, the amount of taxes paid and residence in a certain place for a specific period of time.[288] Over the course of the nineteenth century and the beginning of the twentieth century, suffrage was extended by parliaments to all men and women – a development that has been attributed by some to the economic growth of that time.[289]

---

283 Jan-Werner Müller, *Contesting Democracy. Political Ideas in Twentieth-Century Europe* (Yale University Press 2011) 9.

284 John Torpey, *The Invention of the Passport. Surveillance, Citizenship and the State* (Cambridge University Press 2000) 56.

285 John Torpey, 'The Great War and the Birth of the Modern Passport System' in Jane Caplan & John Torpey (eds), *Documenting Individual Identity. The Development of State Practices in the Modern World* (Princeton University Press 2001) 256.

286 Mira L Siegelberg, *Statelessness. A Modern History* (Harvard University Press 2020) 15.

287 Jan-Werner Müller, *Contesting Democracy. Political Ideas in Twentieth-Century Europe* (Yale University Press 2011) 11.

288 Cf Stefano Bartolini, 'Enfranchisement, Equality and Turnout in the European Democratisation Process: A Preliminary Comparative Analysis' (1996) EUI Working Paper No. 121 <https://www.icps.cat/archivos/WorkingPapers/WP_I_121.pdf?noga=1> accessed 12 September 2021.

289 Roger D Congleton, 'Economic Development and Democracy: Does Industrialization lead to Universal Suffrage?' (2004) 21 Homo Oeconomicus 283; Albert O Hirschman, 'The On-and-Off Connection Between Political and Economic Progress' (1994) 84 The American Economic Review, Papers and Proceedings of the Hundred and Sixth Annual Meeting of the American Economic Association 343.

In 1880, it was widely recognized that the state "was the political expression of the nation" in Europe, with the Austro-Hungarian Empire and the Ottoman Empire as the clear exceptions.[290] These nation-states developed in the course of – mainly – the nineteenth century, mostly "through hegemonic unification" and sometimes "through evolution toward autonomy" (e.g. the end of the dynastic union of Sweden and Norway) or even "through revolutionary breakaway of a colony" (in Europe only revolutionary breakaways from empires were witnessed in the Balkans, and later by the Irish Free State).[291] The importance of nationalism with regard to the rise of the nation-state is often highlighted in the sense that nationalism can be defined as the pursuit for the 'nation' as the system to govern people.[292] At the same time, this phenomenon relates to national identity:

> "Nationalism is perhaps best understood as a kind (or degree) of national identity, urged by individuals or pursued by groups, aiming for a stringent 'congruence between culture and polity' and demanding 'cultural homogeneity within political units and cultural heterogeneity between them'."[293]

It is therefore important to observe that in the decades immediately preceding World War I, nationalism had rapidly gained ground as a transformed concept, which emphasized the ethnic and linguistic elements thereto more.[294] Confirmation of a transformed conception of nationalism can be found for instance in the writings of Jürgen Osterhammel, who, when discussing the differences between the empire and the nation-state, notes that the nation-state is based on citizens belonging to it, "with a general status based on equal rights and political inclusion". At the same time, however, minorities needed to battle to obtain special rights.[295] Others mention how nationalism changed in the second half of the nineteenth century from "a sense of community with one's fellow nationals into aggressive feelings of superiority over other nations"[296] – in other words: some people (or nations) feel that they are better than others. Joep Leerssen finds that there are different elements that push nationalism towards the 'right':

---

290 JM Roberts, *A General History of Europe. Europe 1880–1945* (Longman 1970) 17. The Austro-Hungarian Empire and the Ottoman Empire "could not accept the identity of state and nation" (ibid 19).

291 Jürgen Osterhammel, *The Transformation of the World: Global History of the Nineteenth Century* (transl Patrick Camiller, Princeton University Press 2014) 407, 412.

292 Cf Douglas Bradburn, 'Nation, Nationhood, and Nationalism' in Trevor Burnard (ed) *Oxford Bibliographies in Atlantic History* (Oxford University Press) last modified: 29 June 2011 <www.oxfordbibliographies.com/view/document/obo-9780199730414/obo-9780199730414-0070.xml> accessed 12 September 2021.

293 John Carter Wood, '"Blessed is the Nation"? Christianity and National Identity in Twentieth-Century Europe' in John Carter Wood (ed), *Christianity and National Identity in Twentieth-Century Europe. Conflict, Community, and the Social Order* (Vandenhoeck & Ruprecht 2016) 11–31, 20.

294 Eric J Hobsbawm, *Nations and Nationalism since 1780* (2nd edn, Cambridge University Press 1990) 101–130.

295 Jürgen Osterhammel, *The Transformation of the World: Global History of the Nineteenth Century* (transl Patrick Camiller, Princeton University Press 2014) 423.

296 Andreas Dorpalen, *Europe in the 20th Century. A History* (Macmillan 1968) 3.

> "Most fundamentally, nationalism changed in status from an anti-government opposition force to a propaganda tool wielded by governments to justify hegemonism; also, national thought was infected by the discourse of biological determination, race, the spectre of 'decadence' and degeneration, and the new cult of the authoritarian leader."[297]

Different commentators demonstrate that nationalism in this sense, and when applied to the nation-state, contributes to making distinctions between different groups and defining citizenship, which could eventually result in exclusion and might be a possible precursor to the emergence of statelessness on a large scale. Rogers Brubaker demonstrates that defining citizenship – citizenship law – is influenced by nationalism using the examples of the France and Germany: France's "state-centred, assimilationist understanding of nationhood" corresponds with "an expansive definition of citizenship", whereas Germany's "ethnocultural, differentialist understanding of nationhood" is articulated by "a definition of citizenship that is remarkably open to ethnic German immigrants from Eastern Europe and the Soviet Union, but remarkably closed to non-German immigrants".[298] Making distinctions, for instance between those of a certain ethnicity and those who are not, was easily justified in national thought. Furthermore, ethnic homogeneity became an aspiration of any strong and capable state after 1870: ethnicity and descent are now used as criteria for determining the nation. This form of ethnic nationalism, which included hierarchical distinctions being drawn between nationals and minorities, and could lead to exclusion of foreigners, led – amongst others – to a different attitude towards cross-border cooperation.[299] As a corollary, the attitudes towards freedom of movement changed too. States wanted to be able to distinguish between citizens and non-citizens more and more and no longer accepted everyone within their borders. The only manageable way to accomplish this would be to require documentation from individuals.[300] This bureaucratization of distinction was further stimulated by the advance of the processes of democratization through the extension of suffrage that was mentioned, which led to a closer connection between citizens and states. This, in turn, resulted in

> "an intensified preoccupation with determining who is 'in' and who is 'out' when it came to enjoying the benefits – both political and economic – of membership in those states. This is one of the ways that democratization promoted bureaucratization, a dynamic that Weber noted long ago. In the process, passports became essential to the bureaucratic administration of modern mass migration, just as identity cards have become something like the 'currency' of domestic administration, marking out eligibles from ineligibles in the areas of voting, social services, and much more besides."[301]

---

297 Joep Leerssen, *National Thought in Europe. A Cultural History* (Amsterdam University Press 2006) 215–216.

298 Rogers Brubaker, *Citizenship and Nationhood in France and Germany* (Harvard University Press 1992) 2.

299 Marie-Janine Calic, *Südosteuropa. Weltgeschichte einer Region* (CH Beck 2016) 366.

300 John Torpey, *The Invention of the Passport. Surveillance, Citizenship and the State* (Cambridge University Press 2000) 93.

301 Ibid, 121.

Ethnic nationalism, including its shift to the right, and the bureaucratization of membership thus clearly point towards a trend of exclusion of those who do not 'belong' to the nation – or even to no nation at all. That these developments contributed to – or even were the root cause – of statelessness developing into a significant problem for states is confirmed when considering literature that focuses on statelessness more explicitly. William Conklin, for instance, says: "Hannah Arendt and Margaret Somers have especially decried how the conquest of the state by the ethnic nation has factored into the stateless condition".[302] Not only does this provide a background to World War I, it also relates to the emergence of statelessness on a larger scale than ever before in the context of this war in that it led to further demarcation between people of certain ethnicity and prioritization of the principle of nationality – articulating the belonging to a nation, also in the peace agreements after this war.[303] The account by John Roberts of the period of 1880–1945 confirms how fundamental the principle of nationality was for the structure of Europe, as well as to political changes: "[i]ts spread had already produced great wars and upheavals; even greater ones were still to come."[304]

In terms of administration and controlling movement of people, it was already touched upon that the late nineteenth century saw the relaxation of passport controls (which had existed in some countries) because of economic prosperity. In view of mass migration taking place at the end of the 19th century, legal norms were deemed important by some to address this. Indeed,

> "[i]n the 1880s and 1890s, the Institut de Droit International[305] codified standards for the treatment or removal of refugees and for the power of the state to determine entry and exit. The group put forward a set of recommendations to mitigate the harsh consequences of mass migration and the conflict of nationality laws, recommending that states refrain from forbidding entrance to those without national status and condemning mass expulsion of minority groups."[306]

The Institut de Droit International also held that denationalization could never be imposed as a punishment.[307] There was already legal thinking at the international level

302 William E Conklin, *Statelessness. The Enigma of the International Community* (Hart Publishing 2015) 11.

303 Cf EJ Hobsbawm, *Nations and Nationalism since 1780* (2nd edn, Cambridge University Press 1990) 123.

304 JM Roberts, *A General History of Europe. Europe 1880–1945* (ed Denys Hay, 2nd ed, Longman 1977) 19. He also notes that separating one nationality from the other was much more difficult in eastern Europe.

305 The Institut de Droit International is an independent institution that aims to contribute to the development of international law. It was founded in 1873 and still exists today. See also <https://www.idi-iil.org/en/> accessed 19 September 2021.

306 Mira L Siegelberg, *Statelessness. A Modern History* (Harvard University Press 2020) 36. For instance, Institut de Droit International, 'Règles Internationales sur l'Admission et l'Expulsion des Étrangers' (1892) Session de Genève <https://www.idi-iil.org/app/uploads/2017/06/1892_gen_01_fr.pdf> accessed 19 September 2021.

307 Institut de Droit International, 'Résolutions Relatives aux Conflits de Lois en Matière de Nationalité (Naturalisation et Expatriation)' (1896) Session de Venise, Art 6 <https://www.idi-iil.org/app/uploads/2017/06/1896_ven_02_fr.pdf> accessed 19 September 2021.

about questions of nationality, in- and exclusion before the start of the 20th century. Nonetheless, in the years immediately preceding the Great War, there were also movements countering large-scale migration and relaxed passport controls – not in the last place because of the rising nationalistic sentiments described above. Indeed, with the start of the Great War, passport controls were reinstated and documentary evidence of identity and nationality became important to both foreigners and nationals in light of the "intensified documentary surveillance during the Great War".[308]

The period just before World War I saw the usage of nationality as a way to in- and exclude people. A logical consequence thereof, which was already elaborated upon above, was the rising importance of proving nationality and 'belonging' with the right documentation.[309] Against this background, statelessness – having no nationality and usually no papers – rose to be an issue that needed to be addressed. And it was in these times, when the established order was challenged, disputes arose, people were displaced and borders shifted, that World War I and its aftermath made statelessness a substantial question for European states to deal with.[310] Indeed, this major historical event is the direct cause for statelessness to assume "unprecedented proportions,"[311] but as the above account shows, the development towards exclusion through nationality appears to have started well before that time. It goes beyond the scope of this book to investigate this in more depth, but it would be an interesting topic for further research.

2.3. WORLD WAR I AND ITS AFTERMATH

World War I (1914–1918) was "a war of extraordinary intensity".[312] Notorious for its battles, such as the battle of the Marne, the battle of Gallipoli, the battle of the Somme, the battle of Ypres *(Ieper)* and the battle of Verdun, World War I raged not only in Europe, but – for a large part because of Europe's empires and influence – was also considered to be a global war, as its name suggests. The involvement of the United States and Japan confirm this image, even though it should be recognized that a number of countries were not involved. These countries, nonetheless, also faced the consequences of the war to some extent. The Netherlands, for instance, remained neutral during

308 John Torpey, 'The Great War and the Birth of the Modern Passport System' in Jane Caplan & John Torpey (eds), *Documenting Individual Identity. The Development of State Practices in the Modern World* (Princeton University Press 2001) 257.

309 Cf Miriam Rürup, 'Lives in Limbo. Statelessness after Two World Wars' (2011) 49 Bulletin of the German Historical Institute 113.

310 United Nations Department of Social Affairs, 'A Study of Statelessness' (1949, E/1112/ Add. 1) 5; Marc Vishniak, 'The Legal Status of Stateless Persons' in AG Duker (ed), *Pamphlet Series: Jews and the Post-War World* (No. 6, American Jewish Committee 1945) 15. See also Hannah Arendt, *The Origins of Totalitarianism* (Harvest Book – Harcourt & Brace Company 1979) 277 (n20); Miriam Rürup, 'Lives in Limbo. Statelessness after Two World Wars' (2011) 49 Bulletin of the German Historical Institute 113.

311 United Nations Department of Social Affairs, 'A Study of Statelessness' (1949, E/1112/ Add. 1) 5.

312 Hew Strachan, 'Introduction' in Hew Strachan (ed), *The Oxford Illustrated History of the First World War* (new ed, Oxford University Press 2014) 1–10, 9.

World War I and received large numbers of Belgian refugees that crossed the border to safety.[313]

The enormous devastation caused by the war on the fighting fronts and beyond, but also the aftermath of the war, caused large-scale movements and evacuation of people. It was furthermore considered a war that was different from any war before because of the number of casualties, the immense destruction that it caused, but also because it kick-started innovation in some areas, and had all kinds of economic and social consequences as well.[314] Importantly for this study, it resulted in statelessness on a large scale. Below, this chapter addresses the main causes of the emergence of mass statelessness in Europe and the (legal) responses thereto by European states, also discussing the different groups of people that became stateless.

The scale on which statelessness emerged in the context of World War I was new. In his piece on the legal status of stateless people in World War I and II, Marc Vishniak distinguished between individual causes of statelessness and causes of mass statelessness.[315] Individual causes of statelessness, such as people who remain stateless at birth or who become stateless by marriage, are the result of conflicts of law and were not considered 'new' – these had already existed before the War. Whereas these causes of statelessness certainly contributed to the creation of statelessness, they were not the important causes for statelessness becoming a large-scale problem. These were, *inter alia*, related to the preoccupation of states to determine 'who is in and who is out' using documents, registrations and controlling movements of people. Indeed, John Torpey writes how actions directed towards that goal during World War I "led to the consolidation of views about foreigners and methods for restricting their movements that would prove to be an enduring part of the world"[316] and how

> "[t]he (re)imposition of passport controls by numerous West European countries and the United States during the First World War and their persistence after the war was an essential aspect of [a] 'révolution identificatoire' that vastly enhanced the ability of governments to identify their citizens, to distinguish them from non-citizens, and thus to construct themselves as 'nation-states'".[317]

Because of the war, large numbers of people fled and had been evacuated all over Europe: refugees became an international problem for states and policy-makers in the

313 On the Netherlands during World War I, see for instance Paul Moeyes, *Buiten Schot. Nederland tijdens de Eerste Wereldoorlog 1914–1918* (digital ed, Uitgeverij De Arbeiderspers 2011).

314 Andreas Dorpalen, *Europe in the 20th Century. A History* (Macmillan 1968) 13.

315 Marc Vishniak, 'The Legal Status of Stateless Persons' in AG Duker (ed), *Pamphlet Series: Jews and the Post-War World* (No. 6, American Jewish Committee 1945). Note that Vishniak defines statelessness as "an individual's lack of nationality" (7) and stateless people as "individuals who are not connected with any country by ties of citizenship or nationality" (11). This definition resembles the current definition of statelessness in international law, which also highlights the lack of nationality.

316 John Torpey, *The Invention of the Passport. Surveillance, Citizenship and the State* (Cambridge University Press 2000) 111.

317 Ibid, 121.

beginning of the 20th century.[318] While fleeing war, many of these people had lost their identification documents. This could result in statelessness later, because they could not prove their identity and former country of residence.[319] Furthermore, states deliberately excluded people and made them 'stateless'. Relevant in the context of World War I was the withdrawal of nationality to 'punish' an individual for disloyalty or otherwise. Both Miriam Rürup and Marc Vishniak provide examples of this deprivation of nationality, for instance for accepting an official post in a foreign state, evasion of military service or serving in a foreign military, but also for the failure of an official abroad to comply with their superior's orders to abandon his position.[320] Furthermore, many European countries practiced 'denaturalization' on grounds of national security, such as fraud, residence abroad, etc.[321]

In the context of the War, many foreigners or non-citizens in countries involved in the War, such as (former) Germans in the UK, were (mis)labelled as 'enemy aliens', and were denied naturalization, but could also be subjected to internment. They had for instance renounced their nationality or severed their links with their (former) country of nationality or had been denationalized. They therefore wanted to claim a status as a person with no nationality – stateless. The *Stoeck* case that is described by Mira Siegelberg illustrates this issue.[322] She says:

> "In the years immediately following the war, individuals […] across Europe sought recognition from the courts that they did not possess any national status. After the victors of World War I set out the punitive terms of the Versailles Peace Treaty, there was an even greater clamor among former subjects of enemy powers – including Germany, Austria and Hungary – residing in the British Empire to be formally recognized as stateless in order to avoid the Versailles penalties."[323]

The actions of states against their own nationals did certainly cause statelessness, but after the conclusion of World War I, statelessness increased so massively that more was evidently happening.[324] Indeed, big changes were made to the map of Europe – empires collapsed and new states emerged, which resulted in the creation of 'new' ethnic minorities. Inconsistent nationality laws of the different (new) countries in Europe had the consequence that some people were left without a nationality or a nation to belong

---

318 Claudena M Skran, *Refugees in Inter-War Europe. The Emergence of a Regime* (Clarendon Press 1995) 13–14.

319 Marc Vishniak, 'The Legal Status of Stateless Persons' in AG Duker (ed), *Pamphlet Series: Jews and the Post-War World* (No. 6, American Jewish Committee 1945) 15; also cf John Torpey, *The Invention of the Passport. Surveillance, Citizenship and the State* (Cambridge University Press 2000) 123.

320 Miriam Rürup, 'Lives in Limbo. Statelessness after Two World Wars' (2011) 49 Bulletin of the German Historical Institute 113, 118–119; Marc Vishniak, 'The Legal Status of Stateless Persons' in AG Duker (ed), *Pamphlet Series: Jews and the Post-War World* (No. 6, American Jewish Committee 1945) 13–14.

321 William E Conklin, *Statelessness. The Enigma of the International Community* (Hart Publishing 2015) 107.

322 Mira L Siegelberg, *Statelessness. A Modern History* (Harvard University Press 2020) 12–25.

323 Ibid.

324 See also ILC, 'Report on Nationality, Including Statelessness by Mr Manley O Hudson, Special Rapporteur' (1952) A/CN.4/50, 19.

to.[325] The ethnic minorities were furthermore sometimes excluded by the states to which they belonged, creating flows of migration throughout Europe.[326] Against this background, the mass denationalization of people for political or other reasons during the interwar-period should be considered, such as the case of the Armenians. They were, amongst others, denationalized by Turkey in 1927 by a decree and in some cases by individual administrative decision for political and social reasons.[327] Indeed, this is but one example of how "[d]enationalizaton became a powerful weapon of totalitarian politics".[328] Denationalization contributed heavily to the creation of statelessness on a large scale and was employed for instance in the newly established Soviet Union after the revolutionary events in Russia, as well as fascist Italy and Turkey. After Hitler's rise to power in 1933, Germany started to expatriate and deprive Jews and others that it found to be 'undesirable' citizens, because they had allegedly displayed disloyalty for instance, of their nationality.[329] According to Marc Vishniak:

> "At the beginning of World War II the stateless comprised mainly the Armenians who had escaped from Kurdish and Turkish massacres; Russians who had fled from the Soviet Union; the inhabitants of the Saar who had voted for France or for the League of Nations at the time of the Saar plebiscite; the Assyro-Chaldeans and Assyrians who had left Iraq after the massacres in that country; the Jews, democrats and socialists who had fled Nazi Germany; Austrian Jews, monarchists, democrats and socialists; Rumanians who had opposed the dictatorship, and Rumanian Jews; anti-Fascist Italians and Italian Jews; Spanish Republicans, Czechoslovakian democrats, etc."[330]

What (legal) instruments or responses were turned to after the Great War to address statelessness? World War I ended in 1918 with Allied victory and resulted in the collapse of empires, such as the Ottoman and Austrian-Hungarian empires, as well as massive territorial changes. It also resulted in a number of legal instruments: the peace treaties that were signed at/after the Paris Peace Conference in 1919, of which the Treaty of Versailles between the victors of the war and Germany is probably known best among the public at large. Another outcome was the establishment of the LoN in 1920. In politics after World War I, the principle of self-determination – the right of self-determination

325 Miriam Rürup, 'Lives in Limbo. Statelessness after Two World Wars' (2011) 49 Bulletin of the German Historical Institute 113, 119.

326 Bülent Kaya, *The Changing Face of Europe – Population Flows in the 20th Century* (Council of Europe Publishing 2002) 15.

327 Louise W Holborn, 'The Legal Status of Political Refugees, 1920–1938' (1938) 32 The American Journal of International Law 680; see also Ayse Kadioglu, 'Denationalization of Citizenship? The Turkish Experience' (2007) 11 Citizenship Studies 283.

328 Hannah Arendt, The Origins of Totalitarianism (Harvest Book – Harcourt & Brace Company 1979) 269.

329 Marc Vishniak, 'The Legal Status of Stateless Persons' in AG Duker (ed), *Pamphlet Series: Jews and the Post-War World* (No. 6, American Jewish Committee 1945) 20–33.

330 Ibid, 34. In 1938, the Nansen office reported 600,000 Russians, Armenians, Assyro-Chaldeans, Turks, and Saarlanders as still remaining under LoN protection because of statelessness, see Jane Perry Clark Carey, 'Some Aspects of Statelessness Since World War I' (1946) 40 The American Political Science Review 113, 115.

of peoples – played an important role. James Crawford points out that "the Treaty of Versailles and the counterpart peace treaties of 1919–23 paid regard to the principle of self-determination in some respects".[331] To deal with the exclusion of ethnic minorities, the peace treaties and the LoN-system complemented the principle of self-determination with the protection of minority rights[332], which included ensuring citizenship in the country in which people were.[333] The protection of minorities was subject to limitations though, because the stability in the states was not to be threatened by minorities, and should certainly not result in the establishment of new political entities.[334]

Marc Vishniak believes that "[t]hose who created the new order in Europe and drafted the peace treaties were fully conscious of the injustice inherent in statelessness", evidenced by the inclusion of specific provisions to prevent statelessness in, for instance, the Treaty of St. Germain (with Austria) and the Treaty of Trianon (with Hungary).[335] The problem with these kinds of provisions was, however, that they were interpreted in a restrictive manner and insufficiently implemented by changes in the domestic laws.[336] Indeed, it was clear at the time, from the treaties concluded, but also from the decisions and opinions of the Permanent Court of International Justice (PCIJ), that states retained their power to regulate the acquisition and loss of nationality in their national laws.[337] Nonetheless, the problems of statelessness and of refugees were recognized by states. This was evidenced by some of the other legal instruments of the interwar period. In 1922, for instance, the Rome Convention attempted to alleviate the problems arising from the break-up of the Austrian-Hungarian Empire. This series of treaties included a treaty on nationality matters and attempted to prevent statelessness in successor states of Austria-Hungary, but still was unable to address the plight of minorities that no state felt were their citizens. Since the treaty lacked comprehensiveness and ratifications by states, because governments simply did not seem interested, it was never applied generally but rather as a bilateral treaty between the two countries that ratified the instrument: Austria and Italy.[338] Its influence was therefore limited.

---

331 James Crawford, 'The Right of Self-Determination in International Law: Its Development and Future' in Philip Alston (ed), *Peoples' Rights* (Oxford University Press 2001) 7–67, 14.

332 See also James Crawford, 'The Right of Self-Determination in International Law: Its Development and Future' in Philip Alston (ed), *Peoples' Rights* (Oxford University Press 2001) 14.

333 Marc Vishniak, 'The Legal Status of Stateless Persons' in AG Duker (ed), *Pamphlet Series: Jews and the Post-War World* (No. 6, American Jewish Committee 1945) 16.

334 Eg Melina Grizo, 'The Versailles System of Peace Treaties and the Minority Protection in Southeast Europe. The Bulgarian-Greek Convention for the Exchange of Population of 1919' (2010) 3 Belgrade Law Review 67–72.

335 Marc Vishniak, 'The Legal Status of Stateless Persons' in AG Duker (ed), *Pamphlet Series: Jews and the Post-War World* (No. 6, American Jewish Committee 1945) 16.

336 Ibid, 16–18.

337 William E Conklin, Statelessness. The Enigma of the International Community (Hart Publishing 2015) 105. See also eg *Acquisition of Polish Nationality* (Advisory Opinion) 1923 PCIJ Rep Series B No 7; *Exchange of Greek and Turkish Populations* (Advisory Opinion) 1925 PCIJ Rep Series B No 10.

338 Marc Vishniak, 'The Legal Status of Stateless Persons' in AG Duker (ed), *Pamphlet Series: Jews and the Post-War World* (No. 6, American Jewish Committee 1945) 42–43.

The large numbers of refugees[339], already noted above and among which certainly were stateless people, remained a cause for concern among states. It is worth noting in this regard that the responses towards stateless people and refugees in principle protected both groups, often without making a distinction between them.[340] In the context of the LoN, the aforementioned concern of states was met with the appointment of a High Commissioner for Russian Refugees in September 1921: Fridtjof Nansen. His task was to identify and repatriate over a million Russian refugees.[341] He managed to build up institutions to this end, which essentially were a blueprint for the later established UNHCR.[342] Indeed, the foundation of the High Commissioner has been viewed as "a critical turning point in the long aftermath of the war, because it was the first formal acknowledgement of international responsibility for refugees".[343] An important achievement relevant to the stateless was the introduction of the so-called 'Nansen passport', which was (at first) a special identity certificate for Russian refugees. The majority of these refugees, who had fled Russia because of the Civil War, were stateless and faced a multitude of problems such as lack of freedom of movement and of diplomatic protection.[344]

The statelessness of the Russian refugees was an issue of political debate at the time. They were formally deprived of their citizenship in December 1921 by the Bolshevik government. Recognition of statelessness of the former Russian subjects by officials of other European states was viewed as acceptance of the new Russian government as it would acknowledge the government's right to deprive nationality of its citizens.[345] Nansen had therefore emphasized that any action to address the plight of the refugees should be regarded as "humanitarian and therefore politically neutral".[346]

The Nansen passport, made possible through the Arrangement with respect to the Issue of Certificates of Identity to Russian Refugees[347], gave the Russian refugees some form of legal status and a travel document. Furthermore, it made burden sharing among host countries easier. In 1924, the Nansen passport was extended also to Armenian refugees – often also stateless – by the Plan for the Issue of a Certificate of

339 For a short overview of the formation of modern international refugee law in the interwar period see also Eric Fripp, *Nationality and Statelessness in the International Law of Refugee Status* (Hart Publishing 2016) 104–108.

340 Carol A Batchelor, 'Stateless Persons: Some Gaps in International Protection' (1995) 7 International Journal of Refugee Law 232, 240.

341 Claudena M Skran, 'Profiles of the First Two High Commissioners' (1988) 1 Journal of Refugee Studies 277, 280.

342 Ibid, 280–281.

343 Mira L Siegelberg, *Statelessness. A Modern History* (Harvard University Press 2020) 62.

344 Claudena M Skran, *Refugees in Inter-War Europe. The Emergence of a Regime* (Clarendon Press 1995) 102–103; Peter Fitzmaurice, 'Between the wars – The Refugee Convention of 1933: A Contemporary Analysis' in David Keane & Yvonne McDermott (eds), *The Challenge of Human Rights. Past, Present and Future* (Edward Elgar 2012) 236–255, 242–243.

345 Mira L Siegelberg, *Statelessness. A Modern History* (Harvard University Press 2020) 62–63.

346 Ibid, 63.

347 Arrangement with respect to the Issue of Certificates of Identity to Russian Refugees (signed 5 July 1922) 30 LNTS 238 (No. 855).

Identity to Armenian Refugees.[348] This Plan and the aforementioned Arrangement were complemented and clarified by the 1926 Arrangement relating to the Issue of Identity Certificates to Russian and Armenian Refugees, Supplementing and Amending the previous Arrangements dated July 5, 1922, and May 31, 1924[349] and the 1928 Arrangement Relating to the Legal Status of Russian and Armenian Refugees.[350] Furthermore, an additional Arrangement in 1928 extended the protection measures for the Russian and Armenian refugees also to "Turkish, Assyrian, Assyro-Chaldaean and other assimilated refugees".[351] These instruments were not legally binding but basically contained 'rules of conduct' for states.[352] Whereas these 'soft law' measures – after all, they were not legally binding – were a significant step in improving the situation of certain stateless refugees, other groups were left out, even when they repeatedly asked the High Commissioner to extend the measures to them too.[353] For instance, people from the Central European successor states "petitioned the Office of the High Commission for Refugees to include former imperial subjects without national citizenship".[354] It should also be noted that for these instruments, indeed, it was about lack of protection and not about what caused this (i.e. statelessness or being a refugee similar to the standards we know today), so no real distinction was made between stateless people and refugees.[355] At the same time though, legal theorists like Marc Vishniak and Alexandre Gorovtsev were already beginning to see how stateless people could be viewed as a separate group in international law.[356]

Against the background of economic decline in the late 1920s and in the 1930s, attitudes toward refugees – and foreigners in general – changed and states became (again) more protective of who they considered their 'own'. This resulted, for instance, in more restrictive rules on the employment of aliens. With the conditions for refugees worsening in Europe, efforts to enact a comprehensive treaty on refugees were made, because "with the exception of the Nansen passport, the existing so-called arrangements are producing practically no effect upon the position of the refugees".[357]

---

348 Plan for the Issue of a Certificate of Identity to Armenian Refugees (signed 31 May 1924) 7–10 LoN Official Journal 969.

349 Arrangement relating to the Issue of Identity Certificates to Russian and Armenian Refugees, Supplementing and Amending the previous Arrangements dated July 5, 1922, and May 31, 1924 (signed 12 May 1926) 89 LNTS 48 (No. 2004).

350 Arrangement Relating to the Legal Status of Russian and Armenian Refugees (signed 30 June 1928) 89 LNTS 55 (No. 2005).

351 Arrangement Concerning the Extension to Other Categories of Certain Measures Taken in Favour of Russian and Armenian Refugees (signed 30 June 1929) 89 LNTS 65 (No. 2006), which also provides definitions of these groups of refugees.

352 Claudena M Skran, *Refugees in Inter-War Europe. The Emergence of a Regime* (Clarendon Press 1995) 104–105.

353 Marc Vishniak, 'The Legal Status of Stateless Persons' in AG Duker (ed), *Pamphlet Series: Jews and the Post-War World* (No. 6, American Jewish Committee 1945) 44.

354 Mira L Siegelberg, *Statelessness. A Modern History* (Harvard University Press 2020) 107.

355 Cf Michelle Foster & Hélène Lambert, *International Refugee Law and the Protection of Stateless Persons* (Oxford University Press 2019) 21.

356 Mira L Siegelberg, *Statelessness. A Modern History* (Harvard University Press 2020) 105–107.

357 Secretariat memorandum of 3 February 21933, LNA R5614/686, as quoted in Claudena M Skran, *Refugees in Inter-War Europe. The Emergence of a Regime* (Clarendon Press 1995) 124 (n 70).

Only a few years before the outbreak of World War II, the Convention of 28 October 1933 relating to the International Status of Refugees was adopted. This instrument was aimed at ensuring that refugees could enjoy civil rights, free and ready access to the courts, security and stability as regards establishment and work, facilities in the exercise of the professions, of industry and of commerce, and in regard to the movement of people, admission to schools and universities.[358] Even if this treaty does not mention statelessness explicitly anywhere in its text, the Convention was to be applied to Russian and Armenian refugees[359], among whom certainly were stateless people. There were some problems with applying the Convention[360], such as the inability to respond to refugees from Germany[361], but the 1933 Refugee Convention was certainly an achievement – in itself and because of the standards of refugee treatment that it set.[362] To respond to the situation of the German refugees, which was getting more critical[363], further instruments of protection were developed: a 1936 Provisional Arrangement[364] and the subsequent 1938 Convention concerning the Status of Refugees Coming from Germany.[365] Article 1(1) of the 1938 Convention read as follows:

> For the purposes of the present Convention, the term "refugees coming from Germany" shall be deemed to apply to:
> (a) Persons possessing or having possessed German nationality and not possessing any other nationality who are proved not to enjoy, in law or in fact, the protection of the German Government;
> (b) Stateless persons not covered by previous Conventions or Agreements who have left German territory after being established therein and who are proved not to enjoy, in law or in fact, the protection of the German Government.

---

358 Convention of 28 October 1933 relating to the International Status of Refugees (adopted 28 October 1933, entered into force 13 June 1935) 159 LNTS 3663 (1933 Refugee Convention).

359 Art 1 of the 1933 Refugee Convention.

360 Marc Vishniak, 'The Legal Status of Stateless Persons' in AG Duker (ed), *Pamphlet Series: Jews and the Post-War World* (No. 6, American Jewish Committee 1945) 49–55.

361 Michelle Foster & Hélène Lambert, *International Refugee Law and the Protection of Stateless Persons* (Oxford University Press 2019) 22.

362 Claudena M Skran, *Refugees in Inter-War Europe. The Emergence of a Regime* (Clarendon Press 1995) 124–130; Peter Fitzmaurice, 'Between the wars – The Refugee Convention of 1933: A Contemporary Analysis' in David Keane & Yvonne McDermott (eds), *The Challenge of Human Rights. Past, Present and Future* (Edward Elgar 2012).

363 See more elaborately Michelle Foster & Hélène Lambert, *International Refugee Law and the Protection of Stateless Persons* (Oxford University Press 2019) 22–24.

364 Provisional Arrangement concerning the Status of Refugees coming from Germany (signed 4 July 1936) 171 LNTS 77 (No. 3952).

365 Convention concerning the Status of Refugees coming from Germany (signed 10 February 1938) 192 LNTS 61 (No. 4461). This treaty was concluded between Belgium, the United Kingdom of Great Britain and Northern Ireland, Denmark, Spain, France, Norway and the Netherlands, but in practice, no state wanted to welcome them. See for instance Paul R Bartrop, *The Evian Conference of 1938 and the Jewish Refugee Crisis* (Palgrave MacMillan 2018) 1–4. The only states that had ratified this treaty before World War II broke out, were Belgium and Great Britain (in 1939), see also David Fraser & Frank Caestecker, 'Jews or Germans? Nationality Legislation and the Restoration of Liberal Democracy in Western Europe after the Holocaust' (2013) 31 Law and History Review 391, 395.

Even though the 1936 and 1938 instruments still did not make a real distinction between refugees and stateless people in terms of the protection they could claim, the latter document contained "one of the first explicit references to stateless people in an international instrument".[366]

With stateless refugees still existing today, the development of the international refugee regime after World War I remains a defining moment for the protection of stateless and refugees. The legal protection system that was created had its shortcomings, for instance because protection only applied to specific groups of refugees, but it was important because "refugees became defined as a special category of international migrant".[367] Also, the fact that institutions were created which could act on behalf of refugees on the international plane was innovative and would turn out to be relevant to the protection of the stateless later.

One more legal instrument should be highlighted when considering responses to statelessness after World War I: the 1930 Hague Convention.[368] The relevant content of this instrument was already discussed shortly in paragraph 1.5.1. In the context of the LoN, it had been found that it would be desirable and possible to attempt to come to international agreement on conflict of nationality laws, a conference to codify international rules on nationality matters was convened.[369]

> "[L]egal experts at the League identified international codification as a more limited way of addressing the growing numbers of petitions they received from people who claimed to be stateless since the war. They identified the problem of statelessness within the domain of the conflict of laws and avoided addressing it as a wider international or humanitarian crisis resulting from mass denationalization or exclusionary national legislation. Infringing on nationality law would directly threaten the delicate boundary the League had created between new forms of international authority and the sovereign right if states."[370]

The 1930 Hague Convention and three protocols[371] were the result of this conference. Of the three protocols, two concerned statelessness. One related to a specific case of statelessness among children and provided that when nationality was not acquired based on birth in the territory, a person born in its territory of a mother possessing the nationality of that state and of a father without nationality or of unknown nationality

366 Michelle Foster & Hélène Lambert, *International Refugee Law and the Protection of Stateless Persons* (Oxford University Press 2019) 23.

367 Claudena M Skran, *Refugees in Inter-War Europe. The Emergence of a Regime* (Clarendon Press 1995)144–145.

368 1930 Hague Convention.

369 United Nations, 'Documents on the Development and Codification of International Law', Supplement to (1947) 41(4) American Journal of International Law <http://legal.un.org/ilc/documentation/english/ASIL_1947_study.pdf> accessed 19 September 2021.

370 Mira L Siegelberg, *Statelessness. A Modern History* (Harvard University Press 2020) 131.

371 Special Protocol concerning Statelessness, Protocol relating to a Certain Case of Statelessness, Protocol relating to Military Obligations in Certain Cases of Double Nationality.

shall have the nationality of the said state.[372] The other protocol only entered into force in 2004 and is therefore not relevant here, as it could – from a legal perspective – not really contribute to addressing statelessness after World War I. Overall, the protocols, even if they were specifically directed at statelessness, were much less significant to the issue than the 1930 Hague Convention.

The 1930 Hague Convention did not deal with the causes of mass statelessness after World War I: as we saw in chapter 1, it addressed statelessness where it was a consequence of nationality issues relating to birth and marriage. Furthermore, the treaty does not mention stateless refugees at all. The Convention was an expression of the conviction of states "that it is in the general interest of the international community to secure that all its members should recognise that every person should have a nationality" and an attempt directed towards "the abolition of all cases (...) of statelessness", which was aware that it was at the time not possible to find an immediate and "uniform solution of all the above-mentioned problems".[373] Nonetheless, the 1930 Hague Convention was a great achievement, in particular because is provided that even though it is for each state to determine under its own law who are its nationals, this law shall only be recognized by other states in so far as it is consistent with international conventions, international custom, and the principles of law generally acknowledged with regard to nationality.[374] Furthermore, even if it did not have direct implications for stateless refugees, the Convention was significant because it was the first legal instrument on matters of nationality of a general nature.[375] The importance and continuing relevance of the 1930 Hague Convention to matters of nationality and statelessness is underlined by contemporary commentators. According to Carol Batchelor, the Convention is one of "the primary international instruments which serve as reference points for the principles relating to the right to a nationality and the problem of statelessness".[376] Indeed, "the adoption of the 1930 Hague Convention heralded the onset of a gradual trend towards the acceptance of limitations to the exclusive competence of states" in nationality matters.[377]

In conclusion, for the emergence of statelessness in Europe, the devastating Great War – World War I – is the point in history that marks the occurrence of the issue for the first time on a large scale. This was caused by various events, such as the War itself that created large numbers of refugees, as well as the response to the displacement, and the collapse of empires. Combined with the exclusion of ethnic minorities and states denying or depriving nationality of undesirable people for various reasons, statelessness

---

372 Art 1 Protocol relating to a Certain Case of Statelessness (adopted 12 April 1930, entered into force 1 July 1937) 179 LTS 115.

373 Preamble 1930 Hague Convention.

374 Art 1 1930 Hague Convention.

375 Marc Vishniak, 'The Legal Status of Stateless Persons' in AG Duker (ed), *Pamphlet Series: Jews and the Post-War World* (No. 6, American Jewish Committee 1945) 41.

376 Carol A Batchelor, 'Statelessness and the Problem of Resolving Nationality Status' (1998) 10 International Journal of Refugee Law 156, 158.

377 Laura van Waas, *Nationality Matters. Statelessness under International Law* (School of Human Rights Research Series, Vol 29; Intersentia 2008) 38.

assumed unprecedented proportions in Europe. States were, however, not blind to the stateless and in the context of the LoN the first important steps were taken to address statelessness and stateless refugees but stopped short of addressing root causes or imposing solutions. Importantly, the developments demonstrate a realization of states that "international politics were needed to overcome the issue of not being a national of any nation-state, whereas being a national of a nation-state had had to be defined at the nation-state level".[378]

2.4. WORLD WAR II

Despite the international cooperation that was achieved in the context of the LoN, international politics were swiftly drawn into conflict again. With increasing aggression from Nazi Germany and Fascist Italy, dark clouds were rolling into Europe and in 1939, the continent – and the world – was again the stage of a terrible war. World War II was, as its name suggests, a worldwide war, but "the war that began in 1939 had at its heart the same struggle as that of 1914–18, the overcoming of Germany".[379] It should, however, not be regarded as a European war that grew out to be a world war because "it had worldwide aspects and participants from the beginning".[380] After World War II, Europe was not only literally in ruins because of warfare and extensive bombings, but the continent had also witnessed such atrocious events that it would leave a long-lasting imprint.

In the wake of World War II, in which the protection of minority rights so horribly failed, the formula of self-determination of nations in combination with the protection of minority rights was abandoned in Europe. Instead, the focus shifted to the protection of human rights. At the international level, this change of direction was underlined by the establishment of the UN, with the aim "to maintain international peace and security, to develop friendly relations among nations and to achieve international co-operation in solving international problems of an economic, social, cultural or humanitarian character"[381], and particularly evidenced by the adoption of the UDHR in 1948. World War II and its aftermath certainly had an impact on statelessness in Europe. In the paragraphs below, the important developments as regards causes and responses to statelessness are discussed.

As considered in paragraph 2.3, statelessness already had become a massive issue for states to deal with and was caused by various factors, in particular large-scale denationalization or denial of nationality against a background of displacement and

---

378 Miriam Rürup, 'Lives in Limbo. Statelessness after Two World Wars' (2011) 49 Bulletin of the German Historical Institute 113, 123.

379 JM Roberts, *A General History of Europe. Europe 1880–1945* (ed Denys Hay, 2nd ed, Longman 1977) 525.

380 Gerhard L Weinberg, *World War II. A Very Short Introduction* (Oxford University Press 2014) 2.

381 AJ Grant & Harold Temperley, revised and edited by Lillian M Penson, *Europe in the Nineteenth and Twentieth Centuries (1789–1950)* (Longmans, Green and Co Ltd 1961) 583.

dissolution of the European empires following World War I. This paragraph follows the developments described above and shows how the problems deepened further in the context of World War II.

According to Marc Vishniak, "[s]tateless people are restricted in their rights in time of peace, and infinitely more so in time of war".[382] It seems his point is true when reading his account of how stateless people who were born in 'enemy countries' were still treated as 'enemy aliens', even though they did not possess the nationality of that state anymore during the War.[383] That some people had raised this already in the inter-war period and may or may not have been recognized as stateless, did not take away from the sentiments that continued to exist. In her famous book written directly after World War II, Arendt discusses the difficulty that stateless people face:

> "[It] is not that they are deprived of life, liberty, and the pursuit of happiness, or of equality of the law and freedom of opinion – formulas which were designed to solve problems *within* given communities – but that they no longer belong to any community whatsoever. Their plight is not that they are not equal before the law, but that no law exists for them; not that they are oppressed but that nobody wants even to oppress them."[384]

If we were to describe statelessness during and just after World War II in terms of causes, then "large-scale displacement and denationalisation of people"[385] are probably an apt summary of the main challenges that states faced in this regard. It should be noted that many of the causes of statelessness that existed before World War II persisted, because they were not sufficiently addressed by the legal responses designed in the inter-war period, as elaborated in paragraph 2.3.

A population that was most affected by denationalization in the context of the (run-up to) World War II, were the Jews and others who were considered enemies – some of the international responses to this practice in the inter-war period were already considered above. Where Germany first resorted to denationalization of German Jews based on individual decisions, it eventually took a collective approach in this regard. This becomes clear from "a series of three laws adopted in 1933, 1935 and 1941".[386] The law of 14 July 1933 made revocations of previous naturalizations (1918–1933) possible if these were considered "undesirable" and made deprivation of nationality possible for citizens abroad who had acted "contrary to the duty of fidelity of the Reich".[387] The ordinance on the execution

---

382 Marc Vishniak, 'The Legal Status of Stateless Persons' in AG Duker (ed), *Pamphlet Series: Jews and the Post-War World* (No. 6, American Jewish Committee 1945) 56.

383 Ibid, 56-57.

384 Hannah Arendt, *The Origins of Totalitarianism* (Harvest Book – Harcourt & Brace Company 1979) 295–296.

385 Laura van Waas, 'A 100-year (Hi)Story of Statelessness' (*Peace Palace Library Blog*, 25 August 2016) <https://peacepalacelibrary.nl/blog/2016/100-year-history-statelessness> accessed 19 September 2021.

386 Lester N Salwin, 'Uncertain Nationality Status of German Refugees' (1946) Minnesota Law Review 372.

387 Lawrence Preuss, 'International Law and Deprivation of Nationality' (1935) 23 Georgetown Law Journal 250.

of this law contained explicit reference to Eastern Jews to be considered in particular for revocation of nationality.[388] The Reich Citizenship Law of 1935 reduced Jews to second-class citizens, and it

> "moved away from the individualized denaturalization and denationalization model and applied a collective approach to Germans of Jewish origin. The distinction between subject and citizen, between German Jews and so-called Aryans, laid the ground work for the series of exclusionary measures passed as supplementary decrees to the Citizenship Law. These successive supplementary decrees progressively separated Jewish Germans from their fellow countrypeople, legally, economically, psychologically, and physically. The process culminated with the 11th Decree of November 24, 1941, which stripped all German Jews who had left the German Reich of their nationality".[389]

The obvious groups of people that were stateless after World War II thus included those who were heavily persecuted during the war: the surviving Jews and Roma.[390] At the same time, there was a lot of uncertainty regarding nationality status throughout Europe: the status of ethnic Germans who were forced to leave Eastern Europe after the war was uncertain, and many other people around Europe were displaced with undetermined nationalities.[391]

The aftermath of World War II presented the world with many issues to address and these were answered to by different (legal) responses. One thing was clear though: the great wars of 1914–1918 and 1939–1945 should not be repeated. It should be noted that this was all quite centered around the experience in Europe and that there was a dominant role of European states in the international legal developments that followed – that was already the case in the context of the LoN of course, but also within the UN. With the foundation of the UN, the international community was determined

> "to save succeeding generations from the scourge of war, which twice in our lifetime has brought untold sorrow to mankind, and to reaffirm faith in fundamental human rights, in the dignity and worth of the human person, in the equal rights of men and women and of nations large and small, and to establish conditions under which justice and respect for the obligations arising from treaties and other sources of international law can be maintained, and to promote social progress and better standards of life in larger freedom (...)."[392]

---

388 Ibid, 252.

389 David Fraser & Frank Caestecker, 'Jews or Germans? Nationality Legislation and the Restoration of Liberal Democracy in Western Europe after the Holocaust' (2013) 31 Law and History Review 391, 395.

390 See for an overview on how statelessness was created and caused by the laws and policies of different European countries also Jane Perry Clark Carey, 'Some Aspects of Statelessness Since World War I' (1946) 40 The American Political Science Review 113,116–122.

391 Miriam Rürup, 'Lives in Limbo. Statelessness after Two World Wars' (2011) 49 Bulletin of the German Historical Institute 113, 124.

392 Preamble Charter of the United Nations (adopted 26 June 1945, entered into force 24 October 1945) 1 UNTS XVI (UN Charter).

The specific situation of formerly German Jews who had been deprived of their nationality was an issue of separate concern after the war. Even if the Nazi nationality laws were revoked in 1945 by the Allied Control Council with Control Council Law No. 1, the nationality question remained a complicated one – not least because many people deprived of their nationality did not want their German nationality back.[393] The German Basic Law eventually made it possible for everyone, including their descendants, who had been deprived of their German nationality between 30 January 1933 and 8 May 1945 on political, racial or religious grounds to restore their nationality upon application. And if they had taken up residence in Germany after 8 May 1945 and have not indicated anything to the contrary, they were considered to have never have been deprived of this nationality.[394]

The aftermath of World War II also saw the 'genesis' of human rights as we know them today with at its core two developments: responding to the post-war refugee question and the adoption of the (non-legally binding and therefore not so controversial) UDHR, which paved the way for the adoption of legally binding human rights treaties.[395]

With regard to the latter, the UN set a common human rights standard for states to aspire to with the 1948 UDHR. For the stateless, whose rights had so often been violated, this document was certainly relevant. Even if the UDHR was not legally binding, it included the right that is most directly violated by statelessness itself: the right to a nationality. The impact that this right has had on the issue of statelessness and how it developed is part of the discussions in paragraph 1.5 on the international framework for preventing and solving statelessness. Legally binding treaties were not adopted until later: the ICCPR and the International Covenant on Economic, Social and Cultural Rights (ICESCR)[396] were, for instance, adopted in 1966. As we saw in paragraph 1.5, the UN human rights system has had a significant impact on preventing and solving statelessness.

At the same time, further cooperation of states on different matters on the international plane was needed to rebuild the world, and Europe in particular, after the devastation of World War II. The pressing issue the international community had to deal with were refugees and the stateless. In the context of the UN, this was responded to by creating the International Refugee Organisation (IRO) in 1947, which also

393 David Fraser & Frank Caestecker, 'Jews or Germans? Nationality Legislation and the Restoration of Liberal Democracy in Western Europe after the Holocaust' (2013) 31 Law and History Review 391, 400ff.

394 Art 116(2) German Basic Law (Constitution) – Basic Law for the Federal Republic of Germany in the revised version published in the Federal Law Gazette Part III, Classification No. 100–1, as last amended by Article 1 of the Act of 28 March 2019 (Federal Law Gazette I, 404).

395 Eg G Daniel Cohen, 'The "Human Rights Revolution" at Work. Displaced Persons in Postwar Europe' in Stefan-Ludwig Hoffmann (ed), *Human Rights in the Twentieth Century* (Cambridge University Press 2011) 45–61. See more generally also Peter N Stearms, *Human Rights in World History* (Routledge 2012).

396 International Covenant on Economic, Social and Cultural Rights (adopted 16 December 1966, entered into force 3 January 1976) 993 UNTS 3 (ICESCR).

replaced the Intergovernmental Committee on Refugees (IGCR) – a refugee agency that had been founded outside of the LoN system in 1938 in view of the intensifying refugee challenge.[397] IRO was a temporary UN agency (to complete its activities in 1950), designed to help European refugees.[398] Both the IRO and the IGCR were basically tasked with "providing material assistance, and identifying and negotiating political solutions, such as repatriation and resettlement, not with creating a legal framework to impose legal obligations on states vis-à-vis refugees and stateless persons".[399]

To gain more insight in the issue of statelessness, nonetheless, studies were undertaken. Already in 1946, the IGCR looked at statelessness and some of its causes in Europe, noting that the issue was widespread and that international action was needed.[400] More importantly, with a resolution of the Economic and Social Council (ECOSOC) in 1948[401], a study regarding statelessness was commissioned to gain a better understanding of the issue and to investigate the desirability of further international agreements on the matter.[402] The study, prepared by the Secretary-General, gives an overview of relevant legal instruments and addresses both the improvement of the status of stateless people and the elimination of statelessness. Importantly, it recommends the drafting of a new treaty regarding statelessness in cooperation with the IRO.[403]

When the IRO was about to expire, tensions around the world and in the context of the Cold War proved that refugees were not a temporary issue that the international community had to face.[404] At the same time, the IRO had been unable to really complete its activities as thousands of people remained displaced in Europe. In December 1949, it was therefore decided to establish a new organization for refugees: UNHCR[405], which would later play an important role with regard to the Statelessness Conventions.[406]

After the establishment of UNHCR, a number of legal instruments on refugees and the stateless were developed as we saw in paragraph 1.5.1, which considered the content of these instruments. Here, the background to these documents is considered. After the UN study of statelessness, an Ad Hoc Committee on Statelessness and Related Problems was established. They agreed that there was a need for an international treaty for the protection of refugees and stateless people, but some members pressed for separate

397 See also Michelle Foster & Hélène Lambert, *International Refugee Law and the Protection of Stateless Persons* (Oxford University Press 2019) 24–25.

398 On the IRO see for instance also UNCHR, *The State of the World's Refugees 2000. Fifty Years of Humanitarian Action* (UNHCR/Oxford University Press 2000) ch 1.

399 Michelle Foster & Hélène Lambert, *International Refugee Law and the Protection of Stateless Persons* (Oxford University Press 2019) 25–26.

400 IGCR, 'Statelessness and Some of its Causes: An Outline' (1946 Memorandum).

401 ECOSOC Res 116 (VI) D (1948) Resolutions adopted by the Economic and Social Council during its Sixth Session (2 February to 11 March 1948) 18.

402 UN Department of Social Affairs, *A Study of Statelessness* (1949, E/1112/ Add. 1).

403 Ibid.

404 UNCHR, *The State of the World's Refugees 2000. Fifty Years of Humanitarian Action* (UNHCR/Oxford University Press 2000) 17–19.

405 UNGA Res 319 (IV) (3 December 1949) UN Doc A/RES/319(IV).

406 See para 1.5.1.

treatment of refugees and stateless non-refugees.[407] Eventually, the Committee prepared a Draft Convention Relating to the Status of Refugees and a Draft Protocol Relating to the Status of Stateless Persons thereto, which led to the adoption of the Convention Relating to the Status of Refugees in 1951. "This set the refugee and the stateless person, who had until then been cast together in the eyes of the international community, on diverging paths – a move which has had far-reaching consequences for the protection of the stateless to this day".[408] In 1954, at a second conference of plenipotentiaries, it was decided that the Draft Protocol Relating to the Status would become a convention: the Convention Relating to the Status of Stateless Persons.[409] The reasoning behind a separate treaty, instead of a protocol to the 1951 Convention, was to allow states to accede to an instrument for the protection of stateless people without having to become a state party to the Refugee Convention first.[410]

The other statelessness convention, the Convention on the Reduction of Statelessness, was drafted against the background of the existing 1930 Hague Convention and the newly proclaimed right to a nationality in the UDHR.[411] After preliminary work by the ILC, a Conference took place in 1959 to discuss the draft Convention on the Reduction of Future Statelessness as prepared by the ILC.[412] However, negotiations were difficult and states were unable to come to an agreement, in particular as regards deprivation of nationality.[413] The Conference on this matter was therefore reconvened in 1961, where the 1961 Convention was eventually adopted.

When considering all of this together, the conclusion can only be that large-scale denationalization and displacement had led to statelessness only further increasing after World War I and during World War II. At the same time, the continent had witnessed such atrocities that there was a need also for further responses in that regard. The confrontation with all those people who were left displaced, with or without a nationality, led states to adopt specific treaties on refugees and stateless people, as well as recognize the need to legally distinguish them from each other. Indeed, the period after the war included the adoption of the Statelessness Conventions to specifically respond to the issue of statelessness, as well as the establishment of UNHCR. Furthermore, as a response to inhumanity witnessed during the war, we saw the genesis of modern human rights treaties. However, the need to (legally) address the dire situation after the

---

407 Guy S Goodwin-Gill, 'The Rights of Refugees and Stateless Persons' in K P Saksena (ed), *Human Rights Perspective & Challenges (in 1990 and Beyond)* (World Congress on Human Rights, Lancers Books 1994) 378–401, 381.

408 Laura van Waas, 'The UN Statelessness Conventions' in Alice Edwards & Laura van Waas (eds), *Nationality and Statelessness under International Law* (Cambridge University Press 2014) 67.

409 On the 1951 Convention and 1954 Convention and the drafting process see also Michelle Foster & Hélène Lambert, *International Refugee Law and the Protection of Stateless Persons* (Oxford University Press 2019) 31–46.

410 Laura van Waas, 'The UN Statelessness Conventions' in Alice Edwards & Laura van Waas (eds), *Nationality and Statelessness under International Law* (Cambridge University Press 2014) 68.

411 Ibid, 70.

412 Paul Weis, *Nationality and Statelessness in International Law* (2nd ed, Sijthoff & Noordhoff International Publishers 1979) 166.

413 Ibid, 166.

war was not only felt internationally. It was also felt in Europe, at the regional level, as can be seen in paragraph 2.5 below.

2.5. (RE)BUILDING EUROPE AND NATIONALITY MATTERS

Within Europe, cooperation for stability and peace was sought at the regional level. This resulted in the establishment of the two organizations studied here: the CoE and the EU, i.e. initially the European Communities. In this section, the first steps that were taken to enact these organizations are considered with a particular focus on their relevance and instruments regarding nationality and statelessness.

The CoE was, of the two organizations focused on, the first one to be established, in 1949 by the Treaty of London. This organization was founded on the values of human rights, rule of law and democracy.[414] The genesis of the CoE was "part of a Europe-building process which began soon after 1945".[415] It was the outcome of hard negotiations by 'federalist'[416] and 'unionist'[417] Europeans[418] and was heavily influenced by the Cold War and a "new pattern of international relations based on two superpowers – the United States and the Soviet Union".[419]

Important with regard to developments leading up to the establishment of the EU is that a deeper form of cooperation was sought between six European countries – Belgium, France, Germany, Italy, Luxembourg and the Netherlands – as regards economic matters in the European Coal and Steel Community (ECSC) based on the Schuman Declaration of 1950. In 1957, this specific economic cooperation concerning coal and steel is supplemented with respect to other economic sectors by the introduction of the European Economic Community (EEC) with the aim of ensuring that goods, services and people can move freely across the borders of the member states[420], as well as the European Atomic Energy Community (Euratom).

In terms of (legal) responses to some of the challenges faced with regard to nationality and statelessness, we see that the focus on the European regional level is on seeking cooperation between states and rebuilding Europe together. Legal instruments therefore focus on making this (economic) cooperation available, as well as on the establishment

---

414 See also the Statute of the Council of Europe Statute of the Council of Europe (Statute of the CoE, as amended, London, 1949, CETS No. 1).

415 Birte Wassenberg, *History of the Council of Europe* (Council of Europe Publishing 2013) 14.

416 The federalists wanted a supranational organization that had serious political powers.

417 The unionists preferred intergovernmental cooperation and a confederal union.

418 Anita Prettenthaler-Ziegerhofer, 'A Stopover on the Way to a United Europe: On the Creation of the Council of Europe' in Renate Kicker (ed), *The Council of Europe – Pioneer and Guarantor for Human Rights and Democracy* (Council of Europe Publishing 2010) 9–13; Birte Wassenberg, *History of the Council of Europe* (Council of Europe Publishing 2013) 20–21.

419 Birte Wassenberg, *History of the Council of Europe* (Council of Europe Publishing 2013) 19. On historical developments in Europe in different fields (political, economic, cultural, etc.) after 1945, see for instance Mary Fullbrook, *Short Oxford History of Europe. Europe Since 1945* (Oxford University Press 2001).

420 For an overview of the European integration, see eg Desmond Dinan, *Ever Closer Union. An Introduction to European Integration* (4th ed, Palgrave Macmillan 2010).

of individuals rights and freedoms. After 1957, some competition becomes visible between the CoE and the EEC in terms of harmonized European standard setting.

> "The Council of Europe was reduced to using international law while the EEC had its own community law, which was binding on its members. However, although the EEC was able to adopt legislative provisions which were directly applicable in its member states, these were mostly confined to economic matters. To assert its position in the face of competition from the EEC, the Council of Europe therefore decided in the early 1960s to direct its energies towards areas of legal co-operation which were (as yet) unexplored by the Six: civil law, criminal law, administrative law and public international law."[421]

For matters relating to nationality and statelessness, two relevant legal instruments are adopted, both in the context of the CoE. The first is the Convention for the Protection of Human Rights and Fundamental Freedoms (ECHR) in 1950[422], which remains to this day the most influential human rights instrument in Europe and is an important milestone for the protection of human rights, including of stateless people, in Europe, despite not including the right to a nationality explicitly. Secondly, and against the background of the aforementioned focus of the CoE, a treaty focused specifically on multiple nationality was drafted – the Convention on the Reduction of Cases of Multiple Nationality and on Military Obligations in Cases of Multiple Nationality. Both treaties are considered in more depth in paragraph 3.2 of this study. There thus seems to be some willingness to address nationality matters within the CoE, also evidenced by Recommendations of the CoE Committee of Ministers relating to statelessness and nationality in this period.[423] Overall, however, the developments within the CoE and the predecessors of the EU relating to nationality and statelessness are very limited in the years after World War II and during the Cold War.

2.6. THE END OF THE COLD WAR: A NEW EUROPE?

After World War II, we saw an age of tensions between states rising, as well as improving occasionally, with different crises and wars, such as those in Vietnam and the Middle East. It is "[a]gainst this background of strained international relations"[424] that the focus organizations of this study developed.

---

421 Birte Wassenberg, *History of the Council of Europe* (Council of Europe Publishing 2013) 89.

422 Since then, the Convention for the Protection of Human Rights and Fundamental Freedoms (European Convention on Human Rights (ECHR) (CETS No. 005) has been amended several times by the introduction of Protocols to it.

423 Eg CoE CM Recommendation No. R (83) 1 of the Committee of Ministers to the Member States on the Stateless nomads and nomads of undetermined nationality (356th meeting of the Ministers' Deputies, 22 February 1983); CoE CM Recommendation No. R (84) 21 of the Committee of Ministers to the Member States on the acquisition by refugees of the nationality of the host state (377th meeting of the Ministers' Deputies, 14 November 1984). See also para 3.2.2.

424 Birte Wassenberg, *History of the Council of Europe* (Council of Europe Publishing 2013) 19.

Note should be made of the fact that the aftermath of World War II also saw the decline of colonialism as an "integral part of the structural change in the world political constellation which had been developing since the turn of the century".[425] This, of course, had major consequences for the countries that were former colonies and their nationality laws. Within Europe, that influence was perhaps less felt. At the same time, European states saw themselves confronted – from time to time – with complicated situations that needed to be addressed in their nationality laws. There were no specific international standards on decolonization and nationality matters, but the situation could often be considered a situation of state succession and treaties concluded in the period after the war – in particular the 1961 Convention that contains provisions regarding state succession, as well as the 1930 Hague Convention – could provide further guidance. But that is not to say that statelessness would not occur. One example concerns the Moluccans, who were transferred by the Dutch government to the Netherlands in the wake of Indonesian independence (1945–1949) in 1951–1952. They had served in the Dutch Colonial Army and it was understood that the residence of Moluccans in the Netherlands would be temporary. At the time, there was the belief that the Moluccas would become an autonomous state and therefore, most Moluccans in the Netherlands had no interest in acquiring Dutch citizenship. But as they continued to stay in the Netherlands, they had become stateless as their Indonesian nationality was lost due to residence abroad for five years without expressing the wish to remain a national.[426]

> "By the 1970s about 30,000 stateless persons of Moluccan origin lived in the Netherlands. The Dutch Government recognized the need for improvement and in 1976 the Law pertaining to the position of Moluccans ("Faciliteitenwet Molukkers") was approved, granting Moluccans (nearly) the same rights as Dutch nationals, without actually making them citizens. In their passports it was stated that they were to be treated as Dutch nationals on the basis of the 1976 Act. As this gave rise to practical problems, the Dutch Government decided in 1991 that all stateless Moluccans would be Dutch nationals for the purpose of the Passport Act."[427]

An important event that marks further development, in particular with regard to matters relating to nationality and statelessness, is presented by the fall of the Berlin Wall in 1989 and the dissolution of the Soviet Union that followed in 1991. Later in the 1990s, Yugoslavia and Czechoslovakia also dissolved. Not only did this lead to unrest and conflict in certain situations, it also led to statelessness:

> "After the dissolution of the Soviet Union and Czechoslovakia and the break-up of Yugoslavia, millions of people needed to confirm a new citizenship status. Was a former Czechoslovak citizen now Czech or Slovak? Was someone born in Belgrade, raised in

---

425 Rudolf von Albertini, 'The Impact of Two World Wars on the Decline of Colonialism' (1969) 4 Journal of Contemporary History 17, 35.

426 UNHCR, 'Mapping Statelessness in the Netherlands' (2011) 16 <https://www.refworld.org/docid/4eef65da2.html> accessed 26 September 2021.

427 Ibid.

> Sarajevo, now married to someone from Zagreb and living in Ljubliana, a Yugoslav, Bosnian, Croat or Slovene citizen? New states emerging from these dissolutions established their own criteria for citizenship. In some cases, people who did not meet those criteria became 'stateless'; in other cases they failed to acquire citizenship where they lived."[428]

The most notable groups of people that remained stateless in the context of state succession included the Roma[429] – who were not considered nationals, often were discriminated against and were denied nationality and sometimes even registration – as well as the Russian ethnic minorities in the Baltic States. This last group became stateless because these states applied the principle of state continuity, which In terms of law basically turned back time to before the occupation of the territory by the Union of Soviet Socialist Republics (USSR).[430] After its independence from the USSR, Estonia, for instance, reenacted its citizenship law of 1938, last amended in 1940.[431] In view of this law, only people who were Estonian citizens before 16 June 1940 and their direct descendants were considered to be Estonians.[432] In other words, Estonia adhered to the state continuity principle and maintained that nationality had not ceased to exist because of the illegal occupation.[433] For others, who came to Estonia during the Soviet occupation, naturalization was an option. However, this was subject to a number of requirements including knowledge of the Estonian language, which made naturalization practically impossible for the majority of non-Estonians in the territory.[434] At the same time, former citizens of the USSR did not acquire the nationality of the Russian Federation.[435] Thus, a large number of people remained without a nationality in Estonia.

State succession in this context thus created uncertainty about the citizenship status of large groups of people, statelessness and presented states with a significant human rights issue. We also see states differentiating between people: those who met the criteria for citizenship and those who did not, and registering people as such, or even only registering those who acquired citizenship. This particularly created difficulties for ethnic

---

428 UNCHR, *The State of the World's Refugees 2000. Fifty Years of Humanitarian Action* (UNHCR/Oxford University Press 2000) 189.

429 Gay McDougall, 'Minorities and the Discriminatory Denial or Deprivation of Citizenship. Report of the Independent Expert on Minority Issues (15 and 16 December 2008)' in Gay McDougall, *The First United Nations Mandate on Minority Issues* (Brill Nijhoff 2016) 328.

430 See eg Ineta Ziemele, *State Continuity and Nationality: The Baltic States and Russia. Past, Present and Future as Defined by International Law* (Martinus Nijhoff Publishers 2005) 17–43 for an overview of the claims of the three Baltic States to state continuity.

431 Ibid, 146–148; Raivo Vetik, 'The Statelessness Issue in Estonia' in Caroline Sawyer & Brad K Blitz, *Statelessness in the European Union. Displaced, Undocumented, Unwanted* (Cambridge University Press 2011) 230–252, 230–234.

432 Ineta Ziemele, *State Continuity and Nationality: The Baltic States and Russia. Past, Present and Future as Defined by International Law* (Martinus Nijhoff Publishers 2005) 146.

433 Ibid, 153–154.

434 Raivo Vetik, 'The Statelessness Issue in Estonia' in Caroline Sawyer & Brad K. Blitz, *Statelessness in the European Union. Displaced, Undocumented, Unwanted* (Cambridge University Press 2011) 232.

435 Kees Groenendijk, 'Nationality, Minorities and Statelessness. The Case of the Baltic States' (1993) 4 Helsinki Monitor 13, 18.

minorities in relation to nationality matters where states were broken up due to ethnic conflict, as newly established states in such a situation had "less motivation or support for creating liberal citizenship laws or for ratifying treaties that may guarantee citizenship to large populations of ethnic minorities".[436] Indeed, in Yugoslavia for instance,

> "[...] lawful citizens were, overnight, turned into aliens and, in many cases, the stateless. For the most part, they were required to follow naturalization processes reserved for aliens, requiring a certain number of years of continuous residence and certain additional tests. The Ministries of the Interior that were in charge of deciding on the validity of the applications often had no obligation to state the reasons for the refusal; many reports testify widespread discrimination against members of ethnic minorities."[437]

In view of these types of issues arising from the dissolution of states, "[q]uestions of membership have become central to the construction of identity in post-Cold War Europe".[438] In particular within the CoE, steps were taken to provide a (legal) response to these questions, not least because many Eastern European states joined the organization in the 1990s. The content of the legal instruments enacted by the CoE in this period is discussed further in paragraph 3.2, but notable milestones include the adoption of the ECN in 1997[439] and the adoption of the CoE Convention on the Avoidance of Statelessness in Relation to State Succession (ECSS) in 2006[440] to respond to questions regarding nationality matters and statelessness that were raised in the context of the dissolution of states. In particular, the CoE played an important role in specific Central and Eastern European countries. For instance, it has provided assistance on nationality matters to Bosnia and Herzegovina and followed the question of nationality in the Baltic States closely, again providing assistance, for instance in setting up bodies to process applications for residence permits and nationality.[441] From the early 1990s onwards, the CoE thus considered minority rights and citizenship to a greater extent, also pushed by scholars and NGOs, and effectively influenced the European human rights regime, "seeking to create shared understandings of citizenship".[442]

The EU and its predecessor, paid little attention to nationality matters when compared to the CoE. This is perhaps not surprising in view of its focus on economic cooperation. Nonetheless, there were certainly interesting developments that should be

---

436 David S Weissbrodt, *The Human Rights of Non-Citizens* (Oxford University Press 2008) 93.

437 Igor Štiks, *Nations and Citizens in Yugoslavia and the Post-Yugoslav States: One Hundred Years of Citizenship* (Bloomsbury 2015) 160.

438 Jeffrey T Checkel, 'Norms, Institutions, and National Identity in Contemporary Europe' (1999) 43 International Studies Quarterly 83, 93.

439 European Convention on Nationality (Strasbourg, 1997, CETS No. 166) (ECN).

440 Council of Europe Convention on the Avoidance of Statelessness in relation to State Succession (Strasbourg. 2006, CETS No. 200) (ECSS).

441 Margaret Killerby, 'Steps Taken by the Council of Europe to Promote the Modernization of Nationality Laws of European States' in Síofra O'Leary & Teija Tiilikainen (eds), *Citizenship and Nationality Status in the New Europe* (Sweet & Maxwell 1998) 21–37, 36.

442 Jeffrey T Checkel, 'Norms, Institutions, and National Identity in Contemporary Europe' (1999) 43 International Studies Quarterly 83, 93ff.

noted here. Shortly after the fall of the Iron Curtain, the Treaty of Maastricht (1992) established the EU and introduced the notion of EU citizenship – a notion that was seen as potentially enhancing European identity.[443]

> "The Maastricht Treaty first introduced the legal concept of EU citizenship as part of the move from a mainly economic community to a political union. In addition to providing a stronger Treaty basis for the rights of movement, residence and equal treatment of EU nationals, and gathering existing entitlements together under the umbrella of citizenship, Articles 20–25 [of the Treaty on the Functioning of the EU] created a number of new political and electoral rights."[444]

With the notion of EU citizenship, a new form of citizenship was introduced for every person holding the nationality of one of the EU member states: giving citizens of EU states a political role in the EU and complementing national citizenship but not replacing it.[445] Nationality matters of the member states remain – today still – within the exclusive competences of the member states. With the Treaty of Amsterdam of 1997, the policy regarding asylum and migration was incorporated in the community pillar of the EU, giving the EU extensive powers in this domain. In paragraph 4.2, the content of and developments, including case law of the Court of Justice of the EU (CJEU), in these respective areas of EU law – regarding asylum and migration and regarding EU citizenship – is explored further. Statelessness, as a concept relevant to EU law, was only introduced in the Treaty of Lisbon: stateless people are to be treated as third-country nationals.[446] In the context of the EU, states thus start working together more intensively on a broader range of issues: the cooperation is now of a more political nature and geared towards inclusion, and covers the respect for fundamental rights[447] and reserves a specific status for EU citizens. Over time, the EU expanded, with many (new) Eastern European states joining in 2004, 2007 and 2013, culminating in a (supranational) EU with 28 member states – 27 after the UK left, which is also considered further below.

From this, the conclusion can be drawn that the period after the end of the Cold War resulted in a number of interesting developments in view of nationality matters, with specific instruments being adopted in the context of the CoE, and new steps being taken in the context of the EU – in particular through the introduction of citizenship

---

443 Patricia Mindus, *European Citizenship after Brexit. Freedom of Movement and Rights of Residence* (Palgrave Studies in European Union Politics, Palgrave Macmillan 2017) 8.

444 Paul Craig & Gráinne de Búrca, *EU Law. Text, Cases and Materials* (5th edn, Oxford University Press 2011) 819.

445 Art 20(1) of the Treaty on the Functioning of the European Union and Art 9 of the Treaty on European Union (Consolidated versions of the Treaty on European Union (TEU) and the Treaty on the Functioning of the European Union (TFEU) [2016] OJ C202/1).

446 Currently Art 67(2) TFEU – stateless people are to be treated as third-country nationals for the purpose of Title V on the Area of Freedom, Security and Justice.

447 As is evidenced by the adoption of the Charter of Fundamental Rights of the European Union [2016] OJ C202/389 in 2000, which became legally binding with the entry into force of the Lisbon Treaty in 2009.

of the Union. Even though statelessness and nationality questions were on the agenda, this did not mean that statelessness was resolved. Indeed, many of the instruments in question were only adopted *after* new occurrences of statelessness, for instance due to the dissolution of states.

2.7. STATELESSNESS IN EUROPE TODAY

Today, people remain stateless around Europe and face all kinds of problems with accessing basic human rights. This section aims to set out the contemporary context in which the legal instruments discussed in the next chapters have to be placed, identifying the current numbers, challenges and main causes of statelessness. The latest developments in preventing and solving statelessness in Europe using legal instruments are discussed in more depth in Part II of this research (chapters 3 and 4).

Despite efforts aimed at the protection of human rights and inclusion of people in society, a large number of people remain stateless in Europe. Compared to other regions in the world, statelessness is most comprehensively mapped in Europe.[448] It is estimated that over 500.000 people remain stateless in this region. For a number of reasons however, the statistics that have currently been collected with regard to the magnitude of the problem grapple with methodological difficulties in mapping statelessness, gaps in data from a more practical perspective, as well as political and capacity limitations.[449] When taking a closer look at the statistics available, however, persistent causes and challenges as regards statelessness can be uncovered. Generally, causes of statelessness can be divided in technical causes (such as conflict of nationality laws), causes related to state succession and causes linked to discrimination or arbitrary deprivation of nationality.[450] Below, they are discussed from a European perspective together with current challenges and developments and linked to relevant statistics. A more detailed inspection of numbers demonstrates that

> "over 75% of the total reported stateless population in Europe live in just four countries, all successor states of the Soviet Union: Latvia, the Russian Federation, Estonia and Ukraine. Latvia has the largest stateless population, at 224.844, the only European country with a stateless population of over 100.000. Although numbers in each of these countries are declining, nearly a quarter of a century after state succession took place, 414.050 people remain stateless in these four states. In the six states to emerge from the Socialist Federal

---

448 ISI, *The World's Stateless* (Wolf Legal Publishers 2014) 95. This report analyses the statistical reporting (by UNHCR) on statelessness.

449 Ibid; UNHCR, 'UNHCR Statistical Reporting on Statelessness' (2019) UNHCR Statistics Technical Series 2019/1 <https://www.unhcr.org/statistics/unhcrstats/5d9e182e7/unhcr-statistical-reporting-statelessness.html> accessed 26 September 2021. See also ISI, 'Counting the World's Stateless: Reflections on Statistical Reporting on Statelessness' in UNHCR, 'UNHCR Statistical Yearbook 2013' (2014) 41–47.

450 This division is also used in UNHCR and Inter-Parliamentary Union (IPU), *Nationality and Statelessness. Handbook for Parliamentarians No. 22* (2nd ed, UNHCR 2014).

> Republic of Yugoslavia, a total of almost 10.000 stateless persons were reported in 2015, which has fallen just under 6.000 at the end of 2018. Others remain at risk of statelessness due to lack of key forms of documentation".[451]

An issue to be mindful of in relation to statelessness in Europe relates back to the fact that statistics remain incomplete and to administration as discussed in paragraph 1.4.3. Not every person that is stateless is actually registered as such. A number of European countries register and report individuals as being 'of unknown nationality', which blurs the number of people that are truly stateless.[452] One way to address this is to ensure that stateless people are properly identified using a statelessness determination procedure. A few European countries, such as France, Hungary, Latvia and Moldova, have dedicated statelessness determination procedures in law. Some countries have other types of determination procedures, but quite some of these are not capable of providing a proper framework for identification and protection due to procedural issues or lack of awareness. Furthermore, a number of European countries have no mechanism or status for the identification and protection of the stateless at all.[453] Indeed, research has found that "states are largely failing to acknowledge the vulnerabilities associated with statelessness, [and] to put in place effective procedures to identify statelessness and to protect stateless people", also leading to states' failure to prevent the stateless from being arbitrarily detained around Europe.[454] Persistent challenges thus remain with regard to the identification of stateless people, the adoption of statelessness determination procedures and preventing arbitrary detention of stateless people.

When considering the aforementioned numbers of stateless people in Europe in conjunction with the examples of state succession discussed above in paragraph 2.6, the four countries with the largest numbers of stateless people within their borders according to current data are all formerly part of the USSR. Hence, we can conclude that state succession is the main cause of statelessness in Europe. Indeed, when considering literature on the matter it is demonstrated that "[i]n Europe, causes linked to state succession and restoration have been especially prominent".[455] Keeping in mind the dynamic history of Europe with shifting borders and states appearing, disappearing and/or reappearing that is perhaps not surprising.

---

451 ISI, *The World's Stateless: Deprivation of Nationality* (ISI 2020) 91–92.

452 ISI, *The World's Stateless* (Wolf Legal Publishers 2014) 103.

453 ENS, 'Statelessness Index Thematic Briefing: Statelessness Determination and Protection in Europe: Good Practice, Challenges and Risks' (ENS 2021) <https://www.statelessness.eu/sites/default/files/2021-09/ENS-Statelessness_determination_and_protection_in_Europe-Sep_2021.pdf> accessed 26 September 2021.

454 ENS, 'Protecting Stateless Persons from Arbitrary Detention: An Agenda for Change' (ENS 2017) <https://www.statelessness.eu/sites/www.statelessness.eu/files/attachments/resources/ENS_LockeInLimbo_Detention_Agenda_online.pdf> accessed 3 January 2022; see also UNHCR, 'Stateless Persons in Detention: A Tool for Their Identification and Enhanced Protection' (UNHCR 2017) <https://www.refworld.org/docid/598adacd4.html> accessed 3 January 2022.

455 Olivier Vonk, Maarten Vink and Gerard-René de Groot, Protection Against Statelessness: Trends and Regulations in Europe' (GLOBALCIT, EUDO Citizenship Observatory, Country Reports, 2013/01) 11 <http://cadmus.eui.eu//handle/1814/30201> accessed 22 August 2021.

A unified Europe after years of tensions and wars as described in this chapter is not self-evident at the beginning of 2022. Different events have led to increased 'new' nationalism[456], populism and xenophobia, a crisis of multiculturalism and even states turning away from close(r) cooperation on different matters. Key events in this regard include the terrorist attacks of 9/11 and further terrorist attacks around Europe, which sparked the 'War on Terrorism' with all kinds of anti-terrorism measures being taken and a "critique of multiculturalism that focuses on Muslims".[457] But terrorist attacks did not only come from Muslim extremists. From the extreme right we have also seen terrorist attacks, such as the bombing in Oslo and shootings on Utøya in 2011. Even though these events did not lead to statelessness directly, changing, more suspicious attitudes towards foreigners – or anyone who is not a national – could have consequences for stateless people, as they are a foreigner in any state, including discrimination. Such changing views of what behavior, believes or qualities makes a person 'foreign' may generate statelessness and make it harder of people to resolve their statelessness, because these also influence nationality policy. Quite some Western European states, for instance, have adopted measures to deprive (suspected) terrorists of their nationality, which sometimes leads to statelessness.[458] For example "Albania, Austria, Belgium, Bulgaria, Germany, Italy, the Netherlands, Norway, and the UK have [...] amended their legislation since 2010 to make it easier for the competent authorities to deprive individuals of their nationality on security grounds".[459] Another example of this is the deprivation of nationality targeted Turkish citizens living abroad after the failed coup in Turkey in 2017.[460] Some states try to avoid statelessness as a result of such measures, by only applying it to dual nationals for instance, but this raises other human rights concerns, for instance in relation to the principle of non-discrimination.[461]

Discrimination remains the main cause of statelessness globally.[462] Indeed, arbitrary deprivation of citizenship can lead to statelessness on a scale that is quite

---

456 Cf Florian Bieber, 'Is Nationalism on the Rise? Assessing Global Trends' (2018) 17 Ethnopolitics 519.

457 Tariq Modood, 'Multiculturalism, Liberal Citizenship and National Identity: On British Muslims' in Montserrat Guibernau & John Rex (eds), *The Ethnicity Reader: Nationalism, Multiculturalism and Migration* (2nd edn, Polity Press 2010) 243–250, 243.

458 PACE/Tineke Strik, 'Report: Withdrawing Nationality as a Measure to Combat Terrorism: A Human Rights-Compatible Approach? (2019) Doc 14790 <http://assembly.coe.int/nw/xml/XRef/Xref-DocDetails-en.asp?FileID=25241&lang=en> accessed 26 September 2021. On this matter, see also eg Sandra Mantu, 'Terrorist citizens and the human right to a nationality' (2018) 26 Journal of Contemporary European Studies 28.

459 ENS, 'Statelessness Index Thematic Briefing: Deprivation of Nationality and the Prevention of Statelessness in Europe' (ENS 2021) 11–12 <https://www.statelessness.eu/sites/default/files/2021-07/Deprivation%20of%20nationality%20and%20the%20prevention%20of%20statelessness%20in%20Europe%20FINAL.pdf> accessed 3 October 2021.

460 ISI, 'Policy Brief: Arbitrary Deprivation of Nationality and Denial of Consular Services to Turkish Citizens (July 2017) <https://files.institutesi.org/policy-brief-Turkey-arbitrary-deprivation-of-nationality_2017.pdf> accessed 26 September 2021.

461 Cf Principles on Deprivation of Nationality as a National Security Measure (2020) 3 <https://www.refworld.org/pdfid/5f3bf26d4.pdf> accessed 26 September 2021.

462 Eg Olivier Vonk, Maarten Vink and Gerard-René de Groot, Protection Against Statelessness: Trends and Regulations in Europe' (GLOBALCIT, EUDO Citizenship Observatory, Country Reports,

massive and comparable to magnitude of causes related to state succession.[463] An example that could be seen above and that is often mentioned in this relation is the deprivation of nationality of Jews by Nazi-Germany, also in occupied states.[464] However, there are also more contemporary instances where discriminated minorities are deprived of citizenship or never receive it, such as the Rohingya in Myanmar.[465] In Europe, the situation of the Roma minority – the largest minority group in Europe – is considered discriminatory and leading to statelessness, and is often also related to lack of or problems with documentation and civil registration.[466] Also, we see gender discrimination in nationality laws around the world, which can result in statelessness[467], as well as discrimination against people with a disability. This problem perhaps is more

2013/01) 11 <http://cadmus.eui.eu//handle/1814/30201> accessed 22 August 2021.

463 Cf ISI, *The World's Stateless* (Wolf Legal Publishers 2014) 25.

464 Cf Paul Weis, *Nationality and Statelessness in International Law* (2nd ed, Sijthoff & Noordhoff International Publishers 1979) 119–126; David Weissbrodt, *The Human Rights of Non-Citizens* (Oxford University Press 2008) 127.

465 Eg David Weissbrodt, *The Human Rights of Non-Citizens* (Oxford University Press 2008) 98–99; ERT, 'Unravelling Anomaly. Detention, Discrimination and the Protection Needs of Stateless Persons' (July 2010) <www.equalrightstrust.org/ertdocumentbank/UNRAVELLING%20ANOMALY%20small%20file.pdf> accessed 26 September 2021; ERT, 'Burning Homes, Sinking Lives. A Situation Report on Violence Against Stateless Rohingya in Myanmar and their *Refoulement* from Bangladesh' (June 2012) <www.equalrightstrust.org/ertdocumentbank/The%20Equal%20Rights%20Trust%20-%20Burning%20Homes%20Sinking%20Lives.pdf> accessed 26 September 2021; ERT & Institute of Human Rights and Peace Studies, Mahidol University, 'The Human Rights of Stateless Rohingya in Thailand' (February 2014) <www.equalrightstrust.org/ertdocumentbank/The%20Human%20Rights%20of%20Stateless%20Rohingya%20in%20Thailand(small).pdf> accessed 26 September 2021. The Rohingya are also mentioned explicitly in ISI, *The World's Stateless* (Wolf Legal Publishers 2014) 25 and Olivier Vonk, Maarten Vink and Gerard-René de Groot, Protection Against Statelessness: Trends and Regulations in Europe' (GLOBALCIT, EUDO Citizenship Observatory, Country Reports, 2013/01) 11 <http://cadmus.eui.eu//handle/1814/30201> accessed 22 August 2021.

466 ERRC, 'Roma Belong – Discrimination, Statelessness and Marginalisation of Roma in the Western Balkans and Ukraine' (*errc.org,* 26 October 2017) <www.errc.org/uploads/upload_en/file/roma-belong.pdf> accessed 22 August 2021; Annemarie Busser & Peter Rodrigues, 'Staatloze Roma in Nederland' [Stateless Roma in the Netherlands] (2010) 8 *Asiel & Migrantenrecht* 384; Jessica Parra, 'Stateless Roma in the European Union: Reconciling the Doctrine of Sovereignty concerning Nationality Laws with International Agreements to Reduce and Avoid Statelessness' (2011) 34 *Fordham International Law Journal* 1666; Ivanka Kostic, 'Discrimination and Statelessness – the Roma in the Western Balkans' (*Statelessness.eu*, ENS Kick-Off Seminar 19–21 November 2012) <www.statelessness.eu/sites/www.statelessness.eu/files/attachments/resources/ENS%20kick-off%20seminar%202012%20-%20Discrimination%20and%20statelessness,%20the%20Roma%20in%20the%20Western%20Balkans.pdf> accessed 26 September 2021; Julija Sardelic, 'Romani Minorities on the Margins of Post-Yugoslav Citizenship Regimes' (2013) Citsee Working Paper 2013/31 <http://papers.ssrn.com/sol3/papers.cfm?abstract_id=2388859> accessed 26 September 2021; Ivan Kochovski, 'Statelessness and Discriminatory Nationality Laws: The Case of the Roma in Bosnia and Serbia' (LLM thesis, Tilburg University 2013); Joanne van Selm, 'Stateless Roma in Macedonia' (2014) 32 *Forced Migration Review* 46. See also ISI, *The World's Stateless* (Wolf Legal Publishers 2014) 27.

467 Eg Laura van Waas & Zahra Albarazi, 'Towards the Abolition of Gender Discrimination in Nationality Laws' (2014) 46 *Forced Migration Review* 49; Women's Refugee Commission & Tilburg University, 'Our Motherland, Our Country. Gender Discrimination and Statelessness in the Middle East and North Africa (June 2013) <www.refworld.org/docid/51c02a084.html> accessed 26 September 2021.

prominent in other regions of the world, but European states can still be confronted with such issues in view of migration.

In 2014 and 2015, Europe faced what has been termed a 'European migrant crisis' or 'refugee crisis' with increased migration to the region, and with the EU struggling to respond to the large numbers of migrants arriving. During this crisis, "European immigration officers [...] face[d] the particular yet confusing case of stateless people seeking asylum in Europe, with the result that stateless people regularly face long periods of immigration detention waiting to be identified in need of international protection as stateless persons".[468]

Migrants can become stateless in the process of migrating, can already be stateless before coming to Europe or can give birth to stateless children after settling in Europe. Stateless people – in particular those who suffer from discrimination and marginalization – might furthermore attempt to find a safer place to stay and could end up in Europe or in another European country. Rashid's story below illustrates their plight:

> "Rashid was born in Myanmar. He fled to Bangladesh aged 12 with his mother in 1992 after his father, who was a Muslim rights activist, was killed and his sister was arrested. He lived in Bangladesh for 20 years, first in a refugee camp and then in several villages. Before Rashid's mother passed away in 2002, she explained to Rashid that he did not possess a valid identity document because the Rohingya of Myanmar had been deprived of their Myanmar nationality.
> Rashid travelled irregularly to the Netherlands in 2012. He applied for asylum twice and his request was refused both times. After the second rejection he was kept in immigration detention for 8 months. He was eventually released after being presented to the Bangladeshi and Myanmar authorities, both of which refused to accept him as a national. However, following his release he was unable to regularize his stay and he remains without status and sleeps in a homeless shelter. He has lived with instability his entire life and now finds himself alone in a foreign country suffering from nightmares, psychological issues and high blood pressure (even though he is still a young man). He cannot lead a normal life in the Netherlands but equally he cannot go and live anywhere else."[469]

The Rohingya are an example of people who are already stateless before coming here, thus demonstrating that statelessness can be a reason to migrate as it is an indicator of the problems and violations of rights that a stateless person could face. In the context of the Syrian Civil War that started in 2011, the already stateless Kurds were among the refugees that came to Europe.[470] However, the fact that a person has migrated can

---

468 Katalin Berényi, 'Statelessness and the Refugee Crisis in Europe' (2016) 53 Forced Migration Review 69.

469 ENS, 'Still Stateless, Still Suffering. Why Europe Must Act Now to Protect Stateless Persons' (ENS 2014) 5 <www.statelessness.eu/sites/www.statelessness.eu/files/ENS_Still_Stateless_Still_Suffering_online%20version_2.pdf> accessed 26 September 2021.

470 On this matter see Thomas McGee, 'Statelessness Displaced: Update on Syria's Stateless Kurds' (2016) Statelessness Working Paper Series No. 2016/02 <www.institutesi.org/WP2016_02.pdf> accessed 26 September 2021.

also create statelessness. Syrian refugee children, for instance, are at risk of statelessness because of the application of Syrian nationality laws and difficulties with proving their nationality and discriminatory nationality laws in the country of origin.[471]

The EU was faced with another challenge when the UK left the EU in January 2020, after long negotiations as a result of the 2016 referendum in which the majority of UK voters indicated that they would like to leave the EU. Shortly after, in March 2020, Europe was confronted with yet another crisis: COVID-19. A dangerous virus quickly infected parts of the population, forcing states to take far-reaching measures to contain it. Many European states went into lockdown, meaning that people were no longer allowed to go to work, to school or to restaurants and shops, and should stay at home. But it also meant that many states closed their borders. In this global pandemic, those who are already vulnerable, including the stateless, "are at heightened risk".[472] Indeed, stateless people face different consequences and issues as a result of this crisis, including problems surrounding access to rights (healthcare, education, shelter, work and food), increased discrimination, lack of accessible information for stateless people and a general lack of visibility and attention to the needs of the stateless specifically in media, political and other discussions as well as responses.[473]

At the same time, the issue of statelessness was more firmly brought (back) into the spotlights in recent years[474] by a dedicated campaign by UNHCR to end statelessness by 2024.[475] Academic scholarship on statelessness increased[476], as well as attention by civil society with dedicated non-governmental organizations on statelessness being established.[477] This has significantly increased the current body of knowledge on the issue. As chapter 1 showed, statelessness is clearly an issue of interest for the international community. This is evidenced by, for instance, the UNHCR issuing

471 Cf ISI & Norwegian Refugee Council, 'Understanding Statelessness in the Syria Refugee Context. Research Report' (2016) <https://www.nrc.no/globalassets/pdf/reports/understanding-statelessness-in-the-syria-refugee-context.pdf> accessed 26 September 2021.

472 OHCHR, IOM, UNHCR & WHO, 'The Rights and Health of Refugees, Migrants and Stateless Must Be Protected in COVID-19 Response' (*UNHCR*, 31 March 2020) <https://www.unhcr.org/news/press/2020/3/5e836f164/rights-health-refugees-migrants-stateless-must-protected-covid-19-response.html> accessed 26 September 2021.

473 ISI, 'Together We Can: The COVID-19 Impact on Stateless People & a Roadmap for Change' (ISI 2021) <https://files.institutesi.org/together_we_can_report_2021.pdf> accessed 26 September 2021; ENS, 'Position Paper: "Even before the pandemic, statelessness has been invisible" – Involving stateless people in Europe's COVID-19 response' (ENS 2020) <https://www.statelessness.eu/resources/even-pandemic-statelessness-has-been-invisible-involving-stateless-people-europe-s-covid> accessed 26 September 2021.

474 Eg Laura van Waas, 'Are We There Yet? The Emergence of Statelessness on the International Human Rights Agenda' (2014) 32 Netherlands Quarterly of Human Rights 342.

475 See also para 1.5.1.

476 Maria Jose Recalde Vela, Sangita Jaghai-Bajulaiye & Caia Vlieks, 'The State of Statelessness Research: 5 Years Later (2019) 24 Tilburg Law Review 139.

477 For instance, the European Network on Statelessness (ENS), established in 2012, an open and growing civil society alliance with 150 members in over 40 countries, committed to ending statelessness and ensuring that the estimated 600,000 people living in Europe without a nationality are protected under international law; and the Institute on Statelessness and Inclusion (ISI), established in 2014, the first and the only human rights NGO dedicated to working on statelessness at the global level.

guidelines on the interpretation of the Statelessness Conventions[478] and reference being made to statelessness by different UN treaty bodies.[479] At the European, regional level we also see new case law on statelessness emerging, both from the European Court of Human Rights (ECtHR) relating to the ECHR and from the CJEU concerning EU law.[480] This case law considers issues and gaps in nationality laws in European states as well.

Indeed, technical causes, relating to the conflict of and gaps in nationality laws, still cause statelessness in Europe today. This is also related to Europe's preference for *jus sanguinis* as the main principle of nationality acquisition, as described in paragraph 1.4.2 as well. This means that children born to parents that have no, an unknown or foreign nationality in Europe may be more vulnerable to problems in acquiring a nationality. Research has shown that some European states do not provide adequate safeguards in their laws to prevent statelessness among children born on the territory and ensure every child's right to acquire a nationality, for instance because they only provide safeguards for children who are born in the country and have legal residence, or because they leave children with an undetermined or unknown nationality.[481] Indeed, when considering the national laws of European states on granting nationality to otherwise stateless children born in the territory of the state, problems can indeed be encountered: not all European states provide a (complete) a safeguard.[482] Most European states have a safeguard that provides for the grant of citizenship to foundlings of unknown parentage found in the territory of the country though.[483] Cyprus, however, has no safeguards for children born on the territory who would otherwise be stateless, nor for foundlings. And not too long ago, the ECtHR had to take a strong stance on nationality laws concerning children born out of wedlock in Malta, because this amounted to differential treatment in violation of the ECHR.[484] Further challenges with regard to nationality matters of a more technical nature are presented by modern reproductive techniques, such as surrogacy, as well as adoption and foundlings.[485]

---

478 See para 1.5.1.

479 See para 1.5.1.

480 See ch 3 & 4.

481 ENS, 'No Child Should Be Stateless' (ENS 2015) <https://www.statelessness.eu/sites/www.statelessness.eu/files/ENS_NoChildStateless_final.pdf> accessed 26 September 2021.

482 Cf ENS, 'Statelessness Index' (2021) <https://index.statelessness.eu/> accessed 3 October 2021. Theme 'Prevention and Reduction' was selected, and note that only 27 countries are included; Olivier Vonk & Maarten Vink, 'Global Protection Against Statelessness Database' (EUI Research Data 2015) <https://cadmus.eui.eu/handle/1814/64601> accessed 3 October 2021. 'Mode S01: born stateless' was used and only member states of the CoE were selected. Unfortunately, six European states are not included (Andorra, Armenia, Azerbaijan, Georgia, Monaco, San Marino).

483 Cf ENS, 'Statelessness Index' (2021) <https://index.statelessness.eu/> accessed 3 October 2021. Theme 'Prevention and Reduction' was selected; Olivier Vonk & Maarten Vink, 'Global Protection Against Statelessness Database' (EUI Research Data 2015) <https://cadmus.eui.eu/handle/1814/64601> accessed 3 October 2021. 'Mode S02: foundling' was used and only member states of the CoE were selected.

484 *Genovese v Malta* App No 53124/09 (ECHR, 11 October 2011) ECLI:CE:ECHR:2011:1011JUD005312409. See also para 3.3.1.

485 Cf Case C-490/20 *V.M.A. v Stolichna Obshtina, Rayon 'Pancharevo'* [2021] ECLI:EU:C:2021:1008, discussed further in para 4.3.1.

It is clear that statelessness in Europe is caused by a multitude of factors, which relate to (recent) factual and political developments and new crises or threats to nationality, as well as to gaps and issues with current nationality laws and registration of citizenship. All of the general categories of causes of statelessness can thus be found in Europe: technical causes as well as causes relating to discrimination or arbitrary deprivation can be found. The largest numbers of stateless people in Europe, however, remain stateless due to the state dissolution that took place after the end of the Cold War.

2.8. CONCLUSION

This chapter aimed to demonstrate the broader context in which the regional European instruments studied in this research need to be placed. What causes were there for statelessness occurring, and how and why did states respond to it, in particular through law-making? The picture of Europe that has been sketched above demonstrates how the continent's history has unfolded in this regard, with its own particularities and practices, which were – at the same time – intertwined with major developments globally. It demonstrated that reasons for statelessness occurring in such ways that it demanded a response in law from states were often closely related to different historical events.

Already in the 19th century, nationality and registration became more important, paving the way towards exclusion based on these elements. World War I and its aftermath, however, made statelessness appear on a large scale in Europe. The LoN, founded after the war, took some first steps in recognizing and addressing the issue, but addressed only technical root causes and not the more practical ones, which eventually caused further problems. Displacement and denationalization in the context of World War II further deepened and added to the existing statelessness. The atrocities of war and the complications that ensued from this did not only result in a focus on human rights and the adoption of legal instruments on this; but also translated into concern for statelessness, with the UN Statelessness Conventions being adopted in 1954 and 1961. One of the ways in which Europe in particular responded to the devastation of war, was with the establishment of cooperation mechanisms (or the predecessor thereof) that are studied further in the chapters that follow. Legal progress on nationality and statelessness matters in the context of the CoE and the predecessors of the EU was relatively low after World War II and during the Cold War though. The period immediately after the end of the Cold War presented more development with the CoE adopting distinct legal instruments on nationality and statelessness, and – later – the EU introducing the notion of EU citizenship.

The exploration in this chapter demonstrated the relevance of these two European cooperation mechanisms. This is evident when considering their areas of focus and work: the CoE and its focus on human rights and the EU based on cooperation, inclusion and free movement and even the development of an own EU citizenship.

Both thereby show their commitment to connecting between people and states, beyond borders so that everyone can enjoy their rights. Where nationality was always viewed as a confirmation of a bond between the person and a state, in Europe it is considered as a way to establish a bond between a person and a state that is essential for being included in European society. Statelessness as such is therefore undesirable, but it does not take away from the fact that large numbers of people remain excluded from society and from (certain) rights. How to mitigate this tension between in- and exclusion using the legal concept of nationality is therefore a question that the continent continues to be faced with.

Today, statelessness still affects hundreds of thousands of people in Europe and different factors, including issues around discrimination, migration, registration and administration contribute to this. When considering the numbers on statelessness in Europe, causes relating to state succession remain most prevalent, despite specific legal instruments on this. Statelessness thus remains a widespread phenomenon at European level, despite efforts to reduce it through the adoption of legal instruments. At the same time, continued challenges presented by history taking another turn and crises emerging put further pressure on questions of nationality, identity and registration. Developments, also legally, to respond to these issues and to address statelessness remain ongoing.

Think back also to the situation of the Grynszpan family from 1938 that was described at the beginning of this chapter. When comparing this to the account of Rashid in 2014 as included in paragraph 2.7, there are major differences between them of course. But both stories do have similarity: they concern people that for reasons of no state feeling responsible for them were or are left in difficult situations in which they suffer. Despite all historical and legal developments, despite the fact that the key legal instruments were adopted years ago by states, people remain trapped in situations of misery, uncertainty and rightlessness without a nationality. This begs the question where we currently stand at a European, regional level from a legal perspective in addressing statelessness and what more would be needed to truly solve statelessness in Europe. The efforts of the CoE and EU in this regard are explored in Part II of this research.

This chapter furthermore served to help uncover any changes that would need to be made to the analytical framework as set out in paragraph 1.5.3. This framework was based on the exploration of international legal instruments and legal instruments from other regions in the world relating to the right to a nationality and statelessness. It helps to provide proper analysis of the European legal instruments in the chapters that follow, taking into account the context in which these were developed and operate. A couple of questions were visible from the analysis in chapter 1, such as whether norms addressing the nationality of women would amount to a separate category and whether norms relating to nationality matters and preventing statelessness in the context of state succession really needed to be included as distinct from the other categories. From this chapter, no urgent reason arose to include women's nationality rights separately.

On state succession – which already was an independent category in the analytical framework presented earlier – this chapter proved that it remains a key cause and worry in relation to statelessness in Europe, which is why a separate category regarding norms on this is useful. Another specific concern with regard to statelessness, that features throughout the history of statelessness and nationality questions in Europe, is that of statelessness in the context of mass displacement. Displacement, however, is not (always) in itself the cause of statelessness, but is an important context that should be acknowledged. The analytical framework allows for this, as issues arising from mass displacement, such as children of migrants being born stateless in Europe, or solving statelessness of migrants can be addressed in the various categories: childhood statelessness and acquisition of nationality respectively for the examples mentioned. In view of the analytical framework, no further questions were raised by this chapter that would require changes. Therefore, the analytical framework for studying the CoE and the EU in the next two chapters continues to consist of five categories of substantive legal norms on preventing and solving statelessness:

- legal norms aimed at preventing and solving *childhood statelessness*;
- legal norms concerning solutions to *conflicts of nationality law* and preventing *loss / (arbitrary) deprivation / denial of nationality* (later in life – in order to prevent statelessness);
- nationality matters and reduction of statelessness in the context of *state succession*;
- legal norms aimed at the *right to a nationality* and *acquisition of a nationality for people who became stateless in the past and remain stateless today and/or who arrive to a country stateless* (in order to solve statelessness);
- legal norms ensuring *non-discrimination* and *equality before the law* in nationality matters (acquisition and loss and (arbitrary) deprivation of nationality – in order to prevent and solve statelessness).

PART II

EUROPEAN LAW ON NATIONALITY AND STATELESSNESS

CHAPTER 3
THE COUNCIL OF EUROPE

"The price to pay for the perpetuation of statelessness is high not only for the persons affected, but also for the countries in which stateless persons live. Statelessness prevents participation in socioeconomic, but also in public affairs, and results in the alienation of entire groups from society, which is passed on from generation to generation."
– Nils Muižnieks, former CoE Commissioner for Human Rights[486]

3.1. INTRODUCTION

As the above quote of a former Council of Europe (CoE) Commissioner for Human Rights demonstrates, statelessness should be a concern of the 47 countries that are members of this organization for cooperation between states on issues concerning human rights, democracy and the rule of law, even today. The CoE "has been working very actively on questions relating to nationality"[487], demonstrating the importance and value of this organization to this study. Different CoE legal instruments explicitly addressing questions relating to nationality and statelessness have been adopted, but people still remain without any nationality today. This chapter therefore studies the legal instruments that are available to address the issue: it is dedicated entirely to the CoE and its legal instruments that can contribute to preventing and solving statelessness in Europe. It also considers what these legal instruments on preventing and solving statelessness add to our understanding of the legal concept of nationality.

In analyzing the different legal instruments of the CoE, this chapter is mindful of the differences between 'key', legally binding instruments and other instruments. This distinction is thus made based on the instruments' relevance to the prevention and resolution of statelessness, their legal force and importance within the CoE. This allows the chapter to feature those instruments that are key more prominently, in particular in the deeper analysis in section 3.3.

---

486 Nils Muižnieks, 'Stateless but Not Rightless: Improving the Protection of Stateless Persons in Europe', Keynote Speech at the Conference organized by UNHCR and ENS in Strasbourg, 8 April 2014, CommDH/Speech(2014)6.

487 Margaret Killerby, 'Steps Taken by the Council of Europe to Promote the Modernization of the Nationality Laws of European States' in Síofra O'Leary & Teija Tiilikainen, *Citizenship and Nationality Status in the New Europe* (Institute for Public Policy Research, Sweet & Maxwell 1998) 21–37, 21.

Each of the (key) instruments is analyzed in a similar manner, studying the instrument and explanatory background documents and, where appropriate, case law and/or related legal documents, as well as literature and commentaries from academics and, if relevant and as a complementary source, studies from civil society organizations and other institutions. An important source that is used to provide more background to the provisions of CoE treaties are the associated explanatory reports. Note that explanatory reports of the CoE are drafted by the committee of experts that was also responsible for a draft of the respective treaty. They are published with the convention when it is adopted by the Committee of Ministers (CM). Explanatory reports are not an authoritative interpretation of the treaty they concern, but could facilitate the interpretation and implementation of the provisions of the convention. As such they provide a good background to any CoE treaty.[488] The CoE legal instruments are available on the CoE website through the Treaty Office[489], and for specific recommendations and resolutions of the Parliamentary Assembly (PACE) and the CM relating to nationality and statelessness separate searches were also conducted in the databases with documents of the respective bodies.[490] All literature is selected based on their relevance and quality.

This chapter first explores more generally the different instruments, actors and trends in relation to nationality and statelessness in the CoE in section 3.2. Section 3.3 provides a deeper analysis of the relevant legal instruments on preventing and solving statelessness, in line with the analytical framework as developed in earlier chapters. As such, the aspects of the different instruments relating to childhood statelessness; conflicts of nationality law, or loss or (arbitrary) deprivation of nationality; the right to a nationality and acquisition of nationality; nationality matters and statelessness in relation to state succession; and non-discrimination are considered thoroughly. Concluding remarks on the contribution of European law made by the CoE to the prevention of and solutions to statelessness can be found in section 3.4, which also reflects on how these observations help us to understand the legal concept of nationality today.

488 See CoE, 'About Conventions in the Council of Europe Treaty Series (CETS)' <www.coe.int/en/web/conventions/about-treaties> accessed 24 May 2021.

489 CoE, 'Treaty Office' <www.coe.int/en/web/dlapil/treaty-office> accessed 24 May 2021.

490 CoE, 'Committee of Ministers – Documents' <www.coe.int/en/web/cm/documents> accessed 24 May 2021; CoE, 'Parliamentary Assembly – Documents' <https://pace.coe.int/en/pages/official-documents> accessed 24 May 2021. Key words and subjects that were used for instance: nationality, stateless person, stateless, statelessness.

3.2. THE COUNCIL OF EUROPE AND NATIONALITY MATTERS: INSTRUMENTS, ACTORS AND TRENDS

3.2.1. INTRODUCTION

The CoE is an international organization consisting of 47 states in Europe.[491] It was founded in 1949 and its start "inevitably bore the stamp of the immediate post-war years", which was visible in its clear focus on the establishment of rights and freedoms for individuals, as well as economic recovery.[492] The aim of the organization "is to achieve a greater unity between its members for the purpose of safeguarding and realizing the ideals and principles which are their common heritage and facilitating their economic and social progress".[493] Also, according to the Statute of the CoE, CoE members "must accept the principles of the rule of law and of the enjoyment by all persons within its jurisdiction of human rights and fundamental freedoms [...]"[494] – thus referring to some of the foundational values of the CoE. Indeed, the CoE's work today is divided into different strands[495]: human rights, including promoting and protecting human rights, as well as social rights specifically; democracy, with a focus on democratic governance and sustainable democratic societies; and rule of law, considering justice, common standards and policies in this area, as well as threats to the rule of law, such as corruption and cybercrime.

The CoE has different institutions and bodies that allow it to operate and "can be described as a standard-setting organization, although these standards do not all have a binding character. Over 200 international treaties, hundreds of recommendations and policy guidelines provide precious advice to public authorities in a range of areas".[496] According to the Statute of the CoE, the aims of the organization

> "shall be pursued through the organs of the Council by discussion of questions of common concern and by agreements and common action in economic, social, cultural, scientific, legal and administrative matters and in the maintenance and further realisation of human rights and fundamental freedoms".[497]

The CM can consider actions required to realize the aims of the CoE, either on recommendation of the PACE or at its own initiative, which may lead to "the conclusion of conventions or agreements and the adoption by governments of a common policy with regard to particular matters".[498]

---

491 See also para 1.4.4 on how 'Europe' is defined for the purposes of this research.

492 *The Council of Europe: Structure, Aims and Achievements* (Council of Europe Directorate of Press and Information 1970) 47.

493 Art 1(a) Statute of the Council of Europe (Statute of the CoE, as amended, London, 1949, CETS No. 1).

494 Art 3 Statute of the CoE.

495 See also the CoE's website: <https://www.coe.int/en/web/portal/home> accessed 24 May 2021.

496 Irena Guidikova, 'General Introduction' in Tanja EJ Kleinsorge, *The Council of Europe* (Kluwer International 2019) §3, para 10.

497 Art 1(b) Statute of the CoE.

498 Art 15(a) Statute of the CoE. On the conclusion of CoE treaties, see also Jörg Polakiewicz, *Treaty-making in the Council of Europe* (Council of Europe Publishing 1999).

CoE institutions and bodies

The CoE of Europe has different bodies and institutions. Some of these are considered as relevant below. Two important bodies were already mentioned in this chapter: the Committee of Ministers (CM) and the Parliamentary Assembly (PACE).[499]

The CM (Chapter IV of the Statute of the CoE) is the decision-making body of the CoE and consists of the Ministers of Foreign Affairs of the Member States (or their permanent representatives/deputies) and decides on the CoE's policy. It furthermore supervises execution of judgments of the ECtHR by the Member States, and for instance determines what actions should be taken as regards recommendations from the PACE. The decisions of the CM are expressed in CoE conventions and treaties, which are legally binding on the states parties to them, as well as in declarations, resolutions and recommendations.

The PACE, formerly the Consultative Assembly (Chapter V of the Statute of the CoE), is the deliberative body of the CoE and consists of members of parliament from the 47 member states of the CoE. It can recommend action to be taken, is a forum for debate, can monitor states and observe elections. Furthermore, the PACE for instance elects the Secretary General of the CoE, as well as the judges of the European Court of Human Rights (ECtHR). Although this body has no legislative power, it has played and continues to play an active and important role within the CoE.

Other institutions and bodies of the CoE[500] include the CoE secretary-general, elected by PACE for five years, responsible for the CoE work program and leading the organization. There is also the Congress of Local and Regional Authorities, which works on strengthening local and regional democracy in the member states. The CoE Commissioner for Human Rights, also elected by PACE, can furthermore independently highlight human rights concerns, and the Conference of International NGOs connects the CoE's work with the public and civil society.

The CoE Commissioner for Human Rights, quoted at the start of this chapter, is a non-judicial institution that promotes human rights as enshrined in the CoE human rights instruments. It was established in 1999 and functions independently and impartially. To fulfil the role, the Commissioner visits the CoE member states to evaluate the human rights situation, may conduct thematic work on topics important to human rights protection in the CoE, and raises awareness about human rights. PACE elects the Commissioner by majority, based on a list of three people made by the CM, and for a term of six years (see also CM Resolution 99 (50) on the Council of Europe Commissioner for Human Rights).

---

499 For a more elaborate introduction to the institutions and bodies of the CoE, please refer for instance to Aline Royer, *The Council of Europe* (Council of Europe Publishing 2010).

500 See also CoE, 'Structure' <https://www.coe.int/en/web/about-us/structure> accessed 24 May 2021.

The ECtHR is the CoE's permanent judicial body, which oversees the interpretation and implementation of the European Convention on Human Rights (ECHR) (Article 32 ECHR). The ECtHR has 47 judges (Article 20 ECHR) who are elected by PACE (Article 22 ECHR).

Two further bodies of the CoE that are relevant to this research are the European Commission for Democracy through Law (CDL) – also called the Venice Commission (VC) because its plenary session are held in Venice – and the European Committee on Legal Co-operation (CDCJ).

The CDL is an independent consultative body, which cooperates with its members (Article 1 Revised Statute of the European Commission for Democracy through Law). These members are all CoE member states, but also other countries, such as Brazil, Morocco, and the United States. The CDL is composed of independent experts and aims to promote rule of law, human rights and democracy, as well as common constitutional heritage, providing legal advice to its member states.[501] Since its establishment in May 1990, the CDL has furthermore regularly commented on national laws of the member states concerning nationality or related matters.[502] Nationality is thus clearly a topic that has also been considered within this body and to which other CoE bodies refer (e.g. PACE Resolution 1989 (2014) on access to nationality and effective implementation of the ECN) – thus contributing to legal development in the CoE on nationality and statelessness.

The CDCJ was established in 1963 under Art 17 of the Statute of the CoE by the CM. It engages in standard-setting activities as well as cooperation projects and has competence in private and public law. As a steering committee, it reports to the CM, proposes texts for adoption to the CM and proposes priorities in its fields of competence, which include nationality matters.[503]

The CoE Conference of Ministers of Justice are furthermore important to the preparation of new legal standards and addressing new developments. All Ministers of Justice of the CoE member states participate in these conferences, which aim to present proposals for joint action to the governments of the different member states.[504]

---

501 See also CoE, 'The Venice Commission of the Council of Europe' <https://www.venice.coe.int/WebForms/pages/?p=01_Presentation&lang=EN> accessed 24 May 2021.

502 Eg CDL, 472/2008 – Law on Double citizenship of Moldova (2008); full list available <https://www.venice.coe.int/WebForms/documents/by_opinion.aspx?v=all> accessed 1 July 2021.

503 See also CoE, 'European Committee on Legal Co-operation' <https://www.coe.int/en/web/cdcj/home> accessed 24 May 2021.

504 See also CoE, 'Ministerial Conferences' <https://www.coe.int/en/web/human-rights-rule-of-law/ministerial-conferences> accessed 1 July 2021.

The work of the CoE regarding nationality is part of its promotion of the values of human rights, democracy and the rule of law. A closer look reveals that this work is closely related to the functioning and coordination of (national) legal systems.

> "In fact, the very values which the Council of Europe supports and promotes, as well as the recent drastic expansion of the membership of the Council, contribute to the increasing need of co-ordination in determining who is the national of which State or, perhaps, which States. This need for co-ordination becomes crucial in situations when incompatible nationality legislation in two or more States might create problems for individuals and pose a threat to democratic stability".[505]

This demonstrates that democratic stability and the need for coordination in nationality matters are seen to be connected. After all, a democratic state needs people to function. Furthermore, it shows that there is an understanding within the CoE that nationality matters, and issues related to it, such as statelessness, are not solvable without cooperation and coordination. Indeed, the CoE has proven that it can provide a platform for these activities, which can be seen throughout this chapter. At the same time, it should be remembered that this statement was made in the late '90s. In the 1990s, a number of Eastern European states, including successor states of the USSR and the Socialist Federal Republic of Yugoslavia (SFRY), in which questions and problems concerning nationality matters arose, became members of the CoE. In that sense, there was an immediate reason for the CoE to consider these matters.

The CoE acknowledges that the right to a nationality is a fundamental right: everyone's right to a nationality is included in the principles of the ECN, adopted in 1997.[506] On nationality, different instruments have been enacted, some of which explicitly address statelessness. Indeed, the ECSS, adopted in 2006, explicitly addresses statelessness in the state succession context. A 'stateless person' in the CoE context aligns with the international definition of the 1954 Convention – the explanatory reports to the ECN and the ECSS both make reference to the international definition when defining statelessness.[507] The efforts of the CoE on nationality matters are, however, not as new as the dates of these treaties may suggest. There are further treaties and other legal instruments that consider nationality and statelessness. These are introduced more elaborately in paragraph 3.2.2.

The CoE does not include the right to a nationality in its important and authoritative human rights instrument: the ECHR. However, that does not mean that nationality matters have not been considered in jurisprudence in relation to this instrument

---

505 Hans Christian Krüger (Deputy Secretary General of the CoE), 'Opening Speech' in CoE, *1st European Conference on Nationality: Trends and Developments in National and International Law on Nationality – Proceedings* (Strasbourg, 18–19 October 1999, CONF/NAT PRO 1) 9.

506 Art 4 ECN.

507 CoE, *Explanatory Report to the European Convention on Nationality* (Strasbourg, 6 November 1997, CETS No. 166) para 33; CoE, *Explanatory Report to the Council of Europe Convention on the Avoidance of Statelessness in relation to State Succession* (Strasbourg, 19 May 2006, CETS No. 200) para 9.

by the ECtHR. In this light, and given the human rights perspective of this study on preventing and solving statelessness, paragraph 3.2.3 looks at the efforts of the CoE in the area of human rights in relation to nationality matters and statelessness. Paragraph 3.2.4 provides some concluding remarks, before turning to the deeper analysis in section 3.3 of this chapter.

3.2.2. NATIONALITY AND STATELESSNESS

Issues of nationality and statelessness have been addressed specifically in various legal instruments that were developed in the context of the CoE. Already in 1954, the question of perhaps concluding a specific European treaty on statelessness and multiple nationality was put on the agenda of the CoE by the Assembly.[508] In light of the international legal developments at the time – the adoption of the 1954 Convention specifically – it was felt that it was unnecessary to pursue this further. Still, the CoE has adopted a number of relevant instruments over time. Below, these different instruments are introduced, starting as early as 1963 with the Convention on the Reduction of Cases of Multiple Nationality[509] and including also later efforts of the CoE, such as the CM Recommendation on the nationality of children of 2009.[510] The overview of key instruments is provided in chronological order, so as to also demonstrate the development of law on nationality and statelessness over time. At the end, an overview is given of 'other' legal instruments on nationality and statelessness, including CM Recommendations and other efforts on these matters.

1963 Convention on the Reduction of Cases of Multiple Nationality and on Military Obligations in Cases of Multiple Nationality

In 1963, the Convention on the Reduction of Cases of Multiple Nationality and on Military Obligations in Cases of Multiple Nationality (1963 CoE Convention) was adopted. Later, a number of Protocols were added[511], which considered the communication between states about acquisition of nationality, as well as addressing developments since adoption of the

508 PACE Recommendation 87 (1955): Statelessness (adopted by the Assembly at its 24th Sitting on 25 October 1955).

509 Convention on the Reduction of Cases of Multiple Nationality and on Military Obligations in Cases of Multiple Nationality (Strasbourg, 1963, CETS No. 043).

510 Recommendation CM/Rec (2009) 13 of the Committee of Ministers to member states on the nationality of children (adopted by the Committee of Ministers on 9 December 2009 at the 1073rd meeting of the Ministers' Deputies).

511 Protocol amending the Convention on the Reduction of Cases of Multiple Nationality and Military Obligations in Cases of Multiple Nationality (Strasbourg, 1977, CETS No. 095); Additional Protocol to the Convention on the Reduction of Cases of Multiple Nationality and Military Obligations in Cases of Multiple Nationality (Strasbourg, 1977, CETS No. 096); Second Protocol amending the Convention on the Reduction of Cases of Multiple Nationality and Military Obligations in Cases of Multiple Nationality (Strasbourg, 1993, CETS No. 149). See also Alfred M Boll, *Multiple Nationality and International Law* (Martinus Nijhoff Publishers 2007) 199–203.

treaty. These included clarifying the meaning of certain provisions, for instance making reservations with regard to married woman to the Convention impossible and making new provisions for allowing an individual to retain their nationality of origin in certain circumstances, such as marriage between nationals of different state parties.

When this treaty was adopted, the – then only Western and Southern European – member states of the CoE agreed that multiple nationality was undesirable and should be reduced. Such reduction can, however, only be achieved when states work together. Hence, the introduction of a treaty on this matter was a logical step. Even though the instrument is focused on the reduction of cases of multiple nationality, it allows for multiple nationality in limited situations, thereby recognizing state discretion in these matters.[512] It further considers the consequences of cases of multiple nationality, in particular as regards military obligation of the individual concerned. It provides, for example, that "[p] ersons possessing the nationality of two or more Contracting Parties shall be required to fulfil their military obligations in relation to one of those Parties only".[513]

Nonetheless, the CoE and Europe changed a lot after 1963. It was found that multiple nationality and other issues relating to nationality were not adequately addressed by the original 1963 CoE Convention, as also evidenced by the adoption of the later Protocols that were mentioned above, and in particular the 1993 Protocol.[514] Multiple nationality is no longer necessarily viewed as something that is to be avoided. Important is therefore the general treaty on nationality that was introduced later: the ECN.[515] Even if the 1963 CoE Convention is of no to little significance to preventing and solving statelessness, it deserves some attention here, because the ECN cannot be properly introduced without mentioning 1963 CoE Convention.[516] As Horst Schade, at the time involved with the CoE, explains in his article on the draft ECN:

> "(...) in particular, mobility and migration and the principle of equality between women and men has meant that, in practice, there are many cases of dual nationality, and for the purposes of integration, some countries see dual nationality as desirable."[517]

---

512 See also Margaret Killerby, 'Steps Taken by the Council of Europe to Promote the Modernization of the Nationality Laws of European States' in Síofra O'Leary & Teija Tiilikainen, *Citizenship and Nationality Status in the New Europe* (Institute for Public Policy Research, Sweet & Maxwell 1998) 21–37, 32.

513 Art 5(1) 1963 CoE Convention.

514 Second Protocol amending the Convention on the Reduction of Cases of Multiple Nationality and Military Obligations in Cases of Multiple Nationality (Strasbourg, 1993, CETS No. 149), which recognized changing circumstances in its preamble, noting in particular migration and integration of second-generation migrants, mixed marriages, and conservation of nationality of origin.

515 See also this para, under 'European Convention on Nationality'.

516 See also Horst Schade, 'The Draft European Convention on Nationality' (1995) 49 Austrian Journal of Public International Law 100. The 1963 CoE Convention is not very relevant anymore, yet still has 12 ratifications. Many of these states have however denounced chapter I on the reduction of cases of multiple nationality, which demonstrates this treaty's decreased relevance, access through CoE, 'Details of Treaty No. 043' <www.coe.int/en/web/conventions/full-list/-/conventions/treaty/043> accessed 26 May 2021.

517 Horst Schade, 'The Draft European Convention on Nationality' (1995) 49 Austrian Journal of Public International Law 100. Similar considerations are found in the Explanatory Report to the ECN: CoE,

Horst Schade's article, however, is from 1995 and development has continued. Research has shown that

> "[i]n Europe, the change from restrictive attitudes towards dual citizenship to dual citizenship
> tolerance follows the global trend, with 47 per cent of states having tolerant policies in 1960 to over 70 per cent in 2017".[518]

Dual or multiple nationality is, however, not always viewed as unproblematic or uncontroversial in European countries. In 2007, for instance, much attention was paid to the dual nationality of Dutch politicians. Geert Wilders, leader of the Dutch Party for Freedom, criticized different politicians with dual nationality. He viewed their dual nationality as undesirable and unacceptable because it could appear as if these people have dual loyalty, which could lead to conflicts of interests.[519] In light of what the Dutch Constitution says on these matters in its provisions regarding suffrage and the right to be elected or appointed to a public office[520], these objections are, however, constitutionally unjustified.[521]

How did the ECN then deal with these developments regarding the desirability of dual and multiple nationality? The answer seems perfectly tailored for a more general legal instrument relating to nationality matters that should be able to coexist with the 1963 CoE Convention[522] and take into account developments on multiple nationality: the ECN remains neutral towards multiple nationality.[523] As such, states can be parties to both the ECN and the 1963 CoE Convention; the ECN "neither modifies nor is incompatible with the 1963 [CoE] Convention".[524]

Explanatory Report to the European Convention on Nationality (Strasbourg, 6 November 1997, CETS No. 166) para 8.

518 Maarten Vink, Arjan Schakel, David Reichely, Ngo Chun Luk & Gerard-René de Groot, 'The International Diffusion of Expatriate Dual Citizenship' (2019) 7 Migration Studies 362, 369.

519 *Kamerstukken II* 2006/07, 30891, no. 22.

520 See Arts 3 & 4 of the Dutch Constitution (Grondwet voor het Koninkrijk der Nederlanden, *Stb.* 2019, 33).

521 See also Ernst Hirsch Ballin, 'Commentaar op artikel 3 van de Grondwet' in Ernst Hirsch Ballin & Gert-Jan Leenknegt, *Artikelsgewijs Commentaar op de Grondwet [Commentary on the Constitution]* (Nederlandrechtsstaat.nl 2021) <www.nederlandrechtsstaat.nl/grondwet/artikel.html?artikel=3##artikel3> accessed 26 May 2021; Gert-Jan Leenknegt, 'Commentaar op artikel 4 van de Grondwet' in Ernst Hirsch Ballin & Gert-Jan Leenknegt (eds), *Artikelsgewijs Commentaar op de Grondwet [Commentary on the Constitution]* (Nederlandrechtsstaat.nl 2021) <www.nederlandrechtsstaat.nl/grondwet/artikel.html?artikel=4&categorie=&auteur=&trefwoord=&l=1##artikel4> accessed 26 May 2021.

522 Note that 12 states ratified the 1963 CoE Convention. The majority of these states have, however, denounced the treaty or denounced chapter I of it. See in more detail CoE Treaty Office, 'Chart of Signatures and Ratifications of Treaty 043' <https://www.coe.int/en/web/conventions/full-list/-/conventions/treaty/043/signatures?p_auth=cn3Ehlrw> accessed 26 May 2021.

523 See eg Lisa Pilgram, *International Law and European Nationality Laws* (EUDO Citizenship Observatory 2011) 5, 7; CoE, *Explanatory Report to the European Convention on Nationality* (Strasbourg, 6 November 1997, CETS No. 166) para 97.

524 CoE, *Explanatory Report to the European Convention on Nationality* (Strasbourg, 6 November 1997, CETS No. 166) para 12, see also Art 26 ECN and the corresponding paras 137–139 of the aforementioned Explanatory Report.

European Convention on Nationality

The European Convention on Nationality (ECN) is *the* treaty of the CoE on nationality. The ECN was born out of the CoE's desire "to consolidate in a single text the new ideas which have emerged as a result of developments in internal law and in international law".[525] At the same time, the treaty attempts to also contribute to the developments in international law regarding nationality. The ECN opened for signature on November 6, 1997 and entered into force on March 1, 2000. As it stands in January 2022, the ECN has been ratified by 21 European states, with the majority of these states making reservations and/or declarations. The most recent addition to the states parties to the ECN is Luxembourg, which ratified the treaty in 2017. Another eight states have signed the ECN, but never ratified it.[526]

Besides the 1963 CoE Convention, other efforts regarding nationality of the CoE, including recommendations, as well as the increase in international legal provisions relating to nationality were reasons for the adoption of a general European treaty on nationality.[527] An inquiry was even launched in 1988 in order to investigate whether the right to a nationality could be introduced by adding it to the ECHR or by any other means.[528] As discussed in paragraph 3.2.3 as well, adding a protocol on this subject to the ECHR was rejected, but in light of the results of a questionnaire on this matter, the idea of a stand-alone treaty was explored further. This indeed led to the adoption of such a convention.[529] In view of its aim, the ECN drew inspiration from and attempted to integrate a number of international treaties that contain standards regarding nationality, including Article 8 of the ECHR.[530] Against this background, it was believed that the ECN could not only achieve "some harmonization" regarding the rules relating to the acquisition and loss of nationality, but could also – in particular for the "new democracies in Eastern Europe since 1989" – provide basic provisions in the area of nationality.[531]

---

525 CoE, *Explanatory Report to the European Convention on Nationality* (Strasbourg, 6 November 1997, CETS No. 166) para 11.

526 CoE, 'Chart of Signatures and Ratification of Treaty 166 – European Convention on Nationality' <www.coe.int/en/web/conventions/full-list/-/conventions/treaty/166/signatures?p_auth=D4IQ7AR9> accessed 26 May 2021.

527 CoE, *Explanatory Report to the European Convention on Nationality* (Strasbourg, 6 November 1997, CETS No. 166) para 11.

528 Mónika Ganczer, 'The Right to a Nationality as a Human Right?' (2014) Hungarian Yearbook of International Law and European Law 15–33, 22; Hans Ulrich Jessurun d'Oliveira, 'Het Europees Verdrag inzake Nationaliteit, Straatsburg, 6 november 1997. Een verkenning' in Hans Ulrich Jessurun d'Oliveira (ed), *Trends in het nationaliteitsrecht. Nationaal en Internationaal [Trends in Nationality Law. National and International]* (Sdu Uitgevers 1998) 7–47, 8. In more depth, see Johannes Chan, 'The Right to a Nationality as a Human Right. The Current Trend towards Recognition' (1991) 12 Human Rights Law Journal 1–14, 7–10.

529 Hans Ulrich Jessurun d'Oliveira, 'Het Europees Verdrag inzake Nationaliteit, Straatsburg, 6 november 1997. Een verkenning' in Hans Ulrich Jessurun d'Oliveira (ed), *Trends in het nationaliteitsrecht. Nationaal en Internationaal* (Sdu Uitgevers 1998)7–47, 8.

530 See Preamble ECN, see also para 3.2.3.

531 Gerard-René de Groot, 'The European Convention on Nationality: A Step towards a *Ius Commune* in the Field of Nationality Law' (2007) 7 Maastricht Journal of European and Comparative Law 117, 119.

The ECN is a treaty that lays down principles and rules relating to all aspects of the nationality of individuals.[532] It contains a number of human rights principles concerning nationality.[533] These can be found in the ECN's general principles, which provide a basis for the laws on nationality of each state party to the ECN: a) everyone has the right to a nationality; b) statelessness shall be avoided; no one shall arbitrarily be deprived of his or her nationality; and d) neither marriage nor the dissolution of a marriage between a national of a state party and an alien, nor the change of nationality by one of the spouses during marriage, shall automatically affect the nationality of the other spouse.[534] Furthermore, the principle of non-discrimination in nationality matters is included separately in the ECN.[535] At the same time, however, one of the ECN's general principles – and, like the other principles, a guiding principle in international public law – is that each state determines under its own law who its nationals are, thus explicitly respecting state sovereignty and authority in matters regarding nationality.[536] Nonetheless, the national laws of a state that regulate nationality issues are only to be respected by other states insofar as they comply with international (human rights) standards.[537] This means that states do not have to respect domestic laws that, for instance, outright discriminate in nationality matters: laws like those used in Nazi Germany to deprive individuals of their nationality on political, racial, or religious grounds.

After a preamble and introductory articles setting out the object of the convention, definitions[538] – including a definition of 'nationality'[539] – and general principles, the ECN sets out rules relating to the acquisition and loss of nationality, as well as procedures relating to nationality.[540] A separate chapter of the treaty is devoted to multiple nationality, as well as to military obligations in cases of multiple nationality.[541] As was discussed already, the ECN remains neutral as regards the desirability of multiple nationality and is able to coexist with the 1963 CoE Convention. In fact, the ECN's provisions concerning military obligations in cases of multiple nationality are copied from the 1963 CoE Convention and the Protocol amending the 1963 CoE Convention.[542] The ECN is furthermore particularly innovative in its chapter that relates specifically to nationality and state succession. It can be viewed as the ECN's

532 Cf Art 1 ECN.

533 Laura van Waas, *Nationality Matters. Statelessness under International Law* (School of Human Rights Research Series Vol. 29, Intersentia 2008) 61.

534 Art 4 ECN.

535 Art 5 ECN.

536 Art 3(1) ECN, see also CoE, *Explanatory Report to the European Convention on Nationality* (Strasbourg, 6 November 1997, CETS No. 166) para 28.

537 Art 3(2) ECN, see also ibid, para 29.

538 Art 2 ECN.

539 Art 2(a) ECN.

540 Chapters III & IV ECN.

541 Chapters V & VII ECN.

542 See also CoE, *Explanatory Report to the European Convention on Nationality* (Strasbourg, 6 November 1997, CETS No. 166) para 124.

clearest attempt to contribute to progress in international law on nationality.[543] Furthermore, the ECN lays down rules about the procedures relating to nationality.[544]

Besides the obligatory chapters on the application of the convention and final clauses, the ECN also contains an interesting chapter on cooperation between the states parties to the ECN, which relates to continuing the development of laws relating to nationality matters within Europe.[545] Pursuant to these provisions, the competent authorities of the states parties shall provide the Secretary General of the CoE and, when requested, each other with information about their internal laws regarding nationality as well as developments concerning the application of the ECN.[546] Also, the provisions speak more elaborately about cooperation and of exchange of information relating to voluntary acquisition of nationality.[547] The results of the aforementioned obligation to provide information to the CoE should, according to the Explanatory Report, be compiled by the European Documentation Centre on Nationality in a European Bulletin on Nationality.[548] The European Bulletin on Nationality used to be publicly available, but the last update is from 2004.[549] It is unclear whether this information is still being collected and distributed in the context of the CDCJ, which is the CoE body which remains concerned with questions around nationality and statelessness.[550] It looks like no real cooperation or exchange of information has been taking place, even though renewed efforts, like the 2021 Conference Statelessness and the Right to a Nationality in Europe: Progress, Challenges and Opportunities[551], are a step in the right direction. From the ECN is, nonetheless, evident that such reporting should happen. According to the second paragraph of the same Article 23 of the ECN, the states parties are to cooperate with each other and within the framework of the CoE with the aim to deal with any problems that may arise and to promote progressive development of legal principles relating to nationality. Again, the Explanatory Report provides further explanation, and names the Committee of Experts on Nationality (CJ-NA) as the appropriate body for cooperation within the CoE.[552]

543 Gerard-René de Groot, 'The European Convention on Nationality: A Step towards a *Ius Commune* in the Field of Nationality Law' (2007) 7 Maastricht Journal of European and Comparative Law 117, 120.

544 Chapter IV ECN.

545 Chapter VIII ECN.

546 Art 23(1) ECN.

547 Arts 23(2) & 24 ECN. For more information, see CoE, *Explanatory Report to the European Convention on Nationality* (Strasbourg, 6 November 1997, CETS No. 166) paras. 131–133.

548 CoE, *Explanatory Report to the European Convention on Nationality* (Strasbourg, 6 November 1997, CETS No. 166) para 129.

549 CDCJ, 'Nationality' <https://www.coe.int/en/web/cdcj/completed-work/standard-setting/nationality> accessed 26 May 2021.

550 See also CDCJ, 'Statelessness' <https://www.coe.int/en/web/cdcj/statelessness> accessed 26 May 2021.

551 This Conference and technical meeting of experts took place on 23–24 September 2021 in Strasbourg, were organized by the CDCJ and UNHCR, and were aimed at strengthening efforts to end statelessness in Europe. See also <https://www.coe.int/en/web/cdcj/statelessness-and-the-right-to-a-nationality-in-europe-progress-challenges-and-opportunities> accessed 27 September 2021.

552 CoE, *Explanatory Report to the European Convention on Nationality* (Strasbourg, 6 November 1997, CETS No. 166) para 131.

CoE institutions and bodies: expert bodies on nationality

The Committee of Experts on Nationality (CJ-NA) was a dedicated expert group established by the CoE in the course of the development of legal instruments relating to nationality. The CJ-NA – formerly the Committee of Experts on Multiple Nationality (CJ-PL)[553] – was a subordinate committee of the CDCJ[554] and was in charge of intergovernmental cooperation in the area of nationality matters. The CJ-NA brought together officials with (practical) expertise on citizenship issues from each Member State, but also observers from other states and international organizations. Their work (and that of its Working Party (CJ-NA GT)) included the preparation of proposals for legal instruments that could be adopted in the field of nationality, as well as the organization of the European Conferences on Nationality[555] and proposals for follow-up[556] and preparing and updating the European Bulletin on Nationality. As such, this Committee provided a forum for cooperation and legal development for nationality issues. The CJ-NA existed up to 2005, but its work was discontinued after that due to issues with funding.[557]

In 2008, the CM set up an *ad hoc* advisory group with the purpose of following up on the Action Plan of the CDCJ as regards nationality matters in particular: the Group of Specialists on Nationality (CJ-S-NAT).[558] The CJ-S-NAT fell under the authority of the CDCJ and its task was to promote and contribute "to the reinforcement of the existing instruments of the Council of Europe in the field of nationality and to make proposals to the CDCJ".[559] It also was to propose themes to the CDCJ for the 4th European Conference on Nationality. The CJ-S-NAT consisted of nine experts on nationality matters. The Group presented its final report in 2009[560], which demonstrates that a large part of the work of the CJ-S-NAT was devoted to drafting a proposal for a non-binding recommendation on the nationality of children[561], which is introduced below. Furthermore, the Group came

553 Cf ibid, para 4.

554 On the CDCJ, see also F. Th. Zilverentant, 'Bericht uit Straatsburg' in Hans Ulrich Jessurun d'Oliveira (ed), *Trends in het nationaliteitsrecht. Nationaal en Internationaal [Trends in Nationality Law. National and International]* (Sdu Uitgevers 1998) 49–51, 49.

555 A total of four Conferences on Nationality have been organized in the context of the CoE: 1st European Conference on Nationality 'Trends and Developments in National and International Law on Nationality' (1999); 2nd European Conference on Nationality 'Challenges to National and International Law on Nationality at the Beginning of the New Millennium' (2001); 3rd European Conference on Nationality 'Nationality and the Child' (2004); 4th European Conference on Nationality 'Concepts of Nationality in a Globalised World' (2010).

556 See for instance CoE, 'Revised Terms of Reference of the Committee of Experts on Nationality (CJ-NA) (Appendix 8, Item 10.1a)' (1999) Official Gazette of the Council of Europe (Committee of Ministers part-volume) 96 (under c).

557 See CJ-NA, 'Report of the 21st Meeting', CDCJ (2004) 21 / CJ-NA (2004) 5 rev., para 75; CJ-NA GT, 'Report of the 26th Meeting', CJ-NA GT (2005) 2, para 7.

558 CoE, 'Group of Specialists on Nationality. Terms of Reference for 2008', CJ-S-Nat (2008) 1.

559 Ibid.

560 CJ-S-NAT, 'Final Report', CJ-S-NAT (2008) 24.

561 This resulted in Recommendation CM/Rec(2009)13 of the Committee of Ministers to Member States on the Nationality of Children (1073rd meeting of the Ministers' Deputies, 9 December 2009).

up with some tools for improving visibility, availability of information and accession to the CoE nationality conventions[562], as well as a proposal for the 4th European Conference on Nationality, which took place in 2010. It also recommended to the CDCJ that that CJ-NA should be reinstated as soon as possible in light of the importance of the work of the CoE in the area of nationality.[563] The CJ-NA was, however, not reinstated and the CDCJ remains the responsible organ in this field.

In short, a specialized organ on nationality was abandoned and cooperation is to take place in the context of a more general CoE body. In itself, that is not contrary to the ECN, nor is reporting in a less public way, but it is at least questionable whether this is in the interests of progressive development of legal principles and practice concerning nationality and related matters, such as statelessness – an issue that remains of importance to the CDCJ. At the same time, the CDCJ has listed its standard-setting on nationality as one of its completed standard setting activities.[564]

The ECN remains important in that it consolidates the obligations and ideas that have emerged as a result of international and internal laws on nationality matters in a single and concrete document that is ready to be implemented in states' nationality laws.[565] Although the ECN cannot be considered to be a 'real' human rights document, it can be viewed as an important contribution to (European) human rights law. This is related to the fact that the right to a nationality itself is a human right and that the possession of a nationality paves the way for the enjoyment of other (human) rights. As such, it has been held that the ECN is "a significant and welcome advance in the process of transforming the Universal Declaration's call for a right of all persons to possess a nationality into a substantive legal norm".[566] At the same time, the ECN has not even been ratified by half of the CoE member states, thereby roughly representing barely a third of the European population, and some of the ambitions for development and cooperation within the context of this legal instrument are not as actively pursued as they used to be. Still, the legal standards that this instrument provides are relevant for a large number of European countries and can thus aid in reducing statelessness in Europe.

---

562 These included a proposal for a website (which existed for a while, but is no longer online), as well as a draft brochure which provides states ten good reasons for acceding to the European nationality conventions. These are attached in the appendixes to the Final Report (CJ-S-NAT, 'Final Report', CJ-S-NAT (2008) 24).

563 CJ-S-NAT, 'Final Report', CJ-S-NAT (2008) 24.

564 CDCJ, 'Standard Setting – Completed Activities' <https://www.coe.int/en/web/cdcj/standard-setting-completed-activities> accessed 26 May 2021.

565 See also Gerard-René de Groot, 'The European Convention on Nationality: A Step towards a *Ius Commune* in the Field of Nationality Law' (2007) 7 Maastricht Journal of European and Comparative Law 117, 120; Laura van Waas, 'Fighting Statelessness and Discriminatory Nationality Laws in Europe' (2012) 14 European Journal of Migration and Law 243, 247.

566 Stephen Hall, 'The European Convention on Nationality and the Right to Have Rights' (1999) 24 European Law Review 586, 600.

Convention on the Avoidance of Statelessness in Relation to State Succession

The Council of Europe Convention on the Avoidance of Statelessness in Relation to State Succession (ECSS) concerns the specific topic of the avoidance of statelessness and the particular context of state succession. As such, other causes of statelessness or situations in which statelessness can arise are not addressed, and other aspects relating to state succession are not considered. According to Roland Schärer, this enabled the member states of the CoE to reach consensus on "clearly defined obligations for States Parties".[567] The Treaty was born out of the importance of avoiding statelessness – it being one of the main concerns of the international community in the field of nationality according to the preamble – and state succession being one of the principal causes of statelessness, in particular in Europe. At the same time, however, it clearly attempted to fill a gap in standard setting concerning state succession, as other international legal instruments do not address important points as regards state succession – they are too general – or are not legally binding, and statelessness in relation to state succession remained an issue.[568] As such, the ECSS is another unique instrument that addresses statelessness. The Convention opened for signature on 19 May 2006 and entered into force on 1 May 2009 after ratification by three member states. As of January 2022, the ECSS has been ratified by seven member states of the CoE: Austria, Hungary, Luxembourg, Moldova, Montenegro, the Netherlands, and Norway. Both Germany and Ukraine have signed it, but these signatures have not been followed by ratification. None of the states parties have made a declaration or reservation as regards this Convention.[569]

All of the states parties to the ECSS are parties to the ECN as well. The ECSS is clearly related to the ECN, as is noted in the preamble:

> "In order to give effect to the principles established in the European Convention on Nationality that everyone has the right to a nationality and that the rule of law and human rights, including the prohibition of arbitrary deprivation of nationality and the principle of non-discrimination, must be respected in order to avoid statelessness, [...]."[570]

When considering the ECN in relation to the ECSS, one may remember that the ECN in fact included a number of provisions on the avoidance of statelessness and even

567 Roland Schärer, 'The Council of Europe and the Reduction of Statelessness' (2006) 25 Refugee Survey Quarterly 33, 34. Roland Schärer was Head of the Swiss Nationality Section, Federal Office for Migration, Bern, Switzerland. He was the Chair and a member of the CJ-NA.

568 Council of Europe Convention on the Avoidance of Statelessness in relation to State Succession (Strasbourg, 2006, CETS No. 200), Preamble. See also Ineta Ziemele, 'State Succession and Issues of Nationality and Statelessness' in Alice Edwards & Laura van Waas (eds), Nationality and Statelessness under International Law (Cambridge University Press 2014) 217–246, 226.

569 CoE, 'Chart of Signatures and Ratification of Treaty 200 – Council of Europe Convention on the Avoidance of Statelessness in relation to State Succession' <www.coe.int/en/web/conventions/full-list/-/conventions/treaty/200/signatures?p_auth=wylJwIfo> accessed 26 May 2021.

570 Council of Europe Convention on the Avoidance of Statelessness in relation to State Succession (Strasbourg, 2006, CETS No. 200), Preamble.

a separate chapter on state succession. Why was a separate instrument necessary and would it not have been easier to just add a protocol to the ECN? As the ECN only contains general principles concerning statelessness in relation to state succession and, in light of "recent practical experiences" – likely to refer to the dissolution of the USSR, the SFRY and Czechoslovakia – the addition of "specific rules applicable to the particular situation of statelessness in relation to state succession" was deemed important.[571] The idea, however, was at first to draft an additional protocol to the ECSS, or perhaps even a recommendation as a precursor to a protocol.[572] CoE documents show that in 2002, the CJ-NA was given a mandate to develop an additional protocol to the ECN, which would further develop the provisions already present in the ECN.[573] That the CoE in the end chose to draft a treaty was the result of considerations of a procedural nature. Any new states that come into existence should be able to accede to the ECSS immediately so that statelessness caused by state succession can be addressed effectively as soon as possible: "in order to allow as many States as possible to accede to this new instrument, including States which had not yet ratified the ECN, the Committee of Experts decided that the Protocol should be (technically) independent from the ECN".[574] If a state would have to accede to the more elaborate ECN first, this would take up much more time, which did not seem appropriate to the CoE.[575]

The attention to this specific issue within the CoE was not new, as the relation with the ECN already demonstrates. But as was mentioned above, in 1996, the CDL also adopted a Declaration on the Consequences of State Succession for the Nationality of Natural Persons. The ECSS is furthermore based on a number of other legal instruments. These include the legally binding 1961 Convention, and the 'soft law' instruments that are not legally binding: the ILC Draft Articles on Nationality of Natural Persons in relation to the Succession of States and the CM Recommendation on the Avoidance and Reduction of Statelessness, which is discussed further below. These instruments indeed are either not binding or are not specifically dealing with state succession. At the same time, this evidences how the CoE instrument is again an attempt to bring together rules, in this case on a very specific topic and situation, in one legally binding instrument.

The ECSS's structure is in some ways quite similar to that of the ECN, even though it does not include a chapter structure. After a preamble, the Treaty introduces a number of general provisions in Articles 1–4. These commence with definitions,

---

571 Ibid.

572 Roland Schärer, 'Statelessness in relation to State Succession: The Necessity of an Additional Instrument to the European Convention on Nationality' in CoE, *2nd European Conference on Nationality "Challenges to National and International Law on Nationality at the Beginning of the New Millennium" (Strasbourg, 8 and 9 October 2001): Proceedings* (CoE 2001) CONF/NAT (2001) PRO, 173–188, 188.

573 PACE, 'Draft Protocol on the Avoidance of Statelessness in Relation to State Succession – Parliamentary Assembly Opinion No. 258', 7 February 2006, GR-J(2006)3. The Opinion also considers the change of name of the instrument: from protocol to convention.

574 Ibid.

575 Roland Schärer, 'The Council of Europe and the Reduction of Statelessness' (2006) 25 Refugee Survey Quarterly 33, 38–39.

including a definition of state succession. State succession is defined in accordance with what has been accepted in other international legal instruments on the matter[576]: it is the replacement of one state by another in the responsibility for the international relations of territory.[577] Another important point that follows from the definitions of this Convention, is that even though statelessness is defined in the same way as in Article 1(1) of the 1954 Convention, the ECSS is only relevant to those situations in which statelessness occurred or will occur as a consequence of state succession. It thus does not concern people who are already stateless before state succession or who become stateless after state succession due to causes that are not related to state succession.[578] The other general provisions contain principles that are similar to those contained in the ECN: the right to a nationality (Article 2), the prevention of statelessness (in particular in the context of state succession, Article 3) and the principle of non-discrimination (Article 4).

The articles that lie at the heart of the ECSS, are Articles 5 and 6. Article 5 considers the responsibility of the successor state and Article 6 deals with the responsibility of the predecessor state. Other articles of the ECSS concern issues relating to the avoidance of statelessness in the context of state succession. They include respect for the expressed will of an individual, rules of proof, facilitated acquisition of nationality, avoidance of statelessness at birth, the provision of information and procedural guarantees. Furthermore, Articles 13 and 14 of the ECSS stress the importance of international agreement and international cooperation. Also, the Convention provides that it is not retroactive (unless declared otherwise by the state in question)[579] and does not prejudice more favorable provisions, the application of the ECN and its more general provisions on state succession in chapter VI, or other binding international instruments insofar as they are compatible with the ECSS in the relations between states bound by these instruments.[580]

What is striking throughout the rules provided in the ECSS, is that they are in many ways similar to or based on the provisions of the ECN. As such, it is clearly relevant to the prevention and resolution of statelessness from a more general perspective, but it is also of limited relevance because it only concerns statelessness resulting from state succession. These matters are discussed more elaborately in section 3.3.

---

576 The Vienna Convention on the Succession of States in Respect of Treaties (1978), the Vienna Convention on the Succession of States in respect of State Property, Archives and Debts (1983), the ILC Draft Articles on Nationality of Natural Persons in relation to the Succession of States (1999). See also CoE, *Explanatory Report to the Council of Europe Convention on the Avoidance of Statelessness in relation to State Succession* (Strasbourg, 19 May 2006, CETS No. 200) para 6 <https://rm.coe.int/CoERMPublicCommonSearchServices/DisplayDCTMContent?documentId=09000016800d3815> accessed 26 May 2021.

577 Art 1(a) ECSS.

578 Art 1(c) ECSS; CoE, *Explanatory Report to the Council of Europe Convention on the Avoidance of Statelessness in relation to State Succession* (Strasbourg, 19 May 2006, CETS No. 200) para 9.

579 Art 15 ECSS.

580 Art 16 ECSS.

Other instruments on nationality and statelessness

Resolutions and recommendations of both the CM and the PACE on nationality and statelessness and related topics can be regularly encountered since the CoE was founded.

CoE Resolutions and Recommendations: legal status

CoE resolutions and recommendations have a different legal status than the treaties. They are not legally binding on the member states, whereas treaties or conventions are legally binding – though only on the states that have ratified them.[581] Recommendations by the CM are, nonetheless, legal instruments that have legal significance.[582] They are intended to further the aims of the CoE, and concern measures that are recommended in this light by the legislative body of the CoE. That is not to say that the resolutions and recommendations by PACE are not significant. Even though the PACE recommendations, for instance, are directed to the CM, these are – just like the PACE resolutions – of importance from a legal perspective. They signal developments in the (legal) attitude towards certain issues, as these documents contain the views and suggestions of the CoE's deliberative body. Essentially, the instruments of the CM and PACE can be qualified as soft law.[583] Given the particular significance of recommendations by the CM to the issue of statelessness, this chapter discusses mainly such recommendations.

The CM has made the following recommendations on nationality and statelessness:

- Recommendation on stateless nomads and nomads of undetermined nationality (1983)[584];

---

581 Cf CoE CM Texts of a statutory character adopted by the Committee of Ministers in the course of its 8th and 9th Sessions with a view to their ultimate inclusion in a revised Statute of the Council of Europe (Strasbourg, 1951, CETS No. 008): I – Resolution adopted by the Committee of Ministers at its 8th Session (May 1951), see Powers of the Committee of Ministers, Article 15 of the Statute. That this text can be read as part of the Statute, is clarified in the details of the Statute as provided by the CoE Treaty Office, see <www.coe.int/en/web/conventions/home> accessed 26 May 2021.

582 Grégor Puppinck, 'Status of the Recommendations of the Committee of Ministers in the Legal Field of Council of Europe – Synthesis' (European Centre for Law and Justice, March 27, 2012) <http://eclj.org/PDF/status-of-the-recommendations-of-the-committee-of-ministers-in-the-legal-field-of-the-council-of-europe%E2%80%93synthesis-english.pdf> accessed 26 May 2021.

583 Soft law can encompass a wide range of instruments, that can at the same time "influence the course or content of international law", cf James Crawford & Martti Koskenniemi 'Introduction' in James Crawford & Martti Koskenniemi (eds), *The Cambridge Companion to International Law* (Cambridge University Press 2012) 11. It is acknowledged by Jörg Polakiewicz that soft law-instruments have gained importance in the Council of Europe and it is even noted that their capacity to modify state behavior is sometimes "not much inferior to that of hard law instruments". He mentions the CM recommendations as an example. See Jörg Polakiewicz, 'Alternatives to Treaty-Making and Law-Making by Treaty and Expert Bodies in the Council of Europe' in Rüdiger Wolfrum & Volker Röbin (eds), *Developments of International Law in Treaty Making* (Springer 2005) 245–290, 287.

584 CoE CM Recommendation No. R (83) 1 of the Committee of Ministers to the Member States on the Stateless nomads and nomads of undetermined nationality (356th meeting of the Ministers' Deputies, 22 February 1983).

- Recommendation on second-generation migrants (1984)[585];
- Recommendation on the acquisition by refugees of the nationality of the host country (1984)[586];
- Recommendation on the avoidance and reduction of statelessness (1999)[587];
- Recommendation on the nationality of children (2009).[588]

Given their direct relevance to preventing and solving statelessness, and their more recent dates, the last two recommendations in this list are discussed more elaborately below.

Recommendation No. R (99) of the CM to the member states on the avoidance and reduction of statelessness[589] recognizes the negative impact of statelessness on individuals and the problems that it creates. This Recommendation was made relatively shortly after the adoption of the ECN. The CM takes into account the importance of the ECN and expresses the hope that many states will soon sign and ratify this treaty. At the same time, the CM says that it realizes "the need for further measures, both at national and international levels, to avoid and reduce cases of statelessness".[590]

As a matter of substance, the Recommendation highlights principles based on the ECN that have a special relevance to the avoidance and reduction of statelessness and adds a number of more elaborate provisions aiming at the avoidance and reduction of cases of statelessness. The latter category is divided into another three further categories: avoiding and reducing statelessness at birth, facilitating the acquisition of nationality by stateless people, and avoiding statelessness as a consequence of loss of nationality. These substantive provisions from the Recommendation are discussed in more depth in section 3.3.

Even though matters regarding the nationality of children are already addressed in the ECN, as well as in some rulings of the European Court of Human Rights – for instance the case of *Genovese v. Malta*, as we will see below – the CM Recommendation

585 CoE CM Recommendation No. R (84) 9 of the Committee of Ministers to the Member States on second-generation migrants (368th meeting of the Ministers' Deputies, 20 March 1984).

586 CoE CM Recommendation No. R (84) 21 of the Committee of Ministers to the Member States on the acquisition by refugees of the nationality of the host state (377th meeting of the Ministers' Deputies, 14 November 1984). This Recommendation can be regarded as the final piece in a row of recommendations and resolutions on this issue, see CoE CM Resolution (70) 2: Acquisition by refugees of the nationality of their country of residence (adopted by the Ministers' Deputies on 26 January 1970), and PACE Recommendation 564 (1969): Acquisition by refugees of the nationality of their country of residence (30 September 1969).

587 CoE CM Recommendation No. R (99) 18 of the Committee of Ministers to the Member States on the avoidance and reduction of statelessness (679th meeting of the Ministers' Deputies, 15 September 1999).

588 Recommendation CM/Rec (2009) 13 of the Committee of Ministers to member states on the nationality of children (adopted by the Committee of Ministers on 9 December 2009 at the 1073rd meeting of the Ministers' Deputies).

589 CoE CM Recommendation No. R (99) 18 of the Committee of Ministers to the Member States on the avoidance and reduction of statelessness (679th meeting of the Ministers' Deputies, 15 September 1999).

590 Ibid.

on the nationality of children[591] can be helpful to preventing and solving childhood statelessness as well.[592] This important 'soft law'-instrument was adopted by the CM in 2009 and stresses the activities of the CoE in the field of nationality law and its competence in these matters. The principles included in this Recommendation and their relevance to preventing and solving statelessness are discussed in section 3.3.

In addition to these important CM recommendations, the PACE has been active on the issue of statelessness, issuing a resolution and recommendation in 2014 on access to nationality and the effective implementation of the ECN.[593] In this resolution, the PACE recommends that the CM:

> "2.1. examine ways and means of promoting accession to the European Convention on Nationality (CETS No. 166), as well as its speedy implementation at national level;
> 2.2. re-establish an expert committee on nationality, which could conduct a study on new trends related to nationality matters, such as the growing acceptance of multiple nationality, acquisition of nationality at birth by children of long-term residents or conditions for naturalisation, including the criterion of residence, and examine the current and continuous relevance of the Convention on the Reduction of Cases of Multiple Nationality and on Military Obligations in Cases of Multiple Nationality (CETS No. 43) and its protocols (CETS No. 95, CETS No. 96 and CETS No. 149);
> 2.3. stimulate and supervise, in co-ordination with the United Nations High Commissioner for Refugees, the member States in the establishment of a statelessness determination procedure at the national level, in accordance with their obligation under the European Convention on Nationality to avoid statelessness;
> 2.4. draft a recommendation on the matters referred to in paragraph 2.1 above."[594]

This showed promise for further development and possibilities as regards nationality (and statelessness). Unfortunately, the reply by the CM was not so promising. Even though the CM welcomed the attention that is drawn to the right to a nationality, re-establishment of the CJ-NA proved not possible for financial reasons, and the CDCJ continues to be the primary organ responsible for the conventions relating to this matter. Concerning a possible recommendation, the CM believes the current framework to be sufficient, but "implementation of the current standards in the Member States

591 Recommendation CM/Rec (2009) 13 of the Committee of Ministers to member states on the nationality of children (adopted by the Committee of Ministers on 9 December 2009 at the 1073rd meeting of the Ministers' Deputies).

592 See also Gerard-René de Groot, 'Children, Their Right to Nationality and Child Statelessness' in Alice Edwards & Laura van Waas (eds), *Nationality and Statelessness under International Law* (Cambridge University Press 2014) 144–168, 156; Brad K Blitz, 'Policy Responses and Global Discourse on the Rights of Non-Citizens and Stateless People' in Caroline Sawyer & Brad K Blitz, *Statelessness in the European Union. Displaced, Undocumented, Unwanted* (Cambridge University Press) 108–138, 122.

593 PACE Resolution 1989 (2014) Final version; PACE Recommendation 2042 (2014) Final version, with reference to PACE Resolution 1989 (2014).

594 PACE Recommendation 2042 (2014) Final version, with reference to PACE Resolution 1989 (2014).

should be promoted and supported".[595] Unfortunately, there are no clear steps included to facilitate and/or monitor such promotion.

The Assembly has also drawn special attention to statelessness among children in Europe in its 2016 resolution on the need to eradicate statelessness of children.[596] In this resolution, the PACE asks member states to take steps to eradicate childhood statelessness. In particular, it urges states to ratify the relevant legal instruments of the CoE as well as the 1954 and the 1961 Conventions. It calls upon states to ensure compliance with the aforementioned legal instruments in their domestic laws, introduce or upgrade statelessness determination procedures, and ensure immediate birth registration, which could aid in preventing and solving statelessness among children. What is particularly interesting is that the PACE also invites states to participate in UNHCR's Global Plan to End Statelessness (2014–2024)[597] and promote the prevention and resolution of statelessness using, for instance, the UN UPR system. This seems to indicate that statelessness among children is not an issue that can be effectively addressed using only regional instruments, but should be addressed using all (legal) means possible.

In terms of childhood statelessness, it is also interesting to note that the PACE has discussed the issue of children's rights related to surrogacy. In the report for the PACE on the matter, it is explicitly noted that "cross-border surrogacy can be a source of statelessness for children".[598] This indicates that any (legal) follow-up to this might include something on the prevention of statelessness among children born as a result of cross-border surrogacy arrangements. Unfortunately, however, the PACE voted against the adoption of a recommendation to the CM[599] on the exploration of the possibility of European guidelines ensuring children's rights in relation to surrogacy arrangement.[600]

Concerns regarding childhood statelessness have furthermore been highlighted in the CoE Action Plan on Protecting Refugee and Migrant Children in Europe. This plan was adopted in May 2017 by the CM and "outlines concrete actions for the benefit of refugee and migrant children, according to their rights and adapted to their specific situations."[601] This plan includes the objective of ensuring that every child has a nationality and proposes that the implementation in practice of the principle of avoiding statelessness in relation to child migrants is to be examined and appropriate solutions should be identified in the form of practical guidance.

---

595 CoE CM Reply to PACE Recommendation 2042 (2014) (1205th meeting of the Ministers' Deputies, 9 July 2014) Doc 13583.

596 PACE Resolution 2099 (2016): The Need to Eradicate Statelessness of Children.

597 See on UNHCR's work also para 1.5.1.

598 PACE, 'Report and Draft Recommendation: Children's Rights Related to Surrogacy', Doc 14140, 23 September 2016, para 21, 25.

599 PACE, 'Children's Rights Related to Surrogacy', Doc 14140, 11 October 2016, compendium of amendments to Draft Recommendation.

600 PACE, 'Vote on Recommendation' <http://assembly.coe.int/nw/xml/Votes/DB-VotesResults-EN.asp?VoteID=36189&DocID=16001&MemberID=> accessed 26 May 2021.

601 CoE CM, 'Action Plan on Protecting Refugee and Migrant Children' (127th Session of the Committee of Ministers, Nicosia, 19 May 2017) CM(2017)54-final.

This has led to further work on statelessness being taken up by the CDCJ, which sees statelessness as one of the topics of its ongoing activities. This renewed interest seems to have background in the migration 'crisis' that Europe faced and which was also considered in paragraph 2.7. Christophe Poirel, Director of Human Rights of the CoE, has indicated for instance that the issue of statelessness became "more acute with the migration crisis".[602] In 2019, an analysis was conducted of the current practices regarding the avoidance and reduction of statelessness by Europe.[603] The presentation of this report led the CDCJ to decide to take on the recommended action and organize an "international conference on statelessness to raise awareness and promote implementation of Council of Europe standards in this field" as well as a "series of technical meetings on statelessness following the conference".[604]

In September 2021, the CDCJ and UNHCR organized an International Conference and Technical Meeting of Experts on statelessness and the right to a nationality in Strasbourg. The technical meeting on the first day was focused on the need for well-functioning statelessness determination procedures as well as preventing and reducing statelessness in Europe, among children in particular.[605] This technical meeting identified a number of points that needed to be taken into account in enacting and improving such procedures and gaps. Highlighted were the need for access to proper legal assistance, shared burden of proof, special attention for people with 'unknown' or 'undetermined' nationalities, access to legal residence and, eventually, naturalization. It was, however, also indicated that confirmation of nationality may be appropriate where people had been resident in the territory for a long time and had previously been treated as a national.[606] There was attention for deprivation of nationality and the need for further guidance on the proportionality test that is to be applied in this context was considered important. With regard to preventing childhood statelessness and ensuring child-friendly procedures, there was attention for specific groups of

602 Translated from the contribution of Christophe Poirel during the High-Level Panel 'Eradicating Statelessness In Europe: Progress, Challenges and Opportunities' of the 2021 Conference Statelessness and the Right to a Nationality in Europe: Progress, Challenges and Opportunities (Strasbourg, 24 September 2021).

603 CDCJ, 'Statelessness: Analysis of the Current Practices and Challenges regarding the Avoidance and Reduction of Statelessness in Europe prepared by Prof. Dr. Gerard-René de Groot' (2019) CDCJ-GT-APA(2019)3 <https://rm.coe.int/analysis-statelessness-/1680990cc5> accessed 27 May 2021.

604 CDCJ, '94th Meeting of the European Committee on Legal Co-operation, Strasbourg, 13–15 November 2019 – Meeting Report' (2019) CDCJ(2019)10, para 9 <https://rm.coe.int/cdcj-2019–10e-meeting-report-cdcj-94/1680a1bf82> accessed 27 May 2021.

605 UNHCR & CoE, 'Identifying and Protecting Stateless Persons in Europe – Technical Meeting of Experts Issue Paper' (2021) <https://rm.coe.int/briefing-paper-session-1-with-coverpage-en-unhcr/1680a3e6a5> accessed 27 September 2021; UNHCR & CoE, 'Realising the Right of Every Child to a Nationality in Europe – Technical Meeting of Experts Issue Paper' (2021) <https://rm.coe.int/session-2-thematic-paper-coverpage-en-final/1680a3e6a1> accessed 27 September 2021.

606 Summarized from the contribution of Professor Gerard- René de Groot during the High-Level Panel 'Eradicating Statelessness in Europe: Progress, Challenges and Opportunities' of the 2021 Conference Statelessness and the Right to a Nationality in Europe: Progress, Challenges and Opportunities (Strasbourg, 24 September 2021), who reported back on practical challenges and recommended actions as a result of the technical meeting of experts of 23 September 2021.

children, such as refugee children, children born on the territory of the member states, and children with links to suspected foreign terrorist fighters. Implementation of CM Recommendation on the nationality of children was highlighted as a necessary step in preventing statelessness, but it was also recognized that some further guidance on migrant or refugee children born aboard might be necessary.[607] Overall, the conclusions of this technical meeting pointed at the need for cooperation, exchange of information and further experts meetings and/or guidance to be developed on the basis of existing legal instruments.[608] The international conference the next day reiterated the need for cooperation between the CoE and CDCJ in particular with UNHCR, civil society organizations, affected people and member state governments. There was a clear belief that the existing standards on statelessness in the CoE were sufficient, but that there was a need for implementation of those, and – as necessary – additional guidance on how to implement these standards. Indeed, as Christophe Poirel pointed out: "The number one priority is implementing legislation".[609] In December 2021, the CDCJ indicated, taking note of the outcomes of the International Conference and Technical Meeting of Experts, that it will "prioritise as follow-up activities […] guidance on child sensitive procedures in administrative and migration law matters for stateless children or children at risk of being stateless and guidance on the establishment of nationality, in particular for children".[610]

Another priority that the CDCJ is currently working on in its standard setting activities, and has some links with statelessness, is that of administrative detention of migrants.[611] Research has shown that stateless people in Europe can (repeatedly) end up immigration detention because of their status.[612] The CDCJ has established a committee of experts working on the issue: the Committee of Experts on Administrative Detention of Migrants (CJ-DAM). The CJ-DAM's main task is to draft a codifying instrument on the administrative detention of migrants, based on existing international and regional standards on this matter.[613] A first draft of this instrument is available[614] and has been commented on by stakeholders and civil society. These comments included the

607 Ibid.

608 Ibid.

609 Translated from the contribution of Christophe Poirel during the High-Level Panel 'Eradicating Statelessness in Europe: Progress, Challenges and Opportunities' of the 2021 Conference Statelessness and the Right to a Nationality in Europe: Progress, Challenges and Opportunities (Strasbourg, 24 September 2021).

610 CDCJ, '97th Meeting of the European Committee on Legal Co-operation, Strasbourg, 1–3 December 2021 – Abridged Meeting Report' (2021) CDCJ(2021)33, para 6.

611 More information and documents available at <https://www.coe.int/en/web/cdcj/activities/administrative-detention-migrants> accessed 27 May 2021.

612 See the research conducted by ENS at <https://www.statelessness.eu/issues/preventing-arbitrary-detention> accessed 27 May 2021.

613 CDCJ, 'Terms of Reference of CJ-DAM', CJ-DAM(2016)1 (adopted by the Committee of Ministers at the 1241st Meeting of Ministers' Deputies, 24–26 November 2015).

614 CDCJ, 'Codifying Instrument of European Rules on the Administrative Detention of Migrants. 1st Draft (Strasbourg, 18 May 2017) <https://rm.coe.int/european-rules-on-the-administrative-detention-of-migrants-draft-codif/1680714cc1> accessed 27 May 2021.

remark that the draft does not specifically deal with (the vulnerabilities of) stateless migrants.[615] Depending on the follow-up to this consultation, it is therefore possible that this instrument, which also refers to the CM Recommendation on the nationality of children, could come to address statelessness in some way – even though this is not the case at the moment.

3.2.3. HUMAN RIGHTS AND MINORITY PROTECTION

Since its inception, the protection of human rights and fundamental freedoms has been at the core of the work of the CoE. As was described in paragraph 2.4, the protection of minorities changed after World War II – the focus was on safeguarding the rights of the individual. The CoE indeed, with the adoption of the ECHR in 1950, demonstrated its commitment to the protection of the human rights of the individual. The right to a nationality is not included in the ECHR, but as is discussed below, the instrument does contribute in some ways to preventing and solving statelessness.

Statelessness affects minorities in Europe, such as the Roma and the Russian ethnic minorities in the Baltic states.[616] Minority rights did not find an explicit place on the ECHR either, but the supervisory bodies have "been prepared to protect the rights of minorities under the ECHR."[617] Later, after the end of the Cold War[618], minorities protection was back on the agenda of the CoE. The important CoE instrument that was developed on minority protection in particular – the Framework Convention for the Protection of National Minorities (FCNM) – should be seen against the background of

> "[t]he revolution that has occurred in Europe since 1989 [that] has reawakened many minority issues that had lain relatively dormant during Soviet domination of the eastern part of the region and a plethora of measures, at the regional and international levels,' have been promulgated to deal with various minority situations and to reinforce the image of Europe as a collection of pluralist, multicultural states".[619]

615 CDCJ, 'Conditions of Administrative Detention of Migrants. Report of the General Rapporteur Mr Christoph Henrichs (Germany) on the Hearing' (Strasbourg, 22 September 2017) para 16 <https://rm.coe.int/report-of-the-hearing-22–23-june-2017/168074ce2f> accessed 27 May 2021; CJ-DAM, 'Analysis of the Results of the Written Consultation on the 1st Draft of the Codifying Instrument of European Rules on the Administrative Detention of Migrants' (Strasbourg, 12 September 2017) para 34 <https://rm.coe.int/publication-document-analysis-of-the-results-of-the-written-consultati/168074ce2e> accessed 27 May 2021.

616 See also para 2.6.

617 Geoff Gilbert, 'The Council of Europe and Minority Rights' (1996) 18 Human Rights Quarterly 160, 173.

618 See also para 2.6.

619 Geoff Gilbert, 'The Council of Europe and Minority Rights' (1996) 18 Human Rights Quarterly 160, 160–161.

Below, the ECHR and key articles relevant to the prevention of and solutions to statelessness are introduced. Furthermore, the broader work of the CoE on the protection of human rights and minorities are considered for its relevance to the topic of this study, particularly looking at the FCNM.

European Convention on Human Rights

The first main instrument of the CoE, the Convention for the Protection of Human Rights and Fundamental Freedoms (ECHR) of 1950, has proven to be relevant in nationality matters – as this chapter demonstrates.[620] The ECHR is the CoE's main human rights document, which is of great importance in Europe. The ECHR was adopted in 1950 in the aftermath of World War II. Currently all 47 Member States of the CoE are party to this Treaty. Moreover, the ECHR has a supervisory mechanism: the European Court of Human Rights (ECtHR). This ECHR and the Court have been quite influential in developing the respect for human rights and supplementing constitutional guarantees in the Member States.[621]

When considering the topics of nationality and statelessness under the Convention, it is first relevant to note that the rights set forth in the ECHR apply also to stateless people in Europe. They can submit an application to the ECtHR claiming that one of the States Parties to the Convention has violated (one of) the rights guaranteed by the ECHR or its Protocols.[622] Case law evidences that, indeed, the Court has protected the rights of stateless people, also rights that relate specifically to their statelessness.[623]

That nationality matters have found a place within the ECHR might at first sight be surprising: the ECHR does not contain a right to a nationality[624] or any reference to nationality matters. It was only later, in 1988, that the Committee of Experts for the Development of Human Rights considered the issue of the right to a nationality as a human right. It was discussed whether such right should be added to the ECHR using a 'Protocol on the Right to Nationality'.[625] This idea was, however, abandoned in 1989. According to Johannes Chan, the reasons for this were political: "States are not prepared to forgo their sovereignty and submit themselves to the supervision of the European

620 Please refer also to section 3.3.

621 Christoph Grabenwarter, for instance, shows how the ECHR and the interpretations thereof by the ECtHR have influenced the development of human rights and supplemented constitutional assurances in Austria: Christoph Grabenwarter, 'The Significance of the European Convention on Human Rights in the Development of Human Rights' in Renate Kicker (ed), *The Council of Europe. Pioneer and Guarantor for Human Rights and Democracy* (Council of Europe Publishing 2010) 39–42.

622 Art 34 ECHR.

623 See for instance *Andrejeva v Latvia* App No 55707/00 (ECHR, 18 February 2009) ECLI:CE:ECHR:2009:0218JUD005570700 and *Kim v Russia* App No 44260/13 (ECHR, 17 July 2014) ECLI:CE:ECHR:2014:0717JUD004426013.

624 Cf *X v Austria* App No 5212/71 (ECHR, 5 October 1972) ECLI:CE:ECHR:1972:1005DEC000521271.

625 Johannes Chan, 'The Right to a Nationality as a Human Right. The Current Trend towards Recognition' (1991) 12 Human Rights Law Journal 1, 7.

Court of Human Rights on the question of nationality".[626] As such, the ECHR remained without a right to a nationality.

Nonetheless, when studying the case law of the Court on nationality matters, it becomes clear that nationality issues have been discussed in the context of Article 8 of the ECHR (right to respect for private and family life) in particular. The introduction of nationality as a topic under Article 8 has been a process of interpretation by the Court (and the European Commission of Human Rights until the entry into force of Protocol No. 11).[627] Even though cases on nationality have been lodged with the relevant supervising body since the 1970s, it was felt that "the regulation of nationality was not a matter on which the ECHR had any bearing".[628] That is perhaps not surprising, as nationality matters are traditionally viewed as a competence of the sovereign state, on which, indeed, international laws in principle do not have bearing.[629] In the 1990s, some development becomes visible in case law. In a case regarding the withdrawal of nationality, resulting in statelessness, the European Commission of Human Rights[630] noted when considering admissibility and in particular Article 8 that "la requête pose de sérieuses questions de fait et de droit qui ne peuvent être résolues à ce stade de l'examen de la requête, mais nécessitent un examen au fond".[631] Even though the decision on the merits of this case did not result in the finding of a violation of the ECHR, a number of other cases followed in which it was acknowledged that, depending on the circumstances, nationality matters may raise an issue under different articles of the Convention, particularly Article 8, but also Articles 3 (prohibition of torture, inhuman and degrading treatment) and Article 14 (prohibition of discrimination).[632]

These cases lead us to a key case as regards the development of nationality matters under the ECHR: the 1999 case of *Karassev v. Finland*. Even though the ECtHR did not find a violation in this case and declared it inadmissible, it is important in the recognition that arbitrary denial of citizenship might raise issues under Article 8 under certain circumstances because of the impact of such denial on the private life of an individual.[633] This demonstrates to some extent an acknowledgement of an aspect

626 Ibid, 9.

627 With Protocol No. 11 to the Convention for the Protection of Human Rights and Fundamental Freedoms, restructuring the control machinery established thereby, CETS No. 155, 1994, a permanent ECtHR replaced the existing part-time Court and European Commission of Human Rights (Commission). Protocol No. 11 entered into force on 1 November 1998.

628 Laura van Waas, 'Fighting Statelessness and Discriminatory Nationality Law in Europe' (2012) 14 European Journal of Migration and Law 243–260, 250. These were decisions of the European Commission on Human Rights, the Court's predecessor.

629 Cf Peter Spiro, 'A New International Law of Citizenship' (2011) 105 American Journal of International Law 694.

630 Hereinafter: the Commission.

631 "The application raises serious questions of fact and law which cannot be resolved at this stage of the examination of the application, but necessitate an examination of the merits" (transl CV). See *Kafkasli c Turquie* App No 21106/92 (European Commission on Human Rights, 22 May 1995, admissibility).

632 Laura van Waas, 'Fighting Statelessness and Discriminatory Nationality Law in Europe' (2012) 14 European Journal of Migration and Law 251–252.

633 *Andrei Karassev and Family v Finland* App No 31414/96 (ECHR, 12 January 1999, admissibility) ECLI: CE:ECHR:1999:0112DEC003141496.

of a right to a nationality in that denial of nationality could amount to a violation of the right to respect for private and family life – where such denial would indeed have consequences for a person's life.[634] The 2011 *Genovese* case[635] is, to date, *the* landmark case as regards nationality under Article 8 of the ECHR, as it explicitly recognized nationality as part of an individual's social identity as protected under the right to private life[636] – which was affirmed in developing case law since. This case and others are considered further in section 3.3.

Framework Convention for the Protection of National Minorities

The Framework Convention for the Protection of National Minorities (FCNM)[637] was adopted in 1995 and entered into force in 1998. As of January 2022, it has been ratified by 39 states.[638] It aims "to specify the legal principles which states undertake to respect in order to ensure the protection of national minorities".[639] According to Article 1 of the FCNM, "[t]he protection of national minorities and of the rights and freedoms of persons belonging to those minorities forms an integral part of the international protection of human rights". Section II of the Framework Convention contains substantive provisions, including the prohibition of discrimination in Article 4. Section III includes guidance on interpretation of the FCNM, as well as the obligations of national minorities themselves. Section IV considers monitoring of the implementation of the Framework Convention. Pursuant to these provisions, the Advisory Committee on the Framework Convention for the Protection of National Minorities (ACFC) was installed by the CM.[640] The ACFC consists of 18 independent experts and monitors the implementation of the FCNM by a reporting procedure for states, adopting country-specific opinions and advising the CM.[641]

Interestingly, the FCNM does not define 'national minorities' anywhere – "[i]t was decided to adopt a pragmatic approach, based on the recognition that at this stage, it is impossible to arrive at a definition capable of mustering general support of all

634 See also Mónika Ganczer, 'The Right to a Nationality as a Human Right?' in Petra Lea Láncos, Réka Varga, Tamás Molnár, Marcel Szabó (eds), *Hungarian Yearbook of International Law and European Law 2014* (Eleven International Publishing 2015) 15–33, 23.

635 *Genovese v Malta* App No 53124/09 (ECHR, 11 October 2011) ECLI:CE:ECHR:2011:1011 JUD005312409.

636 Ibid, para 33.

637 Framework Convention for the Protection of National Minorities (Strasbourg, 1995, CETS No. 157) (FCNM).

638 CoE Treaty Office, 'Chart of Signatures and Ratifications of Treaty 157' <https://www.coe.int/en/web/conventions/full-list/-/conventions/treaty/157/signatures?p_auth=JjR58qcq> accessed 28 May 2021.

639 CoE, *Explanatory Report to the to the Framework Convention for the Protection of National Minorities* (Strasbourg, 1 February 1995, CETS No. 157) para 10.

640 See also Gauthier de Beco & Emma Lantschner, 'The Advisory Committee on the Framework Convention for the Protection of National Minorities (the ACFC)' in Gauthier de Beco (ed), *Human Rights Monitoring Mechanisms of the Council of Europe* (Routledge Research in Human Rights Law, Routledge 2013) 100–126.

641 See also CoE, 'Advisory Committee on the Framework Convention for the Protection of National Minorities' <https://www.coe.int/en/web/minorities/advisory-committee> accessed 28 May 2021.

Council of Europe member states".[642] States have therefore made declarations on how they see this concept in relation to their situation or even announced that the FCNM only applies to a certain minority within their borders (e.g. Denmark stating that the Framework Convention only applies to the German minority in South Jutland).[643] At the same time, inspiration was to be drawn from existing international law on this. Even though there is no authoritative definition of a 'national minority' in international law either, but different attempts at defining this concept have indicated that

> "the minority might need to consist of nationals of the state, it might need to be numerically smaller than the rest of the population, nondominant and loyal to the state, and have objectively distinguishing characteristics based on nationality, ethnicity, religion, language, or culture – or some combination of those elements".[644]

How the FCNM is applied and who are the minorities it applies to, is not up to the states entirely. On the first point, that minorities also need to have the nationality of the state concerned, the ACFC has held that this is not "an *a priori* requirement for the enjoyment of minority rights" and that the inclusion of non-citizens should be considered separately for each article of the Framework Convention.[645] In light of this interpretation of the FCNM, the ACFC has also been able to make observations and recommendations on statelessness. In its Fourth Opinion on Estonia, for example, the ACFC recommended explicitly that Estonia should "continue with efforts to further reduce statelessness and to facilitate access to citizenship for long-term residents in Estonia".[646] In particular, the "Advisory Committee reiterates its call on the authorities to facilitate further the acquisition of citizenship by all stateless persons with the view to enabling their full participation in the political life of the country and relevant decision making processes".[647] The ACFC thus seems to recognize that nationality is important to full participation in society.

Even though the FCNM does not seem to deal with issues of nationality and statelessness in its text, the example above demonstrates that the ACFC is able to address these when monitoring implementation of the Framework Convention. Where making specific recommendations to reduce statelessness and recognizing the importance of nationality to the full enjoyment of rights, the FCNM can thus contribute towards preventing and solving statelessness.

---

642 CoE, *Explanatory Report to the to the Framework Convention for the Protection of National Minorities* (Strasbourg, 1 February 1995, CETS No. 157) para 12.

643 See CoE Treaty Office, 'Reservations and Declarations for Treaty No. 157' <https://www.coe.int/en/web/conventions/full-list/-/conventions/treaty/157/declarations?p_auth=14p5vz9O> accessed 28 May 2021.

644 Geoff Gilbert, 'The Council of Europe and Minority Rights' (1996) 18 Human Rights Quarterly 160, 165.

645 Julie Ringelheim, 'Minority Rights in a Time of Multiculturalism – The Evolving Scope of the Framework Convention on the Protection of National Minorities (2010) 10 Human Rights Law Review 99, 114.

646 ACFC, 'Fourth Opinion on Estonia, Adopted on 19 March 2015', ACFC/OP/IV(2015)002, 28.

647 ACFC, 'Fourth Opinion on Estonia, Adopted on 19 March 2015', ACFC/OP/IV(2015)002, para 99.

Other relevant instruments on human rights and minority protection

A possible area for legal developments relevant to statelessness might also be the CoE work that concerns the Roma. The CoE has adopted various texts and strategic documents in this regard[648], even though statelessness as a separate issue is not usually part of such documents – these focus on inclusion of Roma and Travelers more broadly.[649] In the *Strasbourg Declaration on Roma* of 2010, the member states of the CoE agreed on a number of priorities for inclusion of Roma in Europe, which included one on citizenship: "Take effective measures to avoid statelessness in accordance with domestic law and policy and to grant Roma legally residing in their national territory access to identification papers".[650] That statelessness is a problem for Roma and that it is being addressed in CoE context is acknowledged in a 2012 report that was commissioned by the CoE Commissioner for Human Rights.[651] Particularly interesting is the 2012 Assembly recommendation on Roma migrants to the CM, in which the PACE asks CM – amongst others – to

> "ask member States to take the necessary steps to naturalise stateless Roma and to sign, ratify and implement the European Convention on Nationality (CETS No. 166) and the Council of Europe Convention on the Avoidance of Statelessness in relation to State Succession (CETS No. 200), as well as the United Nations 1954 Convention relating to the Status of Stateless Persons and the 1961 Convention on the Reduction of Statelessness".[652]

Even though the CM welcomes the efforts of the PACE to work towards improving the situation of Roma in Europe, the CM does not consider the abovementioned request of the Assembly in its reply.[653] Nonetheless, it does show that statelessness and reducing this phenomenon among a group of people of which some are (at risk of) statelessness is of concern to the CoE as a whole and provides another avenue for promoting existing standards on preventing and solving statelessness.

The CoE Commissioner for Human Rights has also paid attention to statelessness. The issue is, for instance, considered in reports of country visits. Indeed, in the report of the country visit to Albania in 2018,

> "the Commissioner calls on the authorities to ensure that European and international instruments concerning nationality, prevention and reduction of statelessness, which are

648 CoE, 'Adopted Texts (Roma and Travellers)' <https://www.coe.int/en/web/roma-and-travellers/adopted-texts> accessed 7 October 2021.

649 Eg CoE, 'CoE Strategic Action Plan for Roma and Traveller Inclusion (2020–2025)' (2020) <https://rm.coe.int/coe-strategic-action-plan-for-roma-and-traveller-inclusion-en/16809fe0d0> accessed 7 October 2021.

650 CM, 'The Strasbourg Declaration on Roma' (CoE High Level Meeting on Roma, Strasbourg, 20 October 2010) CM(2010)133 final, pt 21.

651 CoE, *Human Rights of Roma and Travellers in Europe* (Council of Europe Publishing 2012), available online <https://www.coe.int/t/commissioner/source/prems/prems79611_GBR_CouvHumanRightsOfRoma_WEB.pdf> accessed 3 January 2022, see in particular Ch 7.

652 PACE, Recommendation 2003 (2012) final version: Roma Migrants in Europe, para 7.3.

653 CM, Reply to Recommendation 2003 (2012) on Roma Migrants in Europe (1166th Meeting of the Ministers' Deputies, 27 March 2013) Doc 13162.

binding on Albania, are complied with. Special attention should be paid in this context to the situation of Roma children and children born abroad lacking birth registration. Albania should introduce a procedure in law to identify and protect stateless persons in line with the 1954 Convention and UNHCR's Handbook on Protection of Stateless Persons. Albania is also urged to accede to the 2006 Council of Europe Convention for the Avoidance of Statelessness in relation to State Succession".[654]

Furthermore, various human rights comments have been made by the Commissioner: in 2010 on stateless Roma and documentation[655]; in 2011 on statelessness more generally, promoting the ECN and ECSS for instance[656]; in 2013 on stateless children, again calling states to accede to the ECN and ECSS (in addition to the 1954 and 1961 Conventions)[657]; and in 2015 on (the risk of) statelessness in relation to Syrian refugees.[658] Furthermore, in 2019 the Commissioner called on CoE member states to accede to the relevant UN and CoE conventions on statelessness in the context of the UNHCR #IBELONG campaign, also calling for further measures to be taken by states, including enacting statelessness determination procedures, easing naturalization procedures and ensuring birth registration.[659]

Even though not specifically focused on nationality or statelessness, it is also relevant to take note of the work of the European Commission against Racism and Intolerance (ECRI). This CoE human rights monitoring mechanism was set up in 1993 and got a firm legal basis in its own Statute in 2002.[660] It does not oversee the implementation of a specific treaty, but its focus is on issues relating to the fight against racism, discrimination (on grounds of race, ethnic/national origin, color, citizenship,

---

654 CoE Commissioner for Human Rights, 'Report by Dunja Mijatović, Commissioner for Human Rights of the Council of Europe Following Her Visit to Albania from 21 to 25 May 2018' (2018) CommDH/GovRep(2018)10 <https://search.coe.int/commissioner/Pages/result_details.aspx?ObjectId=09000016808d2e22> accessed 2 July 2021.

655 CoE Commissioner for Human Rights, 'Human Rights Comment: Stateless Roma: No Documents – No Rights' (2010) <https://www.coe.int/en/web/commissioner/-/stateless-roma-no-documents-no-righ-1> accessed 2 July 2021.

656 CoE Commissioner for Human Rights, 'Human Rights Comment: Several Hundred Thousand People in Europe are Stateless – They Need Extra Protection' (2011) <https://www.coe.int/en/web/commissioner/-/several-hundred-thousand-people-in-europe-are-stateless-they-need-extra-protecti-1> accessed 2 July 2021.

657 CoE Commissioner for Human Rights, 'Human Rights Comment: Governments Should Act in the Best Interest of Stateless Children' (2013) <https://www.coe.int/en/web/commissioner/-/governments-should-act-in-the-best-interest-of-stateless-childr-1> accessed 2 July 2021.

658 CoE Commissioner for Human Rights, 'Human Rights Comment: Syrian Refugees: 'Reset' Needed in Europe's Approach' (2015) <https://www.coe.int/en/web/commissioner/-/syrian-refugees-reset-needed-in-europe-s-approach> accessed 2 July 2021.

659 CoE Commissioner for Human Rights, 'Statement: Step Up Action Against Statelessness' (2019) <https://www.coe.int/en/web/commissioner/news-2019/-/asset_publisher/Arb4fRK3o8Cf/content/step-up-action-against-statelessness> accessed 2 July 2021.

660 CM Resolution (2002) 8 on the on the statute of the European Commission against Racism and Intolerance (adopted by the Committee of Ministers on 13 June 2002 at the 799th meeting of the Ministers' Deputies, amended by Resolutions CM/Res(2013)12 and CM/Res(2014)2 adopted, respectively, on 9 October 2013 and 19 February 2014 at their 1180th and 1192nd meetings).

religion, language, sexual orientation and gender identity), xenophobia, antisemitism and intolerance in Europe.[661] It monitors these in the member states of the CoE and works on general issues, notably through the development of General Policy Recommendations. ECRI has issued such recommendations for instance with regard to combating anti-Gypsyism and discrimination against Roma[662], and on safeguarding irregularly present migrants from discrimination.[663] It is considered a "unique and particularly successful European human rights monitoring mechanism" in view of its examination of local developments and specific recommendations and dialogue with states, as well as its influence on broader CoE work on these topics.[664] None of ECRI's General Policy Recommendations concern statelessness or nationality matters, but they contribute towards the bigger question of inclusion of people (with or without nationality) in society. In its country monitoring reports, the issue of statelessness is addressed though. In the ECRI country report on Estonia, the reduction of the number of stateless people is considered for instance:

> "In its 4th report, ECRI recommended that the Estonian authorities continue the measures taken thus far to reduce the number of stateless persons, in full consultation with representatives of the persons concerned. As seen above, the number of people with undetermined citizenship has continually fallen over the past five years, as a result of the 2008–2013 integration policy. ECRI notes that while, as acknowledged by representatives of stateless persons, the authorities engaged in broad consultation with the latter when drawing up the new 2020 strategy, this was not sufficiently the case in the implementation of the 2008–2013 strategy as evidenced by the fact that various practical problems persist, for example with regard to the language tests for acquisition of nationality, and the review of language requirements in connection with a particular job."[665]

ECRI goes on to refer back to recommendations made on language testing and language requirements. Preventing and solving statelessness, and the way in which such measures are implemented, in particular as regards minorities such as the Russian ethnic minority (non-citizens) in Estonia, can thus be subject to scrutiny of ECRI.

---

661 See also CoE, 'ECRI – European Commission against Racism and Intolerance' (2019) <https://rm.coe.int/leaflet-ecri-2019/168094b101> accessed 28 May 2021.

662 ECRI General Policy Recommendation No. 13 (revised) on Combating Anti-Gypsyism and Discrimination against Roma (adopted on 24 June 2011 and amended on 1 December 2020) <https://www.coe.int/en/web/european-commission-against-racism-and-intolerance/recommendation-no.13> accessed 28 May 2021.

663 ECRI General Policy Recommendation No. 16 on Safeguarding Irregularly Present Migrants from Discrimination – adopted on 16 March 2016 <https://www.coe.int/en/web/european-commission-against-racism-and-intolerance/recommendation-no.16> accessed 28 May 2021.

664 Lanna Yael Hollo, 'The European Commission against Racism and Intolerance (ECRI)' in Gauthier de Beco (ed), *Human Rights Monitoring Mechanisms of the Council of Europe* (Routledge Research in Human Rights Law, Routledge 2013) 127–149, 127.

665 ECRI, 'ECRI Report on Estonia (Fifth Monitoring Cycle)', CRI(2015)36, para 85–86 <https://rm.coe.int/fifth-report-on-estonia/16808b56f1> accessed 28 May 2021.

3.2.4. CONCLUDING REMARKS

Since the CoE was founded in 1949, the organization has come a long way – not only in a general sense, but also as regards statelessness and nationality in particular. Developments in the 1990s – the end of the Cold War with new states emerging and becoming members of the CoE – have sparked standard setting on nationality. The key instruments for preventing and solving statelessness in Europe were adopted from that moment in time onwards: the ECN and the ECSS, as well as two Recommendations of the CM – on the avoidance and reduction of statelessness and on the nationality of children. But developments relevant to preventing and solving statelessness can also be found in the CoE's protection of human rights and minorities. One of the key instruments in that regard remains the ECHR[666], as new case law regarding nationality matters continues to emerge. Indeed, it was also here, that in the 1990s – after the end of the Cold War and with standards being adopted in CoE context – more developments on nationality could be seen. After the 2009 Recommendation of the CM on the nationality of children, legislative efforts in the field of nationality were marked 'completed' by the CoE, as evidenced by the 'completed activities' of the responsible organ, the CDCJ. However, the CDCJ has taken on 'statelessness' as a new topic of concern, trying to promote CoE standards in this field. Given the activities that the CDCJ still aims to undertake in this field, some further guidance on statelessness issues may be expected, which might in turn, like it did for nationality, also have a broader influence on the interpretation and implementation of existing CoE instruments, including ECHR jurisprudence for instance.

3.3. PREVENTING AND SOLVING STATELESSNESS

This section provides a thematic analysis of the key instruments of the CoE on nationality and statelessness for their contribution to preventing and solving statelessness. The first paragraph analyzes measures aimed at preventing and solving childhood statelessness, and the second paragraph examines norms concerning solutions to conflicts of nationality law and preventing loss / deprivation of nationality. In the third paragraph, the spotlight is on standards regulating nationality matters in cases of state succession. The fourth paragraph considers legal norms aimed at the acquisition of a nationality for people who became stateless in Europe in the past and remain stateless today and/or who arrive in Europe stateless. Provisions ensuring non-discrimination in nationality matters are discussed in the fifth paragraph, and the section is concluded with a summary and concluding observations.

666 See also section 3.3.

3.3.1. CHILDHOOD STATELESSNESS

There is no right to nationality for children included in the treaties of the CoE, nor is there an explicit provision that says that the child's best interests need to be the first consideration in any decisions that concern them. However, a number of the wider CoE legal instruments and provisions do relate to preventing and solving childhood statelessness, as well as their best interests and their right to acquire a nationality. This paragraph sets out the key standards in this regard.

As was briefly considered in paragraph 1.4.2, European states generally apply the *jus sanguinis* principle in their nationality laws, meaning that children usually acquire nationality at birth by descent. Where the ECN establishes that a child of a national should acquire the nationality of his or her parent (*jus sanguinis*) *ex lege*, it helps to ensure that every child acquires a nationality and thus aids in preventing statelessness.[667] Children born to nationals of one of the European countries in the respective country or abroad usually acquire the nationality of their parent(s).[668] At the same time, this is a demonstration of the *jus sanguinis*-bias that Europe has towards the acquisition of nationality; the principle of *jus sanguinis* remains the dominant principle for the acquisition of nationality, and can have both a negative and a positive effect on preventing statelessness:

> "The *jus sanguinis*-principle has some positive effect on the prevention of statelessness: children born to European nationals anywhere in the world are at a minimal risk of statelessness. However, the same principle fosters the assumption that children born to non-European nationals in Europe should be citizens of elsewhere, leaving some of those children at risk of statelessness."[669]

However, the ECN and other CoE instruments recognize that only application of the *jus sanguinis* principle will not prevent statelessness childhood statelessness in all circumstances. To mitigate this, additional safeguards need to be put in place. According to the ECN, a state should provide for its nationality to be acquired by children born in the territory who do not acquire another nationality at birth – who would otherwise remain stateless. States have two options in granting nationality: they can do so *ex lege* or subsequently, to children who remained stateless, upon an

---

667 Art 6(1)(a) ECN; see also Gerard-René de Groot, 'Children, their Right to a Nationality and Child Statelessness' in Alice Edwards & Laura van Waas, *Nationality and Statelessness under International Law* (Cambridge University Press 2014) 144–168, 155.

668 Cf ENS, 'Statelessness Index' (2021) <https://index.statelessness.eu/> accessed 3 October 2021. Theme 'Prevention and Reduction' was selected; Olivier Vonk & Maarten Vink, 'Global Protection Against Statelessness Database' (EUI Research Data 2015) <https://cadmus.eui.eu/handle/1814/64601> accessed 3 October 2021. 'Mode S03: descent (birth in country)' & 'Mode S04: descent (birth abroad)' were used and only member states of the CoE were selected.

669 Caia Vlieks & Katja Swider, 'The *Jus Sanguinis* Bias of Europe and What It Means for Childhood Statelessness' (*ENS Blog*, 17 June 2015) <www.statelessness.eu/blog/jus-sanguinis-bias-europe-and-what-it-means-childhood-statelessness> accessed 3 July 2021.

application being lodged with the appropriate authority, by or on behalf of the child.[670] This provision can be compared with Article 1 of the 1961 Convention. The ECN allows states to require lawful and habitual residence on its territory for a period not exceeding five years immediately preceding the lodging of the application.[671]

In its rules on the acquisition of nationality[672], the ECN also makes provision for foundlings specifically: each state party shall ensure that its nationality is acquired *ex lege* by foundlings found in its territory who would otherwise be stateless.[673] Similar provisions can be found in two older international legal instruments: Article 2 of the 1961 Convention and Article 14 of the 1930 Hague Convention. But who is the foundling who can benefit from this provision in the ECN? The ECN does not define the concept of a 'foundling' in its definitions of Article 2. However, the Explanatory Report to the ECN offers more information: 'foundlings' are new-born infants found abandoned in the territory of a state with no known parentage or nationality who would be stateless if Article 6, paragraph 1, sub-paragraph b, of the ECN was not applied.[674] It is in line with the object and purpose of the ECN, in particular when looking at Article 6, paragraph 2, for states to treat abandoned children[675] in their territory similar to foundlings as regards the acquisition of nationality.[676] In this context, commentators have held that if no child is to be left stateless, this safeguard should, as a minimum, "apply to all young children who are not yet able to communicate accurate information pertaining to the identity of their parents or their place of birth".[677] If applied correctly, and in line with these considerations, this provision could indeed prevent statelessness effectively.

The provisions in Article 6, paragraph 1, sub-paragraph b, and Article 6, paragraph 2, of the ECN thus complement Article 6, paragraph 1, under a, of the ECN, and together attempt to minimalize the risk of any child being born stateless. However, the paragraphs of Article 6 both use a formulation that indicates that they only apply if the child would otherwise be stateless or remains stateless. The question is what that means. Gerard-René de Groot explored this in depth in a chapter on children's right to nationality and child statelessness.[678] He identifies the aforementioned question on ascertaining whether a child would otherwise be stateless as one of specific challenges to children's access to a nationality and demonstrates that guidance on these matters

---

670 Art 6(2) ECN.

671 Art 6(2)(b) ECN.

672 See generally also Roland Schärer, 'The European Convention on Nationality' (1997) 40 German Yearbook of International Law 438, 445–446; Gerard-René de Groot, 'The European Convention on Nationality: A Step towards a *Ius Commune* in the Field of Nationality Law' (2007) 7 Maastricht Journal of European and Comparative Law 117, 129–134.

673 Art 6(1)(b) ECN.

674 CoE, *Explanatory Report to the European Convention on Nationality* (Strasbourg, 6 November 1997, CETS No. 166) para 48.

675 Cf the definition of a 'child' in Art 2(c) ECN.

676 See also Gerard-René de Groot, 'Children, their Right to a Nationality and Child Statelessness' in Alice Edwards & Laura van Waas, Nationality and Statelessness under International Law (Cambridge University Press 2014) 144–168, 161–162.

677 Ibid, 162.

678 Ibid, 158–161.

is to be found in the 1954 Convention and the explanations relating to the definition of statelessness, as well as the determination of statelessness available in the UNHCR Handbook on the Protection of Stateless Persons.[679]

In relation to children, the ECSS also contains a specific provision for avoiding statelessness at birth, in particular to prevent children from becoming stateless because their parents are stateless.[680] Article 10 of this Treaty says that a predecessor or successor state shall grant nationality at birth to a child born following state succession on its territory to a parent who, at the time of state succession, had the nationality of the predecessor state if that child would otherwise be stateless. This provision can be compared with the provision for the prevention of statelessness at birth in Article 6, paragraph 2, of the ECN. However, not only in its scope does the provision in the ECSS differ from that in the ECN: the ECSS provides that nationality shall be acquired by a child *ex lege*, and does not provide states for the possibility of arranging this upon application, which is allowed under the ECN.[681] Furthermore, no reservations can be made to this Article of the ECSS.[682] As such, it should be rather effective in combatting childhood statelessness in the context of state succession and it also demonstrates how *jus soli* elements for addressing statelessness are finding its way into different CoE instruments on nationality and statelessness.

The CM Recommendation on the avoidance and reduction of statelessness (1999) almost repeats the key principles on preventing childhood statelessness from the ECN[683], stating that:

> "Each state should provide for its nationality to be acquired *ex lege* by children one of whose parents possesses, at the time of birth of these children, its nationality. Exceptions made with regard to children born abroad should not lead to situations of statelessness. Each state should ensure that its legislation provides for the acquisition of its nationality by children born on its territory who would otherwise be stateless."[684]

Moreover, the specific CM Recommendation on the nationality of children of 2009[685] contains 23 principles, which are grouped in different categories. The first ten principles deal with the reduction of statelessness of children specifically. The Recommendation

679 UNHCR, 'Handbook on the Protection of Stateless Persons under the 1954 Convention Relating to the Status of Stateless Persons' (Geneva, 2014) <www.unhcr.org/protection/statelessness/53b698ab9/handbook-protection-stateless-persons.html> accessed 3 July 2021.

680 CoE, *Explanatory Report to the Council of Europe Convention on the Avoidance of Statelessness in relation to State Succession* (Strasbourg, 19 May 2006, CETS No. 200) para 42.

681 Ibid, para 43.

682 Art 20 ECSS. Reservations can only be made with regard to Arts 7, 8(2), 12 and 14(2)b.

683 Art 6(1) & 6(2) ECN.

684 CM Recommendation No. R (99) 18 of the Committee of Ministers to the Member States on the avoidance and reduction of statelessness (679th meeting of the Ministers' Deputies, 15 September 1999), paras II.A.a & II.A.b.

685 Recommendation CM/Rec (2009) 13 of the Committee of Ministers to member states on the nationality of children (adopted by the Committee of Ministers on 9 December 2009 at the 1073rd meeting of the Ministers' Deputies).

furthermore highlights, similar to the ECN, the importance of cooperation in childhood statelessness, including exchange of information. What is interesting, is that specific attention is paid to the administration relating to nationality matters. As was considered in paragraph 1.4.3, (stateless) people can be registered with an 'unknown nationality'. This is also true for (stateless) children[686], who should, according to the Recommendation, be registered with an 'unknown' or 'undetermined' nationality "only for as short a period as possible".[687] Also, the situation of adoption is addressed by the 2009 Recommendation, stating that revocation or annulment of adoption and consequent loss of nationality should not lead to statelessness.[688] Other categories deal with nationality as a consequence of a child-parent family relationship, also trying to facilitate acquisition of nationality of children that are adopted or born out of medically assisted reproductive techniques, children born on the territory of a state to a foreign parent, the position of children treated as nationals, the rights of children in proceedings affecting their nationality, and registration of birth – given the importance of birth registration to ensuring the right to a nationality and avoiding statelessness. According to Gerard-René de Groot, scientific expert of the CJ-S-NAT at the time, this Recommendation supplements the ECN and could serve as inspiration for a protocol to the ECN on this topic. He also believes that "[t]he principles are (…) a source of inspiration for other international and regional debates on the improvement of rules avoiding and reducing cases of statelessness".[689] The CM Recommendation on the nationality of children thus presents another more specialized legal instrument in nationality matters, which has the potential to aid states in avoiding statelessness.[690]

As could be seen in paragraph 3.2.3, the ECHR is a relevant instrument in addressing statelessness and nationality matters. This is certainly true with regard to the issue of childhood statelessness, as ECHR jurisprudence elaborates on how the CoE instruments (collectively) understand states' obligations with regard to *jus sanguinis* conferral of nationality. A key decision on nationality matters under the ECHR also relates to children and their nationality: the *Genovese* case.[691] The case concerned the issue of discrimination of children in nationality law.[692] A young British man also

686 ENS, 'No Child Should be Stateless' (ENS 2015) 17 <https://www.statelessness.eu/sites/www.statelessness.eu/files/ENS_NoChildStateless_final.pdf> accessed 3 July 2021.

687 Recommendation CM/Rec (2009) 13 of the Committee of Ministers to member states on the nationality of children (adopted by the Committee of Ministers on 9 December 2009 at the 1073rd meeting of the Ministers' Deputies), para I.8.

688 Ibid, para I.10.

689 Gerard-René de Groot, 'Children, Their Right to Nationality and Child Statelessness' in Alice Edwards & Laura van Waas (eds), *Nationality and Statelessness under International Law* (Cambridge University Press 2014) 144–168, 158.

690 See also ENS, 'Mr. Nils Muižnieks, the Council of Europe's Commissioner for Human Rights, speaks exclusively to ENS' (*ENS Blog*, 15 January 2014) <https://www.statelessness.eu/updates/news/mr-nils-muiznieks-council-europes-commissioner-human-rights-speaks-exclusively-ens> accessed 26 May 2021.

691 *Genovese v Malta* App No 53124/09 (ECHR, 11 October 2011) ECLI:CE:ECHR:2011:1011JUD005312409.

692 Cf William Thomas Worster, 'The Obligation to Grant Nationality to Stateless Children Under Customary International Law' (2019) 27 Michigan State International Law Review 441, 483.

wanted to obtain Maltese nationality. He was, however, born out of wedlock to a British mother and a Maltese father. Because Maltese nationality law treated children born in and out of wedlock differently, Genovese was unable to acquire Maltese nationality, whereas children born in wedlock in the same situation could receive this nationality. He complained to the Court of a violation of Article 14 in conjunction with Article 8 of the Convention. The ECtHR agreed that he was treated differently without reasonable and objective justification contrary to Article 14.[693] This case shows that children in similar situations should not be treated differently in nationality laws and led to law reform in Malta.[694]

Two further important ECHR cases with regard to children and nationality were decided in 2014: *Mennesson* and *Labassee v. France*.[695] These cases both concerned France's refusal to grant legal recognition to the parent-child relationships that were established legally in the United States through a surrogacy arrangement. Because these two cases and the decisions of the Court therein are so similar, the discussion here focuses on the *Mennesson* case solely. In the *Mennesson* case both the French parents and their two children born through the surrogacy arrangement in the US complained to the Court of a violation of Article 8 of the Convention. Their complaint was based on their inability to obtain legal recognition in France – their claims were dismissed up to the French Court of Cassation – of the parent-child relationships established abroad as a result of a surrogacy agreement, which they believed harmed the children's best interests.[696] French law, however, prohibits surrogacy. The French government considers that surrogacy is a moral and ethical issue, which allows the state a wide margin of appreciation in these matters. The Court agrees that there is a lack of consensus regarding the legality of surrogacy arrangements in Europe, which reflects that recourse to a surrogacy arrangement raises sensitive ethical questions. It also confirms that states must in principle be afforded a wide margin of appreciation regarding the decision whether or not to authorize this method of assisted reproduction and whether or not to recognize a legal parent-child relationship between children legally conceived as the result of a surrogacy arrangement abroad and the intended parents.[697] However, the Court also

---

693 *Genovese v Malta* App No 53124/09 (ECHR, 11 October 2011) ECLI:CE:ECHR:2011:1011 JUD005312409, paras 48–49.

694 ENS, 'Preventing Childhood Statelessness in Europe: Gaps, Issues and Good Practices' (ENS 2014) 29 <https://www.statelessness.eu/updates/publication/preventing-childhood-statelessness-europe-issues-gaps-and-good-practices> accessed 3 July 2021.

695 *Mennesson v France* App No 65192/11 (ECHR, 26 June 2014) ECLI:CE:ECHR:2014:0626 JUD006519211; *Labassee c France* App No 65941/11 (ECHR, 26 June 2014) ECLI:CE:ECHR:2014 :0626JUD006594111. See about these cases also Liesbet Pluym, 'Mennesson v. France and Labassee v. France: Surrogate Motherhood Across Borders' (*Strasbourg Observers*, 16 July 2014) <https://strasbourgobservers.com/2014/07/16/mennesson-v-france-and-labassee-v-france-surrogate-motherhood-across-borders/> accessed 3 July 2021; and Claire Achmad, 'European Court of Human Rights: France Violated Child Rights in International Surrogacy Cases' (*Leiden Law Blog*, 28 July 2014) <http://leidenlawblog.nl/articles/european-court-of-human-rights-france-violated-child-rights-in-internationa> accessed 3 July 2021.

696 *Mennesson v France* App No 65192/11 (ECHR, 26 June 2014) ECLI:CE:ECHR:2014:0626 JUD006519211, para 43.

697 Ibid, para 79.

takes into account that an essential aspect of the identity of individuals is at stake where the legal parent-child relationship is concerned. The margin of appreciation afforded to France therefore needs to be reduced. The ECtHR continues:

> "Moreover, the solutions reached by the legislature – even within the limits of this margin – are not beyond the scrutiny of the Court. It falls to the Court to examine carefully the arguments taken into consideration and leading to the solution reached and to determine whether a fair balance has been struck between the competing interests of the State and those directly affected by that solution. In doing so, it must have regard to the essential principle according to which, whenever the situation of a child is in issue, the best interests of that child are paramount."[698]

The Court finds that France overstepped its margin of appreciation by the non-recognition of the legal parent-child relationships for the children as part of their right to respect for private life in light of the consequences thereof. Furthermore, the ECtHR questions the compatibility of that situation with the best interests of the child and states that "a serious question arises as to the compatibility of that situation with the children's best interests, respect for which must guide any decision in their regard".[699] The Court concludes that there has been a violation of Article 8 of the ECHR with regard to the two children in this case.

This case is highly relevant to nationality and statelessness of children because the non-recognition of the legal parent-child relationships in this case had the consequence that – at the time of the judgment – the children had not been granted French nationality. In its reasoning, the Court also recalls its *Genovese* judgment by reminding us of the fact that nationality is an element of a person's identity.[700] Because of non-recognition of the legal parent-child relationships, uncertainty exists as regards the possibility of the children to acquire a nationality, which could have "negative repercussions on the definition of their personal identity".[701] Moreover, in the advisory opinion that the ECtHR issued on this case upon request of the French Court of Cassation, it was clarified that private life under Article 8 ECHR

> "of a child born abroad through a gestational surrogacy arrangement requires that domestic law provide a possibility of recognition of a legal parent-child relationship with the intended mother, designated in the birth certificate legally established abroad as the "legal mother"."[702]

698 Ibid, para 81.
699 Ibid. para 99.
700 Ibid, para 97.
701 Ibid.
702 *Advisory Opinion concerning the Recognition in Domestic Law of a Legal Parent-Child Relationship between a Child Born through a Gestational Surrogacy Arrangement Abroad and the Intended Mother* Request no. P16-2018-001 (ECtHR, 10 April 2019) para 46. On the Advisory Opinion, also refer to Adam Weiss, 'Case Note: Mennesson v France and Advisory Opinion concerning the Recognition in Domestic Law of a Legal Parent-Child Relationship between a Child Born through a Gestational Surrogacy Arrangement Abroad and the Intended Mother' (2019) 1 Statelessness and Citizenship Review 343.

In this regard, considerations regarding nationality were taken into account, as "there is a risk that [...] children [born through surrogacy arrangements] will be denied the access to their intended mother's nationality which the legal parent-child relationship guarantees"[703]

The case as a whole can therefore be read as reinforcing the need to take into account the best interests of the child in any decision regarding them, including decisions on a child's right to nationality.[704] By referencing the 'best interests of the child', a concept drawn from the CRC, the ECtHR invites this treaty into its considerations. One might therefore wonder whether every child's right to acquire a nationality, which is ensured by the CRC[705], is of importance here as well and whether it would not be in the best interests of the child to indeed acquire a nationality, and not to remain stateless – also given the severe effects that this can have on a child's life.[706] As such, the reasoning in this case could help to prevent childhood statelessness. Furthermore, surrogacy – involving international surrogacy arrangements – can be considered to be one of the complex issues relating to statelessness, because such reproductive techniques are not always accommodated in nationality regulations of the countries involved. This could result in a child remaining stateless.[707] In this context, the *Mennesson* case is again of importance in that it demonstrates that "even where domestic law does not regulate this question, states must nevertheless act in such a way as to ensure children's right to a nationality, in line with the best interests of the child".[708] Here, this case aids in preventing childhood statelessness, because every child should be able to acquire a nationality, even where a child is born in the context of a surrogacy agreement. Moreover, the case should also be

> "read more broadly, as requiring states to guarantee that the birth of any child connected to a state has their birth registered by that state. This includes any child born in the territory of the state, as well as children born abroad whose intended parents are citizens."[709]

Note also that in another, similar case, the Court decided in the same way. This case was that of *Foulon et Bouvet c. France* and judgment was delivered in 2016.[710] The case

703 *Advisory Opinion concerning the Recognition in Domestic Law of a Legal Parent-Child Relationship between a Child Born through a Gestational Surrogacy Arrangement Abroad and the Intended Mother* Request no. P16–2018–001 (ECtHR, 10 April 2019) para 40.

704 See also ENS, 'No Child Should be Stateless' (ENS 2015); ISI, *World's Stateless: Children* (Wolf Legal Publishers 2017) 432–433.

705 Art 7 CRC.

706 UNHCR, 'I Am Here, I Belong. The Urgent Need to End Childhood Statelessness' (UNHCR 2015) available at www.unhcr.org/ibelong/wp-content/uploads/2015-10-StatelessReport_ENG15-web.pdf> accessed 3 July 2021.

707 Sanoj Rajan, 'International Surrogacy Arrangements and Statelessness' in ISI, *World's Stateless: Children* (Wolf Legal Publishers 2017) 374–384; Jyothi Kanics, 'Preventing and Addressing Statelessness in the Context of International Surrogacy Arrangements' (2014) 19 Tilburg Law Review 117, 120.

708 ENS, 'No Child Should Be Stateless' (ENS 2015) 24.

709 Adam Weiss, 'Case Note: Mennesson v France and Advisory Opinion concerning the Recognition in Domestic Law of a Legal Parent–Child Relationship between a Child Born through a Gestational Surrogacy Arrangement Abroad and the Intended Mother' (2019) 1 Statelessness and Citizenship Review 343, 349.

710 *Foulon et Bouvet c France* App Nos 9063/14 & 10410/14 (ECHR, 21 July 2016) ECLI:CE:ECHR:2016:07 21JUD000906314.

concerned the refusal of the French authorities to register the births of children born to French nationals in India, because they were suspected to have been born as the result of a surrogacy agreement. As such, the case indeed presents a similar situation as in the *Mennesson* and *Labassee* cases. The ECtHR therefore explicitly refers to these two cases and sees in the circumstances of this case no reason to conclude differently than in these cases.[711] Accordingly, the Court finds a violation of the right to private life as regards the children in this case. This confirmation reaffirms the Court's commitment to the best interests of the child under Article 8 of the Convention.

Various legal instruments regarding the nationality and statelessness of children are thus available in the context of the CoE. These reinforce and elaborate the dominant *jus sanguinis* principle for acquisition of nationality by newborn children, but also try to mitigate the problems that arise from this by introducing *jus soli* elements as additional safeguards, or elaborating on application of *jus sanguinis* in situations that are less straightforward, for instance in cases of surrogacy. As mentioned in paragraph 3.2.2, there has also been some attention paid to childhood statelessness specifically by PACE and in the CoE Action Plan on Protecting Refugee and Migrant Children in Europe. Concrete further guidance or next steps have as of the time of writing not (yet) been introduced. Nonetheless, childhood statelessness remains an issue that is on the agenda of the CoE.

3.3.2. CONFLICTS OF NATIONALITY LAW, LOSS AND DEPRIVATION OF NATIONALITY

The legal bond between a person and a state may be lost or may cease to exist at some point, which could, if a person has no other nationality, result in statelessness. The ECN sets out a number of relevant standards that help to prevent statelessness in such situations.

As regards the loss of nationality, the ECN is clear. Article 7, paragraph 1, of the ECN says that a state party may in its laws not provide for the loss of its nationality *ex lege* or at the initiative of the state except in an exhaustive number of cases.[712] Also, according to Article 7, paragraph 2, ECN, states may include in their national legislation rules for the loss of its nationality by children whose parents lose that nationality, except for cases that concern voluntary service in a foreign military force or conduct that is seriously prejudicial to the vital interests of the state. A child shall, however, not lose that nationality if one of the parents retains it.[713]

711 Ibid, para 47.

712 Art 7(1) ECN; CoE, *Explanatory Report to the European Convention on Nationality* (Strasbourg, 6 November 1997, CETS No. 166) para 58. For a more elaborate overview of the cases of loss of nationality included in Article 7(1) ECN, please consult for instance: Sandra Mantu, *Contingent Citizenship. The Law and Practice of Citizenship Deprivation in International, European and National Perspectives* (Ipskamp Drukkers 2014) 60–64; Roland Schärer, 'The European Convention on Nationality' (1997) 40 German Yearbook of International Law 438–459, 448–452; Gerard-René de Groot, 'The European Convention on Nationality: A Step towards a *Ius Commune* in the Field of Nationality Law' (2007) 7 Maastricht Journal of European and Comparative Law 117–157, 139 ff.

713 Art 7(2) ECN.

Furthermore, and importantly, Article 7, paragraph 3, ECN provides a specific application of the general ECN principle to avoid statelessness. It adds that a state party may not provide in its internal law for the loss of its nationality under paragraphs 1 and 2 of that Article if the person concerned would thereby become stateless. One exception is made: a person can become stateless when he or she acquires the nationality of the state party by means of fraudulent conduct, false information or concealment of any relevant fact attributable to the applicant.[714] Both children and adults can be subject to statelessness under this circumstance.[715] When placing this in light of the obligations that follow from the 1961 Convention in this regard, it can be seen that the prohibition of statelessness of the ECN here goes further than that of the 1961 Convention as the latter allows for loss of nationality with statelessness as a consequence on more grounds.[716]

Because of the particular attention that the ECN pays to multiple nationality, which might lead to conflict of nationality laws, it needs to be addressed here as well in light of the prevention of statelessness. As was seen above in paragraph 3.2.2, the ECN takes a neutral position regarding multiple nationality. It even requires states parties to allow multiple nationality in two cases: children who acquired different nationalities automatically at birth and nationals who possess another nationality where this other nationality is automatically acquired by marriage.[717] States are free to allow for other cases of multiple nationality, but are also free to limit these cases. In comparison to the 1963 CoE Convention, this is an improvement. Attempting to limit all kinds of cases of multiple nationality could in certain situations perhaps lead to statelessness, if laws of another state regarding nationality are misinterpreted for example and a person then acquires no nationality or loses the only nationality he or she had because the state in question thought that he or she possessed the nationality of another state. The fact that the ECN approaches this issue more openly is in light of the prevention of statelessness therefore only to be welcomed.

The CM Recommendation on the avoidance and reduction of statelessness reiterates that nationals should not be arbitrarily deprived of their nationality, and that no form of loss of nationality – whether at the initiative of the state or at the initiative of the individual – should result in statelessness.[718] The Recommendation provides further guidance on provisions of the ECN. Even where a person could be deprived of nationality because of fraud, a state should not necessarily use this measure so as to avoid statelessness as far as possible. It should also consider in such a decision "the gravity of the facts, as well as other relevant circumstances, such as the genuine

---

714 Arts 7(3) conj Art 7(1)(b) ECN.

715 CoE, *Explanatory Report to the European Convention on Nationality* (Strasbourg, 6 November 1997, CETS No. 166) para 77.

716 Cf Art 8 1961 Convention; CoE, *Explanatory Report to the European Convention on Nationality* (Strasbourg, 6 November 1997, CETS No. 166) para 77.

717 Art 14 ECN; CoE, *Explanatory Report to the European Convention on Nationality* (Strasbourg, 6 November 1997, CETS No. 166) para 94.

718 CoE CM Recommendation No. R (99) 18 of the Committee of Ministers to the Member States on the avoidance and reduction of statelessness (679th meeting of the Ministers' Deputies, 15 September 1999) para (c).

and effective link of these persons with the state concerned".[719] With these concrete pointers, the Recommendation thus explicates how statelessness should be avoided as much as possible.

Loss and deprivation of nationality have been considered by the Court in its case law as well. Clearly relevant is the case of *Ramadan v. Malta*[720], because it involves statelessness directly. The applicant in this case is Ramadan, who is stateless. He was an Egyptian citizen, but was allowed to renounce his Egyptian citizenship after he acquired Maltese nationality subsequent to his marriage to a Maltese citizen. After marital problems arose – of a severe nature: the applicant was convicted for assaulting his pregnant wife – a Maltese judge annulled the marriage and held that there had been simulation of marriage.[721] Ramadan did not notify the authorities of the annulment. In 2003, he married a Russian citizen and it was only in that context that the authorities became aware of the annulment of the applicant's first marriage. After a notification and some proceedings, he was deprived of his Maltese nationality in 2007 with immediate effect because it had been obtained fraudulently and he became stateless.[722] In the meantime, two children had been born from his second marriage. They are both Maltese nationals. After unsuccessfully instituting constitutional redress procedures, Ramadan complained to the ECtHR of a violation of Article 8 of the Convention.

> "The applicant complained that the decision to divest him of his Maltese citizenship had not been made in accordance with the law. It had interfered with his right to private and family life and exposed him to the risk of being separated from his family. The decision had not been accompanied by the relevant procedural safeguards as required under Article 8 of the Convention and the State had failed to fulfil its positive obligation to protect his rights under that provision. Lastly, the applicant complained that the decision had left him stateless. He thus had to live in a state of uncertainty, where he could not even leave the country for fear of not being let back in."[723]

From a perspective of the prevention of statelessness, in particular preventing deprivation of nationality, this case presents an opportunity for the Court to make a statement. The ECtHR, however, declares parts of the complaint inadmissible. According to the Court, the applicant could not claim to be a victim of a violation of his rights under Article 8 in relation to his potential removal from Malta, because a removal order had not been issued (yet) and because this order could still be challenged if it were issued. Interestingly, the ECtHR makes a specific observation regarding the statelessness of the applicant:

---

719 Ibid, para II (C)(c).
720 *Ramadan v Malta* App No 76136/12 (ECHR, 21 June 2016) ECLI:CE:ECHR:2016:0621JUD007613612.
721 Ibid, para 14.
722 Ibid, paras 23–24.
723 Ibid, para 49.

> "Moreover, on a more practical level, it appears that the applicant is currently stateless; thus, as the situation stands to date, it cannot be said that he is under a threat of expulsion [...] as there is no guarantee that the Egyptian authorities would accept him, nor is it likely that he could be removed to another country. In any event, such arrangements would take a certain amount of time, and in the event of a removal order being issued and steps being taken in respect of its execution, the applicant would still have a possibility of pursuing the relevant remedies."[724]

Some have observed that it almost seems as if it does not matter that the person has become stateless.[725] Nonetheless, the Court did consider the merits of the complaint regarding the deprivation of citizenship and its consequences under Article 8 of the ECHR. The ECtHR does not distinguish between the situations where acquisition of citizenship is arbitrarily denied (*cf.* the *Karassev* case) or where nationality is revoked[726], such as in the present case, and goes on to establish whether this revocation was arbitrary. It finds that the deprivation was in accordance with the law and accompanied by the necessary procedural safeguards, and is therefore not arbitrary and can as such not raise an issue under Article 8. Also, the Court seems to consider the consequences of the deprivation in this case negligible and attaches significant weight to the applicants' own actions that led to this situation and that could have eased the effects of it on his private- and family life. The ECtHR also seems to question whether the applicant is truly stateless because no official documents were produced.[727] The ECtHR concludes that there has been no violation of Article 8.

In light of the existing international instruments dealing with the loss of nationality resulting in statelessness, this judgment should not have come as a surprise. According to both the 1961 Convention and the ECN – Malta has not ratified these treaties; only signed the ECN – nationality may be lost, even if a person would thereby become stateless, if that nationality was obtained fraudulently.[728] In the absence of a right to a nationality in the ECHR and with – according to the Court – limited impact on the private- and family life of the applicant, the ECtHR was not willing to go beyond its current interpretations of Article 8 of the Convention. In terms of the contribution of this judgment to the discourse under the ECHR relating to nationality and the issue of statelessness, it therefore seems that this decision does not help to address it. However, a closer look at the case demonstrates that the Court reaffirmed its statement from the *Karassev* case[729] and examined the merits of the case, i.e. it considered the arbitrariness

724 Ibid, para 56.

725 Marie-Bénédicte Dembour, 'Ramadan v. Malta: When Will the Strasbourg Court Understand that Nationality is a Core Human Rights Issue?' (*Strasbourg Observers*, 22 July 2016) <https://strasbourgobservers.com/2016/07/22/ramadan-v-malta-when-will-the-strasbourg-court-understand-that-nationality-is-a-core-human-rights-issue/> accessed 4 July 2021.

726 *Ramadan v Malta* App No 76136/12 (ECHR, 21 June 2016) ECLI:CE:ECHR:2016:0621JUD007613612, para 85.

727 Ibid, paras 90, 92.

728 Art 7 ECN; Art 8 1961 Convention.

729 *Ramadan v Malta* App No 76136/12 (ECHR, 21 June 2016) ECLI:CE:ECHR:2016:0621JUD007613612, para 84.

of the revocation and it took into account the situation of the applicant involved. As such, it demonstrated the importance of looking at the consequences and situation of the person affected by loss of citizenship, which is important in nationality matters and can help to address statelessness. More hope can perhaps be seen when turning to the dissenting opinion of Judge Pinto de Albuquerque, who recalls the right to nationality in international human rights law, criticizes the procedures and measures of the Maltese government and emphasizes that "creation and perpetuation of situations of statelessness should be avoided at any cost in a civilised Europe". He concludes: "It is high time for the Court to recognise explicitly that State citizenship belongs to the core of someone's identity, which is protected by Article 8 of the Convention."[730] Even though this represents only the opinion of one of the judges, it might be the direction in which the ECHR and its interpretations by the ECtHR could develop and/or could be encouraged to develop using strategic litigation.[731]

In 2017, the Court decided on a matter regarding deprivation of nationality in the case of *K2 v. the United Kingdom*.[732] Born in Sudan, K2 became a naturalized citizen of the UK in 2000. After being arrested for an offence, he left the UK and travelled to Somalia. Here, he took part in terrorism-related activities. In 2010, he was therefore deprived of his British nationality and excluded from the country. K2 complained under Article 8 that the decisions to deprive him of his UK citizenship and bar him from re-entering the country breached his right to respect for his family and private life and amounted to an attack on his reputation. He further complained that there were inadequate procedural safeguards to ensure effective respect for his Article 8 rights as there was very limited disclosure of the national security case against him and he was unable to participate effectively in the legal proceedings.[733]

In its assessment of the case, the Court recalled that arbitrary denial or revocation of citizenship could in certain circumstances raise an issue under Article 8 of the ECHR, because of its impact on the private life of a person. The ECtHR therefore has to examine whether the revocation was arbitrary and what the consequences thereof were for the applicant.[734] In doing so, the Court clearly sets out (again) the important standards to be taken into account when considering deprivation of nationality:

---

730 Ibid, Dissenting Opinion of Judge Pinto de Albuquerque.

731 Cf efforts to litigate strategically as regards statelessness, and more specific related issues such as statelessness determination and childhood statelessness, eg Maxim Ferschtman, 'Litigating for the stateless – a bumpy, but steady road upwards (*ENS Blog*, 13 July 2013) <https://www.statelessness.eu/updates/blog/litigating-stateless-bumpy-steady-road-upwards> accessed 4 July 2021; ENS, 'Strategic Litigation: An Obligation for Statelessness Determination under the European Convention on Human Rights?' (2014) ENS Discusssion Paper 09/14 <https://www.statelessness.eu/updates/publication/obligation-statelessness-determination-under-european-convention-human-rights> accessed 17 October 2021; ISI, *World's Stateless: Children* (Wolf Legal Publishers 2017) ch 12.

732 *K2 v the United Kingdom* App No 42387/13 (ECHR, 9 March 2017) ECLI:CE:ECHR:2017:0207DEC004238713.

733 Ibid, para 46.

734 Ibid, para 49.

> "In determining arbitrariness, the Court has had regard to whether the revocation was in accordance with the law; whether it was accompanied by the necessary procedural safeguards, including whether the person deprived of citizenship was allowed the opportunity to challenge the decision before courts affording the relevant guarantees; and whether the authorities acted diligently and swiftly (...)."[735]

The ECtHR continues by addressing the applicant's procedural and substantive complaints together and by reviewing the 'conditions' relating to the determination of arbitrariness in this case. It also notes that in view of the consequences of the revocation for the applicant that K2 was not rendered stateless by the decision to deprive him of his British citizenship, and that his claims related to his family life were not well-substantiated, nor seemed to amount to a breach of Article 8.[736] The Court concludes that insofar as the applicant's Article 8 complaint concerns the decision to deprive him of his citizenship, it is manifestly ill-founded and must be rejected. As regards the part of the complaint that addresses his exclusion from the UK, the ECtHR reiterated that, subject to their treaty obligations, states have the right to control the entry, residence and expulsion of aliens.[737] Having regard to the limited nature of the interference of the exclusion with K2's private- and family life, and the extent of his terrorism-related activities, the ECtHR does not consider that the decision to bar him from re-entering the UK was disproportionate to the legitimate aim pursued: namely, the protection of the public from the threat of terrorism.[738] This complaint is therefore also rejected by the Court.

When considering this case from the perspective of addressing nationality matters and statelessness, it is clear that it sheds light on a practice that is increasingly used by states to deal with terrorism: deprivation of nationality. The case is helpful in that it clearly sets out a number of points that are to be taken into account when determining whether revocation of citizenship is arbitrary. It is also clear on the importance of having due regard for the consequences of such revocation for the individual(s) affected by it. In this sense, it presents a straightforward framework on revocation of nationality. Because these guarantees are clearly delineated, it could help in preventing statelessness resulting from deprivation, also because the consequences for the person concerned are considered. That people who become stateless as a result of revocation of nationality will not always be protected by this, was already shown in the analysis of the *Ramadan* case above.

The applicant in this case, however, submitted a complaint under Article 14 read in conjunction with Article 8 as well. According to him, he was treated differently from UK citizens considered a threat to national security who did not hold a second nationality, as they could not be deprived of their British citizenship.[739] This complaint,

---

735 Ibid, para 50.
736 Ibid, para 62.
737 Ibid, para 65.
738 Ibid, para 66.
739 Ibid, para 47.

however, had not been raised before in domestic courts, which meant that K2 had failed to exhaust domestic remedies in this regard. This led this part of the complaint to be rejected by the ECtHR. This part of the complaint, nonetheless, seems to be very interesting and connects to the matter of the creation of different 'classes' of citizenship that is raised in relation to non-discrimination in nationality matters in paragraph 3.3.5 below. It would have been interesting to see what the Court would have done with this matter, given its judgment in the *Biao* case and because it is a clear side effect of these widely used policies to combat terrorism.

Nationality deprivation continues to be an issue that is raised in applications to the ECtHR. In 2020, the the Court decided on a case from France in this regard: *Ghoumid and others v. France.*[740] The case concerned five applicants who all were dual nationals. They were tried and convicted of terrorism-related crimes in 2007. In 2015, they were deprived of their French nationalities. Their arguments to challenge the decision before the ECtHR relied on the right to family life and the right to private life under Article 8 of the Convention, and the *ne bis in idem*-principle as enshrined in Article 4 of Protocol No. 7 to the ECHR (the right not to be tried or punished twice for the same offence).

At the outset of its assessment of the case, the Court declares that the deprivation of nationality which affects the applicants does not constitute an interference with the exercise of their right to respect for their family life, because they can remain in France (at that moment).[741] That seems to indicate that (legal) stay in the country and nationality are not connected – according to the ECtHR. Later on in its judgement, the Court nonetheless acknowledges that deprivation of French nationality has weakened their ability to stay in France.[742] On the impact on the applicants' private life, the ECtHR finds no violation of Article 8 either. In finding no violation, the Court first examines the arbitrariness of the measures taken against the applicants: whether these were lawful, whether they are accompanied by the necessary procedural guarantees, and whether the authorities acted with diligence and promptness.[743] What is particularly interesting here, is that the applicants were deprived of nationality after a long period had passed since they had committed their crimes and were convicted. That no violation was found in this regard in view of the requirement of diligence and promptness, has been criticized[744]:

---

740 *Ghoumid and others v France* App No 52273/16 (ECHR, 25 June 2020) ECLI:CE:ECHR:2020:0625 JUD005227316.

741 Ibid, para 42.

742 Ibid, para 49. See also Karin de Vries & Kees Groenendijk, 'Annotatie [Case Note] Ghoumid e.a. t. Frankrijk (EHRM, nr. 52273/16 e.v.)' (*European Human Rights Cases – Updates* 17 September 2020) para 5 <https://www.ehrc-updates.nl/commentaar/210803?skip_boomportal_auth=1> accessed 4 July 2021.

743 *Ghoumid and others v France* App No 52273/16 (ECHR, 25 June 2020) ECLI:CE:ECHR:2020:0625 JUD005227316, para 44.

744 This standard has been rendered meaningless almost according to some, see Karin de Vries & Kees Groenendijk, 'Annotatie [Case Note] Ghoumid e.a. t. Frankrijk (EHRM, nr. 52273/16 e.v.)' (*European Human Rights Cases – Updates* 17 September 2020) para 7 https://www.ehrc-updates.nl/commentaar/210803?skip_boomportal_auth=1 accessed 4 July 2021. See also *Ghoumid and others v France* App No 52273/16 (ECHR, 25 June 2020) ECLI:CE:ECHR:2020:0625JUD005227316, para 45.

> "[T]he standard of "diligence and promptness" of the European Court case-law is normally designed to prevent any delayed measure. Moreover, as the French Government acknowledged during the proceedings, this delay was entirely caused by the political context. These five nationality revocations were clearly meant to show political action against terrorism, in a climate of uncertainty (after the Charlie Hebdo shooting, before the Paris attacks). Far from issuing any criticism, the judges considered that "given the circumstances of this case" this timeframe did not reveal any arbitrariness. In other words, the political purpose of the revocations had precisely the effect to justify the delay of the measures – where one could have imagined the exact opposite."[745]

On the consequences of the deprivation of nationality on the applicants' private lives, the Court takes into account that – so far – no removal measures have been taken. The ECtHR does acknowledge though that deprivation of nationality constitutes loss of an element of their identity as protected by the right to private life.[746] In its reasoning in relation to this, the Court says it understands the government's considerations for showing a greater firmness as regards terrorism-related crimes, and takes into account the applicants' own actions. The ECtHR also says that it attaches great importance to the fact that all applicants have another nationality, meaning that the decision to deprive does not render them stateless.[747] This seems to indicate that the considerations and finding might have turned out differently if statelessness would have resulted in this case, but certainly signifies the Court's concern with avoiding statelessness in these situations. In conclusion, the consequences of the measures taken against the applicants on their private life are not considered disproportionate by the ECtHR.[748]

The argument regarding the principle of *ne bis in idem*, as included in Article 4 of Protocol No. 7 – meaning that nationality deprivation would constitute a penalty, which is actually based on a previous criminal conviction – had not been submitted to the Court before in this context. The ECtHR, however, finds that the nationality deprivation measures respond to terrorist acts which undermine the very foundation of democracy. The Court further recalls that this measure does not in itself result in the removal from French territory of the applicants and that is not a sanction that could be said to be criminal in nature.[749] The application as regards Article 4 of Protocol No. 7 is therefore declared inadmissible. Commentators have observed that the ECtHR thereby has accepted that deprivation of nationality in a counter-terrorism context is a measure which primarily

745 Jules Lepoutre, 'Ghoumid and others v. France: The Grey Hole of Nationality Revocation' (*GLOBALCIT Blog*, 5 August 2020) <https://globalcit.eu/ghoumid-and-others-v-france-the-grey-hole-of-nationality-revocation/> accessed 4 July 2021.

746 *Ghoumid and others v France* App No 52273/16 (ECHR, 25 June 2020) ECLI:CE:ECHR:2020:0625JUD005227316, para 49.

747 Ibid, para 50.

748 Ibid, para 51.

749 Ibid, para 72.

serves to express the requirements imposed on national – in this case French – citizenship and which is to some extent disconnected from the behavior of those affected.[750]

A case concerning nationality deprivation against the UK is pending before the Court at the time of writing: *Pham v. the UK*.[751] It is a case that involves (the risk of) statelessness. The applicant is a British naturalized citizen who was born in Vietnam. Vietnam does not recognize his Vietnamese citizenship and his British citizenship was deprived for reasons of national security in 2011. He remains married to a British citizen, and they have two children. The complaint before the ECtHR relates to an alleged violation of Article 8 ECHR in view of the UK decision to deprive Pham of his nationality. A third party submission has been made in this case, highlighting the need to take (the risk of) statelessness into account when assessing the consequences of the deprivation measure, as well as the importance of an examination whether statelessness would result from the measure before issuing a decision in view of Article 53 ECHR[752] in conjunction with obligations under the 1954 and 1961 Conventions.[753] As such, the case will be another opportunity for the ECtHR to consider deprivation of nationality and statelessness.

Within the PACE, attention has also been paid to deprivation of nationality. In 2019, a report on withdrawing nationality as a measure to combat terrorism was presented, which approached the issue from a human rights perspective.[754] In contrast with the more permissive stance of the Court, the PACE report critiqued the use of deprivation measures in a counter-terrorism context:

> "In the light of [...] human rights and other considerations, the deprivation of nationality should not occur on grounds of terrorist activities. Nevertheless, those States whose legislation allows it must ensure that deprivation of nationality is not arbitrary. In particular, it should be decided or reviewed by a criminal court, with full respect for all procedural guarantees, should not be discriminatory and should not lead to statelessness. It should be proportionate to the pursued objective and applied only if other measures foreseen in domestic law are not sufficient. The notion of 'conduct seriously prejudicial to the vital interests' must be interpreted narrowly and be based on an individual assessment, and national security interests should be carefully weighed against human rights. Terrorism is indeed a serious threat to our societies, but we should not sacrifice our values because of it.

---

750 Karin de Vries & Kees Groenendijk, 'Annotatie [Case Note] Ghoumid e.a. t. Frankrijk (EHRM, nr. 52273/16 e.v.)' (*European Human Rights Cases – Updates* 17 September 2020) para 10 <https://www.ehrc-updates.nl/commentaar/210803?skip_boomportal_auth=1> accessed 4 July 2021.

751 *Minh Quang Pham v the United Kingdom* App No 37478/20 (ECtHR, communicated on 25 November 2020).

752 Art 53 ECHR contains a safeguard for existing human rights and reads as follows: "Nothing in this Convention shall be construed as limiting or derogating from any of the human rights and fundamental freedoms which may be ensured under the laws of any High Contracting Party or under any other agreement to which it is a party."

753 AIRE Centre & ENS, 'Written Submission on Behalf of the Interveners – Pham v. the UK', 19 April 2021 <https://www.statelessness.eu/sites/default/files/2021-04/Pham_v_UK-TPI_AIRE-Centre-ENS-Apr_2021.pdf> accessed 8 July 2021.

754 CoE PACE/Tineke Strik, 'Report: Withdrawing Nationality as a Measure to Combat Terrorism: A Human Rights-Compatible Approach? (2019) Doc 14790.

Furthermore, deprivation of nationality is not an effective measure to combat terrorism and may even be counter-effective to the goals of counter-terrorism policy."[755]

Such considerations resemble the synthesis of international (human rights) standards on the matter as provided in the Principles on Deprivation of Nationality as a National Security Measure, which also conclude that states should not deprive people of their nationality in a national security context and that any exception to this is subject to limits set by other principles of international law, including non-discrimination and the avoidance of statelessness for instance.[756] PACE furthermore adopted a resolution on the matter, voicing its concern that some states "consider nationality as a privilege and not a right".[757] It urged CoE states to review their laws on this considering international norms on (arbitrary) deprivation of nationality, to provide safeguards against statelessness in such laws, and to avoid (indirect) discrimination against minorities.[758] It also encouraged those states that had not yet ratified the 1954 and 1961 Statelessness Conventions and the ECN to do so.[759] Moreover, PACE has recommended to the CM that they prepare a comparative analysis of the laws of member states on deprivation of nationality in a counter-terrorism context and draft guidelines on deprivation of nationality and measures that could replace such deprivation powers.[760] The CM responded recognizing that deprivation of nationality could impact on the right to a nationality under Article 15 of the UDHR and Article 8 ECHR.[761] The CM believes, however, that the ECN gives enough guidance and guarantees on the matter, and that states should consider ratifying this instrument if they have not already done so.[762] The proposed study could, according to the CM, be included in the prevention activities of the CoE Counter-Terrorism Strategy (2018–2022).[763]

Whereas the considerations above concerned loss of nationality at the initiative of the state, and rules that states may set in this regard, it is also possible that a person wants to renounce their nationality. According to Article 8 of the ECN, loss of nationality that is voluntarily requested by the individual – renunciation of nationality – shall be permitted as long as this individual does not thereby become stateless. This means that in cases where an individual has to meet certain criteria before he or she can acquire a new nationality, but fails to do so and thus fails to obtain this nationality, the state whose nationality was renounced must allow recovery of its nationality or consider

---

755 Ibid, para 52.

756 Principles on Deprivation of Nationality as a National Security Measure (2020) Principle 4 – Basic Rule <https://www.refworld.org/pdfid/5f3bf26d4.pdf> accessed 8 July 2021.

757 PACE Resolution 2263 (2019): Withdrawing Nationality as a Measure to Combat Terrorism: A Human Rights-Compatible Approach?, para 5.

758 Ibid, para 9.

759 Ibid, para 9.9.

760 PACE Recommendation 2145 (2019): Withdrawing Nationality as a Measure to Combat Terrorism: A Human Rights-Compatible Approach?

761 CM Reply to Recommendation 2145 (2019) (359th meeting of the Ministers' Deputies, 5 November 2019) Doc. 15006, para 2.

762 Ibid, para 3.

763 Ibid, para 4; CM, 'Council of Europe Counter-Terrorism Strategy (2019–2022)' (2018) CM(2018)86-addfinal.

that it was never lost.[764] On renunciation, the CM Recommendation on the avoidance and reduction of statelessness furthermore advises that renunciation "without the possession, actual acquisition or guarantee of acquisition of another nationality" should be without effect.[765] Moreover, if it is necessary to first lose nationality before new nationality can be acquired, the state concerned should grant nationality – "even if the previous one is not immediately lost".[766] The relevant CoE instruments are thus clearly geared towards preventing statelessness in (almost) any case.

Overall, it is clear that different legal instruments address loss and deprivation of citizenship in the CoE context. Even though legal principles like the avoidance of statelessness and non-discrimination are well-represented there, it does not necessarily in concrete cases lead to no statelessness at all, as jurisprudence of the ECtHR has shown. The use of deprivation of nationality in a national security context also leads to new cases and challenges in relation to questions of statelessness and nationality.

3.3.3. STATE SUCCESSION

State succession has occurred within or affected a number of states that are members of the CoE today. As we saw above, the CoE has actively sought to address this. This paragraph explores the background and context of the legal efforts in this regard further, as well as the substance of the norms developed.

As could be seen in section 3.2, the Venice Commission contributes to continuing the development of democracy, and "has proved to be relatively effective in providing guidance where politics and law converge".[767] In 1996, the Venice Commission adopted the Declaration on the Consequences of State Succession for the Nationality of Natural Persons and published a report on this matter.[768] This Declaration includes different principles: the avoidance of statelessness, the right of every person to a nationality and the principle that questions relating to nationality fall to the jurisdiction of states within the limits provided by international law.[769] It furthermore contains a number

---

764 CoE, *Explanatory Report to the European Convention on Nationality* (Strasbourg, 6 November 1997, CETS No. 166) para 79.

765 CoE CM Recommendation No. R (99) 18 of the Committee of Ministers to the Member States on the avoidance and reduction of statelessness (679th meeting of the Ministers' Deputies, 15 September 1999) para II (C)(a).

766 Ibid, para II (C)(b).

767 Wolfgang Hoffmann-Riem, 'The Venice Commission of the Council of Europe – Standards and Impact' (2014) 25 European Journal of International Law 579.

768 Declaration on the Consequences of State Succession for the Nationality of Natural Persons adopted by the European Commission for Democracy through Law at its 28th Plenary Meeting (Venice, 13–14 September 1996), published in CDL, 'Consequences of State Succession for Nationality' (Strasbourg, 10 February 1997) CDL-INF (97) 1. This publication also includes the report and an explanatory report to the Declaration. This was later also published as CDL, *Consequences of State Succession for Nationality. Report by the Venice Commission* (Collection Science and Technique of Democracy, No. 23, Council of Europe Publishing 1998).

769 Declaration on the Consequences of State Succession for the Nationality of Natural Persons, Arts 2, 5 & 6. cf Ineta Ziemele, 'State Succession and Issues of Nationality and Statelessness' in Alice Edwards

of situations in which nationality should be granted by the successor state and also provides that the predecessor state shall not withdraw its nationality from its own nationals who have been unable to acquire the nationality of a successor State.[770] This document, however, is not legally binding. Nonetheless, it was taken into account when the 1999 ILC Draft Articles, the ECN and the ECSS were drafted later.[771]

Moving on to one of these instruments, the ECN, it can be seen that part of the ECN is devoted to the specific issue of state succession in relation to nationality. As regards statelessness, the ECN stresses that states parties are to respect a number of principles, in particular in order to avoid statelessness.[772] This really is the primary concern of the provisions of the ECN on state succession and it aims to reinforce Article 10 of the 1961 Convention.[773] While not repeating the message of the 1961 Convention explicitly, the ECN indeed seems to do so by providing more implementable rules for states to work with in cases of state succession. Still, these rules remain very much expressed as (general) principles that are to be taken into account by states. This makes these provisions, in particular Article 18 of the ECN, somewhat vague and general, and not concrete or easily implementable.[774] Apparently no consensus could be reached on more precise standards at that time. Nonetheless, the fact that attention is paid to the issue of state succession separately with the avoidance of statelessness as its main concern is clearly an achievement as regards the prevention of statelessness.

The CM Recommendation on the avoidance and reduction of statelessness does not provide further guidance, but is short on the matter of state succession: "States should endeavour to regulate matters relating to statelessness, where appropriate and in particular in cases of state succession, by international agreement."[775]

Some years after the adoption of this Recommendation and the ECN, the CoE drafted a specific treaty on this issue, to specify its rules on statelessness in the context of state succession: the CoE Convention on the Avoidance of Statelessness in Relation to State

& Laura van Waas (eds), *Nationality and Statelessness under International Law* (Cambridge University Press 2014) 217–246, 223.

770 Declaration on the Consequences of State Succession for the Nationality of Natural Persons, sections III & IV.

771 Francesco Costamagna, 'Statelessness in the Context of State Succession. An Appraisal under International Law' in Alessandra Annoni & Serena Forlati, *The Changing Role of Nationality in International Law* (Routledge 2013) 37–53, 41; Roland Schärer, 'The Council of Europe and the Reduction of Statelessness' (2006) 25 Refugee Survey Quarterly 33, 34.

772 Art 18(1) ECN.

773 CoE, *Explanatory Report to the European Convention on Nationality* (Strasbourg, 6 November 1997, CETS No. 166) paras. 107, 111.

774 See also Gerard-René de Groot, 'The European Convention on Nationality: A Step towards a *Ius Commune* in the Field of Nationality Law' (2007) 7 Maastricht Journal of European and Comparative Law 117–157, 153–154; Ineta Ziemele, 'State Succession and Issues of Nationality and Statelessness' in Alice Edwards & Laura van Waas, *Nationality and Statelessness under International Law* (Cambridge University Press 2014) 217–246, 226. For example, Art 18(1) ECHR reads: "In matters of nationality in cases of State succession, each State Party concerned shall respect the principles of the rule of law, the rules concerning human rights [...]".

775 CoE CM Recommendation No. R (99) 18 of the Committee of Ministers to the Member States on the avoidance and reduction of statelessness (679th meeting of the Ministers' Deputies, 15 September 1999) para I(e).

Succession. The ECSS is, as its name already says, aimed at avoiding statelessness, i.e. making sure that cases of statelessness are limited to a minimum. This treaty's most prominent aim is hence the prevention of statelessness. Its scope is furthermore restricted to statelessness arising from state succession and concerns, in principle, only state succession after the entry into force of the Convention.[776] However, that does not mean that the contribution of the ECSS to the prevention and resolution of statelessness is insignificant. State succession is one of the main causes of statelessness in Europe and preventing statelessness in the context of state succession is therefore important. A closer look at the ECSS's provisions demonstrates how this treaty both prevents and resolves statelessness in relation to state succession.

First and foremost, the ECSS only concerns the prevention of statelessness as a result of state succession – the transfer of territory.[777] It, however, prevents statelessness in this context in different ways, which are discussed in this paragraph. Part of the general rules of the ECSS are the right to a nationality (Article 2) and the prevention of statelessness (Article 3). Predecessor and/or successor states are obliged to take all appropriate measures to prevent people who, at the time of state succession, had the nationality of the predecessor state, from becoming stateless as a result of state succession.[778]

The core Articles 5 and 6 of the Convention provide further explanation as to the implementation of this obligation. In light of the current topic, statelessness in relation to state succession, one can imagine that these two Articles indeed contain the core rules on the matter and complement each other. That they indeed do so, can be seen when taking a closer look at the rules that these Articles lay down, aptly summarized by Sandra Mantu as follows:

> "1) a successor state shall grant its nationality to persons habitually resident in its territory, in particular if they become stateless as a result of state succession;
> 2) a predecessor state shall not withdraw its nationality from its nationals who have been unable to acquire the nationality of a successor state;
> 3) a successor state shall grant its nationality to persons habitually resident in a third state who become stateless as a result of the succession if they were born in the territory which has become the territory of the successor state, had their last habitual residence in it or have any other appropriate connection with the successor state."[779]

Obviously, Article 6 on the responsibility of the predecessor state only applies when the predecessor state continues to exist after state succession. Where the predecessor state ceases to exist or is not a party to the ECSS, only Article 5 applies.[780]

---

776 According to Art 15(2) ECSS a state can, however, declare by notification addressed to the Secretary General of the CoE at the time of expressing its consent to be bound by this Convention, or, at any time thereafter, that it will also apply the provisions of the ECSS to state succession occurring before the entry into force of the ECSS.

777 Cf Art 1(a) ECSS: "'State succession' means the replacement of one State by another in the responsibility for the international relations of territory".

778 Art 3 ECSS.

779 Sandra Mantu, *Contingent Citizenship: The Law and Practice of Citizenship Deprivation in International, European and National Perspectives* (Ipskamp Drukkers 2014) 58.

780 CoE, *Explanatory Report to the Council of Europe Convention on the Avoidance of Statelessness in relation to State Succession* (Strasbourg, 19 May 2006, CETS No. 200) para 29.

Article 5 of the ECSS entails that the successor state should grant nationality to any person who had the nationality of the predecessor state at the time of state succession, and who has or will become stateless if he or she was at the time habitually resident in the territory that has become territory of the successor state, or if they were not habitually resident, but still have an appropriate connection with the successor state. For this Article, habitual residence is an important element. If it is interpreted in a narrow manner, it could still lead to statelessness. The ECSS, fortunately, provides a definition: habitual residence means stable, factual residence[781] and "does not require any formal qualification", thus overcoming any discrepancies between formal and factual concepts of residence.[782] At the same time, it remains a rather open and broad concept, which states still may interpret in a stricter way. Another significant concept in this Article is the appropriate connection. According to Article 5(2) of the ECSS, such a connection can entail a legal bond to the territory of the predecessor state that is now part of successor state, birth on the territory that is now of the successor state, last habitual residence on territory that has now become part of the successor state. This it is not an exhaustive list though.[783] The usage of appropriate connection in this Article resembles a *jus soli* approach, as all of the connections have to do with the territory where a person was born, has a legal connection to or has habitually resided. That is quite remarkable for Europe, as states usually primarily rely on *jus sanguinis* in granting nationality. At the same time, it is a logical approach in attempting to prevent statelessness, as *jus soli* norms are more often used to correct gaps in nationality laws and prevent statelessness, for instance where nationality is to be granted to children born in the territory of a state who would otherwise be stateless.[784] It is also a logical approach given the specific context of state succession and the general principle that the population follows the territory.[785]

Article 6 provides that the predecessor state – if it continues to exist – shall not withdraw its nationality from nationals who do not acquire the nationality of the successor state and who would otherwise become stateless because of the state succession. Subsistence of the predecessor state thus means that they are principally responsible for preventing any cases of statelessness from occurring, because they can only withdraw nationality if a person obtains the nationality of a successor state.

Another way in which the ECSS attempts to prevent statelessness is by setting certain rules of proof in light of the difficulty of fulfilling requirements of (documentary) evidence in order to meet the conditions for acquiring nationality, which may mean that an individual has to prove that he or she has not acquired an(y)other nationality.[786] This

---

781 Art 1(d) ECSS.

782 Roland Schärer, 'The Council of Europe and the Reduction of Statelessness' (2006) 25 Refugee Survey Quarterly 33, 35–36.

783 See also CoE, *Explanatory Report to the Council of Europe Convention on the Avoidance of Statelessness in relation to State Succession* (Strasbourg, 19 May 2006, CETS No. 200) para 24.

784 See also para 3.3.1.

785 See also CoE, *Explanatory Report to the Council of Europe Convention on the Avoidance of Statelessness in relation to State Succession* (Strasbourg, 19 May 2006, CETS No. 200) para 20.

786 Art 8 ECSS.

provision was introduced because past experiences of state succession had demonstrated that too strict requirements lead to statelessness.[787] The first paragraph of Article 8 of the Treaty provides that a successor state shall not insist on standard requirements of proof for granting nationality if the person would become stateless because of state succession and where it is not reasonable to ask such people to meet the standard requirements. The Explanatory Report points out on this matter that successor states should be aware that the circumstances leading to problems with presenting proof do not have to be linked to state succession.[788] Furthermore, it indicates what type of proof would suffice: high probability of proof or an independent testimony that the requirements for granting nationality by the successor state are met.[789] Article 8(2) of the ECSS obliges successor states not to require proof of non-acquisition of another nationality – a practice commonly employed in order to prevent the occurrence of dual nationality – before granting nationality to people habitually resident in the territory of the respective state at the time of state succession who have or would become states as a result of the state succession. This provision is only relevant when the predecessor state has disappeared and all people that had the nationality of this state have lost it as an automatic consequence of this type of state succession.[790] The rules laid down in Article 8 thus make life of people attempting to acquire a nationality somewhat easier and try to avoid states attempting to battle dual nationality in such a way that it could result in statelessness. In this way, it prevents more cases of statelessness from arising.

An interesting clause is the obligation for states to take all necessary steps to ensure the provision of adequate information regarding the rules and procedures relating to the acquisition of nationality to people at risk of statelessness in the context of state succession.[791] Providing information creates awareness and knowledge amongst those affected by state succession, and what this may mean for their nationality or risk of statelessness. Even though the state has a lot of discretion in determining what measures to take in this context, it does have to make sure that people are aware of where to submit an application and who to ask for further information.[792] At a quite practical level, this can be very important in preventing statelessness, because without knowledge of changes and the corresponding rules and procedures, possibilities for the acquisition of nationality could be missed, which may result in statelessness. At the same time, the relevance of this provision to the prevention of statelessness should not be overstated. If a state is not willing to provide this information to certain people or groups of people, for instance by not providing information in minority languages, it

787 Roland Schärer, 'The Council of Europe and the Reduction of Statelessness' (2006) 25 Refugee Survey Quarterly 33, 37.

788 CoE, *Explanatory Report to the Council of Europe Convention on the Avoidance of Statelessness in relation to State Succession* (Strasbourg, 19 May 2006, CETS No. 200) para 34.

789 Ibid, para 35.

790 Ibid, para 36. On the different types of state succession see for instance ILC, 'Draft Articles on Nationality of Natural Persons in relation to the Succession of States with Commentaries' (1999) 2 Yearbook of the International Law Commission (part two) 19, 23.

791 Art 11 ECSS.

792 Cf CoE, *Explanatory Report to the Council of Europe Convention on the Avoidance of Statelessness in relation to State Succession* (Strasbourg, 19 May 2006, CETS No. 200) para 44.

may be able to circumvent this rule as it has a lot of discretion in the determination of the most appropriate measures. According to the Explanatory Report to the ECSS, the only condition is that the information is disseminated in an open and transparent manner.[793]

A further point to be raised is to what extent the rules of the ECSS truly solve statelessness. Everything is aimed at avoiding statelessness, so it seems likely that they do. However, a striking provision that is included is Article 7 concerning respect for the expressed will of a person affected by state succession. This is what it says exactly:

> "A successor state shall not refuse to grant its nationality under Article 5, paragraph 1, sub paragraph b, of the ECSS where such nationality reflects the expressed will of the person concerned, on the grounds that such a person can acquire the nationality of another state concerned on the basis of an appropriate connection with that state".[794]

This will of a person is expressed usually by applying for a certain nationality.[795] Under this provision of the ECSS, people who reside in a third state and have an appropriate connection with more than one successor state, have the right to opt for one of the nationalities. This is not the case for a person habitually residing in one of the successor states: he or she cannot opt for the nationality of another successor state or the predecessor state – if the latter has not disappeared.[796] The limited scope of the ECSS is visible here again. The ECSS does not require states involved in state succession to grant the most appropriate nationality, which equals their "most effective link and their expressed will, but must simply prevent statelessness".[797] From a legal perspective, having a nationality means that statelessness is solved. But again, one may wonder whether that is enough. As explored in paragraph 1.4.2, truly solving statelessness may mean that the nationality obtained should be in line with peoples' life situation and corresponds to the appropriate, effective link between a person and a state, so that he or she can indeed exercise all of his or her rights and the state at the same time gains a citizen that participates in society.[798] When taking this perspective, the ECSS may perhaps be too concerned with avoidance of statelessness, while forgetting that in order to truly solve statelessness, it is necessary that a person is able to access full citizenship and all associated rights, preferably in the state and society that he or she is most connected to. Nonetheless, as is also noted by Roland Schärer, the solution provided by the ECSS in the context of state succession will in many cases correspond with the most appropriate nationality, and the treaty only sets minimal standards.[799]

---

793 Ibid.

794 Art 7 ECSS.

795 See also CoE, *Explanatory Report to the Council of Europe Convention on the Avoidance of Statelessness in relation to State Succession* (Strasbourg, 19 May 2006, CETS No. 200) para 31.

796 See Roland Schärer, 'The Council of Europe and the Reduction of Statelessness' (2006) 25 Refugee Survey Quarterly 33, 36.

797 Ibid 37.

798 Cf Caia Vlieks, Ernst Hirsch Ballin & María José Recalde Vela, 'Solving Statelessness: Interpreting the Right to Nationality' (2017) 35 Netherlands Quarterly of Human Rights 158.

799 See Roland Schärer, 'The Council of Europe and the Reduction of Statelessness' (2006) 25 Refugee Survey Quarterly 33, 37.

3.3.4. ACQUISITION OF NATIONALITY

This paragraph looks at what the CoE can contribute towards the acquisition of nationality by stateless people later in life through (facilitated) naturalization. Acquisition of nationality at birth is discussed in paragraph 3.3.1.

Article 6, paragraphs 3 and 4, of the ECN deal with naturalization. Paragraph 3 says that each state shall provide in its internal law for the possibility of naturalization of people who are lawfully and habitually resident on its territory. States are not allowed to require a period of residence exceeding ten years before an application for naturalization can be lodged. This can be considered as an explication of the 'genuine and effective link': such link – the bond of nationality – "at least exists after a period of lawful and habitual residence of ten years".[800] Of particular interest to the resolution of statelessness is the obligation for states of paragraph 4: in its internal law, states parties shall facilitate the acquisition of its nationality – *inter alia* – for stateless people (and recognized refugees) lawfully and habitually resident on its territory.[801] This standard was inspired by Article 15 UDHR, the 1961 Convention and the 1954 Convention.[802] In commentaries on the provision under Article 6(4)of the ECN it has been held that they "have only a framework character" and are very general.[803] Also, the level of facilitation of naturalization that is required, which may include a reduction of the length of required residence, less stringent language requirements, an easier procedure and lower procedural fees, is disappointing as the Explanatory Report provides an argument for states to escape from this obligation: where the generally required conditions are already very favorable, states are not required to take additional measures.[804] Specifically concerning the rule relating to stateless people, it is emphasized that people who have deliberately become stateless, for example in order to qualify for specific benefits granted to stateless people, cannot rely on Article 6(4)(g) of the ECN for facilitated naturalization.[805]

Another point that should be raised in relation to facilitated naturalization for stateless people under the ECN is the fact that this presupposes that people are identified as being stateless. In many cases, this would mean that statelessness determination[806]

---

800 Roland Schärer, 'The European Convention on Nationality' (1997) 40 German Yearbook of International Law 438–459, 446.

801 Art 6(4)(g) ECN.

802 Cf Art 32 1954 Convention. See also Roland Schärer, 'The European Convention on Nationality' (1997) 40 German Yearbook of International Law 438–459, 448.

803 Roland Schärer, 'The European Convention on Nationality' (1997) 40 German Yearbook of International Law 438–459, 446.

804 CoE, *Explanatory Report to the European Convention on Nationality* (Strasbourg, 6 November 1997, CETS No. 166) para 52; Gerard-René de Groot, 'The European Convention on Nationality: A Step towards a *Ius Commune* in the Field of Nationality Law' (2007) 7 Maastricht Journal of European and Comparative Law 117–157, 135.

805 CoE, *Explanatory Report to the European Convention on Nationality* (Strasbourg, 6 November 1997, CETS No. 166) para 57; Roland Schärer, 'The European Convention on Nationality' (1997) 40 German Yearbook of International Law 438–459, 448.

806 The obligation to determine statelessness is implicit from the 1954 Convention and is elaborated upon in UNHCR, 'Handbook on the Protection of Stateless Persons under the 1954 Convention relating to

is required. Even though some European countries have dedicated statelessness determination procedures and there is a "growing interest" in these mechanisms among European states, it is certainly not (yet) common practice in Europe.[807] The application of this already very general provision regarding the resolution of statelessness is therefore dependent on the identification of stateless persons, which remains an issue as long as statelessness cannot be properly determined in a country. Since only a few European states have statelessness determination procedures in place, it is questionable whether this ECN standard can be applied effectively in practice. Note should also be taken of the fact that even where statelessness has been determined, it does not necessarily mean that a person obtains a legal status in the country that he or she resides in. The fact that the provision of the ECN only ensures (facilitated) naturalization for stateless persons who are lawfully and habitually resident on the territory is in that regard concerning, as persons who are stateless but do not have a legal status have no right to facilitated naturalization nor to naturalization according to the ECN. In light of the international principle of the avoidance of statelessness – which the ECN explicitly reinforces – it would be desirable that any person who is stateless (and is determined as such) has access to facilitated naturalization in the country where he or she is habitually resident (or with which he or she has a connection – where he or she is 'at home'[808]), also in light of Article 32 of the 1954 Convention.[809] It thus is clear this ECN standard concerning the resolution of statelessness is of a very general nature and could benefit from a further explanation as regards its relation with statelessness determination.

The CM Recommendation on the reduction and avoidance of stateless does provide some further explanation in relation to the relevant provisions of the ECN, but not as regards statelessness determination. The Recommendation indicates that "access to the nationality of a state should be possible whenever a person has a genuine and effective link with that State, in particular through birth, descent or residence".[810] As such, a

---

the Status of Stateless Persons' (Geneva, 2014) <www.unhcr.org/protection/statelessness/53b698ab9/handbook-protection-stateless-persons.html> accessed 2 August 2021. See also Gábor Gyulai, 'The Determination of Statelessness and the Establishment of a Statelessness-specific Protection Regime' in Alice Edwards & Laura van Waas, *Nationality and Statelessness under International Law* (Cambridge University Press 2014) 116–143; ENS, 'Statelessness Determination and the Protection Status of Stateless Persons. A Summary Guide of Good Practices and Factors to Consider When Designing National Determination and Protection Mechanisms' (ENS 2013) <www.statelessness.eu/sites/www.statelessness.eu/files/attachments/resources/Statelessness%20determination%20and%20the%20protection%20status%20of%20stateless%20persons%20ENG.pdf> accessed 10 July 2021.

807 UNHCR, 'Good Practice Papers – Action 6: Establishing Statelessness Determination Procedures for the Protection of Stateless Persons' (2020) 5 <https://www.refworld.org/docid/5f203d0e4.html> accessed 10 July 2021.

808 Ernst Hirsch Ballin, *Citizens' Rights and the Right to Be a Citizen* (Developments in International Law Vol. 66, Brill Nijhoff 2014) 141.

809 Art 32 1954 Convention provides: "The Contracting States shall as far as possible facilitate the assimilation and naturalization of stateless persons. They shall in particular make every effort to expedite naturalization proceedings and to reduce as far as possible the charges and costs of such proceedings."

810 CoE CM Recommendation No. R (99) 18 of the Committee of Ministers to the Member States on the avoidance and reduction of statelessness (679th meeting of the Ministers' Deputies, 15 September 1999) para I(b).

genuine and effective link that should be solidified by the legal label of nationality can exist when a person is born in the territory, has (grand)parents that were connected to the territory, or resides in the territory. Furthermore, the "acquisition of nationality by stateless persons should be facilitated and not subject to unreasonable conditions".[811] This standard is elaborated on in the Recommendation and it demonstrates that facilitated naturalization could include more favorable conditions. Such conditions can concern reducing the required period of residence as compared to the normal period required, and employing a different standard with regard to the knowledge of language(s), for instance not requiring more than adequate knowledge of one of the official languages of a state. Moreover, procedures should be accessible, with no delays and reduced fees. Finally, any offences that are relevant to the decision to grant nationality should not unreasonably prevent stateless people from acquiring citizenship.[812]

As was considered in paragraph 3.3.3, the ECSS's main focus is prevention of statelessness in the specific context of state succession. However, in order to resolve statelessness resulting from state succession in spite of the Convention's other provisions, an obligation for facilitated naturalization is included. This provision obliges the successor state to ensure more favorable conditions for acquiring its nationality if a person remained stateless because of state succession and resides lawfully and habitually in the territory.[813] In this way, it attempts to deal with situations where the predecessor state is not a party to the ECSS, where the predecessor state has disappeared, which results in automatic loss of nationality and statelessness, or in the circumstances of state dissolution with different times of state succession for the successor states.[814] When considering this provision and the explanation of it in the Explanatory Report to the ECSS, it can be seen that the 'favorable conditions' that should be applied are not specified. States thus have quite some discretion and concerns with regard to actually ensuring more favorable conditions, similar to those mentioned above with regard to the ECN, apply here as well. The provision also excludes anyone who speculatively changes his or her residence.[815]

Another point that needs to be taken into account is that for facilitated naturalization of someone who is stateless to take place, also if caused by state succession, a person should first be identified as being stateless before he or she can in fact rely on such provision. Statelessness determination is therefore – again – important. In light of the lack of consideration of the ECSS of statelessness determination in relation to facilitated naturalization, even though the rules of proof of the ECSS in Article 8 perhaps go some way in giving guidance on this matter, one may wonder how effective this provision may be. On the other hand, the ECSS presupposes throughout many of its provisions that states are aware of who is stateless or is at risk of statelessness. In the specific context

811 Ibid, para I(d).
812 Ibid, para II(B).
813 Art 9 ECSS.
814 CoE, *Explanatory Report to the Council of Europe Convention on the Avoidance of Statelessness in relation to State Succession* (Strasbourg, 19 May 2006, CETS No. 200) para 38–39.
815 Ibid, para 41.

of state succession, it is not that strange that this is easily presupposed: in particular when the predecessor state disappears, it is evident that all people who previously were nationals of this state are at risk of statelessness, as they lose their nationality because of state succession. Furthermore, it should be taken into account that the specific context of state succession, an *in situ* context, may require a response other than the use of statelessness determination procedures:

> "Some stateless populations in a non-migratory context remain in their "own country" and may be referred to as *in situ* populations. For these groups, determination procedures for the purpose of obtaining status as stateless persons are not appropriate because of their long-established ties to these countries. Based on existing international standards and State practice in the area of reduction of statelessness, such ties include long-term habitual residence or residence at the time of State succession. Depending on the circumstances of the populations under consideration, States might be advised to undertake targeted nationality campaigns or nationality verification efforts rather than statelessness determination procedures."[816]

As such, statelessness determination procedures may not be suitable in the cases of state succession that the ECSS applies to, yet some form of identification or verification may still be necessary. The rules of proof of the ECSS itself already provide some guidance as to what should be taken into account in such cases and what may be expected from the person involved.[817] Alternatively, there may also be people in a migratory context who are affected by a situation of state succession, for instance because they are residing outside or were displaced from their country of nationality at the time of dissolution. In such cases, nationality verification or statelessness determination efforts may be needed as well.

The ECHR does not include a right to a nationality. As we saw above, however, nationality is considered part of an individual's social identity – protected under the right to private life of Article 8. In the 2018 case of *Hoti v. Croatia*[818], however, the Court did consider matters of statelessness, identification, status and nationality. Hoti was born in Kosovo but has resided in Croatia since 1979. He was involved in different procedures on his residence rights in the country, only to result in a temporary residence permit every now and then, and certainly no stable residence permit. Relying on Article 8 ECHR in particular, the applicant therefore complained that he could not regularize his residence status.[819] What is interesting in this case, is how statelessness features specifically as a matter that is of importance in the assessment of the ECtHR. Indeed, the Court accepted the applicant's statelessness without doubting the existing proof for this, and determined that his status of 'stateless migrant' sets him apart from other, 'settled' migrants.[820] The ECtHR

---

816 UNHCR, 'Handbook on the Protection of Stateless Persons under the 1954 Convention relating to the Status of Stateless Persons' (UNHCR 2014) para 58.

817 Cf Art 8 ECSS.

818 *Hoti v Croatia* App No 63311/14 (ECtHR, 26 April 2018) ECLI:CE:ECHR:2018:0426JUD006331114.

819 Ibid, para 3.

820 Ibid, para 127–128.

> "finds it striking that despite being aware that the applicant does not have any nationality, as is evident from his birth certificates issued by the authorities in Kosovo in 1987 and 2009, when extending the applicant's residence status on humanitarian grounds the Croatian authorities insisted that the applicant was a national of Kosovo [...]. As there was no suggestion that the applicant had ever had Kosovo nationality, it is difficult to understand the Croatian authorities' insistence on the fact that the applicant should obtain a travel document from the authorities in Kosovo [...]. It is also noted in this connection that despite the applicant's statelessness, which was apparent from the relevant documents available to the Croatian authorities, they never considered taking the relevant measures, such as providing administrative assistance to facilitate the applicant's contact with the authorities of another country, to resolve the applicant's situation, as provided in the international documents to which Croatia is a party".[821]

The Court therefore finds that the state did not comply with a positive obligation under Article 8 "to provide an effective and accessible procedure or combination of procedures enabling the applicant to have the issues of his further stay and status in Croatia determined with due regard to his private-life interests".[822] It is clear that no right to a particular residence status or nationality exists under the ECHR.[823] Yet, this case shows the need for states to properly identify stateless people and ensure that they are not left in a situation of uncertainly without possibility to regularize their status. Moreover, it has been considered "important that the Court did not assign significance to the potential culpability of the applicant in his lack of citizenship, and insisted that the state of Croatia had nevertheless an obligation to ensure stability of residence for him through any adequate legal status".[824] This could help towards solving status, as a residence status in a country usually a first step towards being able to claim nationality at some point. Moreover, this case more generally also contributed to protecting stateless migrants' social identity and to strengthening "their right to remain, to a legal status and to citizenship based on their center of life".[825] Moreover, the fact that the ECtHR did not assign significance to potential culpability of the applicant might mean that people who have deliberately become stateless should also be able to rely on Article 6(4)(g) of the ECN for facilitated naturalization – despite of what the Explanatory Report to the ECN says.

Similarly, the ECtHR found a violation of Article 8 in the case of *Sudita Keita v. Hungary*.[826] The case concerns a person who is considered stateless, and who, despite

---

821 Ibid, para 138.

822 Ibid, para 141.

823 Also reiterated in this particular case, ibid, para 120–121.

824 Katja Swider, '*Hoti v. Croatia* – A Landmark Decision by the European Court of Human Rights on the Residence Rigths of a Stateless Person' (*ENS Blog*, 3 May 2018) <https://www.statelessness.eu/updates/blog/hoti-v-croatia-landmark-decision-european-court-human-rights-residence-rights> accessed 10 July 2021.

825 Barbara von Rütte, 'Social Identity and the Right to Belong – The ECtHR's Judgment in *Hoti v. Croatia*' (2019) 14 Tilburg Law Review 147, 154.

826 *Sudita Keita v Hungary* App No 42321/15 (ECtHR, 12 May 2020) ECLI:CE:ECHR:2020:0512JUD004232115.

the existing statelessness determination procedure in Hungary[827], is unable to regularize his status, with detrimental consequences for his access to healthcare and employment, and the right to get married. This led the Court to find that the state had not "complied with its positive obligation to provide an effective and accessible procedure or a combination of procedures enabling the applicant to have the issue of his status in Hungary determined".[828] Even though contributing more indirectly to solving statelessness, as explained above, both *Sudita Keita* and *Hoti* have been welcomed as a "line of jurisprudence that has the potential to promote a harmonised and human rights-based interpretation of the core statelessness conventions" and leaves the ECtHR

> "well positioned to develop regional case law on the fundamental rights of stateless persons, demanding states to establish mechanisms and procedures to adequately identify statelessness and provide stateless persons with access to the protection afforded by the 1954 Convention, as well as preventing interference with Art. 8 and other ECHR rights".[829]

Under the ECHR, there is thus no right to acquire a nationality, but Article 8 proves a useful avenue for further litigation, and shows that a first step towards solving stateless, by properly identifying stateless people and affording them with a stable legal status, may be required from states in view of the private life considerations. Such considerations from the ECHR jurisprudence could also help to better understand the provisions in the various CoE instruments on the acquisition of nationality. Indeed, the ECN standard relating to facilitated naturalization is of a very general nature, and similarly, the ECSS includes a provision on this. The CM Recommendation on the reduction and avoidance of stateless provides some further guidance on how these general provisions are to be applied, indicating that access to the nationality of a state should be available when a person has a genuine and effective link with that state and indicating what favorable conditions states might set to facilitate naturalization.

3.3.5. NON-DISCRIMINATION

Non-discrimination is a key principle of human rights law. The ECN includes the principle of non-discrimination among the general principles of the ECN in Article 5. These principles include the right to nationality for everyone, the avoidance of statelessness, the principle that no one should be arbitrarily deprived of his or her nationality and that nationality laws should not be discriminatory. They echo

827 This procedure, however, was until 2015 only for people with lawful residence in the country. On the Hungarian statelessness determination procedure, see for instance Anikó Bakonyi & Gábor Gyulai, 'Awaiting – Stateless Lives in Hungary' (*ENS Blog*, 11 March 2021) <https://www.statelessness.eu/updates/blog/awaiting-stateless-lives-hungary> accessed 10 July 2021.

828 *Sudita Keita v Hungary* App No 42321/15 (ECtHR, 12 May 2020) ECLI:CE:ECHR:2020:0512JUD004232115, para 41.

829 Patrícia Cabral, 'Case Note: *Sudita Keita v Hungary* – European Court of Human Rights Decision on the Right to Private Life of Stateless Persons' (2020) 2 Statelessness and Citizenship Review 324, 330.

the international human rights instruments that contain rules on nationality and statelessness, such as Article 15 of the UDHR, the 1961 Convention, the ICCPR, the ACHR, the CRC, the CEDAW and the CERD.[830] Together these principles should go a long way in ensuring that statelessness is prevented and resolved in Europe. At the same time, the classic principle[831] that every state is free to determine who its nationals are applies, but only as long as it is consistent with international law. And the limits set by international law are already spelled out by these general principles: statelessness shall be avoided, no arbitrary deprivation of nationality and rules on nationality matters may not be discriminatory.[832] In view of the fact that certain communities, such as the Roma and Russian ethnic minorities remain (at risk of) stateless(ness) due to discriminatory practices and nationality deprivation powers grapple with questions around discrimination, the principle of non-discrimination remains important in addressing statelessness.

Article 5 of the ECN in particular provides that domestic laws on nationality matters should "not contain distinctions or include any practice which amount to discrimination on the grounds of sex, religion, race, colour or national or ethnic origin". This provision is echoed in the CM Recommendation on the avoidance of statelessness, which states that "laws and administrative practices relating to the acquisition, retention, loss, recovery or certification of nationality should not contain distinctions that amount to discrimination" on the same grounds.[833]

Note that the principle of non-discrimination of Article 4 of the ECSS is based on the non-discrimination rules of the ECHR.[834] As such, it is broader when compared to the ECN principle on this matter, which only concerns itself with the key components of non-discrimination concerning nationality.[835] Where the ECN only mentions sex, religion, color or national or ethnic origin as grounds, the ECSS prohibits discrimination on any ground such as sex, race, color, language, religion, political or other opinion, national or social origin, association with a national minority, property, birth or other status.[836] Furthermore, it should be kept in mind that the FCNM makes

---

830 See for more elaborate comments Roland Schärer, 'The European Convention on Nationality' (1997) 40 German Yearbook of International Law 438–459, 443–445; Gerard-René de Groot, 'The European Convention on Nationality: A Step towards a *Ius Commune* in the Field of Nationality Law' (2007) 7 Maastricht Journal of European and Comparative Law 117–157, 124–128.

831 See also Stephen Hall, 'The European Convention on Nationality and the Right to Have Rights' (1999) 24 European Law Review 586–602, 600; Art 1 1930 Hague Convention on Certain Questions Relating to the Conflict of Nationality Laws.

832 Cf Laura van Waas, 'Fighting Statelessness and Discriminatory Nationality Laws in Europe' (2012) 14 European Journal of Migration and Law 243–260, 246.

833 CoE CM Recommendation No. R (99) 18 of the Committee of Ministers to the Member States on the avoidance and reduction of statelessness (679th meeting of the Ministers' Deputies, 15 September 1999) para I.b.

834 Art 14 ECHR and Protocol No 12 to the ECHR. See also CoE, *Explanatory Report to the Council of Europe Convention on the Avoidance of Statelessness in relation to State Succession* (Strasbourg, 19 May 2006, CETS No. 200) para 17.

835 Cf Roland Schärer, 'The Council of Europe and the Reduction of Statelessness' (2006) 25 Refugee Survey Quarterly 33, 35.

836 Cf Art 5 ECN and Art 4 ECSS.

special provision in the equal treatment of people belonging to national minorities, including that "any discrimination based on belonging to a national minority shall be prohibited".[837]

The 2011 *Genovese* case[838] is *the* landmark case as regards nationality under Article 8 of the ECHR. The principle of non-discrimination is clearly present in this case, as was already highlighted in the discussion of the facts of the case above.[839] A key question in this case was whether the ECHR protects against discrimination concerning the acquisition – or denial – of nationality and, in particular, whether this was protected by Article 8.[840] According to the Court,

> "the denial of citizenship may raise an issue under Article 8 because of its impact on the private life of an individual, which concept is wide enough to embrace aspects of a person's social identity. While the right to citizenship is not as such a Convention right and while its denial in the present case was not such as to give rise to a violation of Article 8, the Court considers that its impact on the applicant's social identity was such as to bring it within the general scope and ambit of that Article".[841]

As such, the ECtHR was able to find that a nationality provision of a state party to the ECHR was in fact a violation of Article 14[842] in conjunction with Article 8 of this Treaty. At the same time, its statement that nationality is part of a person's social identity that is protected under the notion of private life in the Convention is an assertion that leaves the door open for more nationality laws to be tested against the ECHR. Furthermore, the case of *Genovese v. Malta* clearly demonstrates that a right to citizenship (by descent), something that could in certain circumstances – where a child can for instance only obtain a nationality from one of the parents – prevent or solve statelessness, should be secured without discrimination. Commentators have held that this case may have relevance beyond this specific situation as well, such as in particular cases of loss of nationality[843], which could again prevent statelessness. The *Genovese* case also clarified that discrimination on the grounds of the marital status of the parents is prohibited in the context of nationality rights, which might be seen as expanding the grounds in the ECN and certainly gives further interpretation to 'other status' as used in the non-discrimination standard in the ECSS.[844] Moreover, it has been held that the case could

---

837 Art 4(1) FCNM.

838 *Genovese v Malta* App No 53124/09 (ECHR, 11 October 2011) ECLI:CE:ECHR:2011:1011 JUD005312409.

839 See para 3.3.1.

840 Gerard-René de Groot & Olivier Vonk, 'Nationality, Statelessness and ECHR's Article 8: Comments on Genovese v. Malta (2012) 14 European Journal of Migration and Law 317, 319.

841 *Genovese v Malta* App No 53124/09 (ECHR, 11 October 2011) ECLI:CE:ECHR:2011:1011 JUD005312409, para 33.

842 Article 14 needs to be invoked in relation to other ECHR rights. An independent non-discrimination provision has been introduced later in Article 1 of Protocol No. 12 to the ECHR (2000).

843 Rene de Groot & Olivier Vonk, 'Nationality, Statelessness and ECHR's Article 8: Comments on Genovese v. Malta (2012) 14 European Journal of Migration and Law 317, 323–325.

844 As was noted above, the ECSS was based on the ECHR.

point to an obligation for states to determine statelessness in light of Article 8, as a precondition to the effective implementation of national standards that grant nationality to children who would otherwise be stateless and because of the impact that not establishing a person's nationality or statelessness could have on the life of an individual.[845]

Another case of the ECHR that is relevant here is *Biao v. Denmark*.[846] This case concerns differences in treatment between nationals. Biao was born in Togo and lived in Ghana for a while before coming to Denmark. In 2002, he obtained Danish nationality. Shortly afterwards, he married a Ghanaian woman and the couple applied for family reunification in Denmark. Their application was rejected, because they did not comply with the so-called 'attachment requirement'. Only people who had been Danish nationals for 28 years were exempted from this requirement (the '28-year rule'). The couple did not meet the 'attachment requirement' according to the Danish authorities, because their aggregate ties to Denmark were not stronger than those to Ghana. Also, they could not appeal to the aforementioned exemption. After exhausting domestic remedies, they complained to the ECtHR that the refusal by the Danish authorities to grant them family reunion in Denmark was in breach of Article 8, taken alone and in conjunction with Article 14. They submitted that the '28-year rule' resulted in an unjustified difference in treatment between two groups of Danish nationals: namely those born Danish nationals and those, like Biao, who acquired Danish nationality later in life, and also Danish nationals of Danish ethnic origin and Danish nationals of other ethnic origin.[847] The Grand Chamber of Court agreed with the applicants[848] and held:

> "[T]he Government have failed to show that there were compelling or very weighty reasons unrelated to ethnic origin to justify the indirect discriminatory effect of the 28-year rule. That rule favours Danish nationals of Danish ethnic origin, and places at a disadvantage, or has a disproportionately prejudicial effect on persons who acquired Danish nationality later in life and who were of ethnic origins other than Danish. It follows that there has been a violation of Article 14 read in conjunction with Article 8 of the Convention in the present case."[849]

---

845 ENS, 'Strategic Litigation: An Obligation for Statelessness Determination under the European Convention on Human Rights?' (2014) ENS Discusssion Paper 09/14, 19 <https://www.statelessness.eu/updates/publication/obligation-statelessness-determination-under-european-convention-human-rights> accessed 17 October 2021.

846 *Biao v Denmark* App No 38590/10 (ECHR, 24 May 2016) ECLI:CE:ECHR:2016:0524JUD003859010.

847 Ibid, para 62.

848 Note that the Second Section of the Court in its judgment of 25 March 2014 (ECLI:CE:ECHR:2014:0325JUD003859010) came to a different conclusion and found no violation of Article 8 or Article 14 in conjunction with Article 8. For a discussion of this case and comments on it, see for instance Eva Ersbøll, 'Biao v. Denmark – Discrimination Among Citizens?' (2014) EUI Working Papers RSCAS 2014/79 <http://cadmus.eui.eu/bitstream/handle/1814/32015/RSCAS_ERS%20_2014_79.pdf?sequence=1> accessed 10 July 2021. See also Alix Schlüter, 'Biao v. Denmark: Grand Chamber Ruling on Ethnic Discrimination Might Leave Couples Seeking Family Reunification Worse Off' (*Strasbourg Observers* 13 June 2016) <https://strasbourgobservers.com/2016/06/13/biao-v-denmark-grand-chamber-ruling-on-ethnic-discrimination-might-leave-couples-seeking-family-reunification-worse-off/> accessed 10 July 2021, who compares the Chamber judgment and the Grand Chamber judgment.

849 *Biao v Denmark* App No 38590/10 (ECHR, 24 May 2016) ECLI:CE:ECHR:2016:0524JUD003859010, para 138.

In light of this conclusion, the ECtHR believed that it was not necessary to examine the complaints separately under Article 8 of the Convention. What is striking in this judgment, is how the Court includes the ECN in its considerations regarding Article 14 in conjunction with Article 8.[850] The applicants in the case specifically relied on Article 5(2) of the ECN. This provision indicates that states "shall be guided by the principle of non-discrimination between its nationals, whether they are nationals by birth or have acquired its nationality subsequently". This is perhaps not an outright ban of differential treatment between nationals by birth and naturalized citizens – as is also outlined in the ECN explanatory report – but it does mean that states should, as much as possible, eliminate the discriminatory application of provisions on nationality between nationals by birth and other (naturalized) citizens.[851]

The Court notes in this regard that the ECN has been ratified by 20 Member States of the CoE, including Denmark. Furthermore, the ECtHR refers to the Explanatory Report to the ECN and says that this paragraph of the ECN can be viewed as a declaration of intent, "aimed at eliminating the discriminatory application of rules in matters of nationality between nationals from birth and other nationals, including naturalised persons".[852] According to the Court, this shows a certain trend towards a European standard on these matters that is relevant in this case. This case thus demonstrates the continuing development of ECHR jurisprudence in nationality matters, in particular discrimination based on nationality: between a country's own nationals based on acquisition of nationality (at birth or later in life), which could contribute to preventing and solving statelessness generally by ensuring equal nationality rights. What is furthermore very interesting about this case is what it says about the concept of nationality. Apparently, Denmark attached more privileges to nationality when it has been held for more than 28 years. The aim of the '28-year rule' was to ensure that Danish expatriates with strong and lasting ties with Denmark would be able to obtain family reunion in Denmark. The reasoning was that it would be unproblematic to grant them family reunion with a foreign spouse because the latter would normally be successfully integrated into Danish society, and because they had been unintentionally disadvantaged by the tightness of the attachment requirement.[853] However, the difference that is made between the nationals of the country makes one wonder whether this means that there are classes or levels in nationality based on how it is acquired? Is the bond of nationality in some way stronger after 28 years? However, the Court's decision demonstrates that this constitutes prohibited indirect discrimination between Danish nationals based on ethnic origin, which should put an end to this

---

850 See also Eva Ersbøll, 'Biao v. Denmark: Discrimination Among Citizens?' (*GLOBALCIT Blog* 12 July 2016) <https://globalcit.eu/biao-v-denmark-discrimination-among-nationals/> accessed 10 July 2021.

851 CoE, *Explanatory Report to the European Convention on Nationality* (Strasbourg, 6 November 1997, CETS No. 166) paras 45–46.

852 *Biao v Denmark* App No 38590/10 (ECHR, 24 May 2016) ECLI:CE:ECHR:2016:0524JUD003859010, para 132.

853 Ibid, para 74 & 115.

type of distinction between nationals and appears to demonstrate that the bond of nationality cannot be classified in such a way that it is discriminatory.

The questions raised by this case, as well as in that of *K2* discussed above in paragraph 3.3.2, and the answers given by the Court so far say something about what nationality – and hence, a solution to statelessness – means. The Court says that there can be no difference between a person who obtained a nationality at birth and who acquired this nationality later in life (after naturalization), also drawing on the ECN. Both are to be considered nationals and should be treated as such by the state. This is particularly significant for stateless people, who – if their statelessness is solved – usually obtain a nationality through (facilitated) naturalization. If they, as naturalized citizens, would then still be unable to gain access to certain rights, including family reunification, they would not be enjoying the full range of rights available to a citizen. Therefore, the creation of such 'classes of citizenship' could hinder an effective solution to statelessness.

3.3.6. CONCLUDING REMARKS

In paragraph 2.7, it was demonstrated that at the national level, European states still grapple with effectively preventing and solving statelessness. For instance, guarantees to mitigate the (risk of) statelessness at birth are not present in all countries, and long-standing problems with nationality questions for minorities persist due to discriminatory practices, as well as a lack of safeguards at the time of state succession. Moreover, new challenges, such as nationality deprivation as a counterterrorism measure, may further complicate combating inequalities in nationality matters as well as statelessness. At the same time, the CoE does present a framework to address such questions and challenges, sometimes offering very concrete guidance, albeit fragmented in different instruments, including treaties, recommendations, and jurisprudence.

On childhood statelessness, it is clear that this is an issue of concern for the CoE. Legal instruments reinforce, but also further elaborate the dominant *jus sanguinis* principle for acquisition of nationality at birth. Moreover, the problems that arise from the focus on this principle are mitigated by the introduction of *jus soli* elements as additional safeguards. However, when comparing the CoE standards on acquisition of nationality by children with the international framework, a problem can be uncovered. The ECN allows states to require both habitual and lawful residence for granting their nationality to children who do not acquire another nationality a birth.[854] In comparison, the 1961 Convention only allows for the condition of habitual residence to be imposed.[855] The drafters of the 1961 Convention were concerned that this

854 Art 6(2)(b) ECN.

855 Art 1(2)(b) 1961 Convention. The difference between the 1961 Convention and the ECN on this point is noted for instance by Laura van Waas, *Nationality Matters. Statelessness under International Law* (School of Human Rights Research Series Vol. 29, Intersentia 2008) 61–62, note 55; also Gerard-René de Groot, 'Children, their Right to a Nationality and Child Statelessness' in Alice Edwards & Laura

requirement would lead to states avoiding their obligations.[856] As such, the ECN is stricter than other relevant international instruments, but the stronger commitment – the best protection for the individual – should prevail from a human rights perspective. Moreover, drawing on the international principle of harmonization: "when several norms bear on a single issue, they should, to the extent possible, be interpreted so as to give rise to a single set of compatible obligations".[857] One may wonder why the ECN includes the criterion of lawful residence if international legal instruments, such as the 1961 Convention, inspired it.[858] The Explanatory Report to the ECN, unfortunately, does not answer this question. The later principles of the CM Recommendation on the nationality of children of 2009 unfortunately still, like the ECN, allow the condition of lawful and habitual residence of the parent in the country concerned for the acquisition of nationality of that country by a child who would otherwise be stateless.[859] This can exclude stateless people without legal residence from solving their situation.

As was noted earlier, some European countries have no safeguard that deal with granting nationality to otherwise stateless children born in the territory at all, and other states have provisions that are limited in various ways. For instance, they are limited to people of certain age or require lawful residence.[860] Even though it was discussed above that the ECN allows for the requirement of lawful residence, if a state has other obligations under the 1961 Convention for instance, this condition would be unlawful.[861] Furthermore, one may wonder if it is in the best interests of the child, and their right to acquire a nationality, and thus in line with the CRC, to require lawful residence, in particular when the grave consequences of statelessness for a child are considered.[862] Many countries that are a signatory to both the ECN and the 1961 Convention have – perhaps conveniently – remained ignorant of the fact that they cannot require lawful residence in such cases. The Dutch government, one of these

van Waas, Nationality and Statelessness under International Law (Cambridge University Press 2014) 144–168, 155; Katja Swider & Caia Vlieks, 'Discriminatie van staatloze kinderen zonder wettig verblijf [Discrimination of Children without Legal Residence]' (2016) 4 Asiel & Migrantenrecht 168, 171.

856 Gerard-René de Groot, 'Children, their Right to a Nationality and Child Statelessness' in Alice Edwards & Laura van Waas, Nationality and Statelessness under International Law (Cambridge University Press 2014) 144–168, 155.

857 ILC, 'Conclusions of the work of the Study Group on the Fragmentation of International Law: Difficulties arising from the Diversification and Expansion of International Law' (2006) 2 Yearbook of the International Law Commission 178.

858 See also Katja Swider & Caia Vlieks, 'Discriminatie van staatloze kinderen zonder wettig verblijf [Discrimination of Children without Legal Residence]' (2016) 4 Asiel & Migrantenrecht 168, 171.

859 Recommendation CM/Rec (2009) 13 of the Committee of Ministers to member states on the nationality of children (adopted by the Committee of Ministers on 9 December 2009 at the 1073rd meeting of the Ministers' Deputies), para I.2.

860 Cf ENS, 'Statelessness Index' (2021) <https://index.statelessness.eu/> accessed 3 October 2021. Theme 'Prevention and Reduction' was selected.

861 See also Art 26 ECN.

862 Eg ENS, 'No Child Should Be Stateless' (ENS 2015) <www.statelessness.eu/sites/www.statelessness.eu/files/ENS_NoChildStateless_final.pdf> accessed 3 July 2021; UNHCR, I Am Here, I Belong. The Urgent Need to End Childhood Statelessness (UNHCR 2015) <www.unhcr.org/ibelong/wp-content/uploads/2015-10-StatelessReport_ENG15-web.pdf> accessed 3 July 2021.

countries, for instance, maintained for years that the provision of the 1961 Convention in this regard contained the same norm as the ECN, meaning that they could require habitual and lawful residence.[863] In November 2014, they have changed their view after different reports on this matter, as is evidenced by a letter to parliament that concerned statelessness.[864] Creating awareness of the meaning of certain provisions in the ECN and their relationship with other relevant international legal instruments therefore appears to be important in effectively combating statelessness in Europe. Moreover, other concerns around children's nationality remain. The fact that the safeguard against statelessness for foundlings only applies to newborn infants, may exclude children and leave them (at risk of) statelessness. Also, modern reproductive techniques challenge existing, traditional nationality rules and further guidance on nationality matters in cases of surrogacy can prevent statelessness in such situations.

When it comes to loss and deprivation of nationality in relation to preventing and solving statelessness, the ECN presents a clear and strict standard as compared to international norms in this regard. Indeed, states may not provide for the loss of its nationality under if the person concerned would thereby become stateless. Only one exception is made: in cases of acquisition of this nationality by fraudulent conduct. In this regard, CoE guidance also provides that even where a person could be deprived of nationality because of fraud, a state should not necessarily use this measure so as to avoid statelessness as far as possible and take into account the individual circumstances. ECHR jurisprudence has shown that statelessness can still be the outcome of deprivation of nationality in cases of fraud, but also affirmed the importance of looking at the consequences and situation of the person affected by loss of citizenship. This last standard remains important in preventing statelessness in cases of loss or deprivation of nationality. Furthermore, CoE instruments that concern renunciation of nationality – at the initiative of the individual – permit this only if statelessness does not result and provide further safeguards to prevent statelessness in (almost) any case.

Even though the CoE instrument specifically dealing with state succession, the ECSS, came too late to deal with the major cases of state succession in Europe and has a low number of ratifications, it does present a very detailed and concrete framework on the matter, for instance where it includes rules of proof in relation to acquisition of nationality. This part of the ECSS as well as where the convention sets out that states need to provide information about the rules and procedures relating to the acquisition of nationality to people at risk of statelessness in the context of state succession are rather innovative when compared to universal standards. International standards on state succession, like the ECN provisions on state succession that preceded the ECSS,

---

863 Brief van Minister J.W.E. Spies van Binnenlandse Zaken en Koninkrijksrelaties en Minister G.B.M. Leers voor Immigratie, Integratie en Asiel aan R. Bruin (UNHCR Nederland) of 20 August 2012: Beleidsreactie UNHCR-rapport "Staatloosheid in Nederland", kenmerk 2012–0000395600 [Reaction to UNHCR Report Statelessness in the Netherlands], also Bijlage 377600 of *Kamerstukken II* 2013/14, 19637, 1889, p. 6, 15.

864 *Kamerstukken II* 2014/15, 19637, 1917.

have remained quite general.[865] The ECSS norms on evidence and information show how the CoE has managed to take this a step further, thus contributing important ideas to progressive development of international norms on the prevention of statelessness.

On acquisition to nationality, it was demonstrated that the CoE standards are rather general in nature. States are, however, not allowed to require more than ten years of legal and habitual residence for naturalization. In this regard, the CoE norms go further than the international instruments in setting a concrete timeframe. For stateless people, naturalization should be facilitated with 'more favorable conditions', such as less stringent conditions with regard to residence, language requirements, procedure and fees. States have a lot of discretion in this regard though. In this context, another concern relates to statelessness determination, which is presupposed if stateless people are to benefit from facilitated naturalization. Not all CoE member states have procedures or mechanisms to identify statelessness. Nonetheless, ECHR case law shows promise in addressing the necessity to establish statelessness and providing stateless people with a legal status.

Finally, the principle of non-discrimination is also key within the CoE. Even though the ECN contains a limited number of grounds on which discrimination is prohibited, it should be understood that all grounds are prohibited, including discrimination of minorities or in nationality law based on the parents' marital status. This helps to prevent discriminatory nationality laws that may lead to statelessness. Moreover, it is clear that there can also be no difference between a person who obtained a nationality at birth and who acquired this nationality later in life (after naturalization). This reiterates equal nationality rights and helps to better understand the solution to statelessness – nationality.

3.4. CONCLUSION: THE COUNCIL OF EUROPE'S CONTRIBUTION TO THE LEGAL CONCEPTION OF NATIONALITY

This chapter looked at how the CoE and its legal instruments that can contribute to preventing and solving statelessness in Europe. What perhaps is most striking about the CoE framework, is the lack of a clearly explicated human right to a nationality in its key human rights instrument, the ECHR. Nonetheless, with its various instruments on nationality and statelessness, but also more broadly on human rights, the CoE provides a lot of standards that are relevant to preventing and solving statelessness. The framework is comprehensive in explicitly addressing all of the topics identified as part of the analytical framework: childhood statelessness, deprivation of nationality, state succession, acquisition of nationality through naturalization, and non-discrimination. This signifies that having an expounded human right to a nationality may not be

865 See also para 1.5.1.

necessary to be able to address statelessness, even if this right seems to underlie at least some of the instruments of the CoE. Indeed, in the explanatory reports to various treaties, reference is made to international standards that have inspired the norms that are put forward.

What should be noted with regard to the CoE is that it presents a rather fragmented framework on nationality matters though. On the one hand, there are a couple of instruments that are very directly geared at addressing nationality and preventing statelessness, such as the ECN and the ECSS. On the other hand, different other instruments and the work of bodies that may not seem directly linked to the issue, have proven relevant as well. And of course, the ECHR and the Court's case law have also played an important role in further explaining existing CoE standards. Indeed, it is interesting to see how the ECtHR has sometimes taken the approach to integrate other CoE instruments (as well as international standards) into its considerations, thus providing further interpretation of key human rights obligations. As such, from a human rights perspective, the various CoE standards can be viewed as a living ecosystem in which the Court's jurisprudence also helps to clarify more general principles that can be derived from, for instance, the ECN.

Nonetheless, to fully understand the CoE instruments in this regard, the relation with the national level needs to be taken into account. When considering the implementation of CoE standards in domestic law and policy, it should be acknowledged that the CoE is an autonomous, external actor that wants to influence these. It has limited powers to put pressure on states and is dependent on them signing up to treaties. A fragmented framework is then quite unhelpful, as this blurs the integrated and clear approach that is needed to address statelessness and does not help to show the importance of the various instruments to states. This relates to the important question of implementation that was also raised at the 2021 Conference hosted by the CDCJ. For some CoE instruments, there is a clear lack of ratifications, or a lack of understanding around how to implement certain obligations. Even though further guidance on this may help, guidelines that in particular take into account the interdependency of standards within the CoE and the (larger) ecosystem that continues to be developed would be relevant.

This chapter also demonstrated what these legal instruments on preventing and solving statelessness add to our understanding of the legal concept of nationality. Conceptually, nationality can be interpreted using the CoE instruments on preventing and solving statelessness. According to these, nationality is principally acquired at birth by descent, but if a child would be left stateless, birth on the territory would also warrant granting citizenship. At the same time, there seems to be a preoccupation with habitual *and* legal residence on the territory before nationality may be acquired, seemingly indicating that nationality should always be preceded by legal status or residence on the territory. Nonetheless, the fact that the best interests of the child must prevail, also with regard to nationality decisions, gives more urgency to every child's right to acquire a nationality regardless of their status.

Nationality should not be deprived arbitrarily and statelessness needs to be avoided. At the same time, deprivation of nationality is still viewed as an acceptable measure – thus allowing for the instrumentalization of citizenship in certain contexts, such that of national security – and may even result in statelessness in cases of fraudulent acquisition.

The key CoE instrument on dealing with state succession, the ECSS, contains some interesting points regarding nationality and what this constitutes. First of all, it focuses on habitual (stable, factual) residence on the territory as a basis for granting nationality. Moreover, an appropriate connection may also constitute reason to be able to acquire nationality. Appropriate connection entails, for example, a legal bond to the territory of the predecessor state that is now part of successor state, birth on the territory that is now of the successor state, last habitual residence on territory that has now become part of the successor state. At the same time, the ECSS does not require states involved in state succession to grant the most appropriate nationality, which aligns with their (most) effective link and expressed will – it is all about preventing statelessness and less about the meaning of citizenship status. From a human rights perspective, as explicated in paragraph 1.4.2, however, that may not be desirable and may affect a person's ability to be an active member of society.

The CoE standards on acquisition of nationality later in life, through (facilitated) naturalization, have clarified that the bond of nationality can be deemed to exist after a maximum of ten years of legal and habitual residence in the territory. Furthermore, access to the nationality of a CoE should be possible whenever a person has a genuine and effective link with that State. It has been specified that such link would exist in particular through birth, descent or residence. Various additional conditions for naturalization can be set, including required period of residence, language requirements, as well as procedural requirements and fees. Such demands could be relaxed for stateless people, whose naturalization should be facilitated using more favorable conditions and should not be subject to unreasonable limitations.

Non-discrimination also is a key principle in nationality matters. Important for understanding the concept of nationality is that CoE instruments show that there should be no discrimination between nationals based on how they acquired their nationality (at birth or later in life through naturalization). This tells us that nationality should be one status that is the same for all who have it, and that there should not be different classes of citizenship.

In the CoE context, nationality is thus clearly based on a bond between the person and the state. This bond can exist based on different circumstances. An important question in this regard remains whether the (grand)parent(s) are nationals. But next to this, there is also a focus on birth and/or legal and/or habitual residence on the territory. Indeed, by connecting nationality to lawful residence, a clear link is made with immigration policy, which can present an additional hurdle in solving statelessness and privileges those with documents, registration, status as compared to those without these. Furthermore, there is also some regard for the effectiveness of the link as representing the place where a person is most at home, in particular evidenced in the context of the ECSS. A real recognition of a *jus nexus* seems to be a bridge too far for now, as evidenced for instance by the ECSS' prioritization of preventing statelessness over the expressed will of a person in matters of nationality.

CoE norms also take into account the people's own behavior in nationality matters and want to counter fraud in particular. Where a person has caused problems with regard to their nationality through their own actions, for instance by committing fraud in acquiring nationality or by becoming stateless on purpose, they are excluded from certain safeguards (i.e. may be deprived of nationality even if statelessness results and cannot access naturalization). At the same time, it is interesting that the ECtHR in the *Hoti* case did not assign significance to potential culpability of the applicant, which signifies the need to read such norms differently – at least in certain situations.

The conceptualization of nationality in the context of the CoE furthermore presupposes that states have systems in place that allow for the registration of people as well as fair procedures in matters of nationality. Against the background of nationality matters often depending on the parents (and their nationality) as well as the place of birth, birth registration would seem important. Moreover, mechanisms and procedures on (legal) residence and the identification of stateless persons are relevant. In the absence of statelessness determination procedures, a question arises around whether stateless people will be able to claim facilitated naturalization. After all, if statelessness cannot be determined, how can they utilize facilitated naturalization procedures? And importantly, acquisition of nationality should not be subject to requirements that are unreasonable. If, in the absence of an identification mechanism for stateless people, a stateless person is required to prove their own statelessness, that might be unreasonable depending on what conditions apply.

The CoE thus provides a clear and broad contribution to preventing and solving statelessness, but its instruments are fragmented, its influence is limited and the outcomes in concrete cases of (risk of) statelessness at the national level are uncertain and may vary from one country to the other, dependent on what instruments have been ratified for instance. At the same time, the CoE instruments on preventing and solving statelessness also tell us more about how we can understand the concept of nationality.

CHAPTER 4
THE EUROPEAN UNION

"We have undertaken today to act together on behalf of stateless persons: those who do not have rights, who cannot participate in any political system and who do not have access to any social benefits. [...] We have to unite in our efforts within an EU which stands by its values and protects the weakest."
– Jean Asselborn, Minister of Immigration and Asylum of Luxembourg and President of the Council at the time of the adoption of the Council Conclusions on Statelessness[866]

4.1. INTRODUCTION

The above quote demonstrates that member states of the European Union (EU) are confronted with statelessness and can play an important role in helping to solve it. Indeed, it has been estimated that close to 400.000 people remain stateless in the EU.[867] There is thus still plenty of work to be done to try to minimize the occurrence of statelessness and to ensure the right to a nationality of every person in the EU. At first sight, however, the EU seems an odd organization to look to for help in preventing and solving statelessness when considering the EU structure and competences. Nationality – the legal status that effectively prevents and solves statelessness – is in the exclusive competences of the member states of the EU, meaning that the EU is not allowed to regulate on nationality matters.[868] Nevertheless, "years of cooperation have meant that both legal orders have become so intertwined, that an exclusive Member State competence cannot be separated from an EU competence".[869] Indeed, nationality and statelessness are both mentioned in key EU instruments and are considered more often than one might think in EU context, as elaborated further

866 Council of the EU, 'Press Release: Council Adopts Conclusions on Statelessness' (2015) <https://www.consilium.europa.eu/en/press/press-releases/2015/12/04/council-adopts-conclusions-on-statelessness/> accessed 29 October 2021.

867 European Migration Network (EMN), 'Statelessness in the European Union' (2020) EMN Inform <https://ec.europa.eu/home-affairs/system/files/2020-01/00_eu_inform_statelessness_en.pdf> accessed 17 October 2021.

868 Consolidated versions of the Treaty on European Union (TEU) and the Treaty on the Functioning of the European Union (TFEU) [2016] OJ C202/1, Arts 2–6 TFEU jo Art 5(2) TEU.

869 Helen Oosterom-Staples, 'The Triangular Relationship Between Nationality, EU Citizenship and Migration in EU Law: A Tale of Competing Competences' (2018) 65 Netherlands International Law Review 431, 433.

in sections 4.2 and 4.3 of this chapter. This chapter therefore analyses European law made by the EU[870], aiming to demonstrate how it contributes or could contribute to preventing and solving statelessness in Europe. The legal instruments studied vary from treaties to case law and the chapter looks at how legal concepts are applied and developed. Unlike the instruments of the CoE, the relevant EU instruments are less focused on issues of nationality and statelessness, but could still present interesting and important contributions towards addressing statelessness. These EU instruments are all examined in a similar manner in this chapter, using the analytical framework established in earlier chapters for consistency. Literature and commentary from academics, as well as relevant reports from EU-bodies and NGOs, are used to further deepen the analysis. All literature is selected based on its relevance and quality. Relevant indicators in this regard include year of publication, place of publication, reputation of the author, and in-depth consideration of the topic of study.

In section 4.2, the most important EU instruments that relate to preventing and solving statelessness and the different actors involved are introduced. This section also serves to illustrate general trends that are visible in the EU concerning nationality matters. Section 4.3 explores the substance of the relevant EU instruments in relation to preventing and solving statelessness using the analytical framework that has been set out in previous chapters. Section 4.3 therefore considers EU legal instruments aimed at preventing and solving childhood statelessness; concerning solutions to conflicts of nationality law and preventing loss / (arbitrary) deprivation / denial of nationality; focused on the right to a nationality and acquisition of a nationality for persons who became stateless in the past and remain stateless today and/or who arrive to a country stateless; nationality matters and reduction of statelessness in the context of state succession; legal instruments ensuring non-discrimination and equality before the law in nationality matters. Section 4.4 concludes this chapter with reflections on the contribution of European law made by the EU to preventing and solving statelessness and the legal concept of nationality.

4.2. THE EU AND NATIONALITY MATTERS: INSTRUMENTS, ACTORS AND TRENDS

4.2.1. INTRODUCTION

The EU is an economic and political union and connects 27 member states with each other in a unique way. As we saw in chapter 2, the EU has developed out of economic cooperation into a much closer union with its own supranational legal order – an unprecedented form of cooperation between states. The EU's main treaties are the Treaty on European Union (TEU) and the Treaty on the Functioning of the European

870 With regard to the situation prior to 1 December 2009 (entry into force of the Lisbon Treaty), the European (Economic – until 1 November 1993) Community is also included in this.

Union (TFEU). Furthermore, the EU has its own Charter of Fundamental Rights of the European Union (EU Charter)[871], which is binding for the EU and its institutions and for the member states when implementing EU law.[872] These "provide the constitutional basis for the relationship between its own institutions, between those institutions and the Member States, and between those institutions and the citizens of those Member States".[873] Moreover, there are other legally binding EU instruments such as directives and regulations, which allow the EU to coordinate policies or to take measures or action. These are discussed more elaborately where relevant in the paragraphs below.

A key principle in relation to the EU is the principle of conferral. The EU, as an economic and political union of states, is clearly distinct from a state and does not have the traditional, inherent sovereignty to legislate on matters within its own borders. As the principle of conferral of Article 5 TEU expresses, "[i]ts powers are conferred and limited powers".[874] The principle of conferral clarifies that the EU can only take (legislative) action based on competences conferred upon it by the EU member states to attain the objectives set out therein, and any competences not conferred upon the EU remain with the member states.[875] The latter statement on the competences remaining with the member states, should not be read too strictly though. The EU has been able to expand its competences on topics and policy areas that were not mentioned in the EU Treaties, and member states generally share the competences with the EU where these are not expressly conferred upon the EU.[876]

EU institutions and bodies

The EU has an array of institutions that allow it to operate – its structure is quite complex. Article 13(1) TEU lists the EU's principal institutions. A number of these are shortly introduced here as relevant to this chapter.[877] The European Parliament (EP) engages in the EU's legislative and budgetary process and has the task to hold the executive to account – similar to national parliaments. It is the institution that represents the Union's citizens and it is composed of members (MEPs) who are elected in free elections by universal adult suffrage every five years (Article 14 TEU). The European Commission (EC) possess legislative, administrative, executive, and judicial powers. The Commission, for instance,

871 Charter of Fundamental Rights of the European Union [2016] C202/389 (EU Charter).

872 Art 51(1) EU Charter.

873 Ernst Hirsch Ballin, Emina Ćerimović, Huub Dijstelbloem & Mathieu Segers, *European Variations as a Key to Cooperation* (Research for Policy, WRR/Springer Open 2020) 3.

874 Robert Schütze, 'EU Competences: Existence and Exercise' in Anthony Arnull & Damian Chalmers (eds), *The Oxford Handbook of European Union Law* (Oxford University Press 2015) 75–102, 76.

875 Art 5(2) TEU.

876 Robert Schütze, 'EU Competences: Existence and Exercise' in Anthony Arnull & Damian Chalmers (eds), *The Oxford Handbook of European Union Law* (Oxford University Press 2015) 75–102, 77.

877 For a more elaborate introduction to the institutions of the EU, please refer to Catherine Barnard & Steve Peers, *European Union Law* (2nd edn, Oxford University Press 2017) 37–70; Paul Craig & Gráinne de Búrca, *EU Law: Text, Cases, and Materials* (7th edn, Oxford University Press 2020) 59–101.

has the right of legislative initiative, but also plays an executive role as regards the EU's budget and external relations (Article 17(2) TEU), and can bring action against member states that are in breach of EU law (Article 258 TFEU). The EC is currently composed of 27 commissioners: the College of Commissioners – one from each member state of the EU (Article 17(5) TEU). They are appointed for five years based on suggestions from each of the member states, formally by the European Council, but the entire College is also subject to a vote of approval by the EP (Article 17(3) TEU). Included in the 27 commissioners are the President of the Commission (Article 17(6) TEU & Article 248 TFEU) and the High Representative of the Union for Foreign Affairs and Security Policy (Article 18 TEU). The Council (Council of Ministers / Council of the EU) shares its legislative and budgetary functions with the EP (Article 16(1) TEU). The Council consists of ministers of the governments of EU member states (Article 16(2) TEU). There are no fixed members and the configuration of the Council changes as relevant to the area of policy that is under consideration. The Council should not be confused with the European Council. The European Council has no legislative functions, but defines general political directions and priorities. It consists of the heads of state of the member states, as well as its president and the EC-president. The High Representative of the Union for Foreign Affairs and Security Policy also takes part in its work (Article 15 TEU). The Court of Justice of the EU (CJEU) is the EU's court and has the task to ensure that the law is observed in the interpretation and application of the Treaties. It consists of 27 judges – one judge per member state – and is assisted by Advocates-General (Article 19 TEU). Next to these principal EU-institutions, there are obviously a lot of other organizations and agencies involved in governance and administration of the EU. As a relevant example, the EU Agency for Fundamental Rights (FRA) can be considered. This agency provides different EU institutions and member states with assistance and expertise on fundamental rights when they are implementing EU law.[878]

When it comes to EU action on statelessness specifically, the overall picture "is one of clearly emerging interest, but this has yet to crystallise into a concerted, comprehensive and coordinated vision or response".[879] It has also been held that "the EU institutions' growing commitment to fundamental rights protection should garner support for a novel attempt to 're-person' the stateless residents of Union territory," meaning that they are made "visible again by according a legal status".[880] But before considering EU action on preventing and solving statelessness more elaborately, it is important to have

[878] Art 2 Council Regulation (EC) No 168/2007 of 15 February 2007 establishing a European Union Agency for Fundamental Rights [2007] OJ L53/1.

[879] Laura van Waas, 'Study: Addressing the Human Rights Impact of Statelessness in the EU's External Action' (2014) EXPO/B/2014/2014/07, 5 <https://www.europarl.europa.eu/RegData/etudes/STUD/2014/534983/IPOL_STU%282014%29534983_EN.pdf> accessed 17 October 2021.

[880] Julia Bradshaw, 'Stateless in Europe. The Unbearable Lightness of Being an Unperson in the EU' in Nuno Ferreira & Dora Kostakopoulou (eds), *The Human Face of the European Union. Are EU Law and Policy Humane Enough?* (Cambridge University Press 2016) 260–292, 284.

a sense of some of the background to the key legal instruments in the EU that are of relevance.

The EU is built on the common values of its member states:

> "The Union is founded on the values of respect for human dignity, freedom, democracy, equality, the rule of law and respect for human rights, including the rights of persons belonging to minorities. These values are common to the Member States in a society in which pluralism, non-discrimination, tolerance, justice, solidarity and equality between women and men prevail."[881]

It aims to "promote peace, its values and the well-being of its peoples".[882] Importantly, the EU has tried to strengthen European integration through the introduction of EU citizenship in the Treaty of Maastricht. Indeed, the purpose of EU citizenship is

> "to rationalize (symbolically and institutionally) the disordered array of individual freedoms and faculties linked to the EU and its legal order; [and] to create a new recognizable symbol capable of enhancing, precisely, political integration and mutual bonding among all EU citizens, regardless of nationality."[883]

The EU foundational values are based on the constitutional traditions of the member states, and it can be seen as a common extension of the constitutional structure of the member states. These values are also considered an extension of the constitutional traditions of its member states.[884]

Every person holding the nationality of a member state of the EU also holds European citizenship. EU citizenship does not replace national citizenship, but is additional to it.[885] European citizenship thus also is an extension of national citizenship in the member states. EU citizens are entitled to certain rights, set out in Articles 20–24 TFEU, such as the right to move and reside freely in the member states and the right to vote for the EP. This concept of EU citizenship has also developed since its introduction and has been influenced by the jurisprudence of the CJEU. Indeed, as can be seen in the paragraphs that follow, case law relating to EU citizenship is very relevant to nationality matters and potentially also to addressing statelessness. It has been recognized that "[t]he scope of Union law has been significantly affected by the case law of the Court of Justice in the area of European citizenship[...]".[886] It is, however, important to notice that whereas the EU certainly has influence on EU citizenship, it formally has no power as regards citizenship matters at the national level as these are within the exclusive

881 Art 2 TEU.
882 Art 3(1) TEU.
883 Maurizio Ferrera, 'EU Citizenship Needs a Stronger Social Dimension and Soft Duties' in Rainer Bauböck (ed), *Debating European Citizenship* (IMISCOE Research Series, SpringerOpen 2019) 181.
884 Cf Art 6(3) TEU.
885 Art 9 TEU; Art 20 TFEU.
886 Hanneke van Eijken, *European Citizenship and the Constitutionalisation of the European Union* (Europa Law Publishing 2015) 95.

competence of the member states.[887] Commentators have held that "[t]here is no competence in the Treaties to deal directly with the laws on nationality of the member states".[888] Paragraph 4.2.2 explores the concept of EU citizenship and relevant case law relating to this to further uncover EU influence on nationality matters in the member states and the ways in which this concept is pertinent to preventing and solving statelessness.

Stateless people are explicitly mentioned in the EU treaties. According to Article 67(2) TFEU, stateless people are to be treated as third-country nationals (TCNs), meaning that they are considered not to be EU citizens under the EU's area of freedom, security and justice, which includes "[p]olicies as diverse as border controls, immigration, asylum, European citizenship and freedom of movement, cooperation in criminal justice and police".[889] The absence of internal border checks demanded European cooperation and policies as regards border checks, asylum and immigration. Indeed, this led to the development of a common European asylum system (CEAS), which comprises common procedures, criteria and statuses for third-country nationals in the EU – among which are certainly also stateless people.[890] To better understand the treatment of stateless people and the way in which they are identified (or not) in the EU, it is therefore appropriate to consider the role that the CEAS plays or can play in preventing and solving statelessness in paragraph 4.2.3 of this chapter.

As was explained in chapter 1, this study takes a human rights perspective to preventing and solving statelessness, not in the last place because of the relevance of human rights to this topic. Paragraph 4.2.4 therefore considers the EU's human rights catalogue, the EU Charter. Thereafter, paragraph 4.2.5 introduces any further relevant legal instruments of the EU that could be of relevance to preventing and solving statelessness. Please note that these only include instruments that are of relevance to addressing statelessness within the borders of the EU. This means that the EU external action and policy on human rights, looking at issues in third countries that would never be part of the EU, is not considered, because the focus is on addressing statelessness within the EU. There have been some developments of relevance to statelessness in this area though[891] and the attention to statelessness in EU external action on human rights is perhaps even more reason to make sure that statelessness is (also) adequately

---

887 On the division of competences, please refer to Arts 2–6 TFEU.

888 Hans Ulrich Jessurun d'Oliveira, 'Union Citizenship and Beyond' in Nathan Cambien, Dimitry Kochenov & Elise Muir (eds), *European Citizenship under Stress. Social Justice, Brexit and Other Challenges* (Nijhoff Studies in European Union Law Vol 16, Brill Nijhoff 2020) 38.

889 Elspeth Guild & Sergio Carrera, 'The European Union's Area of Freedom, Security and Justice Ten Years On' in Elspeth Guild, Sergio Carrera & Alejandro Eggenschwiler (eds), *The Area of Freedom, Security and Justice Ten Years On. Successes and Future Challenges under the Stockholm Programme* (Centre for European Policy Studies 2010) 1.

890 Cf Art 78 TFEU.

891 Laura van Waas, 'Study: Addressing the Human Rights Impact of Statelessness in the EU's External Action' (2014) EXPO/B/2014/2014/07 <https://www.europarl.europa.eu/RegData/etudes/STUD/2014/534983/IPOL_STU%282014%29534983_EN.pdf> accessed 17 October 2021. See also eg European Parliament Resolution of 14 June 2018 on the situation of Rohingya refugees, in particular the plight of children [2018] 2018/2756(RSP), in which the EP "[w]elcomes the UN campaign to

addressed within the borders of the EU. This section closes with some concluding remarks on the instruments, actors and trends before thematically analyzing the EU's legal possibilities for the prevention of and solutions to statelessness.

4.2.2. EUROPEAN CITIZENSHIP

The introduction of European citizenship, or EU citizenship, in the 1992 Treaty of Maastricht was the outcome of a process that had already started in the 1970s, when several people involved with the institutions of the European Community already expressed the wish of strengthening integration between member states by enhancing a European identity. It was considered that this could perhaps be accomplished by involving the citizens of the member states in the EU integration process, which resulted in the idea of establishing a particular form of citizenship to this end.[892] It took some time for this idea to get off the ground:

> "It was only later, at the summit in Madrid on the 25th and 26th of June 1989, that the political will to introduce European citizenship became tangible. The heads of state gathered in the Spanish capital stressed how the European Community had failed to realise 'the Europe of citizens' [... and] the European Parliament called for a specific formulation of rights of European citizenship to be included in the future Treaty of Maastricht."[893]

Today, explicit reference to European citizenship can be found both in the TFEU – Article 20 – and in the TEU – Article 9, as part of the provision on the EU's democratic principles. It is also encountered in all articles of Title V of the EU Charter, with the exception of Article 41, which provides the right to good administration to every person. In particular, part two of the TFEU contains further provisions regarding non-discrimination and citizenship of the Union. Articles 18 and 19 TFEU explicate that discrimination on the basis of nationality shall be prohibited, and that the EU can take action against discrimination based on sex, racial or ethnic origin, religion or belief, disability, age or sexual orientation. Article 20 TFEU then announces the establishment of European citizenship, and clearly sets out that every person that holds the nationality of a member state, also is a European citizen. Furthermore, European citizenship shall be additional to national citizenship and does not replace it. At the same time, it seems clear that EU citizenship tries to make European citizens less dependent on their national citizenship, at least for a certain number of rights and for the purpose of EU law.

---

end statelessness by 2024 [and] recalls that the Rohingya are an integral part of the population of Myanmar and must therefore be recognised as such in law".

892 Cf Patricia Mindus, *European Citizenship After Brexit. Freedom of Movement and Rights of Residence* (Palgrave Macmillan 2017) 8.

893 Ibid, 9–10.

That European citizenship resembles nationality of a democratic state in different ways, is affirmed when considering the rights attached to this status and comparing these with the rights generally attached to nationality as considered in paragraph 1.4.2. According to Article 21 TFEU (also referred to in Article 20(2)(a) TFEU and Article 45 EU Charter), every EU citizen has the right to move and reside freely within the territory of the member states, subject to the limitations and conditions laid down in the Treaties and by the measures adopted to give them effect. Indeed, one of the key aspects of nationality today is that it allows you to reside (permanently) on the territory of the state of nationality and that you can also leave and re-enter this territory. Furthermore, the right to vote and stand for election that is attached to nationality in democratic states, is also present for citizens of the Union. According to Article 22 TFEU (also considered in Article 20(2)(b) TFEU and Articles 39 and 40 EU Charter), EU citizens have the right to vote and to stand as candidates in elections to the EP and in municipal elections in their member state of residence, under the same conditions as nationals of that state. Furthermore, the traditional right to consular assistance by the state of nationality in the territory of a third country in which the 'own' member state is not represented is extended in Article 23 TFEU (see also Article 20(2)c TFEU and Article 46 EU Charter) so that EU citizens can then enjoy the protection of the diplomatic authorities of any member state under the same conditions as the nationals of that state. Furthermore, the right of EU citizens to petition the EP, to apply to the European Ombudsman, and to address EU institutions (in any of the Treaty languages) is explicitly included in Article 24 TFEU (also mentioned in Article 20(2)(d) TFEU and see Articles 43 and 44 EU Charter as well). All these rights, however, are complementary to existing rights a person may already have in these areas at national level. But here they are, in addition to the institutions of the EU, sometimes also addressed to the institutions of a state other than the state of nationality, for example with regard to municipal suffrage and consular protection. At the same time, this makes clear that European citizenship is a meaningful status and that it could set back those who do not have access to it even more.

European citizenship and the rights attached to this status have been the subject of considerable jurisprudence of the CJEU. Generally, the Court has held that European citizenship should be seen as "the fundamental status of nationals of the member states, enabling those who find themselves in the same situation to enjoy the same treatment in law irrespective of their nationality".[894] In the case of *Eman and Sevinger*, the latter principle of non-discrimination was confirmed when electoral rights attached to EU citizenship were limited based on place of residence. The Court ruled that "the principle of equal treatment prevents, however, the criteria chosen from resulting in different treatment of nationals who are in comparable situations, unless that difference in treatment is objectively justified".[895] The fundamental nature of the status of European

---

894 Case C-184/99 *Rudy Grzelczyk v Centre public d'aide sociale d'Ottignies-Louvain-la-Neu* [2001] ECLI:EU:C:2001:458, para 31.

895 Case C-300/04 *M.G. Eman and O.B. Sevinger v College van burgemeester en wethouders van Den Haag* [2006] ECLI:EU:C:2006:545, para 61.

citizen was furthermore clarified in the *Baumbast* ruling, which demonstrated that the right to reside in one of the member states of the EU is directly conferred to EU citizens by (currently) Article 21(1) of the TFEU.[896] Moreover, the cases of *Zhu and Chen* and *Ruiz Zambrano* demonstrated that European citizenship as a substantive status also meant that parent(s) or legal guardian(s) of minor EU citizens that are third-country nationals should not be denied residence rights or a work permit.[897] Indeed, the *Ruiz Zambrano* case has been referred to as a "new stage in defining the significance of EU citizenship", as in this case there had even been no usage of the EU rights to free movement or residence, which were before considered to 'trigger' EU law in this sphere.[898] In other case law, the Court has subsequently confirmed and clarified that European citizenship as a substantive status may be invoked in situations where "the application of measures by a Member State that would have the effect of depriving him of the genuine enjoyment of the substance of the rights conferred by virtue of his status as a Union citizen or of impeding the exercise of his right of free movement and residence within the territory of the Member States".[899] Thus, member states and the EU itself are to ensure that EU citizens who are in the same situations are treated equally and "should leave the substantive core of rights under EU citizenship intact".[900] This reference to 'the substance of rights attaching to EU citizenship' has also been held to lead to a significant protection of the right to reside for EU citizens and their TCN parent(s) or legal guardian(s): "it protects not only the physical presence of EU minors and their parents within the territory of the Union, but also their right to take part in the distribution of social goods within the EU political community".[901]

Stephen Coutts analyzes recent case law on expulsion in relation to EU citizenship as a fundamental status and feels that EU citizenship can be considered a contingent citizenship, in between a migration status and full citizenship.[902] This in view of the fact that a person's status can be dependent on conditions and limitations and may even be suspended. But it also remains a status of citizenship because of its rights-based essence. He says:

---

896 Case C-413/99 *Baumbast, R v Secretary of State for the Home Department* [2002] ECLI:EU:C:2002:493, para 84.

897 Case C-200/02 *Kunqian Catherine Zhu and Man Lavette Chen v Secretary of State for the Home Department* [2004] ECLI:EU:C:2004:639, para 47; Case 34/09 *Gerardo Ruiz Zambrano v Office national de l'emploi (ONEm)* [2011] ECLI:EU:C:2011:124, para 45.

898 Pierluigi Simone, 'Nationality and Regional Integration. The Case of the European Union' in Alessandra Annoni & Serena Forlati (eds), *The Changing Role of Nationality in International Law* (Routledge 2013) 169–192, 176–177.

899 Case C-434/09 *Shirley McCarthy v Secretary of State for the Home Department* [2011] ECLI:EU:C:2011:277, para 56.

900 Katerina Kalaitzaki, 'EU Citizenship as a Means of Broadening the Application of EU Fundamental Rights: Developments and Limits' in Nathan Cambien, Dimitry Kochenov & Elise Muir (eds), *European Citizenship under Stress. Social Justice, Brexit and Other Challenges* (Nijhoff Studies in European Union Law Vol 16, Brill Nijhoff 2020) 55.

901 Chiara Raucea, 'Citizenship Inverted: From Rights to Status?' (PhD, Tilburg University 2017) 143–144.

902 Stephen Coutts, 'A Contingent Citizenship – Union Citizenship and Expulsion' in Sandra Mantu, Paul Minderhoud & Elspeth Guild (eds), *EU Citizenship and Free Movement Rights: Taking Supranational Citizenship Seriously* (Immigration and Asylum Law and Policy in Europe, Vol. 47, Brill Nijhoff 2020) 243–264.

> "Union citizens were to be rendered less 'other' in the eyes of the Member States and their governments. Nonetheless, it is telling that in a number of key areas, traditionally deemed the core of citizenship, have resisted this trend. While certain political rights have been extended to non-national Union citizens, the most important – the right to vote in national elections – has not. Similarly, the unconditional right to reside in the state and absolute protection from expulsion has not been extended to non-national Union citizens in an unconditional fashion. Despite the Court's oft-proclaimed mantra that Union citizenship is to become 'the fundamental status of the nationals of the Member States' it would seem that nationality still matters in key respects."[903]

At the same time, the way in which the concept of EU citizenship has evolved, and the way in which third county nationals may rely on it in view of CJEU jurisprudence, means that differences and inequalities between third-country nationals can occur, for instance between those who can rely on the European citizen status of their children and those who cannot. Moreover, there is a clear difference between those with and without a status as EU citizen in view of the fundamental status of this concept. Indeed, it has been held that the EU treaties

> "frame the scope of the beneficiaries of European citizenship exclusively in terms of exclusion. The Member States alone decide who gets to join. While the majority of the Member States' nationals do not actually suffer as a consequence of such a state-centric approach to the definition of the scope of the supranational citizenship, it blocks the way to European citizenship status for all those who, although long-term residents in the EU, are not in possession of any of the twenty-seven Member States' nationality. These people, whose exclusion from the scope of European citizenship status is difficult to justify, are the most obvious victims of the present status allocation system."[904]

As such, it may be argued that European citizenship certainly also creates inequalities: not only between third-country nationals who are able to rely on the EU citizenship of a family member and those who cannot[905], but it also deepens the differences between persons with and without member state nationality and, hence, EU citizenship.

In its jurisprudence regarding European citizenship, CJEU case law has also addressed nationality laws of member states. As was seen earlier in paragraph 4.2.1, the

---

903 Stephen Coutts, 'A Contingent Citizenship – Union Citizenship and Expulsion' in Sandra Mantu, Paul Minderhoud & Elspeth Guild (eds), *EU Citizenship and Free Movement Rights: Taking Supranational Citizenship Seriously* (Immigration and Asylum Law and Policy in Europe, Vol. 47, Brill Nijhoff 2020) 243–264, 258.

904 Dimitry Kochenov, 'The Ius Tractum of Many Faces: European Citizenship and the Difficult Relationship Between Status and Rights' (2009) 15 Colombia Journal of European Law 169, 235–236.

905 See also the difference that is made as regards family reunification, where family members of EU citizens (even when they are third-country nationals) can rely on Directive 2004/38/EC of the European Parliament and of the Council of 29 April 2004 on the Right of Citizens of the Union and their Family Members to Move and Reside Freely within the Territory of the Member States [2004] OJ L 158/77; and family reunification of third-country nationals is governed by Council Directive 2003/86/EC of 22 September 2003 on the Right to Family Reunification [2003] OJ L 251/12.

EU has no (formal) competence as regards nationality laws; these are decided on by the individual member states. Arguably however, there is some EU influence to be seen in the development of the Court's case law, marked by the 1992 *Micheletti*-case. In this case, the Court held that "[u]nder international law, it is for each Member State, *having due regard to Community law*, to lay down the conditions for the acquisition and loss of nationality".[906] It is remarkable that the Court seems to imply that an obligation for member states exists *under international law* to consider EU law in their decisions regarding nationality.[907] But this case shows that there may be boundaries to states' discretion in nationality matters that can be derived from EU law, and in particular, European citizenship.

The landmark case of *Rottmann*[908] provided the CJEU with a direct opportunity to consider the regulation of acquisition and loss of nationality in light of EU law, as it concerned the revocation of naturalization by a member state. This 2011 case concerned Mr. Rottmann, who was an Austrian national and acquired German nationality fraudulently. When the German authorities discovered this fraud, Rottmann had already lost his Austrian nationality and would effectively be made stateless if his German nationality was revoked. It was precisely this fact, that Rottmann would lose his German nationality and that he had no other nationality of an EU member state, that made it possible for the Court to intervene in this case. With his German citizenship, Rottmann would of course also lose his European citizenship and the rights attached to this 'fundamental status'. As such, the Court finds that "a decision withdrawing naturalisation such as that at issue in the[se ...] proceedings, is amenable to judicial review carried out in the light of European Union law".[909] The Court goes on to find that withdrawal of nationality is not necessarily contrary to EU law, but the proportionality of this decision has to be considered in light of EU law. This examination needs

> "to take into account the consequences that the decision entails for the person concerned and, if relevant, for the members of his family with regard to the loss of the rights enjoyed by every citizen of the Union. In this respect it is necessary to establish, in particular, whether that loss is justified in relation to the gravity of the offence committed by that person, to the lapse of time between the naturalisation decision and the withdrawal decision and to whether it is possible for that person to recover his original nationality."[910]

The *Rottmann* case clarified that in view of the fundamental status that European citizenship is meant to be and the connection between nationality and EU citizenship,

---

906 Case C-369/90 *Mario Vicente Micheletti and Others v Delegación del Gobierno en Cantabria* [1992] ECLI:EU:C:1992:295, para 10, emphasis added CV.

907 Cf Hans Ulrich Jessurun d'Oliveira, 'Union Citizenship and Beyond' in Nathan Cambien, Dimitry Kochenov & Elise Muir (eds), *European Citizenship under Stress. Social Justice, Brexit and Other Challenges* (Nijhoff Studies in European Union Law Vol 16, Brill Nijhoff 2020) 37.

908 Case C-135/08 *Janko Rottmann v Freistaat Bayern* [2010] ECLI:EU:C:2010:104.

909 Ibid, para 48.

910 Ibid, para 56.

national rules must "respect the general principles of EU law".[911] In view of the general principles of EU law, it has been argued on the basis of the principle of sincere cooperation between the member states (Article 4(3) TEU) that they "are obliged to inform and consult other member states and the European institutions prior to the adoption of measures on the loss or acquisition of nationality".[912] According to the principle of sincere cooperation, member states need to take appropriate measures to ensure fulfilment of the obligations arising out of the Union Treaties or resulting from the acts of the institutions of the EU. They also need to facilitate the achievement of the Union's tasks and refrain from any measure which could jeopardize the EU's aims. Because national rules on national citizenship may affect the core of European citizenship, such obligation can be distilled. Such an idea of coordination between member states in some way on domestic rules relating to nationality could again be helpful in ensuring that no one falls between the cracks and is left stateless, and could constitute another mechanism to help in preventing statelessness as a result of national rules relating to loss of nationality.

Some have seen the decision of the CJEU in the *Rottmann* case as "judicial error" because under EU law and in the view of other EU institutions, such as the Commission, nationality laws remain within the exclusive competence of the member states.[913] In relation to this, an argument may be made for the need to decouple national citizenship and EU citizenship: "the EU would no longer need the (indirect) authority over the nationality law of the member states that the Court has accorded to it, and that can only serve to benefit the clarity of the relationship between the member states and the EU".[914] Others welcome the CJEU's decision in this case "as a milestone in the sphere of nationality law"[915] and point out the important consequences this has for the member states. Indeed, they assert that "all decisions on acquisition and loss of nationality have to be reasoned in order not to conflict with European law".[916] Even though this case does not explicitly say that it is contrary to EU law to withdraw citizenship, thereby making a person stateless, it does invite further consideration of principles of EU law into national decisions that concern loss and acquisition of nationality.

> "Rottmann firmly establishes the jurisdiction of the ECJ in questions relating to the regulation of nationality. While Rottmann centred on an emerging case of statelessness, for

911 Gareth T Davies, 'The Entirely Conventional Supremacy of Union Citizenship and Rights' in Jo Shaw (eds), *Has the European Court of Justice Challenged Member State Sovereignty in Nationality Law?* (EUI Working Paper RSCAS 2011/62, European University Institute 2011) 5–10, 9.

912 Sergio Carrera & Gerard-René de Groot, 'European Citizenship at a Crossroads. Enhancing European Cooperation on Acquisition and Loss of Nationality' (2014) CEPS Paper in Liberty and Security in Europe No. 72, 3 <https://www.ceps.eu/wp-content/uploads/2015/01/No%2072%20European%20 Citizenship%20at%20Crossroads.pdf> accessed 17 October 2021.

913 Hans Ulrich Jessurun d'Oliveira, 'Decoupling Nationality and Union Citizenship?' (2011) 7 European Constitutional Law Review 138, 145.

914 Ibid, 148.

915 Gerard-René de Groot & Anja Seling, 'The Consequences of the *Rottmann* Judgment on Member State Autonomy – The European Court of Justice's Avant-Gardism in Nationality Matters' (2011) 7 European Constitutional Law Review 150.

916 Ibid, 157.

> which the proportionality test was given paramount importance by the ECJ, future cases may also surround other EU principles. For instance, among the general principles of EU law is the prohibition of discrimination, which may lead the ECJ to scrutinise EU member states' nationality policy as to its discriminatory content or effects."[917]

The 2019 *Tjebbes* case[918] clarifies and expands on the CJEU's reasoning in the *Rottmann* case. The case concerned Dutch laws that provide for automatic loss of nationality due to residence abroad. The case reaffirms some of the Court's earlier considerations regarding EU citizenship in relation to nationality laws of the member states. In particular, the CJEU repeats that member states must have due regard for international and EU law when laying down conditions for acquisition and loss of nationality. The Court also reiterates the importance of the proportionality principle:

> "The loss of the nationality of a Member State by operation of law would be inconsistent with the principle of proportionality if the relevant national rules did not permit at any time an individual examination of the consequences of that loss for the persons concerned from the point of view of EU law."[919]

The Court further explains in this regard that difficulties to travel are relevant to this proportionality test for instance, but does not define the contents of this test exhaustively.[920] What is also interesting in this case, is that the CJEU looks at the concept of nationality more closely. It says that it is legitimate for member states to interpret nationality as an articulation of the genuine link between a person and a state, and that absence thereof can result in losing said nationality[921], and goes on to consider habitual, uninterrupted residence abroad for ten years as an indication that there is no such link.[922] Moreover, the legitimacy of such considerations is, according to the Court, underlined by the fact that there was no risk of persons becoming stateless under the provisions at issue.[923] Statelessness was thus not a concern, whereas it was in the *Rottmann* case. With regard to statelessness specifically, the *Tjebbes* case hence does not seem to say much, but the CJEU's considerations do show "some concern of the Court with avoidance of statelessness"[924], when it considers international instruments on the prevention of statelessness and checks whether statelessness is at issue in this case.

The *Tjebbes* case has been welcomed as a next step in case law on nationality matters in the EU and it did clarify some of the Court's considerations as regards the role of EU

917 Laura van Waas, 'Fighting Statelessness and Discriminatory Nationality Laws in Europe' (2012) 14 European Journal on Migration and Law 243, 257.
918 Case C-221/17 *Tjebbes and Others v Minister van Buitenlandse Zaken* [2019] ECLI:EU:C:2019:189.
919 Ibid, para 41.
920 Ibid, para 46.
921 Ibid, para 35.
922 Ibid, para 36.
923 Ibid, para 37.
924 Caia Vlieks, '*Tjebbes and Others v Minister van Buitenlandse Zaken*: A Next Step in European Union Case Law on Nationality Matters?' (2019) 24 Tilburg Law Review 142, 145.

law in domestic provisions on nationality as well as the proportionality test that is to be applied when a person would lose citizenship of a member state, and thereby European citizenship. However, the Court's decision has also raised questions and has even been characterized as a failure. Indeed, it is questionable in light of the 'genuine link' and the reciprocal bond between the state and the individual that this represents, that the individual needs to take action to maintain this bond by – in this case – reapplying for an official document within a certain period of time, "whereas the state can just 'sit back and relax' and provide for automatic loss of nationality after a certain period of time".[925] Indeed, commentators have held that

> "punishing those who fail to renew a passport worse than known terrorists, jihadists and ISIS wives, denying them the legal connection with the EU and the rights to be enjoyed in the internal market, while opening a possibility to weigh this punishment against the use of the rights they are precisely being deprived of for no reason at all and in the interest of no stated EU-related common good, in the context where such use cannot be hypothetical or merely a possibility is undoubtedly a moment significantly undermining the EU integration project".[926]

It has been argued that European citizenship is or should be developing into an autonomous status, also in view of evolving case law.[927] Some authors have, moreover, considered European citizenship as a potential solution for stateless people in the EU, and more specifically for populations in the EU that have a history of statelessness: the Roma and the non-citizens from the Baltic States. Julia Bradshaw, for instance, promotes the idea of European citizenship being extended to all subjects of the EU – both "aliens and natives". She says:

> "Removing the commitment to nationality and substituting societal interaction would produce a fleshed out and reciprocal iteration of citizenship that promotes the Union, its objectives and opportunities and that could fight the overall apathy exhibited by current citizens towards Union affairs by treating all resident actors as though they had an equal interest in the running of the Union."[928]

Also, it has been theorized that granting European citizenship has additional benefits for stateless people when comparing this to being granted residence status. It has been

---

925 Ibid.

926 Dimitry Kochenov, 'The *Tjebbes* Fail' (2019) 4 European Papers 319, 335–336.

927 See eg the discussion by numerous relevant scholars, arguing *pro* and *contra* autonomous European citizenship in Liav Orgard & Jules Lepoutre (eds), 'Should EU Citizenship Be Disentangled from Member State Nationality?' (2019) EUI Working Paper RSCAS 2019/24 <https://cadmus.eui.eu/bitstream/handle/1814/62229/RSCAS%202019_24rev2.pdf> accessed 17 October 2021.

928 Julia Bradshaw, 'Emerging From the Chrysalis: Union Citizenship Must Escape Its Nationality-Based Shortcomings' (2013) 34 Liverpool Law Review 195, 213. See also Julia Bradshaw, 'Stateless in Europe. The Unbearable Lightness of Being an Unperson in the EU' in Nuno Ferreira & Dora Kostakopoulou (eds), *The Human Face of the European Union. Are EU Law and Policy Humane Enough?* (Cambridge University Press 2016) 260–292.

argued that it could help to mitigate rights-related challenges that stateless people face, including discrimination, and could perhaps aid in indirectly facilitating acquisition of nationality by naturalization.[929]

That conferral of EU citizenship to stateless populations in the EU is not a clear-cut solution in view of the EU treaties and its additional and complementary nature, is at the same time something that many of these authors are aware of. Indeed, in presenting European citizenship as a potential solution for Roma who are (at risk of) stateless(ness) in the EU, authors also show the probable inadequacies and the need for, for instance, strategic litigation to help in making this possible.[930] Dimitry Kochenov and Aleksejs Dimitrovs, however, present a proposal for European citizenship for Latvian non-citizens. This is based on the premise that the status of non-citizen is a separate status, distinct from that of a national and of an alien (refugee or stateless person), and does imply obligations between the non-citizen and the Latvian state.[931] They also argue that "member state nationality for the purposes of EU law can have a different meaning and scope compared with 'citizenship' in national law,"[932] and that such extension of EU citizenship would have no internal effect. Latvia can still decide who its nationals are and could, only for the purpose of EU law, decide that this also applies to those who are non-nationals, which would then immediately extend European citizenship to these persons:

> "A simple declaration clarifying who Latvian nationals are for the purpose of EU law, if issued by the Latvian government, would suffice with immediate effect, to extend EU citizenship to all those in possession of the 'non-citizen of Latvia' status."[933]

This thus challenges the idea that a person needs to be a national of an EU member state to also be considered a European citizen; in national law, these persons would remain non-citizens of Latvia. At the same time, it does rely on the premise that only states can decide on nationality matters. Nonetheless, it provides an example of how persons who have been stateless for years in their 'own' country could access European citizenship – paradoxically by not recognizing their statelessness explicitly.

For now, it is important to remember that EU citizenship as a status may help in addressing some of the issues stateless people face and could potentially even aid in preventing and solving statelessness. However, it also seems that European citizenship as an autonomous status that is granted to stateless people may be a bridge too far. And

---

929 Anne Brekoo, 'Statelessness and the European Union: Exploring the Potential Value of Union Citizenship (2020) 2 Statelessness & Citizenship Review 24, 37.

930 Eg Jessica Parra, 'Stateless Roma in the European Union: Reconciling the Doctrine of Sovereignty Concerning Nationality Laws with International Agreements to Reduce and Avoid Statelessness' (2011) 34 Fordham International Law Journal 1666; Maylis de Verneuil, 'Nationality: Romani; Citizenship: European' (2016) Statelessness Working Paper Series No. 2016/03.

931 Dimitry Kochenov & Aleksejs Dimitrovs, 'EU Citizenship for Latvian "Non-Citizens": A Concrete Proposal' (2016) 38 Houston Journal of International Law 55, 60.

932 Ibid, 62.

933 Ibid, 61–62.

even if EU citizenship were to be an autonomous status, looking at it as a solution to statelessness is beyond the scope of this research, as this looks at nationality (as defined in chapter 1, granted by a state). Furthermore, it is relevant to keep in mind that

> "[...] the EU is at present simply confronted with 27 different nationality policies of States that have a very wide discretion in the domain of nationality law. There are no signs that the EU aspires to acquire competence in this field, but the call for minimum harmonization in academic literature is becoming louder."[934]

The above exploration has shown though that the concept of European citizenship has been and is developing, not least because it has been the subject of CJEU jurisprudence, also influencing EU competence on nationality matters and thereby potentially impacting the regulation of acquisition and loss of nationality in Europe and helping to prevent and solve statelessness.

4.2.3. MIGRATION AND ASYLUM POLICY

Statelessness does not figure prominently in the EU's migration and asylum policy. Indeed, the 2020 EU Pact on Asylum and Migration from the EC does not mention stateless people anywhere[935], even though it has been argued that there are opportunities to address the issue through the Pact.[936] Stateless people are to be treated in the same way as third-country nationals, and over time, "[the EU] has enriched the rights enjoyed by stateless persons residing in the territory of the Member States", for instance as regards social benefits.[937] At the same time, the question of what nationality a person does or does not have is undeniably relevant in this area of law, as third-country nationals are – in principle – the primary targets of EU migration and asylum policy. After all, EU citizens – those who possess the nationality of one of the member states of the Union – have the right to move and

934 Olivier W Vonk, *Dual Nationality in the European Union. A Study on Changing Norms in Public and Private International Law and in the Municipal Laws of Four EU Member States* (Immigration and Asylum Law and Policy in Europe, Brill/Martinus Nijhoff Publishers 2012) 160–161.

935 Communication from the Commission to the European Parliament, the Council, the European Economic and Social Committee and the Committee of the Regions on a New Pact on Migration and Asylum [2020] COM(2020) 609 final.

936 For instance as regards improved identification and recording of (indications of) statelessness at the border: ENS, 'Statelessness and the EU Pact on Asylum and Migration: Analysis and Recommendations' (2021) <https://www.statelessness.eu/sites/default/files/2021-01/ENS-Statelessness_and_the_EU_Pact_on_Asylum_and_Migration-Jan_2021_1.pdf> accessed 17 October 2021.

937 Tamás Molnár, 'Stateless Persons under International Law and EU Law: A Comparative Analysis concerning Their Legal Status, with Particular Attention to the Added Value of the EU Legal Order' (2010) 51 Acta Juridica Hungarica 293, 300; Regulation (EC) 883/2004 of the European Parliament and of the Council of 29 April 2004 on the coordination of social security systems [2004] OJ L166/1.

reside freely within EU territory. Below, the CEAS and other EU instruments used to manage migration are analyzed more closely for their relevance towards preventing and solving statelessness.

The CEAS encompasses the following secondary laws: the Asylum Procedures Directive[938], the Reception Conditions Directive[939], the Qualification Directive[940], the Dublin Regulation[941] and the EURODAC Regulation.[942] For the most part, stateless people are distinguished as a specific group from third-country nationals, but are treated exactly the same (see also Table 1 below).

TABLE 1: STATELESSNESS IN CEAS LEGAL INSTRUMENTS

Directive or Regulation	*Explicit reference to stateless people?*
Directive 2013/32/EU (on asylum procedures)	Stateless persons are mentioned alongside third-country nationals and treated the same way. One difference concerns the concept of safe country of origin, where for stateless persons it concerns the country where (s)he was formerly habitually resident (Article 36(1)(b)) as opposed to country of nationality.
Directive 2013/33/EU (on reception conditions)	Refers to stateless persons in addition to third-country nationals, but these groups are treated in the same way throughout.
Directive 2011/95/EU (on qualification as beneficiaries of international protection)	Stateless persons are consistently mentioned alongside third-country nationals and are defined as beneficiaries of international protection on equal footing. For stateless persons specifically, the Directive states that the 'country of origin' means country of former habitual residence (Article 2(n)) and that they shall cease to be a refugee or cease to be eligible for subsidiary protection if they are able to return to the country of former habitual residence (Article 11(1)(f) / Article 16(3)), again as opposed to country of nationality.
Regulation (EU) No 604/2013 (Dublin – on which member state is responsible for application for international protection)	Refers to stateless persons alongside third-country nationals, but these groups are treated in the same way throughout.
Regulation (EU) No 603/2013 (on EURODAC)	Refers to stateless persons alongside third-country nationals, but these groups are treated in the same way throughout.

938 Directive 2013/32/EU of the European Parliament and of the Council of 26 June 2013 on common procedures for granting and withdrawing international protection (Recast) [2013] OJ L 180/60.

939 Directive 2013/33/EU of the European Parliament and of the Council of 26 June 2013 laying down standards for the reception of applicants for international protection (Recast) [2013] OJ L 180/96.

940 Directive 2011/95/EU of the European Parliament and of the Council of 13 December 2011 on standards for the qualification of third-country nationals or stateless persons as beneficiaries of international protection, for a uniform status for refugees or for persons eligible for subsidiary protection, and for the content of the protection granted (Recast) [2011] OJ L 337/9.

941 Regulation (EU) No 604/2013 of the European Parliament and of the Council of 26 June 2013 establishing the criteria and mechanisms for determining the member state responsible for examining an application for international protection lodged in one of the member states by a third-country national or a stateless person (Recast) [2013] OJ L 180/31.

942 Regulation (EU) No 603/2013 of the European Parliament and of the Council of 26 June 2013 on the establishment of 'Eurodac' [...] [2013] OJ L 180/1.

It is interesting that stateless people or their specific problems, vulnerabilities, rights and status in light of international law are not more explicitly included in the CEAS. This is all the more curious when considering that the CEAS does give effect to the Refugee Convention in the EU, but that there is no equivalent for the 1954 Convention, even though they are similar instruments[943] and the latter is ratified by almost all member states of the EU.[944] With regard to the procedures, the specific vulnerabilities and uncertainties accompanying statelessness, such as vulnerability to trafficking[945], might be a reason to pay more attention to statelessness, for instance by expediting the procedure. It falls beyond the scope of this research to analyze such issues of protection of stateless people more elaborately, but there is certainly more to consider with regard to preventing and solving statelessness.

As the CEAS provides the entry point for many stateless people (and other third-country nationals) to legal residence in one of the EU member states, which is the necessary precursor for acquisition of nationality, it plays an indirect but pivotal role in solving statelessness eventually. Indeed, EU member states hold "the ultimate key to the status of European citizenship for third-country nationals via the[ir] naturalization practices [...]".[946] For instance, European countries generally allow persons recognized as a refugee or as a stateless person to acquire the nationality of the country in which they have been legally resident for a certain number of years by naturalization.[947] Some European countries also provide for facilitated naturalization for stateless people, which means that recognized stateless people would sometimes be able to naturalize and see their statelessness solved sooner than those who are not recognized as stateless, but as a refugee.[948] This not only demonstrates the relevance of the CEAS to eventually solving statelessness, it also points to the importance of proper identification of stateless people to ensure that stateless people are not left in their precarious situation for longer than strictly necessary.

When considering EU migration law more broadly, it is particularly interesting to look at the aspect of return to a country of origin or earlier residence or stay. Return is often more difficult for stateless people, because there is no country of nationality they have a right to return to, but only potentially a country of former habitual residence. This is an important difference between stateless people and (other) third-country

---

943 See also para 1.5.1.

944 For an overview of all parties to the 1954 Convention, please refer to the United Nations Treaty Collection (UNTC) <https://treaties.un.org/pages/ViewDetailsII.aspx?src=TREATY&mtdsg_no=V-3&chapter=5&Temp=mtdsg2&clang=_en> accessed 17 October 2021.

945 Conny Rijken, Laura van Waas, Martin Gramatikov & Deirdre Brennan, *The Nexus between Statelessness and Human Trafficking in Thailand* (Wolf Legal Publishers 2015).

946 Dimitry Kochenov, 'The Ius Tractum of Many Faces: European Citizenship and the Difficult Relationship Between Status and Rights' (2009) 15 Colombia Journal of European Law 169, 233.

947 Cf GLOBALCIT Global Database on Modes of Acquisition of Citizenship (2017) mode A22 (Refugees) & A23 (Stateless or Unclear Citizenship), EU countries <https://globalcit.eu/acquisition-citizenship/> accessed 17 October 2021.

948 In the Netherlands, for instance, stateless people are able to naturalize after three years instead of the common five years; cf Arts 8(1) and 8(4) of the Dutch Nationality Act (*Rijkswet op het Nederlanderschap*).

nationals, and one that is also noted explicitly in some of the CEAS legal instruments as discussed above. Moreover, statelessness often is an indication that a person is at risk of wider human rights abuses.[949] In effectuating return of stateless people, there must therefore be specific regard to the principle of *non-refoulement* under Article 3 of the ECHR.[950] Indeed, "[t]he expulsion of a stateless person to a country of former residence might [...] give rise to a risk of a breach of Article 3 of the ECHR, as statelessness is a relevant indication – a sort of 'marker' – of circumstances that the person might face if expelled, which would violate Article 3"[951], which also points to the importance of ensuring that stateless people are properly identified as such. When looking at the Return Directive[952], stateless people are not mentioned alongside third-country nationals in the same way as many other CEAS instruments – there is no reference to the fact that stateless people do not have a country of nationality to return to (but only a country of former habitual residence perhaps). At the same time, this is perhaps not so surprising given the broad definition of return and countries where a person may return to according to Article 3(3) of the Return Directive. Such countries of return, according to the Return Directive, do not only include the country of origin, but also a country of transit or another third country, to which the third-country national voluntarily decides to return and in which he or she will be accepted.[953] There is also no mention of specific vulnerabilities of stateless people, nor are they considered to be 'vulnerable persons' under the Return Directive's definition.[954] Without attention for the specific situation and problems that stateless people face, this could lead to stateless people who are subjected to the Return Directive remaining in a legal limbo with no possibly to return, nor to regularize their status, and certainly no prospect of their statelessness being solved.

> "[W]ithout adequate legal and policy frameworks in place to identify and determine who is stateless and to provide due protection under the 1954 Convention, they are often trapped in systems that criminalise their irregular migration status and subject them to detention and return procedures, pushing many into destitution without there being any real prospect of either regularisation or return."[955]

949 Eg Lindsey N Kingston, '"A Forgotten Human Rights Crisis": Statelessness and Issue (Non)Emergence' (2012) 14 Human Rights Review 73, 75–76.

950 As well as Art 33 1951 Convention – Art 18 EU Charter refers to the Refugee Convention.

951 ENS, 'Strategic Litigation: An Obligation for Statelessness Determination under the European Convention on Human Rights?' (2014) ENS Discusssion Paper 09/14, 5 <https://www.statelessness.eu/updates/publication/obligation-statelessness-determination-under-european-convention-human-rights> accessed 17 October 2021.

952 Directive 2008/115/EC of the European Parliament and of the Council of 16 December 2008 on Common Standards and Procedures in the Member States for Returning Illegally Staying Third-Country Nationals [2008] OJ L 348/98.

953 Art 3(3) Return Directive.

954 Art 3(9) Return Directive.

955 ENS, 'Statelessness and the EU Pact on Asylum and Migration: Analysis and Recommendations' (2021) 8 <https://www.statelessness.eu/sites/default/files/2021-01/ENS-Statelessness_and_the_EU_Pact_on_Asylum_and_Migration-Jan_2021_1.pdf> accessed 17 October 2021.

From this, it can be concluded that without identification of statelessness it is unclear in what situations there is a need to prevent or solve statelessness, or to afford stateless people with adequate protection. Moreover, migration and asylum policy regulate the first step every third-country national takes within the EU in terms of protection and rights, and in particular legal residence, which is a necessary precursor to naturalization – a solution to statelessness.

There is currently no specific EU legislation regarding the identification, protection, or status of stateless people though. In academic literature, however, there has been a call for this and proposals have been made, based on the argument that there is scope for the EU to legislate on statelessness: "[c]ontrary to the common assumption, the EU does have competence to legislate on certain aspects of statelessness, in particular on the identification and protection of stateless persons."[956] As neither the issue of statelessness, nor the solution to this – nationality – are explicitly mentioned in the EU treaties as an area where the EU may legislate, it is therefore necessary to explore further how the EU might have competence to legislate on the issue.

According to several commentators, an EU Treaty basis for EU legislation on identifying stateless people can be found in Articles 78 and 79 TFEU. The wording of these Articles on adopting legislation in the CEAS and on powers to legislate on other forms of immigration, and the practice of some member states grouping procedures around statelessness together with asylum-related procedures and others grouping it with non-asylum statuses, means that these Articles are suitable and sufficiently flexible to "to serve as a basis for EU legislation on the identification and protection of stateless persons".[957] Indeed, when considering the regime applicable to third-country nationals in the EU under CEAS and Article 67(2) TFEU, it is clear that the EU has "already regulated the position of stateless persons extensively on the basis of Articles 78 and 79 TFEU".[958]

Furthermore, it has been held with regard to the question of subsidiarity that

> "within an area without border controls, decisions on the residence of third-country nationals, including stateless persons, taken by one Member State may have effects on other Member States. [...] Member States' practices and legislation display considerable differences in the treatment of stateless persons. This may have undesirable cross-border effects which can be countered by a common framework for the identification and protection of stateless persons".[959]

---

956 Katja Swider, 'Protection and Identification of Stateless Persons through EU Law' (2014) ACELG Working Paper Series 2014–05, 22.

957 Ibid, 13. See also Gerard-René de Groot, Katja Swider & Olivier Vonk, 'Practices and Approaches in the EU Member States to Prevent and End Statelessness. Study for the LIBE Committee' (2015) 55 <https://www.europarl.europa.eu/RegData/etudes/STUD/2015/536476/IPOL_STU(2015)536476_EN.pdf> accessed 17 October 2021.

958 Katja Swider & Maarten den Heijer, 'Why Union Law Can and Should Protect Stateless Persons' (2017) 19 European Journal of Migration and Law 101, 127.

959 Ibid, 129–130.

Arguments on this matter have also been taken a step further, holding that there could be scope for the EU to legislate on statelessness on the basis of Article 67(2) and Article 352 TFEU[960], bringing in the so-called 'flexibility clause' which allows the EU to take action, if necessary, within the framework of the policies defined in the EU treaties. By mentioning stateless people explicitly in Article 67(2) TFEU "and equating their status to those of third-country nationals [in] the Treaty" statelessness is brought "within the scope of [the EU's] objectives, and while no Article that provides legislative competences to the EU explicitly mentions statelessness, Article 352 can be relied on".[961] However, given the limited room for application of this 'flexibility clause', for instance in view of the unanimity required in the Council as well as the fact that this provision is limited to what is needed to attain the objectives of the EU treaties, it seems unlikely that this could serve as a basis for legislating on this in practice.

Alternatively, it has been held that EU legislative action on identification and protection of stateless people could be based on Article 21(2) TFEU:

> "Article 21(2) [...] TFEU could be used to enact rules on the determination of statelessness for cases where the determination of being (otherwise) stateless has as a consequence that the individual involved possesses or can acquire the nationality of an EU Member State and thereby is or would become a European citizen".[962]

Such a scenario is possible in cases where a stateless person has been able to obtain legal status on the territory of the EU, but it remains impossible to naturalize and become a citizen of one of the member states of the EU, and hence, a citizen of the Union. Many EU member states require certain types of identity documentation, in particular a birth certificate, for a citizenship application.[963] Stateless people are more likely than any other group to be unable to produce these in view of no country recognizing them – also administratively – as their citizen.[964] It might thus be argued that failing to identify a person as stateless, a status which entails facilitated naturalization[965] in which usually no such documentation needs to be produced, can therefore lead to stateless people being denied acquisition of EU citizenship and the rights attached to this status.

---

960 Cf Tamás Molnár, 'Moving Statelessness Forward on the International Agenda' (2014) 19 Tilburg Law Review 194, 198 (footnote 21).

961 Katja Swider, 'Protection and Identification of Stateless Persons through EU Law' (2014) ACELG Working Paper Series 2014–05, 14.

962 Gerard-René de Groot, Katja Swider & Olivier Vonk, 'Practices and Approaches in the EU Member States to Prevent and End Statelessness. Study for the LIBE Committee' (2015) 54 <https://www.europarl.europa.eu/RegData/etudes/STUD/2015/536476/IPOL_STU(2015)536476_EN.pdf> accessed 17 October 2021.

963 EMN, 'Pathways to Citizenship for Third-Country Nationals in the EU. EMN Synthesis Report for the EMN Study 2019' (2020) 25 <https://emn.ie/wp-content/uploads/2020/07/2020_eu_emn_study_synthesis_report_citizenship_final_en_0.pdf> accessed 17 October 2021.

964 Cf David Owen, 'On the Right to Have Nationality Rights: Statelessness, Citizenship and Human Rights' (2018) 65 Netherlands International Law Review 299, 303.

965 See also Art 32 1954 Convention.

There is thus some scope for the EU to legislate on their identification and protection. It is therefore not surprising that there have been calls for enacting an EU directive on statelessness determination.[966] Such proposals often concern the nature of identification or determination of statelessness that needs to take place, as well as protection and rights that should be granted, including the question of residence status. These often draw from and refer to existing guidance and good practices on this.[967] So far, a directive or other form of EU legislation specifically on statelessness has not (yet) materialized. However, recognizing "the importance of exchanging good practices among Member States concerning the collection of reliable data on stateless persons as well as the procedures for determining statelessness", the Council and representatives of the member states adopted conclusions on statelessness in 2015.[968] In these conclusions they pointed to the European Migration Network (EMN)[969] as the platform for exchanging experiences and good practices on the issue of statelessness. In the years that followed, there have been signs of some further cooperation on the matter in Europe, and perhaps even the beginnings of harmonization on the determination of statelessness, as evidenced by EMN reports and informs.[970]

---

966 Eg Gerard-René de Groot, Katja Swider & Olivier Vonk, 'Practices and Approaches in the EU Member States to Prevent and End Statelessness. Study for the LIBE Committee' (2015) 60 <https://www.europarl.europa.eu/RegData/etudes/STUD/2015/536476/IPOL_STU(2015)536476_EN.pdf> accessed 17 October 2021; Katja Swider & Maarten den Heijer, 'Why Union Law Can and Should Protect Stateless Persons' (2017) 19 European Journal of Migration and Law 101, 130; Meijers Committee, 'A Proposal for an EU Directive on the Identification and Protection of Stateless Persons' (2014) <https://www.commissie-meijers.com/sites/all/files/cm1410_proposal_for_an_eu_directive_on_the_identification_and_the_protection_of_stateless_persons.pdf> accessed 17 October 2021. The Meijers Committee was founded in the Netherlands in 1991 and is group of law professors, legal researchers, judges and attorneys that aims to inform European institutions and Dutch Parliament about the impact of European law developments.

967 UNHCR, 'Handbook on the Protection of Stateless Persons under the 1954 Convention relating to the Status of Stateless Persons' (Geneva, 2014) <www.unhcr.org/protection/statelessness/53b698ab9/handbook-protection-stateless-persons.html> accessed 2 August 2021; ENS, 'Statelessness Determination and the Protection Status of Stateless Persons. A Summary Guide of Good Practices and Factors to Consider When Designing National Determination and Protection Mechanisms' (2013) <https://www.statelessness.eu/sites/default/files/2020-09/Statelessness%2520determination%2520and%2520the%2520protection%2520status%2520of%2520stateless%2520persons%2520ENG.pdf> accessed 17 October 2021.

968 Conclusions of the Council and the Representatives of the Governments of the Member States on Statelessness [2015] <https://www.consilium.europa.eu/en/press/press-releases/2015/12/04/council-adopts-conclusions-on-statelessness/> accessed 17 October 2021.

969 The EMN is an EU network of experts on asylum and migration law and policy, which collects information in different European countries and aims to provide objective and comparable data on this <https://ec.europa.eu/home-affairs/what-we-do/networks/european_migration_network_en> accessed 17 October 2021.

970 See the Platform on Statelessness on the EMN/EU website <https://ec.europa.eu/home-affairs/pages/page/platform-statelessness_en> accessed 17 October 2021; EMN, 'Statelessness in the EU' (2016) EMN Inform <https://emn.ie/files/p_201702100930222016_emn_inform_on_statelessness.pdf> accessed 17 October 2021; EMN, 'EMN Platform on Statelessness: A Progress Report' (2017) <https://emn.ie/files/p_20180124121544EMN%20Platform%20on%20Statelessness_Progress%20Report_final_2018.pdf> accessed 17 October 2021; EMN, 'Statelessness in the European Union' (2020)

As we saw, legal status in the EU is the first step for third-country nationals towards becoming a citizen of one of its member states, and thereby, of the EU. Even though there is currently no specific EU legislation on stateless people or their identification, which is key to understanding the need to prevent and solve statelessness, it is clear that EU migration law and policy affects their position. The status of stateless people in the EU is regulated by EU migration law and policy, as this lays down the procedures and requirements for obtaining residence status in the EU.

4.2.4. FUNDAMENTAL RIGHTS

As could be seen in paragraph 4.2.1, the EU is built on fundamental values including the respect for human dignity and human rights and has its own fundamental rights catalogue, the EU Charter. The EU Charter is legally binding and has the same status as the EU treaties[971], making this instrument increasingly important in the activities of the Union and in jurisprudence of the CJEU. This also relates to the relative modernity of the EU Charter when compared to the other key human rights instrument in Europe, the ECHR. Indeed, the EU Charter is not only a more recent and elaborate fundamental rights instrument, but also protects certain 'modern' rights, such as a right to good administration[972], a right to protection of personal data[973], and a right to asylum.[974] Taking a constitutional view on the EU Charter, it has been held that this instrument serves three principal purposes:

> "First, it serves as a source of inspiration for the discovery of general principles of EU law. Second, it serves as an aid to interpretation. Given that the provisions of the Charter are primary EU law, secondary EU law, as well as national law implementing EU law, must be interpreted in the light of those provisions. Finally, it has been relied upon as providing grounds for judicial review. EU legislation that breaches the Charter is to be annulled or declared invalid, and national law implementing EU law that contravenes the fundamental rights enshrined therein must be set aside."[975]

These functions are confirmed when taking a closer look at the EU Charter itself, and in particular at those provisions that govern its application and interpretation.

EMN Inform <https://ec.europa.eu/home-affairs/system/files/2020-01/00_eu_inform_statelessness_en.pdf> accessed 17 October 2021.

971 The EU Charter was proclaimed in 2007, Charter of Fundamental Rights of the European Union (EU Charter) [2007] C303/1, and became legally binding when the Lisbon Treaty entered into force in 2009.

972 Art 41 EU Charter.

973 Art 8 EU Charter.

974 Art 18 EU Charter; see also generally Janneke Gerards, Henri de Waele & Karin Zwaan (eds), *Vijf jaar bindend EU-Grondrechtenhandvest* [Five Years of a Binding EU Charter] (Wolters Kluwer 2015) 2.

975 Koen Lenaerts, 'The Role of the EU Charter in the Member States' in Michal Bobek & Jeremias Adams-Prassl (eds), *The EU Charter of Fundamental Rights in the Member States* (EU law in the Member States Vol 7, Hart Publishing 2020) 19–36, 19–20.

It is important to keep in mind that the rights and principles included in the EU Charter are addressed to the Union itself and to the member states only when they are implementing EU law.[976] 'Implementation of EU law' has, however, been interpreted broadly, most notably evidenced by the case of *Åkerberg Fransson*, in which a more distant 'connection' with EU law was enough to apply the EU Charter.[977] In later jurisprudence, this standard has been clarified further:

> "in order to determine whether a national measure involves the implementation of EU law for the purposes of Article 51(1) of the Charter, it is necessary to determine, inter alia, whether that national legislation is intended to implement a provision of EU law; the nature of the legislation at issue and whether it pursues objectives other than those covered by EU law, even if it is capable of indirectly affecting EU law; and also whether there are specific rules of EU law on the matter or rules which are capable of affecting it".[978]

Commentators have held that "although the Court has interpreted Article 51(1) broadly, the level of discretion available allows it to promote a differentiated understanding of the Charter's scope of application in selected cases".[979] For the topic of this research, preventing and solving statelessness, i.e. nationality matters, need to be brought into the sphere of EU law before the EU Charter can be applicable. As we saw, however, nationality matters in principle fall in the competences of the member states and are not governed by EU law. At the same time, the paragraphs above already demonstrated that these matters are in certain circumstances subject to EU law, in particular where it concerns migration and asylum policy or European citizenship. It has, for instance, been held "that in light of the *Ruiz Zambrano* doctrine, the latest case law moves in the direction of considering the Charter applicable when Article 20 TFEU is applicable".[980] Where this chapter considers the EU Charter, it therefore also looks at the applicability of this instrument to the situation referred to.

Some of the rights of the Charter are thus different or more 'modern' when compared to the ECHR. However, some of these rights also correspond or overlap with rights contained in the ECHR – compare for example the prohibition of torture in Article 4 EU Charter and Article 3 ECHR. The EU Charter, however, explains that where rights in the Charter correspond with those in the ECHR, "the meaning and scope of those rights shall be the same as those laid down by the said Convention".[981] At the same time,

---

976 Art 51(1) EU Charter.

977 Case C-617/10 *Åklagaren v Hans Åkerberg Fransson* [2013] ECLI:EU:C:2013:105. This case concerned national provisions for the penalties applicable to non-compliance with VAT legislation (and the latter was an implementation of an EU directive).

978 Case C198/13 *Julian Hernández and Others* [2014] ECLI:EU:C:2014:2055, para 37.

979 Katerina Kalaitzaki, 'EU Citizenship as a Means of Broadening the Application of EU Fundamental Rights: Developments and Limits' in Nathan Cambien, Dimitry Kochenov & Elise Muir (eds), *European Citizenship under Stress. Social Justice, Brexit and Other Challenges* (Nijhoff Studies in European Union Law Vol 16, Brill Nijhoff 2020) 49.

980 Delia Ferri & Giuseppe Martinico, 'Revisiting the Ruiz Zambrano Doctrine and Exploring the Potential for its Extensive Application' (2021) 27 European Public Law 685, 698.

981 Art 52(3) EU Charter.

however, the ECHR should be seen in this context as affording minimum protection, as the Charter also says that Union law may provide more extensive protection.[982] This is thus important to keep in mind when considering the rights under EU law, but also relevant in view of the ECHR as referred to in chapter 3.

The EU Charter contains various fundamental rights, but not all of these are addressed to everyone. Certain rights refer to specific categories of people that they apply to. For instance, Article 2 says that everyone has the right to life, but other Articles refer specifically to children (Article 24), the elderly (Article 25) and persons with disabilities (Article 26). Furthermore, every worker, for instance, has the right to protection against unjustified dismissal according to Article 30 of the EU Charter, and the family is specifically protected under Article 33. Nationality is also a relevant criterion as regards the applicability of certain fundamental rights under the EU Charter. Title V of the Charter contains citizens' rights, which refers to any or every citizen of the Union as regards most rights, such as the right to vote for the EP (Article 39) or the freedom of movement and residence (Article 45). Interestingly, the right to good administration (Article 41), which is part of the aforementioned Title, is addressed to 'every person'. This provision is formulated in respect of "institutions, bodies, offices and agencies of the Union", so this delimitation of the scope means that it is not likely to be applicable to nationality and statelessness-related procedures. As we already saw as regards EU citizenship and EU migration and asylum policy, nationality is a key aspect. For the EU Charter this is perhaps less true, but a distinction is certainly made based on nationality: there are limits on the rights applicable to stateless people, as they are obviously not considered citizens of the EU.

Several rights included in the EU Charter thus apply to every person, regardless of status or (lack of) nationality. These rights are set out in the Dignity and Freedoms Titles of the instrument in particular.[983] The EU Charter, like the ECHR, does not, however, contain a right to a nationality.[984] Stateless people, at the same time, should be able to "enjoy core fundamental rights" and "the risk of discrimination or unequal treatment" should be reduced.[985] These rights should not only result in adequate protection of stateless people – various rights contained in the Charter may also be able to contribute to preventing and solving statelessness. The section 4.3 discusses some of these in more depth, but a couple of examples are already considered below.

Of relevance to preventing and solving statelessness is Article 7 EU Charter. This provision contains the right to private live and corresponds with Article 8 ECHR. As was considered in chapter 3, the European Court of Human Rights has held that

---

982 Ibid.

983 Titles I & II EU Charter.

984 Also noted by Katja Swider, Guilia Bittoni & Laura van Waas, 'The Evolving Role of the European Union in Addressing Statelessness' in Laura van Waas & Melanie Khanna (eds), *Solving Statelessness* (Wolf Legal Publishers 2016) 375–404, 382.

985 Conclusions of the Council and the Representatives of the Governments of the Member States on Statelessness [2015] <https://www.consilium.europa.eu/en/press/press-releases/2015/12/04/council-adopts-conclusions-on-statelessness/> accessed 17 October 2021.

nationality can be seen as part of a persons' personal identity that is protected as part of the right to private life.[986] It is therefore possible that EU rules that address those who lack any nationality (i.e. third-country nationals) and that, for instance, fail to take into account the specific impact of this on personal identity, or leave people (without proper identification of statelessness) in a situation of uncertainty about their (lack of) nationality, could be challenged using Article 7. This could point, again at the important first step of identifying who is stateless, in order to inform further prevention of and solutions to statelessness.

The right to liberty and security (Article 6), for example, also includes the prohibition of arbitrary detention. Immigration detention is something that stateless people in an irregular migratory context in Europe can be confronted with.[987] The CJEU has held that detention in a migratory context is "a serious interference with [... the] right to liberty, [which] is subject to compliance with strict safeguards, namely the presence of a legal basis, clarity, predictability, accessibility and protection against arbitrariness".[988] The FRA has held that in a "situation of statelessness" there may be practical obstacles to removal which can be "outside [... the migrant's] sphere of influence", and that there may be no real prospect of removal.[989] As a reasonable prospect of removal is necessary to comply with the Return Directive[990], as well as to protect against arbitrariness, statelessness is thus relevant to take into account when assessing detention in relation to removal. Not only can stateless people thus rely on the right to liberty for protection of their rights[991], it also demonstrates the importance of taking into account their specific vulnerabilities and the necessity of determining who is stateless, and not leaving people unidentified in limbo. As we saw earlier, the identification of stateless people presents an important first step in preventing and solving statelessness.

Stateless people furthermore regularly encounter all kinds of procedures, such as migration procedures, but also naturalization procedures, procedures for loss or deprivation of nationality, or other procedures that have to do with administration

---

986 See also Katalin Berényi, 'Addressing the Anomaly of Statelessness in Europe: An EU Law and Human Rights Perspective' (PhD thesis, Ludovika – University of Public Service 2018) 160.

987 Eg ENS, 'Protecting Stateless Persons from Arbitrary Detention: An Agenda for Change' (2017) <https://www.statelessness.eu/sites/default/files/2020-09/ENS_LockeInLimbo_Detention_Agenda_online.pdf> accessed 17 October 2021.

988 Case C-528/15 *Policie ČR, Krajské ředitelství policie Ústeckého kraje, odbor cizinecké policie v Salah Al Chodor, Ajlin Al Chodor, Ajvar Al Chodor* [2017] ECLI:EU:C:2017:213, para 40. On guidelines and safeguards relating to (arbitrary) detention of stateless people see also ERT, 'Guidelines to Protect Stateless Persons from Arbitrary Detention' (2021) <https://www.equalrightstrust.org/ertdocumentbank/guidelines%20complete.pdf> accessed 17 October 2021.

989 FRA, 'Detention of Third-Country Nationals in Return Procedures' (2010) 25 <https://fra.europa.eu/sites/default/files/fra_uploads/1306-FRA-report-detention-december-2010_EN.pdf> accessed 17 October 2021.

990 See Art 15(4) Return Directive, see also para 4.2.3.

991 Cf Tamás Molnár, 'The Charter of Fundamental Rights and the Protection of Stateless People in the EU: A Dormant Giant?' (*ENS Blog*, 28 September 2017) <https://www.statelessness.eu/updates/blog/charter-fundamental-rights-and-protection-stateless-people-eu-dormant-giant> accessed 17 October 2021.

and registration, which are of importance to preventing and solving statelessness.[992] Procedural guarantees relating to a judicial review and effective remedy are therefore also necessary to address statelessness.[993] In view of CJEU case law on EU citizenship and EU legislation on asylum and migration, many of these procedures fall within the scope of application of the Charter, and the Charter offers such procedural guarantees in Article 47, which contains the right to a fair trial and the right to an effective remedy, based on Articles 6(1) and 13 of the ECHR.

The EU Charter thus presents an important instrument on fundamental rights in the EU. Even though its scope of application may be limited, it is clear that stateless people could and should benefit from the provisions, that their vulnerabilities should be taken into account and that it includes rights that are relevant to preventing and solving statelessness, in particular with regard to identification of statelessness. At the same time, it was demonstrated that nationality is a material criterion as regards the enjoyment of certain rights. This distinction between those who are EU citizens and those who are not is therefore further explored below in paragraph 4.3.5 on non-discrimination in relation to prevention of and solutions to statelessness.

4.2.5. OTHER LEGAL INSTRUMENTS

The EU of course has a multitude of legal instruments, of which the most important ones to this research were discussed above to give a clearer idea of the challenges, possibilities and trends in addressing statelessness using EU law. Section 4.3 takes a closer look at some of these instruments with a view to better understanding the relevance and contribution of such instruments to preventing and solving statelessness from a human rights perspective. Outside of the instruments already mentioned that have a closer relation to matters around statelessness and nationality, there are more general provisions in the EU treaties that allow the EU to take (legislative) action on certain topics that impact on EU values and aims. As was explained in chapter 2, statelessness in Europe takes many forms, can be a result of discrimination and discriminatory laws, and has existed for many years, with some people remaining stateless for generations. A situation of people, and children in particular, being left in a limbo, without proper access to rights, could therefore interfere with the EU values of Article 3 TEU, such as promoting the wellbeing of its peoples, combating social exclusion and discrimination, promoting social justice and protection, and protecting the rights of the child.

In this light, the 'flexibility clause' of Article 352 TFEU, already mentioned in paragraph 4.2.3, has been argued to provide a basis for EU action on statelessness, when read together with Article 3 TEU. "As these are termed the 'overall objectives' of the Union, they can be reasonably considered to constitute a ground for invoking

992 See also para 1.4.3.
993 See also para 1.5.3.

Article 352 TFEU."[994] However, using the 'flexibility clause' in practice may be difficult as its constraints "are vigorous enough to curb further [use] [...]", which include the requirement of unanimity in the Council.[995] Indeed, in particular as regards nationality matters, member states have shown, for instance in their interventions in some of the cases that were discussed above in paragraph 4.2.2[996], that they see these as national matters that are not to be interfered with by the EU, which renders Article 352 TFEU an unlikely basis for addressing statelessness.

4.2.6. CONCLUDING REMARKS

This section considered the instruments, actors and trends in EU law as regards nationality matters. Even though there is no direct link between EU law and regulation of nationality, because nationality remains the competence of the member states, it was found that there are different key areas of EU law that relate to preventing and solving statelessness. These include notably European citizenship, fundamental rights, asylum and migration policy. The evolution of case law on EU citizenship demonstrated EU influence over nationality matters of the member states. Furthermore, analysis of EU fundamental rights and asylum and migration policy showed a need for identification of statelessness as a first important step in ensuring that the particular vulnerabilities of stateless people can be taken into account. This includes considerations as regards documentation and procedures to regularize their status, or to eventually become naturalized citizens of one of the member states, and thereby of the EU. The next section looks at these and other EU legal instruments relevant to preventing and solving statelessness in more depth.

4.3. PREVENTING AND SOLVING STATELESSNESS

This section considers the key instruments of the EU that relate to nationality and statelessness and discusses the contribution of these instruments to preventing and solving statelessness thematically. The first paragraph considers measures aimed at preventing and solving childhood statelessness, and the second paragraph analyzes norms concerning solutions to conflicts of nationality law and preventing loss and/or

---

994 Anne Brekoo, 'A Role for the European Union in Addressing Statelessness? Assessing Obligations and Possibilities for Action' (BA Thesis, Tilburg University 2019) 72–73 <http://arno.uvt.nl/show.cgi?fid=149065> accessed 17 October 2021.

995 Theodore Konstadinides, 'Drawing the Line Between Circumvention and Gap-Filling: An Exploration of the Conceptual Limits of the Treaty's Flexibility Clause' (2012) 31 Yearbook of European Law 227, 261.

996 See for instance Case C-135/08 *Janko Rottmann v Freistaat Bayern* [2010] ECLI:EU:C:2010:104, paras 37–38, in which various European governments, supported by the EC, argue that withdrawal of naturalization "cannot fall within the ambit of European Union law".

deprivation of nationality. In the third paragraph, the focus is on standards regulating nationality matters in cases of state succession. The fourth paragraph discusses legal norms aimed at the acquisition of a nationality for persons who became stateless in Europe in the past and remain stateless today and/or who arrive in Europe stateless. Provisions ensuring non-discrimination in nationality matters are examined in the fifth paragraph, and the section is brought to a close with concluding remarks.

4.3.1. CHILDHOOD STATELESSNESS

In 2019, the EP adopted a resolution on the occasion of the 30th anniversary of the CRC. Specific attention was paid to statelessness, with concern expressed that children continue to be born stateless in the EU. As such, the EP called on the member states "for a solution to the issue of stateless children within and outside the EU, in accordance with international law", called on the Commission "to promote universal access to birth registration and the child's right to acquire a nationality, with a view to ending the risk of statelessness", and stressed the need for "an intersectional approach to combating all forms of discrimination affecting children, taking into consideration their vulnerabilities, in particular those of [...] stateless or undocumented children".[997] But what EU legal instruments are helpful in preventing and solving statelessness among children, and in what way? This paragraph explores this question further and does this in particular through the lens of the right of every child to acquire a nationality, which is – as we saw in chapter 1, firmly enshrined in various international legal instruments.

The EU has no legal instruments that pertain to the child's right to a nationality specifically, but the EU Charter does include an important provision in Article 24 in particular. Here, it is held that in all actions relating to children, the child's best interests must be a primary consideration.[998] More generally, Article 7 EU Charter (the right to respect for private and family life) is relevant to preventing and solving statelessness, as also considered above in paragraph 4.2.4. Further legal development regarding childhood statelessness and the nationality of children must be sought in case law primarily. Childhood statelessness as such has not (yet) been the topic of CJEU jurisprudence. Loss of nationality, and thereby European citizenship, by a child was, however, a topic that came up in the Court's case law on EU citizenship, notably in the *Tjebbes* case.[999] In this case, the nationality of children was affected as Dutch law provided for the loss of nationality by a minor in the event that his or her parent loses Dutch nationality.[1000] This rule was based on the desire of the legislator to preserve unity of nationality within the family. The question arose, nonetheless,

997 EP Resolution of 26 November 2019 on Children's Rights on the Occasion of the 30th Anniversary of the UN Convention on the Rights of the Child [2019] paras 38, 40 <https://www.europarl.europa.eu/doceo/document/TA-9-2019-0066_EN.html> accessed 17 October 2021.

998 Art 24(2) EU Charter.

999 Case C-221/17 *Tjebbes and Others v Minister van Buitenlandse Zaken* [2019] ECLI:EU:C:2019:189.

1000 Art 16(1)(d) of the Dutch Nationality Act [Rijkswet op het Nederlanderschap].

"whether it is proportionate to deprive a minor of citizenship of the Union and the rights attaching thereto purely for the sake of preserving unity of nationality within the family, and the extent to which the child's best interests within the meaning of Article 24(2) of the Charter are set to play a role in that regard".[1001]

As discussed in paragraph 4.2.2, the *Tjebbes* case explained the need for an individual examination in order to ensure that loss of EU citizenship is in line with the principle of proportionality. This principle also entails ensuring that loss of nationality is in line with the rights of the EU Charter.[1002] With regard to children specifically, the Court goes on to hold that the individual examination by the authorities should take into account "possible circumstances that the loss of [...] nationality by the minor concerned [...] fails to meet the child's best interests as enshrined in Article 24 of the Charter because of the consequences of that loss for the minor from the point of view of EU law".[1003] This case thus confirms that where EU citizenship of children is at stake, a proportionality test applies to weigh the circumstances and consequences of loss of nationality for the child concerned from the perspective of EU law, and that there should be particular attention for the best interests of the child in assessing this. It has generally been widely recognized that being left stateless, in particular for a longer period of time, as a result of loss of nationality or otherwise, is never in the best interests of the child.[1004] That the principle of best interests of the child thus also applies to loss of EU citizenship could therefore help to prevent statelessness where loss of EU citizenship of a child would result in statelessness. The Guidelines on Involuntary Loss of European Citizenship (ILEC Guidelines) help to interpret EU standards in this regard. They underline the importance of the best interests of the child in any decision relating to loss of nationality, and articulate that extension of loss of nationality by (a) parent(s) to a child should never cause statelessness.[1005]

1001 Case C-221/17 *Tjebbes and Others v Minister van Buitenlandse Zaken* [2019] ECLI:EU:C:2019:189, para 25.

1002 Ibid, para 45.

1003 Ibid, para 47.

1004 Eg *Institute for Human Rights and Development in Africa (IHRDA) and Open Society Justice Initiative on Behalf of Children of Nubian Descent in Kenya v the Government of Kenya* Com No Com/002/2009 (ACERWC, 22 March 2011), para 46; African Committee of Experts on the Rights and Welfare of the Child, 'General Comment No. 2 on Article 6 of the ACRWC: The Right to a Name, Registration at Birth, and to Acquire a Nationality' (2014) AU Doc ACERWC/GC/02; UNHCR, 'Guidelines on Statelessness No. 4: Ensuring Every Child's Right to Acquire a Nationality through Articles 1–4 of the 1961 Convention on the Reduction of Statelessness' (2012) HCR/GS/12/04, para 34; UNHCR, 'I am Here, I Belong. On the Urgent Need to End Childhood Statelessness' (2015) <https://www.unhcr.org/ibelong/wp-content/uploads/2015-10-StatelessReport_ENG16.pdf> accessed 17 October 2021; William Thomas Worster, 'The Obligation to Grant Nationality to Stateless Children under Treaty Law' (2019) 24 Tilburg Law Review 204; Jyothi Kanics, 'Preventing and Addressing Statelessness in the Context of International Surrogacy Arrangements' (2014) 19 Tilburg Law Review 117.

1005 Guidelines on Involuntary Loss of European Citizenship (2015) II.6 & IV.6 <www.ilecproject.eu/sites/default/files/GUIDELINES%20INVOLUNTARY%20LOSS%20OF%20 EUROPEAN%20CITIZENSHIP%20.pdf> accessed 17 October 2021. These Guidelines were developed as part of the project 'Involuntary Loss of European Citizenship (ILEC): Exchanging Knowledge and Identifying Guidelines for Europe', Co-funded by the European Commission's Directorate General for Justice, Citizenship

The *Tjebbes* case, however, was preceded by various other cases on nationality matters under EU law, which considered that member states must have due regard to EU law in laying down conditions for acquiring and losing citizenship.[1006] Indeed, it has been held that

> "[b]ased on these judgments we can conclude that, in general terms, EU law is relevant to procedures related to the acquisition of nationality, and therefore to the procedures aiming at preventing statelessness at birth by conferring an EU Member State's nationality to a child born in the EU".[1007]

The landmark *Rottmann* judgement demonstrates this clearly. It affirmed for the first time the proportionality test as regards loss of nationality, and thereby European citizenship. Whereas the *Rottmann* case concerned loss of nationality, it has also been considered relevant to recovering a previous nationality[1008] and to acquisition of nationality generally.[1009] That it is pertinent to acquisition of nationality for otherwise stateless children born on the territory of a member state becomes clear when considering acquisition of nationality for this group (whether *ex lege* or by registration or option). If the application of such provisions, which allow the child to acquire a nationality *jus soli*, is denied because a child is not considered 'otherwise stateless', statelessness determination and denial of nationality, and thereby EU citizenship, could be subject to EU law and can be considered by the CJEU in a preliminary ruling procedure.[1010] As such, there is scope under EU law to address the prevention of statelessness among children born on the territory of the member states.

At the same time, jurisprudence on EU citizenship and the rights attached to this status may also be the reason that EU member states are hesitant to introduce safeguards for otherwise stateless children born in the territory regardless of their residence status – in line with the relevant international instruments, in particular every child's right to acquire a nationality and Article 1(2) of the 1961 Convention. Under CJEU jurisprudence in cases such as *Ruiz Zambrano*, it became clear that third-

---

and Fundamental Rights, and aim to provide guidance on implementation of international and European standards on involuntary loss of nationality for government officials, legal practitioners, decision-makers and the judiciary in EU member states. The Guidelines were drafted by Gerard-René de Groot, Patrick Wautelet and Maarten Vink on the basis of the Policy Briefs prepared for and discussions during the final conference of the ILEC project on 11–12 December 2014 in Brussels.

1006 See also para 4.2.2.

1007 European Council on Refugees and Exiles (ECRE)/Gábor Gyulai, 'The Right to a Nationality of Refugee Children Born in the EU and the Relevance of the EU Charter of Fundamental Rights' (2017) 7 <https://www.ecre.org/wp-content/uploads/2016/12/refugee-children-nationality-LEAP-leaflet.pdf> accessed 17 October 2021.

1008 Case C-135/08 *Janko Rottmann v Freistaat Bayern* [2010] ECLI:EU:C:2010:104, paras 60–64.

1009 Eg Gerard-René de Groot & Ngo Chun Luk, 'Twenty Years of CJEU Jurisprudence on Citizenship' (2014) 15 German Law Journal 821, 828.

1010 Gerard-René de Groot, Katja Swider & Olivier Vonk, 'Practices and Approaches in the EU Member States to Prevent and End Statelessness. Study for the LIBE Committee' (2015) 55 <https://www.europarl.europa.eu/RegData/etudes/STUD/2015/536476/IPOL_STU(2015)536476_EN.pdf> accessed 17 October 2021.

country nationals without residence status in the EU may derive a right to residence and work from the status of their child(ren) who are citizens of the Union.[1011] Member states may therefore be hesitant in granting nationality to otherwise stateless children born on the territory without legal residence, because of the knock-on effect on the legal status of their parent(s).

Some EU member states only have a safeguard for otherwise stateless children with legal residence.[1012] In the Netherlands, for example, a legislative proposal was introduced at the end of 2020 to extend the right to opt for Dutch nationality from only children with legal residence also to children who are born on the territory without residence rights.[1013] The explanatory memorandum to this proposal demonstrates how cautious the authorities are and how difficult in practice it would be to apply the provision to a child without legal residence who would otherwise be stateless: the provision that is to be introduced includes a number of requirements, including a long period of habitual residence as well as a criterion that requires full cooperation from the parents of the child with the authorities in any migration proceedings. Whereas EU law in relation to citizenship of the Union could thus be helpful in addressing prevention of statelessness among children, it also – perhaps unintentionally – can negatively influence the adoption of further safeguards preventing childhood statelessness in the EU by the member states.

A further case relating to every child's right to a nationality concerned a child born to a same-sex couple in Spain.[1014] The parents are from Bulgaria and the UK (Gibraltar). A birth certificate was issued by Spain when the baby was born, but it does not specify who is the biological mother of the child. When the Bulgarian mother applied for a Bulgarian birth certificate, this was refused by the Bulgarian authorities because there was insufficient information on the child's parentage with regard to the biological mother and because the registration of two female parents on a birth certificate was against public policy, since same-sex marriages are not permitted in Bulgaria.[1015] From the questions referred to the CJEU, it becomes clear that the domestic court is unsure

1011 See also para 4.2.2.

1012 Cf GLOBALCIT Global Database on Modes of Acquisition of Citizenship (2017) mode A03b (Born Stateless), EU countries <https://globalcit.eu/acquisition-citizenship/> accessed 17 October 2021; see also ENS, 'No Child Should Be Stateless' (2015) 12–13 <https://www.statelessness.eu/sites/www.statelessness.eu/files/ENS_NoChildStateless_final.pdf> accessed 17 October 2021.

1013 Amendments to the Dutch Nationality Act and the Passport Acts as well as Withdrawal of Reservations to the Convention on the Status of Stateless Persons in Connection with the Determination of Statelessness [Wijziging van de Rijkswet op het Nederlanderschap en de Paspoortwet alsmede intrekking van voorbehouden bij het Verdrag betreffende de status van staatlozen in verband met de vaststelling van staatloosheid] (21 December 2020) in preparation – January 2022 <https://www.tweedekamer.nl/kamerstukken/wetsvoorstellen/detail?id=2020Z25636&dossier=35688-%28R2151%29> accessed 17 October 2021. The UN Human Rights Committee had also determined that the Netherlands was not doing enough to guarantee the right of every child to acquire a nationality, CCPR, 'Views Adopted by the Committee under Article 5(4) of the Optional Protocol, concerning Communication No. 2918/2016' (20 January 2021) CCPR/C/130/D/2918/2016.

1014 Case C-490/20 *V.M.A. v Stolichna Obshtina, Rayon 'Pancharevo'* [2021] ECLI:EU:C:2021:1008.

1015 Ibid, para 23.

whether refusal of a birth certificate is possible on these grounds, and in particular how a balance can be struck between the national and constitutional identity of the member state (Article 4(2) TEU) and the best interest of the child (Article 7 and 24(2) EU Charter). The referring court also asks whether the refusal to issue a Bulgarian birth certificate for the child constitutes an obstacle to the issue of an identity document for the child by a member state. This may impede the unlimited exercise of her rights as a citizen of the EU.[1016] In the meantime, it had become clear that the child does not acquire Spanish or UK nationality, and that the refusal to issue a Bulgarian birth certificate may thus impact on the child's ability to acquire a nationality. The child may not be able to acquire Bulgarian nationality due to lack of a birth certificate, but without recognition of statelessness she would also be unable to rely on the safeguards in Spanish law, the country where she was born, for protection as a child who would otherwise be stateless.[1017]

Whereas the entry point in this case is birth registration, it quickly becomes clear that the case revolves around questions of discrimination (of children born to same-sex couples), EU citizenship (and the effective enjoyment of the rights attached to this status), the right to private and family life, and child's rights (including best interests of the child, the right to birth registration, and the right of every child to acquire a nationality). As was seen earlier, every child's right to acquire a nationality is firmly enshrined in international law, and the right to private life recognizes nationality as part of a person's social identity, as well as the importance of non-discrimination in this regard.[1018]

There are clear fundamental rights norms that are important to consider. Moreover, some key aspects of EU law are in play with the effective enjoyment of EU citizenship and the principle of non-discrimination.[1019] With this at stake, this case presents an opportunity for the CJEU to at least clarify member state obligations with regard to birth registration – an important factor in proving nationality and an often implicit assumption on the basis of which nationality laws, but also the democratic state, operates[1020] and therefore relevant to preventing childhood statelessness. It also offers potential to address the impact of this on the child's right to a nationality, or to EU citizenship at least, and (risk of) statelessness.[1021]

1016 Ibid, para 26.

1017 See also Patrícia Cabral, Protecting the right to a nationality for children of same-sex couples in the EU – A key issue before the CJEU in V.M.A. v Stolichna Obshtina (C-490/20)' (*ENS Blog*, 3 February 2021) <https://www.statelessness.eu/updates/blog/protecting-right-nationality-children-same-sex-couples-eu-key-issue-cjeu-vma-v> accessed 17 October 2021.

1018 Cf ECtHR jurisprudence on nationality matters as considered in ch 3.

1019 See also David de Groot, 'EU Law and the Mutual Recognition of Parenthood Between Member States: The Case of V.M.A. v Stolichna Obshtina' (2021) RSCAS/GLOBALCIT Special Report <https://cadmus.eui.eu/handle/1814/69731> accessed 17 October 2021.

1020 See also para 1.4.3 of this research.

1021 See also also Patrícia Cabral, Protecting the right to a nationality for children of same-sex couples in the EU – A key issue before the CJEU in V.M.A. v Stolichna Obshtina (C-490/20)' (*ENS Blog*, 3 February 2021) <https://www.statelessness.eu/updates/blog/protecting-right-nationality-children-same-sex-couples-eu-key-issue-cjeu-vma-v> accessed 11 March 2021.

In its judgment, the CJEU does not explicitly go into the question of acquisition of nationality by the child, but does draw on key principles in this regard of the CRC[1022], based on the reference that is made to this treaty by Article 24 of the EU Charter. Indeed, the ruling demonstrates "that the non-recognition of the parent-child relationship in situations involving the exercise of EU free movement rights can amount to a breach of fundamental rights protected under the [EU] Charter and the CRC".[1023] The Court finds that

> "a child, being a minor, who is a Union citizen and whose birth certificate, issued by the competent authorities of the host Member State, designates as that child's parents two persons of the same sex, the Member State of which that child is a national is obliged (i) to issue to that child an identity card or a passport without requiring a birth certificate to be drawn up beforehand by its national authorities, and (ii) to recognise, as is any other Member State, the document from the host Member State that permits that child to exercise, with each of those two persons, the child's right to move and reside freely within the territory of the Member States".[1024]

By holding that EU member states need to recognize familial ties established in another member state between a child and her parents (same-sex couple), the Court's considerations show promise in terms of dealing with the recognition of non-traditional family relationships. This case provides a useful benchmark to help to address challenges in translating these into official registration and documentation, which are relevant to the acquisition of nationality and therefore also to preventing (risk of) statelessness.

On acquisition of nationality at birth and non-discrimination, it has furthermore been held that "questionable distinctions" in this regard or "by establishment of a family relationship" could be contrary to the principle of equality.[1025] This could be the case where differentiations in nationality laws are based on whether a child is born inside or outside of wedlock.

Statelessness has been identified in the EU context as a public policy issue relating to civil status implications of surrogacy as well, but further developments of relevance

1022 Arts 2 & 7 CRC; Case C-490/20 *V.M.A. v Stolichna Obshtina, Rayon 'Pancharevo'* [2021] ECLI:EU:C:2021:1008, paras 63–64.

1023 Alina Tryfonidou, 'The Cross-Border Recognition of the Parent-Child Relationship in Rainbow Families under EU Law: A Critical View of the ECJ's V.M.A. ruling' (*European Law Blog*, 21 December 2021) <https://europeanlawblog.eu/2021/12/21/the-cross-border-recognition-of-the-parent-child-relationship-in-rainbow-families-under-eu-law-a-critical-view-of-the-ecjs-v-m-a-ruling/> accessed 3 January 2022.

1024 Case C-490/20 *V.M.A. v Stolichna Obshtina, Rayon 'Pancharevo'* [2021] ECLI:EU:C:2021:1008, para 69.

1025 Gerard René de Groot & Anja Seling, 'The Consequences of the *Rottmann* Judgment on Member State Autonomy – The European Court of Justice's Avant-Gardism in Nationality Matters' (2011) 7 European Constitutional Law Review 150, 158. Remember also *Genovese v Malta* App No 53124/09 (ECHR, 11 October 2011) ECLI:CE:ECHR:2011:1011JUD005312409, explained in para 3.3.5.

in the EU context are currently not visible.[1026] The importance of identifying stateless children as such, also indicating their nationality or statelessness, has been recognized by the EC in their Communication on the protection of children in migration.[1027] Some of these considerations regarding preventing childhood statelessness with a view to ultimately solving statelessness, also form part of the EU's strategy on the rights of the child 2021–2024.[1028] Recommendations on addressing childhood statelessness were suggested by an alliance of civil society partners who stressed the need to promote birth registration and every child's right to acquire a nationality, paying particular attention to the need for national safeguards to prevent childhood statelessness and facilitating identification and responses to statelessness for children in a migratory context.[1029] However, the EU Strategy on the Rights of the Child has not included all of these recommendations. It does, however, recognize the vulnerabilities of stateless children: "[n]ot having a nationality makes it difficult to access some of the basic services such as healthcare and education, and can lead to situation of violence and exploitation".[1030] Moreover, as part of the EU's child-friendly justice system, the EC invites member states to "promote and ensure universal, free and immediate access to birth registration and certification for all children, [and to …] increase capacity of front-line officials to respond to statelessness and nationality-related problems in the context of migration".[1031] It has been held that the strategy has omitted important areas for addressing childhood statelessness, including concerning legal safeguards in nationality law to prevent childhood statelessness and child-friendly statelessness determination procedures. However, there remain "opportunities to address these gaps, [which] lie in the strategy's implementation, and in the mainstreaming of child rights in other law and policy areas, including asylum and migration, Roma equality and inclusion, and LGBTIQ equality".[1032]

1026 Laurence Brunet, Janeen Carruthers, Konstantina Davaki, Derek King, Claire Marzo & Julie McCandless, 'A Comparative Study on the Regime of Surrogacy in EU Member States. Study Requested by the European Parliament's Committee on Legal Affairs' (2013) 173–174 <https://www.europarl.europa.eu/RegData/etudes/STUD/2013/474403/IPOL-JURI_ET(2013)474403_EN.pdf> accessed 17 October 2021.

1027 Communication from the Commission to the European Parliament and the Council: The Protection of Children in Migration [2017] COM(2017) 211 final 6.

1028 EC, 'The EU Strategy on the Rights of the Child and the European Child Guarantee <https://ec.europa.eu/info/policies/justice-and-fundamental-rights/rights-child/eu-strategy-rights-child-and-european-child-guarantee_en#the-eu-strategy-on-the-rights-of-the-child> accessed 17 October 2021.

1029 'Joint Position Paper on a Comprehensive Child Rights Strategy' (2020) 11 <https://reliefweb.int/sites/reliefweb.int/files/resources/Joint-Position-Paper-in-the-Upcoming-Childs-Rights-Strategy.pdf> accessed 12 March 2021.

1030 Communication from the Commission to the European Parliament, the Council, the European Economic and Social Committee and the Committee of the Regions: EU Strategy on the Rights of the Child [2021] COM(2021) 142 final 14.

1031 Ibid, 15.

1032 Khadija Badri, 'EU Strategy on the Rights of the Child Marks an Important Step towards Addressing Childhood Statelessness' (*ENS Blog*, 8 April 2021) <https://www.statelessness.eu/updates/editorial/eu-strategy-rights-child-marks-important-step-towards-addressing-childhood> accessed 17 October 2021.

When considering both the EU Charter and EU jurisprudence on citizenship of the Union together, it becomes clear that EU law is able to address situations where children are born stateless on the territory of the member states, and no effective safeguards are applied.[1033] EU law can be seen as part of a larger ecosystem of international standards that influence each other, meaning that international standards are used to help understand EU law. Under various legal instruments, such as the CRC, the 1961 Convention and the ECN, member states ought to avoid statelessness by introducing a safeguard that grants nationality, and thereby EU citizenship, to children born on their territory who would otherwise be stateless at birth or soon after birth. If a member state is unsuccessful in doing so, this could constitute denial of European citizenship, and could be construed as impeding the effective enjoyment of EU citizen's rights, so member states are in fact acting within the scope of EU law, and hence, of the EU Charter. Denial of nationality and – thereby – EU citizenship could violate various provisions of the Charter, in particular when these provisions are read together with the parallel provisions in the ECHR. The following EU Charter rights are relevant: the right to private life (Article 7), but also the principle of non-discrimination (Article 21) where the lack of application of safeguards would be based on discriminatory grounds (such as parents' marital status or residence status) and the right to an effective remedy (Article 47) where no judicial review would be available. Moreover, there is potential for a violation of the rights of the child and the member states' obligation to put the best interests of the child first in its considerations (Article 24). Furthermore, where children are left unidentified or are registered with an 'unknown nationality'[1034] for a prolonged period of time, these same Articles are relevant to arguments in favor of proper identification or determination of statelessness.

4.3.2. CONFLICTS OF NATIONALITY LAW, LOSS AND DEPRIVATION OF NATIONALITY

Nationality matters and legislation dealing with conflicts of nationality laws, loss and deprivation of nationality traditionally belong to the competence of the EU member states. But as we saw in paragraph 4.2.2, EU citizenship and related jurisprudence has led to more EU influence on nationality matters in the member states. That means that in particular the loss or deprivation of nationality, where it would also entail loss or deprivation of citizenship of the Union, needs to meet certain standards prescribed by EU law. Moreover, where loss of nationality also leads to loss of citizenship of the Union, this also means that there is a clear link with EU law.

1033 A similar line of reasoning is found in ECRE/Gábor Gyulai, 'The Right to a Nationality of Refugee Children Born in the EU and the Relevance of the EU Charter of Fundamental Rights' (2017) <https://www.ecre.org/wp-content/uploads/2016/12/refugee-children-nationality-LEAP-leaflet.pdf> accessed 17 October 2021.

1034 Cf ENS, 'No Child Should Be Stateless' (2015) 17 <https://www.statelessness.eu/sites/www.statelessness.eu/files/ENS_NoChildStateless_final.pdf> accessed 17 October 2021.

Both the *Tjebbes* and *Rottmann* cases[1035] demonstrated that the consequences of loss of EU citizenship need to be taken into account so as to ensure that loss is in line with the principle of proportionality. The interpretation of the principle of proportionality would be relevant in other contexts of loss and deprivation of nationality as well – such as national security-related cases – because it is a general principle.[1036] The *Rottmann* case specifically also concerned a case in which statelessness played a role: Rottmann would become stateless if his German nationality was revoked, as he had lost his Austrian citizenship. From this case thus follows "that deprivation of nationality with statelessness as a consequence is only allowed after the application of a proportionality test".[1037] Moreover, where a member state claims that a person does not become stateless and/or loses EU citizenship when nationality is lost, the determination of nationality or stateless could also be a concern under EU law, and therefore subject to a preliminary ruling procedure.[1038] The additional requirement that in national decisions on loss of nationality proportionality has to be considered in light of EU law, does add another layer of protection that can help in preventing statelessness in view of the need to take into account the consequences for the person concerned and potentially for his or her family. At the same time, this does not prevent statelessness in all circumstances, as the *Rottmann* case proves. The referring court in this case, the *Bundesverwaltungsgericht*, held that the revocation of German nationality was not disproportionate in Rottmann's case, also not from an EU law perspective.[1039]

The *Rottmann* case, however, also concerned the specific situation in which nationality was obtained fraudulently – the only permissible ground for loss of nationality resulting in statelessness under the ECN.[1040] Member states of the EU are indeed also subject to broader legal instruments, international and European, that influence their discretion to legislate on the loss of nationality. The "effective and consistent application" of such standards in the EU "constitutes a key challenge, with a common-level playing field lacking".[1041] In this light, the ILEC Guidelines[1042], developed as part of the ILEC

1035 Case C-221/17 *Tjebbes and Others v Minister van Buitenlandse Zaken* [2019] ECLI:EU:C:2019:189; Case C-135/08 *Janko Rottmann v Freistaat Bayern* [2010] ECLI:EU:C:2010:104.

1036 Draft Commentary to the Principles on Deprivation of Nationality as a National Security Measure (2020) <https://www.refworld.org/docid/5f3bf2d24.html> accessed 17 October 2021; see also Principles on Deprivation of Nationality as a National Security Measure (2020) <https://www.refworld.org/pdfid/5f3bf26d4.pdf> accessed 17 October 2021.

1037 Gerard-René de Groot, Katja Swider & Olivier Vonk, 'Practices and Approaches in the EU Member States to Prevent and End Statelessness. Study for the LIBE Committee' (2015) 57 <https://www.europarl.europa.eu/RegData/etudes/STUD/2015/536476/IPOL_STU(2015)536476_EN.pdf> accessed 17 October 2021.

1038 Ibid, 57.

1039 BVerwG 5 C 12.10 (2010) ECLI:DE:BVerwG:2010:111110U5C12.10.0.

1040 Art 7(3) ECN.

1041 Sergio Carrera & Gerard René de Groot, 'European Citizenship at a Crossroads. Enhancing European Cooperation on Acquisition and Loss of Nationality' (2014) CEPS Paper in Liberty and Security in Europe No. 72, 2 <https://www.ceps.eu/wp-content/uploads/2015/01/No%2072%20European%20Citizenship%20at%20Crossroads.pdf> accessed 17 October 2021.

1042 Guidelines on Involuntary Loss of European Citizenship (2015) <www.ilecproject.eu/sites/default/files/GUIDELINES%20INVOLUNTARY%20LOSS%20OF%20 EUROPEAN%20CITIZENSHIP%20.pdf> accessed 17 October 2021.

project[1043] and aimed at providing guidance on implementation of international and European standards in this regard, summarize aptly how loss of European citizenship should, as a rule, not result in statelessness – except in cases of fraudulent acquisition, but a proportionality test needs to be applied. These Guidelines also synthesize relevant considerations from the international legal framework as discussed in paragraph 1.5.1 of this book, in particular from Articles 5–9 of the 1961 Convention aiming to prevent statelessness in case of loss, renunciation and deprivation of nationality.

Excerpts from the Guidelines on Involuntary Loss of European Citizenship (2015)[1044]

IV.2.a. "Loss of nationality on the grounds of residence abroad should never cause statelessness."

IV.3.a. "Loss of nationality due to undesirable behavior (e.g. acts seriously prejudicial to the vital interests of the state or foreign military service) should never cause statelessness."[1045]

IV.4.a. "A proportionality test must always be applied when deciding on the deprivation of nationality on the grounds of fraudulent acquisition of the nationality concerned, including in cases where no potential statelessness is at stake."

IV.5.b. "Loss of nationality due to the loss of a family relationship should never cause statelessness."

Comparative analysis of EU member state laws on loss of nationality has shown that there are differences in provisions on loss of nationality and their application in countries, not least because the procedural safeguards and remedies available vary. As such, EU citizens may be treated differently as regards loss of nationality depending on the possession of a nationality of the member state, which could affect or even violate the principle of non-discrimination of Article 21 of the EU Charter, as well as the right to an effective remedy under Article 47.[1046] Such considerations from a fundamental rights perspective could be helpful in preventing statelessness where this would be the result of loss of EU citizenship. This is also considered further in paragraph 4.3.5 below.

1043 ILEC stands for Involuntary Loss of European Citizenship, see also <www.ilecproject.eu> accessed 17 October 2021.

1044 Guidelines on Involuntary Loss of European Citizenship (2015) <www.ilecproject.eu/sites/default/files/GUIDELINES%20INVOLUNTARY%20LOSS%20OF%20 EUROPEAN%20CITIZENSHIP%20.pdf> accessed 17 October 2021.

1045 On deprivation of nationality as a national security measure (applied often in a counter-terrorism context in Europe) also see the similar guideline that is provided by the Principles on Deprivation of Nationality as a National Security Measure (2020) <https://www.refworld.org/pdfid/5f3bf26d4.pdf> accessed 17 October 2021: "5.1. States must not render any person stateless through deprivation of nationality."

1046 Sergio Carrera & Gerard René de Groot, 'European Citizenship at a Crossroads. Enhancing European Cooperation on Acquisition and Loss of Nationality' (2014) CEPS Paper in Liberty and Security in Europe No. 72, 2 <https://www.ceps.eu/wp-content/uploads/2015/01/No%2072%20European%20Citizenship%20at%20Crossroads.pdf> accessed 17 October 2021.

As we saw above in paragraph 4.2.4 when considering the role of EU fundamental rights in relation to preventing and solving statelessness, the right to private and family life of Article 7 of the EU Charter is relevant to such analysis. Indeed, where loss of nationality extends beyond the individual to their children or family, or where loss of family relationship could result in loss of nationality and statelessness. The existing international framework as set out in paragraph 1.5 demonstrates that the nationality rights of women and children should not be made dependent on their family.[1047] In paragraph 4.3.1 above, the importance of considering the child's best interests in any decision regarding their nationality was already highlighted and it was also found that loss of nationality by a parent should by extension never cause statelessness of the child. Moreover, the ILEC Guidelines indicate that loss of nationality due to loss of a family relationship should never cause statelessness. At the same time, CJEU jurisprudence in *Rottmann*, for instance, showed that the proportionality test that needs to be performed in case of loss of EU citizenship needs "to take into account the consequences that the decision entails for the person concerned and, if relevant, for the members of his family with regard to the loss of the rights enjoyed by every citizen of the Union".[1048] In relation to the right to private life, it is furthermore important to note that nationality is part of a person's social identity[1049], meaning that loss of nationality may also invite the right private life and social identity into considerations to withdraw or revoke nationality and European citizenship. Such considerations could, again, be helpful towards preventing situations where a person would be left with no nationality at all.

4.3.3. STATE SUCCESSION

State succession and preventing or solving statelessness in this context is in principle something that the EU Treaties or EU law more generally do not deal with. However, some research has been done on what situations of state succession would mean in an EU context, because there are certain situations in which this might arise – the potential secession of Catalonia, Flanders or Scotland for instance.[1050] These studies do not explicitly pay attention to statelessness or addressing the issue in the context of state succession. The question of European citizenship is considered an interesting characteristic specific to the EU context, and that the fact that the EU Treaties do not deal with state succession may mean that such situations can be dealt with following the international legal framework.[1051] The scenario of a potential state succession within the EU has been studied with a view to EU citizenship:

1047 Cf CEDAW and CRC.

1048 Case C-135/08 *Janko Rottmann v Freistaat Bayern* [2010] ECLI:EU:C:2010:104, para 56.

1049 Cf Art 8 ECHR and related jurisprudence, as considered in para 4.2.4 above and in ch 3.

1050 Paul Dermine, 'Succession and EU Treaty Obligations' in Catherine Brölmann & Thomas Vandamme (eds), *Secession within the Union. Collected Think Pieces* (Amsterdam University 2014); Mario Martini & Matthias Damm, 'Succession of States in the EU' (2014) Ancilla Iuris 159; Robert Schütze, *Foreign Affairs and the EU Constitution: Selected Essays* (Cambridge University Press 2014) 91–119.

1051 Mario Martini & Matthias Damm, 'Succession of States in the EU' (2014) Ancilla Iuris 159, 172–173.

> "Given the state of affairs, citizenship of the Union is not enough, at least from the legal point of view, to defend the automatic accession of the potential newly independent States. These new States cannot circumvent the accession procedure to the EU. Notwithstanding, EU citizenship certainly has a role to play through the influence of EU law on the nationality law of the remaining EU Member States and, especially, the application of the proportionality principle in decisions on loss of nationality".[1052]

As was considered in paragraph 1.5.1, the ILC Draft Articles on Nationality of Natural Persons in relation to the Succession of States[1053] are an important international level guideline that does include provisions to prevent statelessness from occurring. These were adopted by the UNGA in 2000 without a vote (by consensus).[1054] In the preparation of the Draft Articles, there was quite active participation by some EU member states. For instance, as regards the Article that concerned the prevention of statelessness, both Finland and Italy indicated that "[t]he obligation of the states involved in a succession to take all appropriate measures to prevent statelessness is a corollary of the right of the persons concerned to a nationality", and France held that the Article was "satisfactory from the point of view of both form and substance".[1055] Drawing on the international framework in case of a state succession within the EU could therefore be helpful in attempting to address the issue of statelessness properly.

The EU has, moreover, also had influence on the nationality laws of states that (re-)emerged after the dissolution of the SFRY and the USSR in the context of negotiating accession of states to the Union. Research on the rules on naturalization in the ten Central and Eastern European accession states of 2004 and 2007 in light of this accession demonstrates that EU policy was not explicitly encouraging additional restrictions on residence-based naturalization.[1056] At the same time, however,

> "[w]hether the Commission's silence towards restrictive changes in naturalization requirements was a matter of negligence or of silent approval, one can argue that in the conditions of intense pre-accession monitoring this issue should have been addressed".[1057]

1052 Guayasén Marrero González, *Civis Europaeus Sum? Consequences with Regard to Nationality Law and EU Citizenship Status of the Independence of a Devolved Part of an EU Member State* (Wolf Legal Publishers 2017) 230.

1053 ILC, 'Draft Articles on Nationality of Persons in relation to the Succession of States' (1999) 2 *Yearbook of the International Law Commission* 23.

1054 UNGA Resolution 55/153: Nationality of Natural Persons in Relation to the Succession of States (2000) A/RES/55/153.

1055 ILC, 'Nationality in Relation to the Succession of States: Comments and Observations Received from Governments' (1998) Doc A/CN.4/493, 162 <https://legal.un.org/ilc/documentation/english/a_cn4_493.pdf> accessed 17 October 2021.

1056 Katja Swider, 'Pre-Accession Changes to Residence-Based Naturalisation Requirements in Ten New EU Member States' (2011) EUI Working Papers RSCAS 2011/18 <https://cadmus.eui.eu/bitstream/handle/1814/16195/RSCAS_2011_18.corr.pdf?sequence=3&isAllowed=y> accessed 17 October 2021.

1057 Ibid, 14.

As naturalization possibilities are of importance to solving statelessness, a lack of attention to this by the EU does not help in addressing statelessness. Moreover, the failure of the EU to address the 'erasure' in Slovenia in the pre-accession process, does not demonstrate a comprehensive EU pre-accession strategy that helps to prevent and solve statelessness. This 'erasure' removed thousands of people from the Slovenian registry of permanent residents and has been considered a human rights violation, also causing negative effects in relation to statelessness.[1058] Still, there was explicit attention to statelessness in the accession partnerships of the EU with Estonia and Latvia for instance. Here, as part of the political criteria for accession, the EU stated that measures needed to be taken "to facilitate the naturalization process to better integrate non-citizens including stateless children".[1059] This directly helps in preventing childhood statelessness and solving existing cases of statelessness (of non-citizens in Estonia and Latvia, a status that resulted from state succession[1060]) for a specific group of people. This example shows that there is room for the EU to address prevention of and solutions to statelessness directly in its (pre-)accession negotiations. However, there is no clear EU policy in this regard.

4.3.4. ACQUISITION OF NATIONALITY

The member states of the Union are free to decide who their citizens are, so there may seem little room to argue that EU law can play a role in acquisition of nationality for stateless people in order to solve statelessness. However, as we saw above, legal developments have contributed towards greater EU influence on nationality matters at the national level. It has been held that, after the judgment in the case of *Rottmann*, "all decisions on acquisition and loss of nationality have to be reasoned in order not to conflict with European law".[1061] The conditions in the laws of the member states "for the acquisition and loss of nationality must be compatible with the Community rules and respect the rights of the European citizen".[1062] As discussed in previous paragraphs, EU law may thus influence loss and deprivation of nationality if it also leads to loss of EU citizenship. The reverse, however, that states need to take into account EU law

1058 Jo Shaw, 'The Constitutional Mosaic Across the Boundaries of the European Union: Citizenship Regimes in the New States of South Eastern Europe' in Neil Walker, Jo Shaw & Stephen Tierney (eds), *Europe's Constitutional Mosaic* (Hart Publishing 2011) 137–170, 159–160; Katja Swider, 'Pre-Accession Changes to Residence-Based Naturalisation Requirements in Ten New EU Member States' (2011) EUI Working Papers RSCAS 2011/18, 4 <https://cadmus.eui.eu/bitstream/handle/1814/16195/RSCAS_2011_18.corr.pdf?sequence=3&isAllowed=y> accessed 17 October 2021.

1059 Both accession partnerships contain this same phrase. See Estonia: Accession Partnership [1998] OJ C 202/03; Latvia: Accession Partnership [1998] OJ C 202/05.

1060 See also paras 2.6 and 2.7.

1061 Gerard René de Groot & Anja Seling, 'The Consequences of the *Rottmann* Judgment on Member State Autonomy – The European Court of Justice's Avant-Gardism in Nationality Matters' (2011) 7 European Constitutional Law Review 157.

1062 Opinion of Advocate General Poiares Maduro in Case C-135/08 *Janko Rottmann v Freistaat Bayern* [2009] ECLI:EU:C:2009:588, para 23.

and principles with regard to the granting and acquisition of nationality, may also be true, even if the cases before the CJEU so far concerned loss of (EU) citizenship. In this paragraph, we therefore consider how EU law might contribute towards the acquisition of nationality by stateless people in the EU.[1063]

Stateless people – as third-country nationals – fall under EU migration law, as could be seen in paragraph 4.2.3. In order to be able to acquire a nationality through naturalization, a legal residence status in one of the member states of the EU is necessary. EU law regulates a CEAS, which provides for rules and procedures with regard to obtaining residence rights in the EU. There are, however, no specific procedures on residence status of stateless people. They have to make do with the existing asylum and migration policy. The relevance of EU asylum and migration policy to solving statelessness is therefore very limited.

States need to have due regard for EU law when setting the conditions for loss and acquisition of nationality though.[1064] As such, matters of acquisition of nationality for stateless people, including (facilitated) naturalization, may fall within the sphere of EU law, and hence, under the protection of the EU Charter.[1065]

> "Citizenship is seen by Member States as either the culmination of the integration process or as facilitating the integration process. However, in most Member States, third-country nationals are not actively encouraged to apply for citizenship, and support is limited."[1066]

An interesting development with regard to granting nationality and EU citizenship in particular, is that of investor citizenship schemes or 'golden passports'.[1067] In July 2020, the EP called on the member states to discontinue existing citizenship by investment schemes in view of concerns with regard to criminal activity, as well as broader risks to the integrity and security of the EU and Schengen area.[1068] In October 2020, the Commission launched infringement action against Cyprus and Malta because they were found to be selling EU citizenship. According to the EC, allowing people to acquire nationality, and thereby EU citizenship, in exchange for a sum of money "without a genuine link" to the member state is incompatible with the principle of sincere

---

1063 This refers to stateless people in the EU who are not children – on children, please refer to para 4.3.1 above.

1064 Case C-369/90 *Mario Vicente Micheletti and Others v Delegación del Gobierno en Cantabria* [1992] ECLI:EU:C:1992:295, para 10.

1065 Cf Article 51 EU Charter and Case C-617/10 *Åklagaren v Hans Åkerberg Fransson* [2013] ECLI:EU:C:2013:105.

1066 EMN, 'Pathways to Citizenship for Third-Country Nationals in the EU. EMN Synthesis Report for the EMN Study 2019' (2020) 34 <https://emn.ie/wp-content/uploads/2020/07/2020_eu_emn_study_synthesis_report_citizenship_final_en_0.pdf> accessed 17 October 2021.

1067 On investor citizenship more generally, see Jelena Džankić, *The Global Market for Investor Citizenship* (Palgrave McMillan 2019).

1068 EP Resolution of 10 July 2020 on a comprehensive Union policy on preventing money laundering and terrorist financing – the Commission's Action Plan and other recent developments (2020/2686(RSP)) [2020] para 31 <https://www.europarl.europa.eu/doceo/document/TA-9-2020-0204_EN.html> accessed 3 January 2022.

cooperation of Article 4(3) TEU. It also "undermines the integrity of the status of EU citizenship".[1069] Even though such schemes and the response by the EU do not directly contribute to acquisition of nationality for stateless people, it does show that the EU is prepared to intervene in the national rules of states on acquisition of nationality. In this case, the EU felt it necessary to step in because the nationality policy is too expansive – allowing people to acquire EU citizenship without a genuine link – and therefore in violation of EU values. But what if national rules or procedures on acquisition of nationality are inadequate and lack necessary safeguards, thereby not allow people with a genuine link to acquire a nationality?

There are instances where states make it very difficult, if not impossible, for stateless people to acquire nationality. For example, due to lack of proper statelessness determination procedures, states do not register stateless people as such, but for instance with 'unknown nationality'[1070], which eventually leads to problems in naturalization procedures, where they would be asked to produce a (former) passport of a country of former residence or nationality. Indeed, it has been found that "for many aspiring citizens, naturalization can be a lengthy and costly process, with limited available support, and a positive outcome is in general not guaranteed, even where all conditions have been met."[1071] As such, EU states may be obstructing access to procedures under which a person can apply for naturalization. Eventually, lack of adequate procedures, safeguards and/or registration leading to prolonged impediments to accessing naturalization procedures might be construed as denial of nationality, and thereby denial of EU citizenship to stateless people – a status that would ensure that someone can fully become part of European society, particularly realized by the right to vote for the EP. Moreover, as we saw in paragraph 4.2.4, nationality can be seen as part of a persons' personal identity that is protected under the right to private life of Article 8 ECHR and the corresponding Article 7 of the EU Charter. Indeed, it has been held that the (arbitrary) denial of citizenship may impact on private life[1072], bringing acquisition of nationality (or denial thereof by EU member states) firmly within the scope of EU law. As the rights in the EU Charter that correspond to rights guaranteed by the ECHR have the same meaning and scope as in the ECHR, it also relevant to consider that the ECtHR has held in relation to cases involving statelessness that states have a

1069 EC, 'Investor citizenship schemes: European Commission opens infringements against Cyprus and Malta for "selling" EU citizenship' (2020) <https://ec.europa.eu/commission/presscorner/detail/en/ip_20_1925> accessed 3 January 2022.

1070 Eg UNHCR, 'Identifying Stateless Persons in the European Union. Intervention by Vincent Cochetel, UNHCR Director of the Bureau for Europe, on the occasion of the meeting of the Strategic Committee on Immigration, Frontiers and Asylum in Brussels, 25 April 2017' (2017) 4–5 <https://www.refworld.org/pdfid/5911d8c34.pdf> accessed 17 October 2021.

1071 EMN, 'Pathways to Citizenship for Third-Country Nationals in the EU. EMN Synthesis Report for the EMN Study 2019' (2020) 33 <https://emn.ie/wp-content/uploads/2020/07/2020_eu_emn_study_synthesis_report_citizenship_final_en_0.pdf> accessed 17 October 2021.

1072 *Andrei Karassev and Family v Finland* App No 31414/96 (ECHR, 12 January 1999, admissibility) ECLI: CE:ECHR:1999:0112DEC003141496.

> "positive obligation to provide an effective and accessible procedure or a combination of procedures enabling the applicant to have the issue of his status [...] determined with due regard to his private-life interests under Article 8 of the Convention".[1073]

This means that leaving stateless people without a legal status and unidentified for a prolonged time, hence denying them a status that could eventually lead to access to nationality and EU citizenship, may violate the right to private life, also under the EU Charter. This confirms the need for proper identification of stateless people, even pointing to the importance of establishing "a common legal framework for the determination of statelessness in the EU".[1074] Taking this a step further, one may also wonder whether states could be held accountable for denying those who have a legal status but are unable to take the last step through naturalization to a more certain and 'full' status in the EU as citizens. This in view of the concept of EU citizenship as it has developed, and taken together with the applicable fundamental rights and the EU's role in migration law in relation to this, also for instance because they are not offering an effective remedy. At the very least, however, all this entails that procedures relating to the regularization of status and acquisition of nationality are subject to the right to an effective remedy as included in the EU Charter (Article 47 EU Charter).

In September 2012, the EU pledged on the occasion of the UN High-level meeting on the rule of law at the national and international levels that all EU member states were to ratify the 1954 Convention.[1075] With the large majority of EU member states as of January 2022 being a party to this treaty, it has been held that this

> "pledge should also have consequences for the accountability of the European Union for meeting the standards of the Convention by the Member States. This includes the obligation of Member States to provide for facilitated naturalisation of stateless persons living on their territory, as laid down in Article 32 of the 1954 Convention".[1076]

This would directly contribute to solving statelessness, as stateless people should then be able to enjoy facilitated naturalization in EU member states. Furthermore, "stimulating the exchange of information between member states, in particular on policies regarding

---

1073 *Sudita Keita v Hungary* App No 42321/15 (ECHR, 12 May 2020) ECLI:CE:ECHR:2020:0512JUD004232115, para 41; see also *Hoti v Kroatia* App No 63311/14 (ECHR, 26 April 2018) ECLI:CE:ECHR:2018:0426JUD006331114.

1074 Gerard-René de Groot, Katja Swider & Olivier Vonk, 'Practices and Approaches in the EU Member States to Prevent and End Statelessness. Study for the LIBE Committee' (2015) 56 <https://www.europarl.europa.eu/RegData/etudes/STUD/2015/536476/IPOL_STU(2015)536476_EN.pdf> accessed 17 October 2021.

1075 Delegation of the EU to the UN, 'High-level Meeting on the Rule of Law at the National and International Levels. Pledge Registration Form' (19 September 2012) A.4 <https://www.un.org/ruleoflaw/files/Pledges%20by%20the%20European%20Union.pdf> accessed 17 October 2021.

1076 Gerard-René de Groot, Katja Swider & Olivier Vonk, 'Practices and Approaches in the EU Member States to Prevent and End Statelessness. Study for the LIBE Committee' (2015) 56 <https://www.europarl.europa.eu/RegData/etudes/STUD/2015/536476/IPOL_STU(2015)536476_EN.pdf> accessed 17 October 2021.

the prevention and reduction of statelessness and the treatment of stateless persons"[1077] could contribute to further visibility of (solutions) to statelessness and EU member states considering their own and each other's law and policy on stateless people and access to nationality.

4.3.5. NON-DISCRIMINATION

The principle of non-discrimination is not only an important principle in international law, it is also a key value of the EU. However, it has its distinct characteristics, which are important to understand as a background to any further considerations regarding its relevant to preventing and solving statelessness. Whereas equality in certain aspects was viewed as a necessary precondition for economic prosperity with an internal market and free movement, it is now a fundamental right in the EU.

> "Prohibitions of discrimination under EU law are now seen as a fundamental social right that builds European citizenship rights [...]. This is testified by EU non-discrimination law expanding well beyond nationality and gender towards a wide range of protected grounds that do not serve an agenda of economic market integration."[1078]

As explicated in Article 2 of the TEU, non-discrimination and equality, in particular between men and women, are principal values on which the EU has been built. The EU views "non-discrimination through a formal lens that derives discrimination from a difference in treatment in comparable situations"[1079] and has tasked itself to "combat social exclusion and discrimination"[1080] explicitly. Two Equality Directives were introduced in 2000: the Framework Equality Directive[1081] and the Race Equality Directive.[1082] These Directives have a defined scope:

> "The Framework Equality Directive is confined to the employment sphere, while the Race Equality Directive also covers social protection, including social security and healthcare, education, and access to goods and services available to the public, such as housing. The Directives are further constrained because they do not cover the prohibition of discrimination on the basis of nationality."[1083]

1077 Ibid, 56.

1078 Marc de Vos, 'The European Court of Justice and the March towards Substantive Equality in European Union Anti-discrimination Law' (2020) 20 International Journal of Discrimination and the Law 62, 64.

1079 Ibid, 65.

1080 Art 3 TEU.

1081 Directive 2000/78 Establishing a General Framework for Equal Treatment in Employment and Occupation [2000] OJ L 3030/16 (Framework Equality Directive).

1082 Directive 2000/43 Implementing the Principle of Equal Treatment between Persons Irrespective of Racial or Ethnic Origin [2000] OJ L 180/22 (Race Equality Directive).

1083 Uladzislau Belavusau & Kristin Henrard, 'A Bird's Eye View on EU Anti-Discrimination Law: The Impact of the 2000 Equality Directives (2019) 20 German Law Journal 614, 626.

Indeed, Article 3(2) of the Framework Equality Directive states that it does not apply to any treatment resulting from the legal status of third-country nationals and stateless persons. Article 3(2) of the Race Equality Directive contains a similar provision. This research focuses on preventing and solving statelessness, and in this paragraph in particular looks for how the principle of non-discrimination can help ensure that no one loses their nationality and becomes stateless (preventing statelessness), or that people acquire a nationality (at birth or later in life through naturalization, thus preventing or solving statelessness). Given the particular purpose and focus of the aforementioned EU Directives, which is without prejudice to provisions and/or conditions relating to the entry into and residence of third-country nationals and stateless people on the territory of the EU, they are therefore not considered further here.

Important for the recognition of the prohibition of discrimination as a fundamental right is Title III of the EU Charter on equality, which guarantees equality before the law.[1084] It also prohibits any discrimination based on any ground, including on the basis of sex, race, color, ethnic or social origin, language, religion or belief, membership of a national minority, and birth.[1085] In Article 21(2) of the EU Charter, it is specified further that any discrimination on the grounds of nationality is prohibited within the scope of application of the EU Treaties and without prejudice to any of their specific provisions. This second paragraph of the aforementioned provision is explored further below in more detail. First, the EU Charter's non-discrimination provisions and their relevance to preventing and solving statelessness are considered more closely, also in relation to the existing CJEU case law on nationality matters and EU citizenship. In this regard, it should be remembered that within the EU, the ECHR is used as "inspiration when determining the scope of human rights protection under EU law".[1086]

Looking at access to nationality, it is clear that not granting nationality to people who are part of a particular ethnic or minority group contravenes the prohibition of discrimination as laid down in Article 21(1) of the EU Charter.[1087] In this way, it may help to prevent statelessness among minorities due to discriminatory treatment.

Nonetheless, the EU more generally paid not as much attention to the protection of minorities as compared to the CoE for example, and changing that "would mean an extension of competences within the EU".[1088] Still, the EU has taken some action regarding minorities and statelessness in particular. In its Resolution on Minimum Standards for Minorities in the EU, the EP has for instance expressed concern about the number of stateless Roma in Europe and called on the member states to "to abolish

---

1084 Art 20 EU Charter.

1085 Art 21(1) EU Charter.

1086 CoE & FRA, 'Handbook on European Non-discrimination Law' (2010) 17 <https://fra.europa.eu/sites/default/files/fra_uploads/1510-fra-case-law-handbook_en.pdf> accessed 21 October 2021.

1087 Katalin Berényi, 'Addressing the Anomaly of Statelessness in Europe: An EU Law and Human Rights Perspective' (PhD thesis, Ludovika – University of Public Service 2018) 160.

1088 Ulrike Barten, 'The EU's Lack of Commitment to Minority Protection' (2016) 15 Journal on Ethnopolitics and Minority Issues in Europe 104, 120.

statelessness and ensure the enjoyment of fundamental human rights by all".[1089] This does not give a lot of specific guidance on how to work towards abolishing statelessness. The EU Roma Strategic Framework for equality, inclusion and participation (2020–2030) also does not say much about addressing statelessness among Roma, but does indicate that national strategic frameworks that member states need to develop, should set out targets and measures for stateless Roma.[1090] Such measures should aim to contribute to equality, inclusion and participation of Roma, but no mention is made of specific measures relating to the identification, prevention and resolution of statelessness.

Clearer on the matter of statelessness is the Minority Safepack, a European Citizens' Initiative. This initiative aims to improve the protection of people belonging to national and linguistic minorities.[1091] The Minority Safepack has called for amendment of EU law to extend "citizenship-related rights to stateless persons and their families, who have been living in their country of origin for the whole of their lives" – but the EC indicated it does not see the need for such changes.[1092] There is thus some attention for statelessness in the EU efforts on minority protection. But even if changes were made to grant stateless long-term residents more citizenship-related rights, this does not go to the root cause(s) of the disenfranchisement of people living their entire life stateless in an EU country. Such measures do not protect them from passing on statelessness to their children or offer a solution that would really resolve their situation by offering a pathway to citizenship. This may be beyond reach for EU law on minorities, but given that it often concerns exclusion of people who have lived their entire lives in the EU, the EU should be concerned about a group that is clearly part of European society, yet is unable to enjoy full participatory rights, including the right to vote as well as other rights associated with EU citizenship. This is considered in more depth further below.

On loss of nationality, it was already noted in paragraph 3.3 that several European states have provisions on deprivation of nationality that differentiate between dual nationals and/or naturalized citizens. Where a distinction is made between European citizens based on how or when they acquired their EU citizenship (by birth or by naturalization), this could be contrary to the EU legal order and principles.[1093] A similar line of reasoning may be followed where it concerns differentiations between EU citizens and people who have EU citizenship as well as another nationality: there should

---

1089 EP Resolution on of 13 November 2018 on Minimum Standards for Minorities in the EU (2018/2036(INI)) [2018] <https://www.europarl.europa.eu/doceo/document/TA-8-2018-0447_EN.html?mc_cid=1a29410458&mc_eid=7bf481eaf5> accessed 28 October 2021.

1090 Communication from the Commission to the European Parliament and the Council: A Union of Equality: EU Roma Strategic Framework for Equality, Inclusion and Participation [2020] COM(2020) 620 final.

1091 See also 'Minority Safepack Initiative' <www.minority-safepack.eu/> accessed 28 October 2021.

1092 Communication of the Commission on the European Citizens' Initiative 'Minority SafePack – one million signatures for diversity in Europe' [2021] C(2021) 171 final, 12.

1093 Gerard René de Groot & Anja Seling, 'The Consequences of the *Rottmann* Judgment on Member State Autonomy – The European Court of Justice's Avant-Gardism in Nationality Matters' (2011) 7 European Constitutional Law Review 150, 158.

be no distinction between EU citizens in that regard either. That measures of nationality deprivation are applied only to dual nationals would imply that such measures would not result in statelessness. In practice, however, the determination of whether a person has another nationality or would become stateless after being deprived of nationality is problematic and may not always prevent statelessness.[1094] Moreover, citizenship deprivation may also have consequences for the nationality of the child(ren) of the person concerned. As such, it is relevant to explore this issue further with a view to preventing statelessness.

In the *Micheletti* case, the CJEU affirmed that the creation different classes of EU citizenship for the purpose of the freedom of establishment was not permitted:

> "[...] it is not permissible to interpret Article 52 of the Treaty to the effect that, where a national of a Member State is also a national of a non-member country, the other Member States may make recognition of the status of Community national subject to a condition such as the habitual residence of the person concerned in the territory of the first Member State. That conclusion is reinforced by the fact that the consequence of allowing such a possibility would be that the class of persons to whom the Community rules on freedom of establishment were applied might vary from one Member State to another."[1095]

Establishing this also with regard to discrimination based on nationality would fall within the provision of Article 21(2) of the EU Charter, as it would concern a difference in treatment between EU citizens on the basis of nationality. Only where there are 'very weighty reasons' might it be possible to justify such treatment, but this standard set by European non-discrimination law is hard to meet.[1096] Moreover, Article 21(1) of the EU Charter could be of relevance as well, as nationality deprivation of dual nationals in a national security context often concerns people with a migration background or belonging to a(n ethnic) minority. Therefore, nationality deprivation measures that only apply to dual nationals may also raise questions concerning (the prohibition of) ethnic and racial discrimination.[1097]

European citizenship jurisprudence taken together with the EU Charter thus demonstrates that where states arbitrarily keep people from acquiring EU citizenship or depriving them of it on discriminatory grounds, this would be problematic under the EU provisions on equality and non-discrimination. However, a key issue for solving

---

1094 Cf *Minh Quang Pham v the United Kingdom* App No 37478/20 (ECtHR, communicated on 25 November 2020), see also para 3.3.2.

1095 Case C-369/90 *Mario Vicente Micheletti and Others v Delegación del Gobierno en Cantabria* [1992] ECLI:EU:C:1992:295, paras 11–12.

1096 Cf para 3.3.5 and *Biao v Denmark* App No 38590/10 (ECHR, 24 May 2016) ECLI:CE:ECHR:2016:0524 JUD003859010, para 138.

1097 See also Meijers Committee, 'Policy Brief on Differential Treatment of Citizens with Dual or Multiple Nationality and the Prohibition of Discrimination' (2020) <https://www.commissie-meijers.nl/wp-content/uploads/2020/12/cm2016_policy_brief_on_differential_treatment_of_citizens_with_dual_or_multiple_nationality_and_the_prohibition_of_discrimination.pdf accessed 24 October 2021> accessed 24 October 2021.

statelessness, in particular when considering the EU context, is access to a legal status and legal residence in the EU, as this can eventually result in access to naturalization. In view of this, it is necessary to further examine the previously mentioned provision of Article 21(2) which limits the use of nationality as a ground for discrimination to where it is within the scope of application of the EU treaties. Article 18 of the TFEU, in that treaty's section on non-discrimination and citizenship of the Union, is similar to the EU Charter provision: "[w]ithin the scope of application of the Treaties, and without prejudice to any special provisions contained therein, any discrimination on grounds of nationality shall be prohibited". The TFEU provision has been regarded as only applying to EU citizens, being pivotal in guaranteeing free movement, and as a key component of EU citizenship. It does not apply to third-country nationals and it has therefore been held that, "where the right to equal treatment is concerned, the 'soft on the inside, hard on the outside' character of citizenship appears to be reproduced at the EU level".[1098] This entails that arguments around unequal treatment because of lack of any nationality are difficult to make under EU law, including the EU Charter. Nonetheless, commentators have indicated that there might be scope to include third-country nationals, and stateless people in particular, drawing on the ECHR:

> "[...] the nationality-triggered applicability of the non-discrimination clause to stateless persons is still an option within the perimeters of the Charter. It is so especially in light of the case law of the European Court of Human Rights, which prohibits discrimination based on nationality under very strict review, and which case law must be duly taken into account when interpreting Charter rights corresponding to rights guaranteed by the European Convention on Human Rights, as the one at hand. Overall, it clearly provides for an entry point for stateless persons to seek protection under the Charter against unlawful discrimination."[1099]

How could this in any way contribute to solving statelessness? As was elaborated on above, states may effectively be denying EU citizenship by creating (unjustifiable) obstacles to naturalization procedures for stateless people. This because they may be lacking mechanisms to adequately determine statelessness, which may in turn result in stateless people being subject to requirements, for instance with regard to

1098 Evelien Brouwer & Karin de Vries, 'Third-country Nationals and Discrimination on the Ground of Nationality: Article 18 TFEU in the Context of Article 14 ECHR and EU Migration Law: Time of a New Approach' in Marjolein van den Brink, Susanne Burri & Jenny Goldschmidt (eds) *Equality and Human Rights: Nothing but Trouble? Liber Amicorum Titia Loenen* (SIM Special 38, SIM/UU 2015) 123–146, 124.

1099 Tamás Molnár, 'The Charter of Fundamental Rights and the Protection of Stateless People in the EU: A Dormant Giant?' (*ENS Blog*, 28 September 2017) <https://www.statelessness.eu/updates/blog/charter-fundamental-rights-and-protection-stateless-people-eu-dormant-giant> accessed 17 October 2021. See also Evelien Brouwer & Karin de Vries, 'Third-country Nationals and Discrimination on the Ground of Nationality: Article 18 TFEU in the Context of Article 14 ECHR and EU Migration Law: Time of a New Approach' in Marjolein van den Brink, Susanne Burri & Jenny Goldschmidt (eds) *Equality and Human Rights: Nothing but Trouble? Liber Amicorum Titia Loenen* (SIM Special 38, SIM/UU 2015) 123–146, 144.

documentation, that they are unable to meet. In cases where third-country nationals like this have been staying legally in the EU for a long time and participating actively in society, it may – from the perspective of equality and non-discrimination – not be feasible to continue to make a distinction between people with and without EU citizenship with regard to the right to fully participate in European society and being able to vote. After all, and as could be seen in paragraph 1.4.2 as well, "the capacity to participate in an election must be seen as central to the complex notion of citizenship".[1100] At the same time, the importance of participation of third-country nationals has been highlighted as important for democracy, the EU and its societies:

> "The full and equal participation of all members of society in the political decision-making process is crucial for the legitimacy of the democratic political systems of Europe's increasingly diverse societies."[1101]

Drawing on such considerations regarding democracy and political participation, the principle of non-discrimination may help stateless people to challenge unreasonable impediments to naturalization, which could help to resolve their situation.

4.3.6. CONCLUDING REMARKS

A thematic analysis of ways in which EU law may contribute to preventing and solving statelessness from a human rights perspective shows that the EU has options, albeit limited. With regard to childhood statelessness, it could be seen that under the EU Charter in conjunction with the CJEU jurisprudence on Union citizenship, there is some scope to address this. In particular, in any decisions concerning (loss of) nationality of children, an individual assessment needs to be made in which the best interests of the child are a key consideration. It was furthermore found that EU law in relation to citizenship of the Union can be useful in addressing prevention of statelessness among children born on EU territory who would otherwise be stateless, as well as for advocating for proper identification of statelessness. However, jurisprudence relating to EU citizenship may also negatively influence the adoption of further safeguards preventing childhood statelessness in the EU by the member states, due to rights that (illegally staying) TCN parents may be able to derive. Moreover, the EU's action in this specific area remains limited, as evidenced by the EU Strategy on the rights of the child omitting important areas for addressing childhood statelessness,

1100 Jo Shaw, *The Transformation of Citizenship in the European Union. Electoral Rights and the Restructuring of Political Space* (Cambridge University Press 2007) 5.

1101 Jan Niessen, 'The Participation of Immigrants in Political Processes and Institutions' in Kristen Jeffers (ed), Inclusive Democracy in Europe (EUDO/European University Institute 2012) 15 <https://cadmus.eui.eu/bitstream/handle/1814/24334/eBook_InclusiveDemocracyInEurope2012.pdf?sequence=1&isAllowed=y> accessed 28 October 2021.

such as legal safeguards in nationality law to prevent childhood statelessness and child-friendly statelessness determination procedures.

With regard to loss and deprivation of nationality, where it would also entail loss or deprivation of citizenship of the Union, it has become clear that this needs to meet certain standards prescribed by EU law. These standards include a proportionality test, but also the principle of non-discrimination for instance. As such, EU law provides for additional safeguards that may prevent a state from withdrawing nationality leading to statelessness. This in particular because statelessness may lead to severe consequences for the individual, for instance with regard to his or her private life, which may not be proportionate with the aim served by the measure of revoking nationality. These safeguards also mean that states must identify whether statelessness would result from loss or deprivation of nationality, and thereby EU citizenship, to be able to factor this into the aforementioned proportionality test.

There is no EU law on state succession and addressing nationality matters in such a context, and it seems EU citizenship can also not provide an avenue for addressing nationality matters arising from state succession. Nonetheless, and despite no clear policy on this, the EU has influenced prevention of and solutions to statelessness directly in its (pre-)accession negotiations with some (candidate) member states where statelessness was produced by restrictive nationality policy following state succession.

Concerning the acquisition of nationality, which seems a stretch in view of the lack of EU competence in regulating nationality matters, some options that could help in solving statelessness were uncovered. These draw on CJEU case law on EU citizenship and Article 7 of the EU Charter (while mindful of the interpretation of this same right under the ECHR). Leaving stateless people without a legal status and unidentified for a prolonged time, hence denying them a status that could eventually lead to access to nationality and EU citizenship, may violate the right to private life. This indicates a need for identification of statelessness from an EU law perspective. A further question that could be asked was whether states could be held accountable for denying those who have a legal status but are unable to take the last step through naturalization to (EU) citizenship, as denial of citizenship may impact on private life as well. At the very least, stateless people should be offered an effective remedy (Article 47 EU Charter) with regard to procedures for regularizing their status and naturalization, including establishing their statelessness, which can help them claim a nationality and resolve their statelessness.

This section also found that the principles of equality and non-discrimination are key to the EU's legal framework. Where nationality laws discriminate on the basis of race, ethnicity, gender or other ground, there is real scope for EU law to address this in view of the link with EU citizenship. In particular where it concerns loss of nationality of EU citizenship and differentiation between EU citizens in this regard, based on how nationality was acquired for example, EU non-discrimination law can be helpful in addressing this. However, where it concerns unequal treatment on the ground of nationality, EU law is – in principle – limited to EU citizens. This makes it difficult for stateless people, as third-country nationals, to use non-discrimination in the context of rules relating to accessing nationality or rights associated with that. Nonetheless, drawing on the EU Charter and the ECHR, it has been held that there is certainly potential for further litigation on this issue. At the same time, the fact that non-discrimination in this regard is reserved to EU citizens only deepens the distinctions between those with and without (EU) citizenship further.

4.4. CONCLUSION: THE EU'S CONTRIBUTION TO THE LEGAL CONCEPTION OF NATIONALITY

This chapter examined how European law made by the EU contributes to preventing and solving statelessness in Europe and to understanding the notion of nationality. Despite the fact that such matters, which concern nationality of the member states, formally are subject to member state competence only, various areas of EU law offer avenues for addressing the prevention of and solutions to statelessness. These areas of law are that of EU citizenship, fundamental rights and asylum and migration policy. Furthermore, statelessness as an issue has been recognized separately in EU law in Article 67(2) TFEU, which indicates that stateless people are to be treated as third-country nationals. At the same time, the EU Charter does not contain a right to a nationality.

The EU as a mechanism of cooperation and as a legal framework presents a strong and coherent system. This can be explained when considering its relation with national jurisdictions, which includes direct effect of (some) EU law and that the principle of primacy of EU law. As such, the influence of EU law at the national level is very direct. In particular, domestic courts and tribunals can apply EU law, and may decide on conflicts between EU and national law. At the same time, despite some interest and recognition of statelessness in its laws, the EU has not taken a clear stance on the matter nor is there any concerted effort to be found that concerns preventing and solving statelessness specifically.

Still, the EU has laid down relevant principles that may aid in preventing and solving statelessness. In particular where (EU) citizenship would be lost, the principle of proportionality has been articulated as a key consideration. Moreover, it was found that the principles of the best interests of the child and of non-discrimination may be helpful in preventing statelessness. Also, the principle of sincere cooperation between the member states was found the be relevant to preventing statelessness as an obligation to coordinate before adopting new rules relating to acquisition and loss of nationality, as these may affect EU citizenship as well. As such, this principle may to some extent restrain states' freedom to regulate nationality matters in a manner that would generate or perpetuate statelessness.

Moreover, drawing on the three areas of EU law as previously mentioned, a need for identification of statelessness as the first important step in ensuring that the particular vulnerabilities of stateless people can be taken into account was shown. After all, the legal residence status that precedes acquisition of nationality through naturalization is largely regulated by EU law. Moreover, with a view to EU citizenship, additional arguments could be made on the need for adequate naturalization procedures and avoiding denial of EU citizenship to people without any nationality who are long-term residents. This is particularly so because EU citizenship was introduced with the idea of enhancing European identity – attempting to create a sense of community and attaching participatory rights to this status. From that perspective, there is therefore an additional argument to be made that the EU should have something to say about who is able to obtain this status. At the same time, it should be recognized that direct influence of EU law over nationality matters would remain limited – dependent on the relevance to EU citizenship. Addressing nationality matters in a state succession context in a concerted way was shown to be outside of the scope of EU instruments at the moment for example.

While addressing nationality matters and statelessness, the EU has taken into account international (human rights) law obligations in setting and interpreting its standards, also where it concerns nationality matters. This is evidenced by the *Rottmann* case for instance, where the CJEU takes note of relevant provisions from the UDHR, the 1961 Convention and the ECN while explaining EU law on Union citizenship. As such, some of the EU's interpretation and standard-setting can be seen to form part of the larger ecosystem of international norms that address statelessness and nationality.

This chapter furthermore gave an indication about what nationality or citizenship entails under EU law. Distinct to the EU context is of course that a status of EU citizenship has been introduced, seemingly indicating that the notion of nationality can be extended beyond a bond between a person and a state. However, as it does not constitute state citizenship, it would still not be a 'full' status that could 'solve' statelessness as defined in this research. When considering EU citizenship more closely from a perspective of preventing and solving statelessness, it was furthermore uncovered that EU citizenship very much reinforces the existing conception of nationality as a status that exists between a person and a state. In fact, EU citizenship is contingent on national citizenship and is only an addition to it. At the same time though, this is precisely why it is possible for the EU to have some say about domestic laws of the member states that concern nationality: exactly because they affect EU citizenship and rights that are attached to this status. Indeed, with the status of EU citizen come extra protections and rights, such as free movement rights and participatory rights. These protections also extend into nationality matters where an individual assessment of the proportionality of loss of EU citizenship specifically is required before a state may take such a measure. The additional rights and protection that EU citizenship offers can therefore be helpful in preventing statelessness. Nonetheless, it should be remembered that adding this additional layer of rights and protection to having a nationality of an EU member state only further increases the inequality between those privileged to have such a nationality and those without any nationality at all.

As the EU conception of citizenship is still one of nationality as a legal bond between a person and a state, it also relies on domestic systems for regulating this further, thus presupposing that systems for registration are in place at the national level, as well as procedures for naturalization, etcetera. Given the EU's role on asylum and migration policy, however, it has been held that there could be scope for the EU to contribute at least towards the identification of stateless people. This is also needed for helping to further prevent and solve statelessness, for instance contributing towards facilitated naturalization possibilities for stateless people.

The EU's contribution to preventing and solving statelessness in Europe thus remains limited. Even though the principle of proportionality as developed under EU law can be important in preventing statelessness, it does not take away from an overall lack of a clear and coherent effort in addressing statelessness. That is perhaps not too surprising from a competence perspective, but given the attempt to consolidate a European (political) community using EU citizenship, people who remain without any nationality for a prolonged time on the territory of the Union can be a concern that the EU may want to address more clearly. The contribution of EU legal instruments to preventing and solving statelessness thus remains small at the moment, but given their wider influence – also at the national level – there is certainly potential.

PART III
CONCLUSIONS AND REFLECTIONS

CHAPTER 5
COMPARISON AND ANALYSIS

"For me, 'statelessness' is having no identity, no personality.
You have no roots, no state, no house, no home, no identity, no personality."
– Railya, born in the former Soviet Union and currently living in France.
Railya was stateless for 24 years and acquired French nationality in 2015[1102]

5.1. INTRODUCTION

The Council of Europe (CoE) and the European Union (EU) are two organizations in which cooperation between states takes place on different topics and in distinct ways. They are indeed very different from each other in some respects, but also have some similarities and have – for the purpose of this study – both been considered to understand the contribution of European law to the issues of nationality and statelessness. As could be seen in chapters 1 and 2 (Part I of this research), statelessness occurred on a large scale in Europe after the World Wars. And today still, a variety of causes lead to continuing occurrences of statelessness. This despite a number of relevant international and European norms. After looking at both the CoE and EU separately in chapters 3 and 4 (Part II of this research), this chapter takes the two together, studying the sum of the two organizations with regard to preventing and solving statelessness. It looks at similarities and differences to better understand their overall contribution and present a clear overview before turning to a discussion of the findings and conclusions of this research.

The comparison and analysis in this chapter draws on the analytical framework that was formulated in Part I of this research. In paragraph 5.2 below, the various instruments of both organizations are categorized and an overall assessment is given of their relevance and contribution, as well as how they may compare to international norms on preventing and solving statelessness and what standards and principles they represent. Moreover, attention is paid in paragraph 5.3 to the similarities and differences between the CoE and the EU to put the findings into perspective. The chapter finishes with a conclusion before moving on to further reflections on the concept of nationality in chapter 6. As such, this

1102 UNHCR, 'Storytelling: Railya' (2011) <www.youtube.com/watch?v=GUEfwLtBcUY> accessed 17 October 2021. See also UNHCR, 'Stateless in Europe. Ordinary People in Extraordinary Circumstances' (2018) <https://www.refworld.org/docid/5aa79f9d4.html> accessed 17 October 2021.

chapter aims to answer the first half of the main research question on how European law contributes to preventing and solving statelessness in Europe.

5.2. HUMAN RIGHTS ANALYSIS AND NORMS: FINDINGS

This research's human rights approach was translated into an analytical framework in chapters 1 and 2.[1103] This framework consists of five 'categories' of norms, each articulating a different aspect of the human right to a nationality, addressing the prevention of and solutions to statelessness:

- legal norms aimed at preventing and solving *childhood statelessness*;
- legal norms concerning solutions to *conflicts of nationality law* and preventing *loss / (arbitrary) deprivation / denial of nationality* (later in life – in order to prevent statelessness);
- nationality matters and reduction of statelessness in the context of *state succession*;
- legal norms aimed at the *right to a nationality* and *acquisition of a nationality for people who became stateless in the past and remain stateless today and/or who arrive to a country stateless* (in order to solve statelessness);
- legal norms ensuring *non-discrimination* and *equality before the law* in nationality matters (acquisition and loss and (arbitrary) deprivation of nationality – in order to prevent and solve statelessness).

The analysis in Part II considered the European legal instruments developed by the CoE and the EU further. In particular, in the third sections of chapters 3 and 4, the various instruments were examined within the categories of the analytical framework. In annex II, the instruments analyzed have been brought together in a schematic overview of the various European legal instruments according to category and framework (CoE/EU). This overview demonstrates that for both the CoE and the EU, legal instruments could be identified in each category.

Overall, the CoE seems to have more and more targeted instruments at its disposal to prevent and solve statelessness. This is particularly visible for instance in the category that concerns legal norms that concern nationality matters and the reduction of statelessness in the context of state succession. Whereas the EU has no clear instruments to address this, the CoE of has a treaty that is entirely dedicated to preventing statelessness in situations of state succession: the ECSS. At the same time, it should be remembered that both the CoE and the EU do not include an explicit right to a nationality in their respective key fundamental rights standards: the ECHR and the EU Charter. Nonetheless, and given the relation between the two instruments[1104], the right

1103 See paras 1.5.3 and 2.8.

1104 Cf Art 53 EU Charter.

to respect for private and family life as included in Article 8 of the ECHR and Article 7 of the EU Charter has proven an important entry-point in this regard by protecting nationality as part of the notion of social and personal identity. ECHR jurisprudence on this has demonstrated that the ECHR protects against discrimination concerning acquisition of nationality.[1105] Moreover, non-discrimination was found to be a key principle in both frameworks, but with some limitations in the EU context – nationality can be a ground for discrimination only where it is within the scope of application of the EU treaties (Article 21(2) EU Charter). On (arbitrary) denial, deprivation and loss of nationality, important jurisprudence exists both in the CoE (from the ECtHR) and the EU (from the CJEU), which has clarified standards around this matter specifically. ECHR case law set out, for instance, the standards for determining whether deprivation of nationality is arbitrary.[1106] And the CJEU clarified a proportionality test that is to be performed in cases of loss of EU citizenship.[1107] The same cannot be said for acquisition of nationality, but it was uncovered that arguments could be made with regard to statelessness determination, legal residence status, and – ultimately – acquisition of nationality in both frameworks.

What norms can overall be derived from the European legal instruments that address the prevention of and solutions to statelessness? Where it concerns preventing and solving childhood statelessness, it is clear that *jus sanguinis* remains the key principle for granting nationality at birth. To address gaps that may arise, *jus soli* elements have been introduced by the CoE framework so as to avoid that foundlings, and other children born on the territory, would otherwise remain stateless. However, and deviating from international law standards on children, legal and habitual residence may be required for otherwise stateless children born on the territory before they are able to claim the nationality of the state where they were born. Still, it is encouraging that both the ECtHR and the CJEU have included the principle of the best interests of the child in their considerations regarding the nationality of children. This seems to be in keeping with developments at the international level in this regard as well. Furthermore, EU law has explicated how the principle of proportionality requires an individual examination of the situation and consequences for the child in case of loss of (EU) citizenship, also taking into account the best interests of the child. Moreover, the principle of non-discrimination was found to be relevant in both frameworks to cases where children would be unable or denied to acquire the nationality of one of the parents, such as in cases of birth out of wedlock. The situation of children registered with 'unknown' nationality was also considered, finding that the principle of the best interests of the child as well as other human rights norms are at odds with a situation where this happens for a long period, and point towards the importance of proper identification of statelessness. Finally, issues around adoption and surrogacy came up

1105 Cf *Genovese v Malta* App No 53124/09 (ECHR, 11 October 2011) ECLI:CE:ECHR:2011:1011JUD005312409.

1106 Para 3.3.2.

1107 Para 4.3.2.

in this research. Whereas clear and specific guidance on this is limited, the CoE offers some: the CM Recommendation on the nationality of children for instance. According to this Recommendation, children born as a result of medically assisted reproductive techniques should be able to acquire nationality *jus sanguinis* if the parent-child relationship is established.[1108] The principle of the best interests of the child as well as the principle of non-discrimination, taken together with the right to respect for private and family life, indicate that such situations should not lead to children being left stateless and without an important part of their identity.

When considering conflicts of nationality law, loss and (arbitrary) deprivation of nationality, European law sets a clear standard: loss or deprivation of nationality should never result in statelessness, except where nationality was acquired by fraud. Moreover, and even in situations of deprivation because of fraudulent acquisition of nationality, a proportionality test is required when deciding on deprivation of nationality. As explained by the CJEU, this needs to take into account the consequences that the decision entails for the person concerned and, if relevant, for the members of his or her family. Moreover, any measure to deprive a person of his or her nationality must, according to the ECtHR, be in accordance with the law and accompanied by the necessary procedural safeguards, with authorities acting diligently and swiftly in such procedures. In this way, European law thus avoids the occurrence of statelessness further as compared to international norms on the matter[1109], by maintaining stricter grounds for exception to the general rule that loss or deprivation of nationality should not lead to statelessness. Drawing on CoE norms, it is also clear that renunciation of nationality should not lead to statelessness. On conflicts of nationality law and multiple nationality, European law remains relatively quiet and neutral.[1110] At the same time, arguments are to be made both on the basis of the ECN[1111] and the EU principle of sincere cooperation[1112] that European states should cooperate and coordinate on nationality matters, also with a view to ensuring that statelessness does not occur. This may for instance be the case where it concerns renunciation of nationality or the introduction of new grounds for loss or deprivation of nationality in domestic laws.

On norms addressing nationality and statelessness in a state succession context, it was already noted that the EU remains as good as silent. The CoE and the ECSS, however, present clear obligations to avoid statelessness. The successor state should grant nationality to any person who had the nationality of the predecessor state at the time of state succession, and who has or will become stateless if he or she was at the time habitually resident in the territory that has become territory of the successor

1108 Recommendation CM/Rec (2009) 13 of the Committee of Ministers to member states on the nationality of children (adopted by the Committee of Ministers on 9 December 2009 at the 1073rd meeting of the Ministers' Deputies), para 12.

1109 See Arts 7 & 8 1961 Convention.

1110 Cf ECN and CoE, *Explanatory Report to the European Convention on Nationality* (Strasbourg, 6 November 1997, CETS No. 166) para 97.

1111 Arts 23–24 ECN.

1112 Art 4(3) TEU.

state, or if they were not habitually resident, but still have an appropriate connection with the successor state. Moreover, the predecessor state – if it continues to exist – shall not withdraw its nationality from nationals who do not acquire the nationality of the successor state and who would otherwise become stateless. The ECSS is perhaps a bit more precise and more elaborate in its provisions as compared to the key international instrument in this regard – the ILC Draft Articles on the Nationality of Natural Persons in relation to the Succession of States[1113] – but their way of dealing with the avoidance of statelessness is comparable. If in the EU context the ILC Draft Articles would be used should a situation of state succession occur – which cannot be ruled out – it should therefore not lead to problems or inconsistencies. The ECSS would offer more protection though, for instance with regard to the provision of information to people concerned.[1114]

With regard to acquisition of nationality, it is clear that the CoE and EU instruments do not offer a right to acquire a nationality. Both the CoE and the EU furthermore seem to agree that a legal residence status precedes any steps towards acquisition of nationality – the CoE by requiring legal and habitual residence for (facilitated) naturalization[1115] and the EU by setting asylum and migration standards, but not also regulating access to nationality. The CoE is clear that no more than ten years of habitual and legal residence may be required before naturalization is offered. And even though facilitated naturalization is recommended in cases of statelessness, the obligation to apply favorable conditions in such cases remains relatively weak. Nonetheless, and as compared to international standards, it does not necessarily present a lower standard or deviation, as the important international provision on this[1116] is also rather vague. However, and drawing on the right to respect for private and family life in both frameworks, legal arguments on the need for determination of statelessness and a road towards regularization of status can be made. These can contribute towards more clarity of legal status and the necessary first step of legal residence, which can eventually help stateless people in seeing their statelessness solved.

As was mentioned above, non-discrimination is a key principle in both frameworks – similar to how this principle is positioned in international (human rights) law. It is therefore laid down in all of the key instruments of the CoE and the EU, including the ECHR, the ECN, the TFEU and the EU Charter. Both frameworks are pretty clear on ruling out any discrimination on the grounds of gender, race, ethnicity, birth, etc. Discrimination on such grounds is prohibited, also where it concerns rules that relate to acquisition and loss of nationality. As such, it could help to prevent and solve statelessness, as no discriminatory measures or conditions can be applied. Moreover, and particularly important to those nationality laws that only apply to dual citizens or naturalized citizens, no differentiation should be made based on how nationality was acquired or whether you possess another nationality: no discrimination between (EU) citizens should exist according to both

---

1113 ILC Draft Articles on Nationality of Persons in relation to the Succession of States (1999).

1114 Cf Art 11 ECSS.

1115 Cf Art 6(3) & 6(4) ECN.

1116 Art 32 1954 Convention.

the CoE and EU frameworks. At the same time, in EU law, stateless people – as third-country nationals – face some limitations with regard to the non-discrimination principle. Discrimination based on the ground of nationality is reserved for EU citizens, which may make additional arguments around unequal treatment with regard to rights attached to (EU) citizenship, such as the right to vote and participate in society, more difficult to make. However, by relying on the potential of the EU Charter and interpretations of the ECHR, it was found that there may be room to make such arguments in order to help find pathways to citizenship for stateless people who remain without a nationality for a prolonged time.

Taken together, the CoE and EU provide further guidance on existing international norms and offer important safeguards for preventing statelessness, as well as avenues for solving statelessness. There is attention for addressing childhood statelessness in both frameworks, which relies on key principles such as the avoidance of statelessness, non-discrimination and the best interests of the child. On loss and deprivation of nationality, there is a strict standard of it not resulting in statelessness, which allows for almost no exception and is subject to a proportionality assessment. For addressing statelessness in a situation of state succession, the CoE offers the most elaborate binding legal instrument yet: the ECSS, which provides detailed guidance on the matter. On (facilitated) acquisition of nationality, there is consensus that habitual and legal residence are key. Yet, considerations with regard to the right to respect for private and family life demonstrate the need for identification of statelessness and ways to regularize a status at national level – an important first step towards solving statelessness. Discrimination, also in nationality laws, is not allowed on any ground in European law. More broadly with the regard to (the right to a) nationality, European law has also made clear that there should be no distinctions made between citizens, which is important to the status of nationality as a solution to statelessness.

5.3. FRAMEWORKS: FINDINGS

Some of the analysis in paragraph 5.2 highlighted differences between the CoE and the EU. These differences, as well as the similarities identified in the contributions that they make, should be understood against the background of the characteristics of these institutions themselves. The concluding paragraphs of both chapters 3 and 4 have made some remarks on this, considering the type of framework and their relationship with international and domestic law. What is important to remember, is that the CoE and the EU as actors have different aims and adopt different methods to achieve these.

The EU has produced a legal order in the EU treaties and further case law that is an extension and assessment framework of the national legal order. This is visible in how law in the EU is made as well. The involvement of an elected EP mimics national level lawmaking and can lead to immediately binding rules for states. And if states do not adhere to these rules, action can be undertaken, as was seen for instance when the EC started infringement action because of investor citizenship schemes. As was explained earlier, CJEU case law on EU citizenship – based on prejudicial questions from national judges – has provided an important avenue for further development of any EU law on matters of nationality and statelessness. If there are such new legal developments in case law for instance, then that is very similar to how national case law would be viewed in relation to national law and the national legislator – now just at a European level. And such interpretations are then also immediately part and parcel of EU law, as the consequences are the same as those attached to national case law for legislators. There is thus a sense of common legal development between the EU and its member states.

The CoE has developed standards more autonomously, on certain topics that the organization sees as important and that would further its aims. The legal framework also appears to be somewhat fragmented, with various different instruments on similar, yet distinct topics. As an external actor, the CoE thus wants to influence the legal systems of the member states, and only has limited and indirect means to oblige states to fulfil their obligations, within the margin of appreciation of states. And states are free – in principle – to sign up to the relevant treaties. So even if the treaties are negotiated within the institutional framework of the CoE, they are only legally enforceable if states ratify them. Certainly, for some of the key CoE instruments regarding nationality and statelessness, this has been problematic, as ratifications by member states remain low.[1117] Furthermore, the CoE lacks a judicial institution that can interpret the full body of CoE instruments – similar to the CJEU's role in EU law. The ECtHR can play this role to some extent, and it has indeed included other CoE and international standards in its interpretation of ECHR rights, but formally, this Court only oversees the ECHR and its Protocols. The influence of the CoE on domestic law therefore has a different character in comparison to the (in principle) direct and binding influence of the EU.

Another difference in approach between the two organizations can be seen when considering human rights. Where the CoE and the ECHR explicitly refer to human rights, the EU and the EU Charter concern fundamental rights, encompassing both human rights and citizens' rights. In the analysis above, it was shown that despite the EU Charter with a majority of provisions that apply to everyone, more emphasis on the EU citizen arises from the scope of EU law. As could be seen, this focus on citizen's rights is also visible in fundamental principles like non-discrimination. To some extent, that also translates into and explains the difference between minority protection by the CoE and the EU. For the CoE, minority protection is an important subject that relates to the core of its activities and has resulted in a separate and dedicated legal instrument – the FCNM.[1118] For the EU, the principles of equality and non-discrimination are paramount: all European citizens are equal and it should not matter whether you belong to a minority or not. At the same time, there has been a realization within the EU that minority inclusion needs more attention from the EU. Indeed, an EU Roma Strategic Framework was developed and further efforts are being sparked by the Minority Safepack initiative.[1119]

1117 Cf the ECN and the ECSS, see also para 3.2.2.
1118 See also para 3.2.3.
1119 See also para 4.3.5.

In some ways, the two frameworks of the CoE and the EU could therefore be considered incomparable. This challenge was overcome in this research by studying both organizations and their legal instruments using an analytical framework derived from international (human rights) law on the human right to a nationality to uncover each framework's distinct contribution. It should be recognized that both the CoE and the EU have – despite their differences in approach – protecting people's fundamental rights at the core of their activities. And in both systems, there is regard for international (human rights) norms in interpretation of CoE or EU standards. Significantly, the EU has also taken into account interpretations of ECHR rights in its system of fundamental rights. Both organizations are thus part of a larger, living ecosystem of evolving (human rights) norms that concern the prevention of and solutions to statelessness.

5.4. CONCLUSION

How has European law contributed to preventing and solving statelessness in Europe? As this chapter has demonstrated, both the CoE and the EU have a(n) (bigger or smaller) array of legal instruments on nationality matters and statelessness. Often, such instruments were developed as a response to factual events or questions that arose, such as the break-up of the Soviet Union or the occurrence of cases that relate to new reproductive techniques such as surrogacy. The CoE and the EU together contribute a variety of norms on preventing and solving statelessness, that usually provide further interpretation of or even additional safeguards relating to existing international norms. Sometimes they deviate from international standards in a negative way. Such issues, however, can be resolved as long as the various norms on the matter are viewed as a living ecosystem – a perspective that the approach taken by the relevant judicial bodies, the ECtHR and the CJEU, seems to support.

Overall, it is clear that the CoE offers a greater range of more targeted and specific instruments on the prevention of and solutions to statelessness. The EU's engagement is limited, also explained by the question of competence that arises in that context. However, when assessing the overall contribution of each of the organizations studied, the focus and limitations of each of them should be taken into account. The CoE has limited influence on its states, and is dependent on ratifications of the key treaties on nationality and statelessness. As such, its bigger contribution does not necessarily translate into changes in domestic laws or make a difference for people that might benefit from the standards it has produced. The EU's influence at the national level is much more direct, which leads to a small contribution, such as the introduction of the proportionality test in nationality matters, having a significant effect. Together – and in particular with case law developing on nationality matters – the CoE and the EU can go a long way in preventing statelessness, and have a positive influence on solutions to statelessness.

CHAPTER 6
DISCUSSION AND CONCLUSIONS

"Everyone has the right to a nationality.
No one shall be arbitrarily deprived of his nationality
nor denied the right to change his nationality."
– Article 15 of the Universal Declaration of Human Rights

6.1. INTRODUCTION

Chapter 5 answered the first half of this study's research question by analyzing and considering the contribution of the legal instruments of the Council of Europe (CoE) and the European Union (EU) to preventing and solving statelessness. The underlying sub questions A, B and C were answered in chapters 2, 3 and 4. This chapter examines the second part of the main question and sub question D more closely, and provides an answer to what the findings of this research can contribute to the understanding of the legal concept of nationality in Europe today. It also reflects on the main research question.

In paragraph 6.2 below, the outcomes of this study are discussed with a view to explaining (aspects of the) notion of nationality. Paragraph 6.3 gives an overall conclusion to the research, addressing the main research question:

> *How does European law contribute to preventing and solving statelessness in Europe and what does this contribution add to the understanding of nationality today?*

It reflects on Europe's stance towards the right to a nationality and the context and developments with regard to the contribution of European law to preventing and solving statelessness. Recommendations that can be made to the CoE and the EU based on this research, as well as final reflections on broader questions around the law, solutions to statelessness and further research are presented in paragraph 6.4.

6.2. DISCUSSION: THE CONCEPT OF NATIONALITY

In Part I of this research, it was identified that nationality is a legal bond between a person and a state. That is still true today, but where the concept was first used to regulate the relationships between states, it has also been proclaimed a human right and has been understood as a gateway for enjoying further rights. That legal bond, however, has various aspects to it, which were also discussed in chapters 1 and 2. Below, the findings of this research are considered for these different characteristics of nationality as a legal concept, looking at it from the perspective of preventing and solving statelessness in Europe.

First of all, there is a question of how nationality is granted and what is necessary for that to happen. There are two key principles for granting nationality at birth: *jus sanguinis* and *jus soli*. Furthermore, *jus domicilii* generally regulates nationality acquisition later in life based on (legal) residence, and *jus nexus* – acquisition of nationality based on rootedness – has been proposed by commentators to align claims to nationality with the place where people's life unfold and where they take part in society.[1120] Moreover, for nationality to be recognized – whether it is at birth or later in life – there is a need for proof, usually legal documents or registrations, which demonstrates the link between a person and a state – whether based on the parent(s), birth or (legal) residence on the territory. This highlights the need for systems of identification and registration.[1121]

In the analysis of the CoE legal instruments on preventing and solving statelessness, it was found that its standard setting on nationality matters departs from a *jus sanguinis* perspective – the dominant principle for nationality acquisition at birth in Europe. It is good to remember in this regard that a *jus sanguinis* system presupposes that a person acquires nationality from his or her parent(s). So even when you immigrate to European territory, it is believed that you would – in principle – have acquired nationality from your parents and that you children will acquire it from you. By introducing additional norms to mitigate the consequences of this approach, for instance where the parents are unknown or cannot pass on nationality, the CoE framework has recognized the limitations of the *jus sanguinis* approach to nationality and seen the need to guarantee nationality to others who would otherwise remain stateless. In contrast with some of the international norms on the matter, however, legal residence may be required even where it concerns nationality acquisition at birth. With regard to acquisition of nationality through naturalization, it can be seen that legal and habitual residence of maximum ten years needs to precede this. This focus on legal residence as a prerequisite to obtaining nationality demonstrates that nationality can – at least to some extent – be seen as an extension of migration policy. It can also be read to reinforce that the *jus sanguinis*, ethnicity-based system for acquisition of nationality at birth appears to make the community not very receptive of immigrants. This conception of nationality may furthermore be more susceptible to nationalism and xenophobia whereby the state (or nation) is to be protected from intruders. This view on nationality, even if other key standards such as around non-discrimination

1120 See also para 1.4.2.
1121 See also para 1.4.3.

and avoidance of statelessness exist, may therefore still present risks and concerns with regard to the inclusion of those without a(ny) nationality.

As could be seen, ten years of legal residence on the territory is used as a criterion for understanding whether a legal bond between a person and a state is such that it qualifies for granting nationality. But this is not the only standard used. CoE instruments make reference to a genuine and effective link between a person and a state, which can exist on the basis of birth, descent or residence. There relevance of this link to nationality questions was also recognized by the CJEU, which furthermore held that habitual, uninterrupted residence abroad for ten years can serve as an indication that there is no (longer) such link. The ECSS introduces the notion of appropriate connection, which has elements that hint at a *jus nexus* approach of citizenship, including such considerations as respect for the expressed will of the person concerned with regard to his or her nationality.[1122] The CoE thus certainly clings to the more traditional views on nationality and its acquisition, but with its most recent comprehensive legal instrument on nationality and statelessness, the ECSS, has also taken into account more progressive stances on nationality and the individual's rights in relation to it. As such, this might signify somewhat of a shift in the conceptualization of nationality, and at least sensitivity of the CoE towards what nationality means to states *and* individuals. That could also translate into the administrative side of nationality questions. With the traditional principles for granting nationality, it is key that information about birth, descent, place of residence, status, etcetera, are properly registered and documented. The expressed will of a person, however, concerns a wholly different criterion that is not something that has to be documented similar to the characteristics – place of birth and parents – previously mentioned. As such, this may also challenge the administrative side of citizenship questions in that it is more difficult to objectify and register.

With regard to the EU instruments, there is less of a clear stance on nationality acquisition that can immediately be drawn from them though. That relates to the fact that the EU framework does not legislate on nationality and statelessness as directly and explicitly as the CoE. A closer look, however, reveals a preoccupation with legal residence and with the *jus sanguinis* principle. The EU's internal openness of borders and free movement, as well as its conception of EU citizenship rely – in essence – on a conception of nationality based on descent. Indeed, there would be less of a need for elaborate procedures on who can claim a legal residence status, if everyone born here would become a citizen of a member state and would thereby also be an EU citizen. And, by creating the additional categories of EU citizen and third-country national, dependent also on national determination of who is a citizen, there is again a real need for proper registration and documentation of nationality of every person, as well as their place of residence and birth. Thus, the EU also reinforces the administrative side of nationality in its dealings with the concept.

Moreover, certain rights are attached to having a nationality, which are reserved for citizens only but are important for enfranchisement. The CoE remains silent on

[1122] Cf Art 7 ECSS.

rights attached to nationality as such[1123] and the ECHR principally concerns human rights, which apply regardless of nationality. For the protection of stateless people, that is of course very important and means that they can claim these rights regardless of whether they are a national. At the same time, the CoE has created various instruments on nationality and statelessness specifically, "[r]ecognising that, in matters concerning nationality, account should be taken both of the legitimate interests of States and those of individuals".[1124] This demonstrates that regard for the interests of individuals, including those relating to rights, enfranchisement, participation in society and identity, is also important to how nationality is viewed as a concept by the CoE. It can be seen as tacit recognition of the enduring significance of nationality though, in spite of human right protection that is grounded in a wider principle of jurisdiction. The EU framework presents a further concern in this regard. By attaching additional rights to EU citizenship status, which is only for those people that are nationals of EU member states, the EU creates an even bigger gap in terms of rights – including participatory rights, such as the right to vote for the EP – between EU citizens and stateless people that the EU does not (yet) address through taking an interest in statelessness-specific policy.

This last point on rights attached to nationality also relates to another aspect of nationality that was touched upon earlier in chapter 2. Nationality has been historically used to include and protect those people who are considered to be part of the community and society that is organized in a state. At the same time, that also means that nationality as a legal concept excludes those people who do not 'belong' to the state and are not considered its citizens. Nationality was – certainly in the 19th and the beginning of the 20th century – and is still used as a way to protect the people that belong to the state and to keep out anyone who might be perceived as compromising that common identity. Both CoE and EU legal instruments on preventing and solving statelessness reflect this line of thought. Within the CoE there is almost a suspicion when you are not able to acquire nationality by descent, which translates into additional requirements that may be added before you are found to 'deserve' nationality based on birth on the territory. Similarly, requirements that 'test' your bond with the state can be set, and even where naturalization should be facilitated for stateless people, the level of facilitation is not specified and is left to states to fill in. However, once you have nationality, it is not easy to be deprived of it or lose it – and it should (almost) never result in statelessness. Even if there is regard for the legitimate interests of the individual with regard to nationality, that does not take away from the key point that some of the exclusionary aspects of citizenship are emphasized in accessing it by the CoE framework, thus still concerning itself with the protection of the state and its (existing) citizens. Nonetheless, some pathways towards inclusion are offered.

1123 Even Art 3 Protocol No 3 ECHR is silent on who should be able to participate in free elections, leaving it up the national legislator. Only Art 3 of Protocol No 4 ECHR includes the right of nationals to enter and not to be expelled from the territory of the state of which they hold nationality.

1124 Preamble of the ECN.

This focus on the exclusionary nature of nationality is – from the perspective of preventing and solving statelessness – also true for the EU, and perhaps even more so. As could be seen in chapter 4, the EU sets important standards on migration and asylum policy, thereby regulating the first step of people who want to see their statelessness resolved by naturalizing in one of the EU member states. However, when it comes to actually acquiring nationality of one of the member states, and also EU citizenship, the EU remains mostly silent. Whereas EU citizenship adds an additional dimension to having a nationality in the territory of the EU, by extra protection, participatory and free movement rights, third-country nationals are excluded from this and the EU has little to no influence on who is able to acquire EU citizenship. Nationality matters largely remain only within the competence of the EU member states and EU citizenship is contingent on national citizenship. This is interesting, as these questions define who would help to shape the EU as a community. At the same time, once you are an EU citizen, your status is more protected and loss or deprivation of nationality is subjected to an additional proportionality test from the perspective of your rights as a citizen of the Union. Both aspects of in- and exclusion with regard to nationality are thus present in the conceptualization of nationality that the EU represents, with those outside of the community as non-citizens clearly being excluded and by presenting no real avenues to inclusion. As such, the expression 'fortress Europe' that is sometimes used in the migration context, which depicts Europe, and the EU in particular, as an almost impregnable fortress, certainly holds true. Coming to the EU and getting a legal status is difficult, but becoming a full and equal part of the community as an EU citizen, with all the rights that it entails, requires the individual to walk down yet another path towards naturalization, filled with obstacles that states are more or less free to set, even for stateless people.

6.3. CONCLUSION

Drawing on the findings in chapter 5 and paragraph 6.2 above, one can but wonder: does Europe believe in a right to a nationality? And how does Europe deal with the dichotomy[1125] between the conception of nationality as part of the sovereignty of states and the individual's right to a nationality in international (human rights) law? As was mentioned on various occasions throughout this book, the CoE and EU frameworks both do not explicitly recognize the individual's right to a nationality as a human right in their respective human rights catalogues, unlike some of their other regional counterparts, such as the Inter-American system. Looking at the contribution of European law to preventing and solving statelessness, it can also be distilled that nationality is not approached as a right for everyone. Rather, it is a right for people who have a nationality not to lose it without adequate safeguards, and deprivation should in most cases not lead to statelessness. Furthermore, nationality is a safeguard for children,

[1125] See also para 1.4.2.

who should not be victimized or be left stateless as a consequence of nationality issues. The right to a nationality can also be seen in the principle that guarantees equality and non-discrimination between citizens and in nationality matters, and that aims at avoiding statelessness in circumstances of conflicts of nationality laws, including state succession contexts. And nationality itself has – in terms of a right – been defined as a part of an individual's personal or social identity that is protected by the right to respect for private and family life.

There is no doubt that the underlying principle of all of these norms is very clearly every person's right to a nationality – the importance of nationality for the individual is not questioned. And in various instruments, this background is even expressly mentioned. At the same time, by nowhere explicitly defining nationality as a human right for the individual to claim, both the CoE and the EU are leaving nationality matters in the hands of states in the first place. This could be seen as a compromise on the dichotomy between right and state sovereignty in this regard: as long as the right to a nationality is not proclaimed, there is nothing that clashes with the sovereignty of states. But the norms produced by both frameworks show that laws on preventing and solving statelessness, whether or not in human rights language, are encroaching on states' freedom to decide on who their nationals are. A dichotomy between nationality as an individual right and as part of states' sovereignty is thus certainly also present in Europe and more emphasis seems to be placed on state sovereignty in this regard. At the same time, by refusing to take a clear stance on this in law, the dichotomy may deepen further, creating uncertainty for both states and individuals. Moreover, Europe is certainly not placing itself at the forefront of nationality rights and addressing statelessness.

However, in order to provide a complete picture of Europe's contribution to preventing and solving statelessness, the broader context of causes of statelessness in Europe and the reactions of states to them, should also be considered. Despite historical and legal developments and instruments adopted by states, people remain trapped in difficult situations of rightlessness without a nationality today.[1126] To what extent do the norms address the causes of statelessness that were identified[1127] and where does that leave stateless people in Europe? In the European context, various causes of statelessness are present and different instruments have been enacted to address them. Often these were developed as a response to events or cases involving statelessness occurring, i.e. after the fact. As such, the instruments often came too late to prevent statelessness. In solving statelessness, states have a lot of freedom still. With the stronger norms on preventing and solving childhood statelessness, however, statelessness should not be passed down from generation to generation. And the norms on loss and deprivation of nationality should limit occurrences of statelessness as a result to a minimum. Furthermore, specific situations that have created large-sale statelessness in Europe in the past, including large-scale deprivation of nationality on discriminatory grounds and in the context of

1126 See also para 2.8.
1127 See also ch 2.

state succession, should have been remedied with the non-discrimination principle that has been entrenched in European legal instruments so clearly, as well as with the most detailed treaty on statelessness and state succession to date. There are thus no obvious gaps in the existing standards. One concern that was identified, however, is the identification or determination of statelessness as a necessary precondition for effectively applying the various norms for preventing and solving statelessness. As discussed, statelessness is not always adequately identified. In both frameworks, this could be addressed by providing additional guidance to existing instruments, drawing also on the larger legal ecosystem of norms and international law on this. For the CoE this could be part of their renewed efforts within the CDCJ, which focus on promoting the existing instruments and explaining them further. For the EU, this could take place within their current competences on migration and asylum law in particular, and where there may even be room to further legislate on statelessness determination.

Another shortcoming of existing European law on the prevention of and solutions to statelessness comes to light when considering a hypothetical scenario. Imagine that a state in Europe would dissolve again into two or more states. Would statelessness be avoided in such a case? If the norms of the ECSS would be followed, no new statelessness should occur. However, it is unlikely that the state in question would follow these rules, as the ECSS has a notoriously low number of ratifications. As such, even with a sophisticated legal instrument focusing on a particular cause of statelessness in Europe, it is uncertain that statelessness would be prevented if this cause would present itself again. At the same time, it should be acknowledged that large-scale discriminatory deprivation of nationality, as was practiced in the context and aftermath of the World Wars, would be a far-fetched scenario today in view of the broad and strong norms on non-discrimination. Looking at the complete picture, European law presents all the important standards to prevent and solve statelessness in Europe, which form part of a larger ecosystem of norms on the right to a nationality and statelessness.

6.4. FINAL REFLECTIONS AND RECOMMENDATIONS

Drawing on the conclusion above, some concerns and limitations of the current legal instruments and conception of nationality were uncovered. With regard to further legal steps that may be taken to address these, some suggestions were already made. In sum, these would lead to the following recommendations to the CoE and the EU:

- Promote (ratification of) *existing* instruments on preventing and solving statelessness in the CoE and provide further guidance on their place within the larger ecosystem of legal norms addressing nationality and statelessness, as well as on the identification of statelessness as a necessary precondition to effectively implementing the current standards so as to provide the highest level of protection to the individual.

- Mainstream the issue of statelessness in EU law and provide additional guidance on the identification of statelessness as a necessary precondition to the protection, participation and inclusion of stateless people.

The conclusions of this study raise an important question with regard to nationality itself: is nationality the proper solution to statelessness? Or is a rights-based approach to statelessness[1128] an option that should be preferred over the acquisition of a nationality? And does Europe need an explicit right to a nationality for people to claim? What this research makes clear, is that at least aspects of the right to a nationality can be claimed in Europe and that there is still a preoccupation with nationality as a gateway to full and equal participation in society. An explicit recognition of every person's right to a nationality in Europe could therefore have an important symbolic value in underlining its importance to the state *and* the individual, and may make it easier to develop further coherent litigation and jurisprudence on the matter specifically. But in essence, the instruments necessary for limiting the occurrence of statelessness as much as possible and solving it where it does arise, are at one's disposal. These are, however, questions that this research cannot answer alone. They need the input from the broader field of statelessness research, providing also other disciplinary perspectives, as well as guidance from stateless people themselves.

Similarly, what is necessary in Europe to prevent and solve statelessness eventually is not just a legal question. One thing that this research has also undoubtedly shown, is the limits of what law can do. Numerous legal instruments may be enacted, but if no state – which in Europe is normally the expression of its people – is willing to abide by them and apply them, that leaves people excluded. The fact that people today, in Europe, remain without a nationality, disenfranchised and rightless, is therefore painful in light of the findings of this research on the legal instruments available. Further research on uncovering the deeper motives behind the exclusion of people and pushing them to the margins of society by leaving or making them stateless, would therefore be welcome also with a view to improving (legal) responses to the issue. Indeed, even though I wish there was a treaty we could sign, there is need for broader action to prevent and solve statelessness.

1128 Katja Swider, 'A Rights-based Approach to Statelessness' (PhD thesis, University of Amsterdam 2018).

ANNEXES

ANNEX I

Schematic overview of relevant provisions from international and other regional instruments in different substantive categories on preventing and solving statelessness[1129]

	Preventing and solving childhood statelessness	Preventing and solving conflicts of nationality laws & preventing loss, (arbitrary) deprivation and denial of nationality	Right to a nationality and acquisition of nationality for stateless people	Nationality matters and reduction of statelessness in the context of state succession	The principle of non-discrimination relating to nationality matters
1930 Hague Convention	×	×			
UDHR	×	×	×		×
1951 Refugee Convention			×		×
1957 Convention		×			
1954 Convention	×	×	×	×	×
1961 Convention	×	×	×	×	×
1999 ILC Draft Articles	×			×	×
ICERD			×		×
ICCPR	×				×
CEDAW	×	×			×
CRC	×	×			
ICMW	×				×

1129 Note that only the main other regional instruments that are comparable to European legal instruments in terms of legal status and supervisory bodies have been added to the table. This annex accompanies chapter 1.

	Preventing and solving childhood statelessness	Preventing and solving conflicts of nationality laws & preventing loss, (arbitrary) deprivation and denial of nationality	Right to a nationality and acquisition of nationality for stateless people	Nationality matters and reduction of statelessness in the context of state succession	The principle of non-discrimination relating to nationality matters
CRPD	×	×	×		×
ACHR	×	×	×		×
ACHPR		×	×		×
ACRWC	×				

ANNEX II

Schematic overview of legal instruments of the Council of Europe and the European Union in different substantive categories on preventing and solving statelessness[1130]

	Council of Europe	European Union
Preventing and solving childhood statelessness	– ECN (Article 6, paragraphs 1 and 2) – ECSS (Article 10) – ECHR (Article 8, *Genovese v. Malta, Mennesson v. France*) – CM Recommendation on the Nationality of Children	– EU Charter (Articles 7 and 24) – TFEU (Article 20), *Tjebbes, Rottmann, Ruiz Zambrano, V.M.A. v. Stolichna Obsthina, Rayon 'Pancharevo* – EC Communication on the Protection of Children in Migration – EU Strategy on the Rights of the Child
Preventing and solving conflicts of nationality laws & preventing loss, (arbitrary) deprivation and denial of nationality	– ECN (Articles 7, 8 and 14) – ECHR (Article 8, *Karassev v. Finland, Ramadan v. Malta, K2 v. the United Kingdom, Ghoumid and others v. France*) – CM Recommendation on the avoidance and reduction of statelessness	– EU Charter (Article 7) – TFEU (Article 20), *Tjebbes, Rottmann* – TEU (Article 4(3))
Nationality matters and reduction of statelessness in the context of state succession	– ECN (Articles 18–20) – ECSS – CM Recommendation on the avoidance and reduction of statelessness – Venice Commission Declaration on the Consequences of State Succession for the Nationality of Natural Persons	– *EU (pre-)accession agreements*

[1130] This overview is based on the analysis in chapters 3 and 4. It accompanies the comparison and analysis in chapter 5. Only key instruments as elaborately examined in the third sections of chapters 3 and 4 are included.

	Council of Europe	European Union
Right to a nationality and acquisition of nationality for stateless people	– ECN (Article 6, paragraphs 3 and 4) – ECSS (Article 9) – ECHR (Article 8, *Hoti v. Croatia, Sudita Keita v. Hungary*) – CM Recommendation on the avoidance and reduction of statelessness	– EU Charter (Articles 7 and 47) – TFEU (Article 20), *Rottmann* – *EU pledge on ratification of the 1954 Convention*
The principle of non-discrimination relating to nationality matters	– ECN (Article 5) – ECSS (Article 4) – ECHR (Article 14 *conj.* Article 8, *Genovese v. Malta, Biao v. Denmark*)	– EU Charter (Article 21) – TFEU (Articles 18 and 20), *Micheletti* – TEU (Article 2)

SUMMARY

The world today is divided into (nation-)states, making belonging to – and being able to enter, reside in, and leave – a state important. To prove and legally qualify the bond between a person and a state, the legal concept of nationality, rules on acquiring and losing nationality, and the passport were introduced. At the same time, some people have been excluded from nationality, left out, or forgotten by this system. They remain disenfranchised, without any nationality, stateless. This research explores, attempts to understand and place into context the legal approaches that states have taken together, at the regional level in Europe – within the Council of Europe (CoE) and the European Union (EU) – to address statelessness. In particular, this study considers the role that European law can play in preventing and solving statelessness in Europe. The main research question of this project is therefore as follows:

> *How does European law contribute to preventing and solving statelessness in Europe and what does this contribution add to the understanding of nationality today?*

This study first introduces the issue of statelessness, the relevance of this research, and the methods and sources used. It shows how statelessness and nationality or citizenship can be understood from a legal perspective, and how the strength of connections between a person and a state, as well as administration, registration and identification play an important role in this. What becomes clear, is that there is a link between nationality and (human) rights, and protection thereof. An examination of the legal norms on these matters at the international level and in regions outside Europe demonstrates that obligations for states have been created in relation to nationality matters and the reduction of statelessness. There is clear 'rights language' visible in the international standards on these topics: individuals, and in particular children, have been given a right to a nationality to claim. Another human rights dimension to preventing and solving statelessness has, for example, been created with the principle of non-discrimination, which applies to nationality laws and can be helpful in addressing gender discrimination in such laws or laws that discriminate against minorities. Drawing on such norms, an analytical framework containing the human rights aspects of the right to a nationality and preventing and solving statelessness with 'categories' of substantive legal norms is constructed to help with the examination of European law. The analytical framework consists of the following categories: norms addressing childhood statelessness, deprivation of nationality, state succession, the acquisition of nationality through naturalization, and non-discrimination. This research thus takes a human rights perspective in order to understand properly European legal norms on preventing and solving statelessness, as well as the legal categorizations of reality through the concepts of nationality and statelessness.

This research goes on to demonstrate the broader, distinctive context in which the regional European instruments analyzed in this research need to be placed, as well as the relevance of the European cooperation mechanisms studied. It also confirms the categories of substantive legal norms previously identified in the analytical framework. It is demonstrated how the continent's history has unfolded, with its own particularities and practices, which were – at the same time – intertwined with major developments globally. Reasons for statelessness occurring in such ways that it demanded a response in law from states were often closely related to different historical events. World War I and its aftermath made statelessness appear on a large scale in Europe. Displacement and denationalization in the context of World War II further deepened and added to the existing statelessness. The atrocities of war and the complications that ensued from this did not only result in a focus on human rights and the adoption of legal instruments on this, but also translated into concern for statelessness, with the Statelessness Conventions being adopted in 1954 and 1961. One of the ways in which Europe in particular responded to the devastation of war, was with the establishment of the European cooperation mechanisms (or the predecessor thereof) that are the focus of this study. Today, statelessness remains a widespread phenomenon in Europe, with causes relating to state succession being most prevalent, and despite efforts to reduce it through the adoption of legal instruments. Further challenges presented by history taking another turn and crises emerging put more pressure on questions of nationality, identity and registration. Developments, also legally, to respond to these issues and to address statelessness remain ongoing.

Against this background, the legal instruments of the CoE and the EU are analyzed separately. Based on this extensive analysis, it becomes clear that the CoE and the EU provide further guidance on existing international norms and offer important safeguards for preventing statelessness, as well as avenues for solving statelessness. To better understand these findings, the sum of the two organizations with regard to preventing and solving statelessness is studied by looking at similarities and differences to better understand their overall contribution in the analytical categories mentioned above. Accordingly, it appears that there is attention for addressing childhood statelessness in both frameworks, which relies on key principles such as the avoidance of statelessness, non-discrimination and the best interests of the child. On loss and deprivation of nationality, there is a strict standard of it not resulting in statelessness, which allows for almost no exception and is subject to a proportionality assessment. For addressing statelessness in a situation of state succession, the CoE offers the most elaborate binding legal instrument yet: the CoE Convention on the Avoidance of Statelessness in relation to State Succession (ECSS), which provides detailed guidance on the matter. On (facilitated) acquisition of nationality, there is consensus that habitual and legal residence are a key prerequisite. Yet, considerations with regard to the right to respect for private and family life demonstrate the need for identification of statelessness and ways to regularize a status at national level – an important first step towards solving statelessness through acquisition of nationality. Discrimination, also in nationality laws, is not allowed on any ground in European law.

Overall, it is clear that the CoE provides a greater range of more targeted and specific instruments on the prevention of and solutions to statelessness. The EU's engagement is limited, also explained by the question of competence – nationality matters are not an EU competence, but a competence of the member states – that arises in that context. However, when assessing the overall contribution of each of the organizations studied, the focus and limitations of each of them should be taken into account. The CoE has limited influence on its member states, and is dependent on ratifications of the key treaties on nationality and statelessness. As such, its bigger contribution in terms of specific legal instruments does not necessarily translate into changes in domestic laws or make a difference for people that might benefit from the standards it has produced. The EU's influence at the national level is much more direct, which leads to a small contribution, such as the introduction of the proportionality test in nationality matters, having a significant effect. Together – and in particular with case law developing on nationality matters – the CoE and the EU can go a long way in preventing statelessness, and have a positive influence on solutions to statelessness. European law on the matter can also be viewed as part of a larger living ecosystem, including international norms on the matter – a perspective that the approach taken in relevant case law by the European Court of Human Rights and the Court of Justice of the EU seems to support.

This research finds no obvious gaps in the existing standards on preventing and solving statelessness in Europe. One concern that is noted, however, is the identification or determination of statelessness as a necessary precondition for effectively applying the various norms for preventing and solving statelessness. In both frameworks, this could be addressed by providing additional guidance to existing instruments, drawing also on the larger legal ecosystem of norms and international law on this. For the CoE this could be part of their renewed efforts within the European Committee on Legal Co-operation, which focuses on promoting the existing instruments and explaining them further. For the EU, this could take place within their current competences on migration and asylum law in particular, where there may even be room to further legislate on statelessness determination. Another concern arose around the lack of ratifications of existing key instruments, including the aforementioned ECSS, which point to the need to promote accession to these instruments by states. Accordingly, the following recommendations are made:

- Promote (ratification of) *existing* instruments on preventing and solving statelessness in the CoE and provide further guidance on their place within the larger ecosystem of legal norms addressing nationality and statelessness, as well as on the identification of statelessness as a necessary precondition to effectively implementing the current standards so as to provide the highest level of protection to the individual.

- Mainstream the issue of statelessness in EU law and provide additional guidance on the identification of statelessness as a necessary precondition to the protection, participation and inclusion of stateless people.

On nationality as a legal concept, from a perspective of preventing and solving statelessness in European law, this research finds that the principle of *jus sanguinis* (law of the blood) underlies the view on nationality regulation and acquisition of nationality at birth in particular. Furthermore, European law makes reference to nationality as genuine and effective link between a person and a state, which can exist on the basis of birth, descent or residence. Ten years of legal residence on the territory would constitute a genuine link between a person and a state, whereas habitual, uninterrupted residence abroad for ten years can serve as an indication that there is no (longer) such link. Within the CoE, the ECSS furthermore introduces the notion of appropriate connection, which has elements that hint at a *jus nexus* approach of citizenship, including such considerations as respect for the expressed will of the person concerned with regard to his or her nationality. As for the rights attached to nationality, both CoE and EU instruments demonstrate recognition of the enduring significance of nationality, in spite of human rights protection that is grounded in a wider principle of jurisdiction. The EU in particular, by attaching additional rights to EU citizenship status – only for those people that are nationals of EU member states – creates an even bigger gap in terms of rights between EU citizens and stateless people, which the EU does not (yet) address through taking an interest in statelessness-specific policy.

Nationality was – certainly in the 19th and the beginning of the 20th century – and is still used as a way to protect the people that belong to the state and to keep out anyone who might be perceived as compromising that common identity. Both CoE and EU legal instruments on preventing and solving statelessness reflect this line of thought. The CoE framework emphasizes exclusionary aspects of nationality where it concerns acquisition of nationality and the EU has little to no influence on who is able to acquire (EU) citizenship. At the same time, those who have a nationality and are included, enjoy additional rights (under EU citizenship) and safeguards that prevent them from losing nationality in almost any case.

The conclusions of this study raise an important question with regard to nationality itself: is nationality the proper solution to statelessness? Or is a rights-based approach to statelessness an option that should be preferred over the acquisition of a nationality? And does Europe need an explicit right to a nationality for people to claim? What this research makes clear, is that at least aspects of the right to a nationality can be claimed in Europe and that there is still a preoccupation with nationality as a gateway to full and equal participation in society. An explicit recognition of every person's right to a nationality in Europe could therefore have an important symbolic value in underlining its importance to the state *and* the individual, and may make it easier to develop further coherent litigation and jurisprudence on the matter specifically. But in essence, the instruments necessary for limiting the occurrence of statelessness as much as possible and solving it where it does arise, are at one's disposal. These are, however, questions that this research cannot answer alone. They need the input from the broader field of statelessness research, providing also other disciplinary perspectives, as well as guidance from stateless people themselves.

One thing that this research also shows, is the limits of what law can do. Numerous legal instruments may be enacted, but if no state – which in Europe is normally the expression of its people – is willing to abide by them and apply them, that leaves people excluded. The fact that people today, in Europe, remain without a nationality, disenfranchised and rightless, is therefore painful in light of the findings of this research on the legal instruments available. Further research on uncovering the deeper motives behind the exclusion of people and pushing them to the margins of society by leaving or making them stateless, would therefore be welcome also with a view to improving (legal) responses to the issue.

SAMENVATTING (NEDERLANDS)

De wereld is onderverdeeld in (natie-)staten, waardoor het behoren tot – en het kunnen betreden, verblijven in en verlaten van – een staat belangrijk is. Om de band tussen een persoon en een staat te bewijzen en juridisch te kwalificeren, werd het juridische begrip nationaliteit geïntroduceerd, evenals regels voor het verkrijgen en verliezen van nationaliteit en het paspoort. In dit systeem zijn sommige mensen echter uitgesloten van nationaliteit of vergeten. Zij blijven veelal rechteloos, zonder enige nationaliteit – staatloos. Dit onderzoek verkent en probeert inzicht te krijgen in de juridische benaderingen die staten samen hebben gekozen op Europees, regionaal niveau – binnen de Raad van Europa (RvE) en de Europese Unie (EU) – om staatloosheid aan te pakken. In het bijzonder staat dit onderzoek stil bij de rol die Europees recht kan spelen bij het voorkomen en oplossen van staatloosheid in de regio. De centrale onderzoeksvraag van dit project luidt dan ook als volgt:

> *Hoe draagt Europees recht bij aan het voorkomen en oplossen van staatloosheid in Europa en wat voegt deze bijdrage toe aan het begrip van nationaliteit?*

Dit onderzoek introduceert eerst het onderwerp staatloosheid, de relevantie van dit onderzoek en de gebruikte methoden en bronnen. Het laat zien hoe staatloosheid en nationaliteit of burgerschap vanuit juridisch perspectief kunnen worden begrepen. Daarbij is ook te zien hoe de binding tussen persoon en staat, evenals administratie, registratie en identificatie hierin een rol spelen. Wat duidelijk wordt, is dat er een verband bestaat tussen nationaliteit en (mensen)rechten, en de bescherming daarvan. Een nadere beschouwing van de rechtsnormen op dit gebied op internationaal niveau en in de regio's buiten Europa toont aan dat er verplichtingen voor staten zijn gecreëerd met betrekking tot vraagstukken rondom nationaliteit en het terugdringen van staatloosheid. In de instrumenten in het internationale recht over deze onderwerpen is duidelijke 'rights language' zichtbaar: individuen, en in het bijzonder kinderen, kunnen een recht op een nationaliteit claimen. Een andere mensenrechtendimensie met betrekking tot het voorkomen en oplossen van staatloosheid is bijvoorbeeld gecreëerd met het non-discriminatiebeginsel, dat van toepassing op nationaliteitswetgeving en nuttig kan zijn bij het aanpakken van genderdiscriminatie of discriminatie van minderheden. Op basis van dergelijke normen wordt een analytisch kader geconstrueerd dat de mensenrechtenaspecten van het recht op een nationaliteit en het voorkomen en oplossen van staatloosheid omvat. Dit wordt gedaan door middel van de formulering van categorieën van materiële rechtsnormen, die vervolgens de analyse van het Europees recht kunnen systematiseren en uniformeren. Het analytisch kader bestaat uit de volgende categorieën: normen betreffende (het voorkomen van) kinderstaatloosheid, ontneming van nationaliteit, staatopvolging, verkrijging van nationaliteit door middel van naturalisatie, en non-discriminatie. Het onderzoek gebruikt aldus een mensenrechtelijk perspectief om de Europese normen betreffende het voorkomen en oplossen van staatloosheid te begrijpen, evenals de juridische categorisering van de werkelijkheid door middel van de concepten 'nationaliteit' en 'staatloosheid'.

Deze studie laat vervolgens de bredere, onderscheidende context zien waarin de in dit onderzoek bestudeerde regionale Europese instrumenten moeten worden geplaatst, en de relevantie van de Europese samenwerkingsmechanismen die onder de loep worden genomen. Het bevestigt ook de categorieën van materiële rechtsnormen die eerder in het analytisch kader werden geïdentificeerd. Er wordt getoond hoe de geschiedenis van het continent zich heeft ontwikkeld, met zijn eigen bijzonderheden en praktijken, die tegelijkertijd verweven waren met grote ontwikkelingen wereldwijd. Redenen voor staatloosheid die zich op zodanige wijze voordeden dat het een juridische reactie van staten vereiste, hielden vaak nauw verband met verschillende historische gebeurtenissen. Door de Eerste Wereldoorlog en de nasleep daarvan, verscheen staatloosheid op grote schaal in Europa. De migratie en vlucht van mensen gedurende de Tweede Wereldoorlog, evenals denationalisatie, verdiepten en vergrootten de bestaande staatloosheid. De wreedheden van de oorlog en de complicaties die daaruit voortvloeiden, leidden niet alleen tot aandacht voor mensenrechten en verdragen hierover, maar vertaalden zich ook in internationale zorgen rondom staatloosheid specifiek. Dit mondde uit in de vaststelling van de Staatloosheidsverdragen in 1954 en 1961. Een van de manieren waarop Europa in het bijzonder reageerde op de verwoesting die de oorlog had gebracht, was met de oprichting van de Europese samenwerkingsmechanismen (of de voorloper daarvan) die de focus van deze studie vormen. Vandaag de dag blijft staatloosheid een wijdverbreid fenomeen in Europa, waarbij staatopvolging een belangrijke oorzaak is, en ondanks pogingen om dit terug te dringen door middel van verschillende juridische instrumenten. Door nieuwe wendingen in de geschiedenis en crisissen wordt steeds opnieuw weer druk gezet op vragen die samenhangen met nationaliteit, identiteit en registratie. Europese ontwikkelingen, ook juridisch, om deze uitdagingen en staatloosheid het hoofd te bieden, blijven gaande.

Tegen deze achtergrond worden de juridische instrumenten van de RvE en de EU afzonderlijk van elkaar onderzocht. Op basis van deze uitgebreide analyse wordt duidelijk dat de RvE en de EU verdere richtlijnen geven over bestaande internationale normen betreffende staatloosheid en nationaliteit, en belangrijke waarborgen bieden om staatloosheid in Europa te voorkomen, evenals mogelijkheden om staatloosheid op te lossen. Om deze bevindingen beter te begrijpen, wordt de som van de twee organisaties met betrekking tot het voorkomen en oplossen van staatloosheid bestudeerd door te kijken naar overeenkomsten en verschillen. Hierbij zijn de bovengenoemde analytische categorieën van belang. Dienovereenkomstig lijkt er in de juridische kaders van beide organisaties aandacht te zijn voor het aanpakken van kinderstaatloosheid, waarbij wordt uitgegaan van principes als het voorkomen van staatloosheid, non-discriminatie en het belang van het kind. Bij verlies en ontneming van nationaliteit geldt er de strikte norm dat dit niet mag leiden tot staatloosheid, die bijna geen uitzondering toelaat. Daarnaast dient ontneming van nationaliteit te worden onderworpen aan een evenredigheidsbeoordeling. Voor de aanplak van staatloosheid in de context van staatopvolging biedt de RvE het meest gedetailleerde verdrag tot nu toe: het Verdrag inzake het voorkomen van staatloosheid met betrekking tot statenopvolging (ECSS). Als het gaat om (gefaciliteerde) verkrijging van nationaliteit, door middel van naturalisatie, is men het erover eens dat gewoon *en* legaal verblijf belangrijke voorwaarden zijn. Toch tonen overwegingen met betrekking tot het recht op respect voor privé- en gezinsleven de noodzaak aan voor staten om staatloosheid te identificeren en om manieren te bieden om status op nationaal niveau te regulariseren – belangrijke eerste stappen in de richting van het oplossen van staatloosheid door middel van het verkrijgen van een nationaliteit. Discriminatie, ook in nationaliteitswetgeving, is in principe op geen enkele grond toegestaan in het Europees recht.

De analyse van de twee Europese samenwerkingsmechanismen maakt duidelijk dat de RvE een groter scala aan meer gerichte en specifieke instrumenten biedt voor het voorkomen en oplossen van staatloosheid. De betrokkenheid van de EU rondom deze onderwerpen is beperkt, wat ook wordt verklaard door het competentievraagstuk dat in dat verband aan de orde komt – nationaliteitskwesties behoren tot de bevoegdheden van de EU-lidstaten. Bij het beoordelen van de bijdrage van elk van de onderzochte organisaties moet echter rekening gehouden worden met de focus en de beperkingen van elk van hen. De RvE heeft beperkte invloed op haar lidstaten en is afhankelijk van de ratificatie van de belangrijke verdragen betreffende staatloosheid en nationaliteit. Als zodanig vertaalt de grotere bijdrage van de RvE in termen van specifieke juridische instrumenten zich niet noodzakelijkerwijs in veranderingen in de nationale wetgeving of maakt het een verschil voor de mensen die baat kunnen hebben bij de normen die de organisatie heeft opgesteld. De invloed van de EU op nationaal, juridisch niveau is veel directer. Hierdoor heeft een kleine bijdrage, zoals de invoering van de evenredigheidstoets in het licht van het EU burgerschap, een significant effect. Samen – en in het bijzonder gelet op de jurisprudentie die zich ontwikkelt rondom nationaliteitskwesties – kunnen de RvE en de EU een grote bijdrage leveren aan het voorkomen van staatloosheid en een positieve invloed hebben op oplossingen voor staatloosheid. Het Europees recht op dit gebied kan tevens worden gezien als onderdeel van een groter juridisch ecosysteem van normen, waartoe ook de relevante internationale normen behoren, die in beweging zijn en zich blijven ontwikkelen. Dit is een perspectief die door de benadering van het Europees Hof voor de Rechten van de Mens en het Hof van Justitie van de EU in de jurisprudentie rondom nationaliteit en staatloosheid lijkt te worden ondersteund.

Dit onderzoek vindt geen duidelijke leemten in de bestaande normen voor het voorkomen en oplossen van staatloosheid in Europa. Een zorg die wel wordt gesignaleerd, betreft de identificatie of vaststelling van staatloosheid als noodzakelijke voorwaarde voor het effectief toepassen van de verschillende normen voor het voorkomen en oplossen van staatloosheid in het Europees recht. Zowel in de RvE als de EU zou dit kunnen worden aangepakt door meer richting te geven aan bestaande instrumenten, daarbij ook voortbouwend op het grotere juridische ecosysteem van (internationale) normen betreffende nationaliteit en staatloosheid. Binnen de RvE zou dit onderdeel kunnen zijn van de hernieuwde inspanningen van de European Committee on Legal Co-operation, die zich richt op het promoten van de bestaande instrumenten van de RvE en het nader uitleggen ervan. Voor de EU zou dit kunnen plaatsvinden binnen de huidige bevoegdheden op het gebied van het migratie- en asielbeleid in het bijzonder, waar er zelfs ruimte zou kunnen zijn om verdere regelgeving op te stellen rondom de vaststelling van staatloosheid. Een ander punt van zorg is het gebrek aan ratificaties van bestaande belangrijke verdragen, waaronder de eerdergenoemde ECSS. Dit wijst erop dat de toetreding van staten tot deze instrumenten moet worden bevorderd. Daarom worden op basis van dit onderzoek de volgende aanbevelingen gedaan:

- Bevorder en promoot (de ratificatie van) *bestaande* instrumenten voor het voorkomen en oplossen van staatloosheid van de RvE en geef aanvullende informatie over hun samenhang en interpretatie gelet op het grotere ecosysteem van rechtsnormen die nationaliteit en staatloosheid betreffen, evenals over de identificatie van staatloosheid als noodzakelijke voorwaarde voor effectieve implementatie van de huidige normen om het hoogste niveau van bescherming aan het individu te waarborgen.
- Mainstream staatloosheid in het EU-recht en geef aanvullende richtlijnen rondom de identificatie van staatloosheid als noodzakelijke voorwaarde voor de bescherming, participatie en inclusie van staatlozen.

Wat betreft nationaliteit als juridisch concept, zoals bekeken in dit onderzoek vanuit het perspectief van het voorkomen en oplossen van staatloosheid, kan worden vastgesteld dat het *jus sanguinis*-principe (recht van het bloed) ten grondslag ligt aan de visie op nationaliteitsregulering en het verkrijgen van nationaliteit bij geboorte in het bijzonder. Bovendien verwijst het Europees recht naar nationaliteit als een echte en effectieve band tussen een persoon en een staat, die kan bestaan op basis van geboorte, afkomst of verblijfplaats. Tien jaar legaal verblijf op het grondgebied zou de voorgenoemde effectieve band tussen persoon en staat aantonen, terwijl een gewoon, ononderbroken verblijf in het buitenland gedurende tien jaar een indicatie kan zijn dat een dergelijke band niet (meer) bestaat. Binnen de RvE introduceert het ECSS tevens het begrip 'appropriate connection', dat elementen bevat die duiden op een *jus nexus*-benadering van burgerschap, waaronder overwegingen als respect voor de uitgesproken wil van betrokkene rondom zijn of haar nationaliteit. Als het gaat om de rechten die aan nationaliteit zijn verbonden, tonen zowel de RvE- als de EU-instrumenten aan dat de (blijvende) betekenis van nationaliteit wordt erkend, ondanks de bescherming van mensenrechten, gebaseerd op een breder bevoegdheidsbeginsel. Met name de EU creëert door het toekennen van extra rechten aan de status van EU-burgerschap – alleen voor mensen die burger zijn van EU-lidstaten – een nog grotere kloof tussen EU-burgers en staatlozen, wat de EU (nog) niet aanpakt door specifiek beleid rondom staatloosheid.

Nationaliteit werd – zeker in de 19de en het begin van de 20ste eeuw – en wordt nog steeds gebruikt als een manier om mensen die tot een staat behoren te beschermen en om iedereen buiten te houden die deze gemeenschappelijke identiteit zou kunnen compromitteren. De juridische instrumenten betreffende het voorkomen en oplossen van staatloosheid van zowel de RvE als de EU weerspiegelen deze gedachtegang. De RvE legt de nadruk op de uitsluitende aspecten van nationaliteit als het gaat om het verkrijgen van nationaliteit en de EU heeft weinig tot geen invloed op wie het (EU-) burgerschap kan verwerven. Tegelijkertijd genieten degenen die een nationaliteit hebben en zijn opgenomen in de gemeenschap aanvullende rechten (gelet op het EU-burgerschap) en waarborgen die in bijna alle gevallen voorkomen dat zij hun nationaliteit verliezen.

De conclusies van dit onderzoek roepen ook een belangrijke vraag op met betrekking tot nationaliteit zelf: is het wel de juiste oplossing voor staatloosheid? Of is een op rechten gebaseerde benadering van staatloosheid een optie die de voorkeur verdient boven het verkrijgen van een nationaliteit? En heeft Europa een expliciet recht op een nationaliteit nodig waarop mensen aanspraak kunnen maken? Wat dit onderzoek duidelijk maakt, is dat in ieder geval aspecten van het recht op een nationaliteit in Europa kunnen worden opgeëist. Daarnaast wordt nationaliteit veelal nog altijd gezien als een voorwaarde voor volledige en gelijke participatie in de samenleving. Een expliciete erkenning van het recht van elke persoon op een nationaliteit in Europa zou daarom een belangrijke symbolische waarde kunnen hebben door het belang ervan voor de staat *en* het individu te onderstrepen. Het zou het tevens gemakkelijker kunnen maken om meer samenhangende Europese jurisprudentie over deze kwestie te ontwikkelen. In wezen staan echter de instrumenten ter beschikking die nodig zijn om staatloosheid zoveel mogelijk te beperken en op te lossen als het zich voordoet. De voorgenoemde vragen zijn niet door dit onderzoek alleen te beantwoorden. Deze verdienen tevens input van het bredere onderzoeksveld op het onderwerp, dat ook andere disciplinaire perspectieven kan bieden, evenals de inbreng van staatlozen zelf.

Dit onderzoek laat ook de grenzen zien van wat het recht kan doen. Er kunnen tal van juridische instrumenten worden opgesteld, maar als geen enkele staat – wat in Europa normaal gesproken de uitdrukking is van een volk – bereid is ze na te leven en toe te passen, blijven regels betekenisloos en kan dat tot gevolg hebben dat mensen worden uitgesloten. Het feit dat er op dit moment in Europa nog altijd mensen verstoken zijn van nationaliteit en (bijbehorende) rechten, is daarom pijnlijk in het licht van de bevindingen van dit onderzoek naar de beschikbare juridische instrumenten. Verder onderzoek dat de diepere motieven achter uitsluiting van mensen door hen te marginaliseren en staatloos te laten of maken, is daarom van belang, ook met het oog op het verbeteren van de (juridische) respons.

BIBLIOGRAPHY

LEGAL SOURCES (TREATIES, UN/COE/EU RECOMMENDATIONS, RESOLUTIONS AND DOCUMENTS, AND OTHER LEGAL SOURCES)

ACERWC, General Comment No 2 on Article 6 of the African Charter on the Rights and Welfare of the Child, ACERWC/GC/02 (2014)

ACFC, 'Fourth Opinion on Estonia, Adopted on 19 March 2015', ACFC/OP/IV(2015)002

Additional Protocol to the Convention on the Reduction of Cases of Multiple Nationality and Military Obligations in Cases of Multiple Nationality (Strasbourg, 1977, CETS No. 096)

African (Banjul) Charter on Human and Peoples' Rights (adopted 27 June 1981, entered into force 21 October 1986) OAU Doc. CAB/LEG/67/3 rev. 5, 21 I.L.M. 58 (1982) (ACHPR)

African Charter on the Rights and Welfare of the Child (adopted 11 July 1990, entered into force 29 November 1999) OAU Doc. CAB/LEG/24.9/49 (1990) (ACRWC)

AG/RES. 2826 (XLIV-O/14) *Prevention and Reduction of Statelessness and Protection of Stateless Persons in the Americas* (adopted at 2nd plenary session, 4 June 2014

Amendments to the Dutch Nationality Act and the Passport Acts as well as Withdrawal of Reservations to the Convention on the Status of Stateless Persons in Connection with the Determination of Statelessness [Wijziging van de Rijkswet op het Nederlanderschap en de Paspoortwet alsmede intrekking van voorbehouden bij het Verdrag betreffende de status van staatlozen in verband met de vaststelling van staatloosheid] (21 December 2020) *currently in preparation* <https://www.tweedekamer.nl/kamerstukken/wetsvoorstellen/detail?id=2020Z25636&dossier=35688-%28R2151%29> accessed 17 October 2021

American Convention on Human Rights – 'Pact of San José' (adopted 22 November 1969, entered into force 18 July 1978) OAS Treaty Series No 36 (ACHR)

Arab Charter on Human Rights (adopted 22 May 2004, entered into force 15 March 2008) reprinted in (2005) 12 Int'l Hum Rts Rep 893 (ArCHR)

Arrangement Concerning the Extension to Other Categories of Certain Measures Taken in Favour of Russian and Armenian Refugees (signed 30 June 1929) 89 LNTS 65 (No. 2006)

Arrangement relating to the Issue of Identity Certificates to Russian and Armenian Refugees, Supplementing and Amending the previous Arrangements dated July 5, 1922, and May 31, 1924 (signed 12 May 1926) 89 LNTS 48 (No. 2004)

Arrangement Relating to the Legal Status of Russian and Armenian Refugees (signed 30 June 1928) 89 LNTS 55 (No. 2005)

Arrangement with respect to the Issue of Certificates of Identity to Russian Refugees (signed 5 July 1922) 30 LNTS 238 (No. 855)

ASEAN Human Rights Declaration (adopted 19 November 2012)

Basic Law (Constitution) for the Federal Republic of Germany, revised version published in the Federal Law Gazette Part III, Classification No. 100–1, as last amended by Article 1 of the Act of 28 March 2019 (Federal Law Gazette I, 404)

Brazil Declaration, 'A Framework for Cooperation and Regional Solidarity to Strengthen the International Protection of Refugees, Displaced and Stateless Persons in Latin America and the Caribbean', Brasilia, 3 December 2014 <https://www.refworld.org/docid/5487065b4.html> accessed 5 September 2021

CCPR, 'General Comment No. 17: Article 24 (Rights of the Child)' (1989) 35th Session

CCPR, 'Views Adopted by the Committee under Article 5(4) of the Optional Protocol, concerning Communication No. 2918/2016' (20 January 2021) CCPR/C/130/D/2918/2016

CDCJ, '94th Meeting of the European Committee on Legal Co-operation, Strasbourg, 13–15 November 2019 – Meeting Report' (2019) CDCJ(2019)10 <https://rm.coe.int/cdcj-2019-10e-meeting-report-cdcj-94/1680a1bf82> accessed 27 May 2021

CDCJ, '97th Meeting of the European Committee on Legal Co-operation, Strasbourg, 1–3 December 2021 – Abridged Meeting Report' (2021) CDCJ(2021)33

CDCJ, 'Codifying Instrument of European Rules on the Administrative Detention of Migrants. 1st Draft (Strasbourg, 18 May 2017) <https://rm.coe.int/european-rules-on-the-administrative-detention-of-migrants-draft-codif/1680714cc1> accessed 27 May 2021

CDCJ, 'Conditions of Administrative Detention of Migrants. Report of the General Rapporteur Mr Christoph Henrichs (Germany) on the Hearing' (Strasbourg, 22 September 2017) <https://rm.coe.int/report-of-the-hearing-22-23-june-2017/168074ce2f> accessed 27 May 2021

CDCJ, 'Statelessness: Analysis of the Current Practices and Challenges regarding the Avoidance and Reduction of Statelessness in Europe prepared by Prof. Dr. Gerard-René de Groot' (2019) CDCJ-GT-APA(2019)3 <https://rm.coe.int/analysis-statelessness-/1680990cc5> accessed 27 May 2021

CDCJ, 'Terms of Reference of CJ-DAM', CJ-DAM(2016)1 (adopted by the Committee of Ministers at the 1241st Meeting of Ministers' Deputies, 24–26 November 2015)

CDL, 472/2008 – Law on Double citizenship of Moldova (2008)

CEDAW Committee, 'General Recommendation No. 21: Equality in Marriage and Family Relations' (1994) 13th Session

CEDAW Committee, 'General Recommendation No. 32 on on the Gender-related Dimensions of Refugee Status, Asylum, Nationality and Statelessness of Women' (2014) CEDAW/C/GC/32

CERD, 'General Recommendation 30: Discrimination Against Non-Citizens' (2004) CERD/C/64/Misc.11/rev.3

Charter of Fundamental Rights of the European Union [2016] OJ C202/389 (EU Charter)

Charter of the United Nations (adopted 26 June 1945, entered into force 24 October 1945) 1 UNTS XVI (UN Charter)

CJ-DAM, 'Analysis of the Results of the Written Consultation on the 1st Draft of the Codifying Instrument of European Rules on the Administrative Detention of Migrants' (Strasbourg, 12 September 2017) <https://rm.coe.int/publication-document-analysis-of-the-results-of-the-written-consultati/168074ce2e> accessed 27 May 2021

CJ-NA GT, 'Report of the 26th Meeting', CJ-NA GT (2005) 2

CJ-NA, 'Report of the 21st Meeting', CDCJ (2004) 21 / CJ-NA (2004) 5 rev.

CJ-S-NAT, 'Final Report', CJ-S-NAT (2008) 24

CM, 'Council of Europe Counter-Terrorism Strategy (2019–2022)' (2018) CM(2018)86-addfinal

CMW & CRC, 'Joint General Comment No. 3/22 on the General Principles regarding the Human Rights of Children in the Context of International Migration' (2017) CMW/C/GC/3-CRC/C/GC/22

CMW & CRC, 'Joint General Comment No. 4/No. 23 on State Obligations regarding the Human Rights of Children in the Context of International Migration in Countries of Origin, Transit, Destination and Return' (2017) CMW/C/GC/4-CRC/C/GC/23

CoE CM Recommendation No. R (83) 1 of the Committee of Ministers to the Member States on the Stateless nomads and nomads of undetermined nationality (356th meeting of the Ministers' Deputies, 22 February 1983)

CoE CM Recommendation No. R (84) 21 of the Committee of Ministers to the Member States on the acquisition by refugees of the nationality of the host state (377th meeting of the Ministers' Deputies, 14 November 1984)

CoE CM Recommendation No. R (84) 9 of the Committee of Ministers to the Member States on second-generation migrants (368th meeting of the Ministers' Deputies, 20 March 1984)

CoE CM Recommendation No. R (99) 18 of the Committee of Ministers to the Member States on the avoidance and reduction of statelessness (679th meeting of the Ministers' Deputies, 15 September 1999)

CoE CM Reply to PACE Recommendation 2042 (2014) (1205th meeting of the Ministers' Deputies, 9 July 2014) Doc 13583

CoE CM Reply to Recommendation 2145 (2019) (359th meeting of the Ministers' Deputies, 5 November 2019) Doc 15006

CoE CM Resolution (2002) 8 on the on the statute of the European Commission against Racism and Intolerance (adopted by the Committee of Ministers on 13 June 2002 at the 799th meeting of the Ministers' Deputies, amended by Resolutions

CM/Res(2013)12 and CM/Res(2014)2 adopted, respectively, on 9 October 2013 and 19 February 2014 at their 1180th and 1192nd meetings)

CoE CM Resolution (70) 2: Acquisition by refugees of the nationality of their country of residence (adopted by the Ministers' Deputies on 26 January 1970)

CoE CM, 'Action Plan on Protecting Refugee and Migrant Children' (127th Session of the Committee of Ministers, Nicosia, 19 May 2017) CM(2017)54-final

CoE CM, 'The Strasbourg Declaration on Roma' (CoE High Level Meeting on Roma, Strasbourg, 20 October 2010) CM(2010)133 final

CoE CM, Reply to Recommendation 2003 (2012) on Roma Migrants in Europe (1166th Meeting of the Ministers' Deputies, 27 March 2013) Doc 13162

CoE Commissioner for Human Rights, 'Human Rights Comment: Governments Should Act in the Best Interest of Stateless Children' (2013) <https://www.coe.int/en/web/commissioner/-/governments-should-act-in-the-best-interest-of-stateless-childr-1> accessed 2 July 2021

CoE Commissioner for Human Rights, 'Human Rights Comment: Several Hundred Thousand People in Europe are Stateless – They Need Extra Protection' (2011) <https://www.coe.int/en/web/commissioner/-/several-hundred-thousand-people-in-europe-are-stateless-they-need-extra-protecti-1> accessed 2 July 2021

CoE Commissioner for Human Rights, 'Human Rights Comment: Stateless Roma: No Documents – No Rights' (2010) <https://www.coe.int/en/web/commissioner/-/stateless-roma-no-documents-no-righ-1> accessed 2 July 2021

CoE Commissioner for Human Rights, 'Human Rights Comment: Syrian Refugees: 'Reset' Needed in Europe's Approach' (2015) <https://www.coe.int/en/web/commissioner/-/syrian-refugees-reset-needed-in-europe-s-approach> accessed 2 July 2021

CoE Commissioner for Human Rights, 'Report by Dunja Mijatović, Commissioner for Human Rights of the Council of Europe Following Her Visit to Albania from 21 to 25 May 2018' (2018) CommDH/GovRep(2018)10 <https://search.coe.int/commissioner/Pages/result_details.aspx?ObjectId=09000016808d2e22> accessed 2 July 2021

CoE Commissioner for Human Rights, 'Statement: Step Up Action Against Statelessness' (2019) <https://www.coe.int/en/web/commissioner/news-2019/-/asset_publisher/Arb4fRK3o8Cf/content/step-up-action-against-statelessness> accessed 2 July 2021

CoE Convention on the Avoidance of Statelessness in relation to State Succession (Strasbourg. 2006, CETS No. 200) (ECSS)

CoE Recommendation CM/Rec (2009) 13 of the Committee of Ministers to member states on the nationality of children (adopted by the Committee of Ministers on 9 December 2009 at the 1073rd meeting of the Ministers' Deputies)

CoE, 'Group of Specialists on Nationality. Terms of Reference for 2008', CJ-S-Nat (2008) 1

CoE, 'Revised Terms of Reference of the Committee of Experts on Nationality (CJ-NA) (Appendix 8, Item 10.1a)' (1999) Official Gazette of the Council of Europe (Committee of Ministers part-volume) 96 (under c)

Commentary to the Principles on Deprivation of Nationality as a National Security Measure (2020) <https://www.refworld.org/docid/5f3bf2d24.html> accessed 17 October 2021

Commonwealth of Independent States Convention on Human Rights and Fundamental Freedoms (adopted 26 May 1996, entered into force 11 August 1998) reprinted in (1996) 3 Int'l Hum Rts Rep 1, 212 (CIS Convention on Human Rights and Fundamental Freedoms)

Communication from the Commission to the European Parliament and the Council: A Union of Equality: EU Roma Strategic Framework for Equality, Inclusion and Participation [2020] COM(2020) 620 final

Communication from the Commission to the European Parliament and the Council: The Protection of Children in Migration [2017] COM(2017) 211 final

Communication from the Commission to the European Parliament, the Council, the European Economic and Social Committee and the Committee of the Regions: EU Strategy on the Rights of the Child [2021] COM(2021) 142 final

Communication from the Commission to the European Parliament, the Council, the European Economic and Social Committee and the Committee of the Regions on a New Pact on Migration and Asylum [2020] COM(2020) 609 final

Communication of the Commission on the European Citizens' Initiative 'Minority SafePack – one million signatures for diversity in Europe' [2021] C(2021) 171 final

Conclusions of the Council and the Representatives of the Governments of the Member States on Statelessness [2015] <https://www.consilium.europa.eu/en/press/press-releases/2015/12/04/council-adopts-conclusions-on-statelessness/> accessed 17 October 2021

Consolidated versions of the Treaty on European Union (TEU) and the Treaty on the Functioning of the European Union (TFEU) [2016] OJ C202/1

Constitution of the Kingdom of the Netherlands (Grondwet voor het Koninkrijk der Nederlanden, *Stb.* 2019, 33)

Convention concerning the Status of Refugees coming from Germany (signed 10 February 1938) 192 LNTS 61 (No. 4461)
Convention for the Protection of Human Rights and Fundamental Freedoms (European Convention on Human Rights) (ECHR) (CETS No. 005)
Convention of 28 October 1933 relating to the International Status of Refugees (adopted 28 October 1933, entered into force 13 June 1935) 159 LNTS 3663 (1933 Refugee Convention)
Convention on Certain Questions relating to the Conflict of Nationality Laws (adopted 12 April 1930, entered into force 1 July 1937) 179 LTS 89 (1930 Convention)
Convention on the Elimination of All Forms of Discrimination against Women (adopted 18 December 1979, entered into force 3 September 1981) 1249 UNTS 13 (CEDAW)
Convention on the Nationality of Married Women (adopted 20 February 1957, entered into force 11 August 1958) 309 UNTS 65 (1957 Convention)
Convention on the Reduction of Cases of Multiple Nationality and on Military Obligations in Cases of Multiple Nationality (Strasbourg, 1963, CETS No. 043).
Convention on the Reduction of Statelessness (with Final Act of the United Nations Conference on the Elimination or Reduction of Future Statelessness held at Geneva from 24 March to 18 April 1959, and Resolutions I, II, III and IV of the Conference) (adopted 30 August 1961, entered into force 13 December 1975) 989 UNTS 175 (1961 Convention)
Convention on the Rights of Persons with Disabilities (adopted 13 December 2006, entered into force 3 May 2008) 2515 UNTS 3 (CRPD)
Convention on the Rights of the Child (adopted 20 November 1989, entered into force 2 September 1990) 1577 UNTS 3 (CRC)
Convention Relating to the Status of Refugees (adopted 28 July 1951, entered into force 22 April 1954) 189 UNTS 137 (1951 Convention/Refugee Convention)
Convention relating to the Status of Stateless Persons (adopted 28 September 1954, entered into force 6 June 1960), 360 UNTS 117 (1954 Convention)
Council Directive 2003/86/EC of 22 September 2003 on the Right to Family Reunification [2003] OJ L 251/12
Council Regulation (EC) No 168/2007 of 15 February 2007 establishing a European Union Agency for Fundamental Rights [2007] OJ L53/1
Covenant on the Rights of the Child in Islam (adopted June 2005) OIC/9-IGGE/HRI/2004/Rep. Final (CRCI)
Declaration on the Consequences of State Succession for the Nationality of Natural Persons adopted by the European
Commission for Democracy through Law at its 28th Plenary Meeting (Venice, 13–14 September 1996), published in CDL, 'Consequences of State Succession for Nationality' (Strasbourg, 10 February 1997) CDL-INF (97) 1
Directive 2000/43 Implementing the Principle of Equal Treatment between Persons Irrespective of Racial or Ethnic Origin [2000] OJ L 180/22
Directive 2000/78 Establishing a General Framework for Equal Treatment in Employment and Occupation [2000] OJ L 3030/16
Directive 2004/38/EC of the European Parliament and of the Council of 29 April 2004 on the Right of Citizens of the Union and their Family Members to Move and Reside Freely within the Territory of the Member States [2004] OJ L 158/77

Directive 2008/115/EC of the European Parliament and of the Council of 16 December 2008 on Common Standards and Procedures in the Member States for Returning Illegally Staying Third-Country Nationals [2008] OJ L 348/98

Directive 2011/95/EU of the European Parliament and of the Council of 13 December 2011 on standards for the qualification of third-country nationals or stateless persons as beneficiaries of international protection, for a uniform status for refugees or for persons eligible for subsidiary protection, and for the content of the protection granted (Recast) [2011] OJ L 337/9

Directive 2013/32/EU of the European Parliament and of the Council of 26 June 2013 on common procedures for granting and withdrawing international protection (Recast) [2013] OJ L 180/60

Directive 2013/33/EU of the European Parliament and of the Council of 26 June 2013 laying down standards for the reception of applicants for international protection (Recast) [2013] OJ L 180/96

Draft Commentary to the Principles on Deprivation of Nationality as a National Security Measure (2020) <https://www.refworld.org/docid/5f3bf2d24.html> accessed 17 October 2021

Draft International Covenants on Human Rights, Report of the Third Committee, 17th Session, 10 December 1961, A/5655

Draft text of the Protocol to the ACHPR on the Specific Aspects of the Right to a Nationality and the Eradication of Statelessness in Africa <https://www.achpr.org/public/Document/file/English/draft_citizenship_protocol_en_may2017.pdf> accessed 5 September 2021

Dutch Nationality Act (Rijkswet op het Nederlanderschap, *Stb.* 1984, 628)

ECOSOC Res 116 (VI) D (1948) Resolutions adopted by the Economic and Social Council during its Sixth Session (2 February to 11 March 1948) 18

ECRI General Policy Recommendation No. 13 (revised) on Combating Anti-Gypsyism and Discrimination against Roma (adopted on 24 June 2011 and amended on 1 December 2020) <https://www.coe.int/en/web/european-commission-against-racism-and-intolerance/recommendation-no.13> accessed 28 May 2021

ECRI General Policy Recommendation No. 16 on Safeguarding Irregularly Present Migrants from Discrimination – adopted on 16 March 2016 <https://www.coe.int/en/web/european-commission-against-racism-and-intolerance/recommendation-no.16> accessed 28 May 2021

ECRI, 'ECRI Report on Estonia (Fifth Monitoring Cycle)', CRI(2015)36, para 85–86 <https://rm.coe.int/fifth-report-on-estonia/16808b56f1> accessed 28 May 2021

EP Resolution of 10 July 2020 on a comprehensive Union policy on preventing money laundering and terrorist financing – the Commission's Action Plan and other recent developments (2020/2686(RSP)) [2020] <https://www.europarl.europa.eu/doceo/document/TA-9–2020–0204_EN.html> accessed 3 January 2022

EP Resolution of 14 June 2018 on the Situation of Rohingya Refugees, in particular the Plight of Children [2018] 2018/2756(RSP)

EP Resolution of 26 November 2019 on Children's Rights on the Occasion of the 30th Anniversary of the UN Convention on the Rights of the Child [2019] <https://www.europarl.europa.eu/doceo/document/TA-9–2019–0066_EN.html> accessed 17 October 2021

EP Resolution on of 13 November 2018 on Minimum Standards for Minorities in the EU (2018/2036(INI)) [2018] <https://www.europarl.europa.eu/doceo/document/TA-8-2018-0447_EN.html?mc_cid=1a29410458&mc_eid=7bf481eaf5> accessed 28 October 2021

Estonia: Accession Partnership [1998] OJ C 202/03

European Convention on Nationality (Strasbourg, 1997, CETS No. 166) (ECN)

Explanatory Report to the Council of Europe Convention on the Avoidance of Statelessness in relation to State Succession (Strasbourg, 19 May 2006, CETS No. 200)

Explanatory Report to the European Convention on Nationality (Strasbourg, 6 November 1997, CETS No. 166)

Explanatory Report to the to the Framework Convention for the Protection of National Minorities (Strasbourg, 1 February 1995, CETS No. 157)

Framework Convention for the Protection of National Minorities (Strasbourg, 1995, CETS No. 157) (FCNM)

Global Compact for Safe, Orderly and Regular Migration (2018) UN Doc A/CONF/231/3 <https://refugeesmigrants.un.org/sites/default/files/180713_agreed_outcome_global_compact_for_migration.pdf> accessed 5 September 2021

Global Compact on Refugees (2018) UN Doc A/73/12 (Part II) <https://www.unhcr.org/gcr/GCR_English.pdf> accessed 5 September 2021

Guidelines on Involuntary Loss of European Citizenship (2015) <www.ilecproject.eu/sites/default/files/GUIDELINES%20INVOLUNTARY%20LOSS%20OF%20 EUROPEAN%20CITIZENSHIP%20.pdf> accessed 17 October 2021

IGCR, 'Statelessness and Some of its Causes: An Outline' (1946 Memorandum)

ILC, 'Conclusions of the work of the Study Group on the Fragmentation of International Law: Difficulties arising from the Diversification and Expansion of International Law' (2006) 2 Yearbook of the International Law Commission 178

ILC, 'Draft Articles on Diplomatic Protection (with Commentaries)' in UNGA, Supplement No. 10: Report of the International Law Commission, 58th Session (2006) A/61/10

ILC, 'Draft Articles on Nationality of Natural Persons in relation to the Succession of States with Commentaries' (1999) 2 Yearbook of the International Law Commission (part two) 19; annex to UNGA Res 55/153 (12 December 2000) A/RES/55/153

ILC, 'Nationality in Relation to the Succession of States: Comments and Observations Received from Governments' (1998) A/CN.4/493, 162 <https://legal.un.org/ilc/documentation/english/a_cn4_493.pdf> accessed 17 October 2021

ILC, 'Report on Nationality, Including Statelessness by Mr Manley O Hudson, Special Rapporteur' (1952) A/CN.4/50

Institut de Droit International, 'Règles Internationales sur l'Admission et l'Expulsion des Étrangers' (1892) Session de Genève <https://www.idi-iil.org/app/uploads/2017/06/1892_gen_01_fr.pdf> accessed 19 September 2021

Institut de Droit International, 'Résolutions Relatives aux Conflits de Lois en Matière de Nationalité (Naturalisation et Expatriation)' (1896) Session de Venise <https://www.idi-iil.org/app/uploads/2017/06/1896_ven_02_fr.pdf> accessed 19 September 2021

International Convention on the Elimination of All Forms of Racial Discrimination (adopted 21 December 1965, entered into force 4 January 1969) 660 UNTS 195 (ICERD)

International Convention on the Protection of the Rights of All Migrant Workers and Members of their Families (adopted 18 December 1990, entered into force 1 July 2003) 2220 UNTS 3 (ICMW)

International Covenant on Civil and Political Rights (adopted 16 December 1966, entered into force 23 March 1976) 999 UNTS 171 (ICCPR)

International Covenant on Economic, Social and Cultural Rights (adopted 16 December 1966, entered into force 3 January 1976) 993 UNTS 3 (ICESCR)

Latvia: Accession Partnership [1998] OJ C 202/05

Montevideo Convention on the Rights and Duties of States (Inter-American) (adopted 26 December 1933, entered into force 26 December 1934) 165 LNTS 19 (1933 Montevideo Convention)

Netherlands parliamentary documents, Brief van Minister J.W.E. Spies van Binnenlandse Zaken en Koninkrijksrelaties en Minister G.B.M. Leers voor Immigratie, Integratie en Asiel aan R. Bruin (UNHCR Nederland) of 20 August 2012: Beleidsreactie UNHCR-rapport "Staatloosheid in Nederland", kenmerk 2012–0000395600 [Reaction to UNHCR Report Statelessness in the Netherlands], also Bijlage 377600 of *Kamerstukken II* 2013/14, 19637, 1889, 6

Netherlands parliamentary documents, *Handelingen II* 1952/53, 17 April 1953, 2251

Netherlands parliamentary documents, *Kamerstukken II* 2006/07, 30891, 22

Netherlands parliamentary documents, *Kamerstukken II* 2014/15, 19637, 1917

PACE Recommendation 2003 (2012) final version: Roma Migrants in Europe

PACE Recommendation 2042 (2014) Final version: Access to Nationality and the Effective Implementation of the European Convention on Nationality

PACE Recommendation 2145 (2019): Withdrawing Nationality as a Measure to Combat Terrorism: A Human Rights-Compatible Approach?

PACE Recommendation 564 (1969): Acquisition by refugees of the nationality of their country of residence (30 September 1969)

PACE Recommendation 87 (1955): Statelessness (adopted by the Assembly at its 24th Sitting on 25 October 1955)

PACE Resolution 1249 (2001) Co-existence of the Convention on Human Rights and Fundamental Freedoms of the Commonwealth of Independent States and the European Convention on Human Rights

PACE Resolution 1989 (2014) Final version: Access to Nationality and the Effective Implementation of the European Convention on Nationality

PACE Resolution 2099 (2016): The Need to Eradicate Statelessness of Children

PACE Resolution 2263 (2019): Withdrawing Nationality as a Measure to Combat Terrorism: A Human Rights-Compatible Approach?

PACE, 'Children's Rights Related to Surrogacy', Doc 14140, 11 October 2016, compendium of amendments to Draft Recommendation

PACE, 'Draft Protocol on the Avoidance of Statelessness in Relation to State Succession – Parliamentary Assembly Opinion No. 258', 7 February 2006, GR-J(2006)3

PACE, 'Report and Draft Recommendation: Children's Rights Related to Surrogacy', Doc 14140, 23 September 2016

PACE/Tineke Strik, 'Report: Withdrawing Nationality as a Measure to Combat Terrorism: A Human Rights-Compatible Approach? (2019) Doc 14790 <http://assembly.coe.int/nw/xml/XRef/Xref-DocDetails-en.asp?FileID=25241&lang=en> accessed 26 September 2021

Plan for the Issue of a Certificate of Identity to Armenian Refugees (signed 31 May 1924) 7–10 LoN Official Journal 969

Principles on Deprivation of Nationality as a National Security Measure (2020) <https://www.refworld.org/pdfid/5f3bf26d4.pdf> accessed 4 September 2021

Protocol amending the Convention on the Reduction of Cases of Multiple Nationality and Military Obligations in Cases of Multiple Nationality (Strasbourg, 1977, CETS No. 095

Protocol relating to a Certain Case of Statelessness (adopted 12 April 1930, entered into force 1 July 1937) 179 LTS 115

Protocol relating to Military Obligations in Certain Cases of Double Nationality adopted 12 April 1930, entered into force 25 May 1937) 178 LTS 227

Protocol relating to the Status of Refugees (adopted 31 January 1967, entered into force 4 October 1967) 606 UNTS 267

Provisional Arrangement concerning the Status of Refugees coming from Germany (signed 4 July 1936) 171 LNTS 77 (No. 3952)

Regulation (EC) 883/2004 of the European Parliament and of the Council of 29 April 2004 on the coordination of social security systems [2004] OJ L166/1

Regulation (EU) No 603/2013 of the European Parliament and of the Council of 26 June 2013 on the establishment of 'Eurodac' for the comparison of fingerprints for the effective application of Regulation (EU) No 604/2013 establishing the criteria and mechanisms for determining the Member State responsible for examining an application for international protection lodged in one of the Member States by a third-country national or a stateless person and on requests for the comparison with Eurodac data by Member States' law enforcement authorities and Europol for law enforcement purposes, and amending Regulation (EU) No 1077/2011 establishing a European Agency for the operational management of large-scale IT systems in the area of freedom, security and justice [2013] OJ L 180/1

Regulation (EU) No 604/2013 of the European Parliament and of the Council of 26 June 2013 establishing the criteria and mechanisms for determining the member state responsible for examining an application for international protection lodged in one of the member states by a third-country national or a stateless person (Recast) [2013] OJ L 180/31

Second Protocol amending the Convention on the Reduction of Cases of Multiple Nationality and Military Obligations in Cases of Multiple Nationality (Strasbourg, 1993, CETS No. 149)

Special Protocol concerning Statelessness (adopted 12 April 1930, entered into force 15 March 2004) 2252 UNTS 435

Statute of the Council of Europe (as amended, London, 1949, CETS No. 1)

UN Department of Social Affairs, 'A Study of Statelessness' (1949, E/1112/ Add. 1)

UN, 'Documents on the Development and Codification of International Law', Supplement to (1947) 41(4) American Journal of International Law <http://legal.un.org/ilc/documentation/english/ASIL_1947_study.pdf> accessed 19 September 2021

UNGA Res 302 (IV) (8 December 1949) UN Doc A/RES/302 (IV)

UNGA Res 31/36 (1976) A/RES/31/36

UNGA Res 319 (IV) (3 December 1949) UN Doc A/RES/319(IV)

UNGA Res 3274 (XXIX) (1974) A/RES/3274(XXIX)

UNGA Res 428 (Fifth Session, 14 December 1950) 46

UNGA Res 50/152 (1995) A/RES/50/152

UNGA Res 61/137 (2006) A/RES/61/137

UNGA Res 70/1 (25 September 2015) A/RES/70/1

UNGA Res 55/153 (2000) A/RES/55/153

UNGA, 'Report of the Special Rapporteur on minority issues. Statelessness: a minority issue' (20 July 2018) UN Doc A/73/205

UNGA, 'Resolution Adopted by the Human Rights Council. Human rights and arbitrary deprivation of nationality' (15 July 2016) UN Doc A/HRC/RES/32/5

UNGA, 'Resolution adopted by the Human Rights Council. The right to a nationality: women and children' (16 July 2012) UN Doc A/HRC/RES/20/4

UNHCR ExCom, 'Conclusion on Identification, Prevention and Reduction of Statelessness and Protection of Stateless Persons', No. 106 (LVII) (6 October 2006)

UNHCR, 'Guidelines on Statelessness No. 4: Ensuring Every Child's Right to Acquire a Nationality through Articles 1–4 of the 1961 Convention on the Reduction of Statelessness' (2012) HCR/GS/12/04

UNHCR, 'Guidelines on Statelessness No. 5: Loss and Deprivation of Nationality under Articles 5–9 of the 1961 Convention on the Reduction of Statelessness' (2020) HCR/GS/20/05

UNHCR, 'Handbook on the Protection of Stateless Persons under the 1954 Convention relating to the Status of Stateless Persons' (Geneva, 2014) <www.unhcr.org/protection/statelessness/53b698ab9/handbook-protection-stateless-persons.html> accessed 2 August 2021

Universal Declaration of Human Rights (adopted 10 December 1948 UNGA Res 217 A(III) (UDHR)

Vienna Convention on the Succession of States in respect of treaties (adopted 23 August 1978, entered into force 6 November 1996) 1946 UNTS 3

CASES

Acquisition of Polish Nationality (Advisory Opinion) 1923 PCIJ Rep Series B No 7

Advisory Opinion concerning the Recognition in Domestic Law of a Legal Parent-Child Relationship between a Child Born through a Gestational Surrogacy Arrangement Abroad and the Intended Mother Request no. P16–2018–001 (ECHR, 10 April 2019)

Amnesty International v Zambia Comm No 212/98 (ACmHPR, 5 May 1999)

Andrei Karassev and Family v Finland App No 31414/96 (ECHR, 12 January 1999, admissibility) ECLI:CE:ECHR:1999:0112DEC003141496

Andrejeva v Latvia App No 55707/00 (ECHR, 18 February 2009) ECLI:CE:ECHR:2009:0218JUD005570700

Anudo Ochieng Anudo v United Republic of Tanzania App No 012/2015 (ACtHPR, 22 March 2018)

Biao v Denmark App No 38590/10 (ECHR, 24 May 2016) ECLI:CE:ECHR:2016:0524JUD003859010

BVerwG 5 C 12.10 (2010) ECLI:DE:BVerwG:2010:111110U5C12.10.0

Case C-490/20 *V.M.A. v Stolichna Obshtina, Rayon 'Pancharevo'* [2021] ECLI:EU:C:2021:1008

Case C-221/17 *Tjebbes and Others v Minister van Buitenlandse Zaken* [2019] ECLI:EU:C:2019:189

Case C-528/15 *Policie ČR, Krajské ředitelství policie Ústeckého kraje, odbor cizinecké policie v Salah Al Chodor, Ajlin Al Chodor, Ajvar Al Chodor* [2017] ECLI:EU:C:2017:213

Case C-617/10 *Åklagaren v Hans Åkerberg Fransson* [2013] ECLI:EU:C:2013:105

Case C-434/09 *Shirley McCarthy v Secretary of State for the Home Department* [2011] ECLI:EU:C:2011:277
Case 34/09 *Gerardo Ruiz Zambrano v Office national de l'emploi (ONEm)* [2011] ECLI:EU:C:2011:124
Case C-135/08 *Janko Rottmann v Freistaat Bayern* [2010] ECLI:EU:C:2010:104
Case C-300/04 *M.G. Eman and O.B. Sevinger v College van burgemeester en wethouders van Den Haag* [2006] ECLI:EU:C:2006:545
Case C-200/02 *Kunqian Catherine Zhu and Man Lavette Chen v Secretary of State for the Home Department* [2004] ECLI:EU:C:2004:639
Case C-413/99 *Baumbast, R v Secretary of State for the Home Department* [2002] ECLI:EU:C:2002:493
Case C-184/99 *Rudy Grzelczyk v Centre public d'aide sociale d'Ottignies-Louvain-la-Neu* [2001] ECLI:EU:C:2001:458
Case C-369/90 *Mario Vicente Micheletti and Others v Delegación del Gobierno en Cantabria* [1992] ECLI:EU:C:1992:295
Case of the Expelled Dominicans and Haitians v Dominican Republic Series C No. 282 (IACtHR, 28 August 2014)
Case of the Girls Yean and Bosico v Dominican Republic Series C No 130 (IACtHR, 8 September 2005)
DZ v the Netherlands Com No 2918/2016 (CCPR, 20 January 2021) UN Doc CCPR/C/130/D/2918/2016 (2020)
Exchange of Greek and Turkish Populations (Advisory Opinion) 1925 PCIJ Rep Series B No 10
Foulon et Bouvet c France App Nos 9063/14 & 10410/14 (ECHR, 21 July 2016) ECLI:CE:ECHR:2016:0721JUD000906314
Gelman v Uruguay Series C No. 221 (IACtHR, 24 February 2011)
Genovese v Malta App No 53124/09 (ECHR, 11 October 2011) ECLI:CE:ECHR:2011:1011JUD005312409
Ghoumid and others v France App No 52273/16 (ECHR, 25 June 2020) ECLI:CE:ECHR:2020:0625JUD005227316
Hoti v Croatia App No 63311/14 (ECHR, 26 April 2018) ECLI:CE:ECHR:2018:0426JUD006331114
Institute for Human Rights and Development in Africa (IHRDA) and Open Society Justice Initiative on Behalf of Children of
Nubian Descent in Kenya v the Government of Kenya Com No Com/002/2009 (ACERWC, 22 March 2011)
Ivcher-Bronstein v Peru Series C No 74 (IACtHR, 6 February 2001)
John K Modise v Botswana Comm No 97/93 (ACmHPR, 6 November 2000)
K2 v the United Kingdom App No 42387/13 (ECHR, 9 March 2017) ECLI:CE:ECHR:2017:0207DEC004238713
Kafkasli c Turquie App No 21106/92 (European Commission on Human Rights, 22 May 1995, admissibility)
Kim v Russia App No 44260/13 (ECHR, 17 July 2014) ECLI:CE:ECHR:2014:0717JUD004426013
Labassee c France App No 65941/11 (ECHR, 26 June 2014) ECLI:CE:ECHR:2014:0626JUD006594111
Mennesson v France App No 65192/11 (ECHR, 26 June 2014) ECLI:CE:ECHR:2014:0626JUD006519211

Minh Quang Pham v the United Kingdom App No 37478/20 (ECtHR, communicated on 25 November 2020)
Nottebohm Case (Liechtenstein v Guatemala) [1955] ICJ Rep 4
Open Society Justice Initiative v Côte d'Ivoire Comm No 318/06 (ACmHPR, 28 February 2015)
Q v Denmark Com No 2001/2010 (CCPR, 19 May 2015) UN Doc CCPR/C/113/D/2001/2010 (2015)
Ramadan v Malta App No 76136/12 (ECHR, 21 June 2016) ECLI:CE:ECHR:2016:0621 JUD007613612
Sudita Keita v Hungary App No 42321/15 (ECHR, 12 May 2020) ECLI:CE:ECHR:2020:0512 JUD004232115
Trop v Dulles 356 US 86 (1958)
X v Austria App No 5212/71 (ECHR, 5 October 1972) ECLI:CE:ECHR:1972:1005DEC000521271

LITERATURE (BOOKS AND ARTICLES)

The Council of Europe: Structure, Aims and Achievements (Council of Europe Directorate of Press and Information 1970)
Albertini R von, 'The Impact of Two World Wars on the Decline of Colonialism' (1969) 4 Journal of Contemporary History 17
Aleinikoff TA & Klusmeyer D (eds), *Citizenship Today. Global Perspectives and Practices* (Carnegie Endowment for International Peace 2001)
Andreassen BA, Sano HO & McInerney-Lankford S (eds), *Research Methods in Human Rights. A Handbook* (Handbooks of Research Methods in Law, Edward Elgar Publishing 2018)
Arendt H, *The Origins of Totalitarianism* (Harvest Book – Harcourt & Brace Company 1979)
Arendt H, *Eichmann in Jerusalem. A Report on the Banality of Evil* (revised and enlarged edn, The Viking Press 1964)
Barnard C & Peers S, *European Union Law* (2nd edn, Oxford University Press 2017)
Barten U, 'The EU's Lack of Commitment to Minority Protection' (2016) 15 Journal on Ethnopolitics and Minority Issues in Europe 104
Bartolini S, 'Enfranchisement, Equality and Turnout in the European Democratisation Process: A Preliminary Comparative Analysis' (1996) EUI Working Paper No. 121 <https://www.icps.cat/archivos/WorkingPapers/WP_I_121.pdf?noga=1> accessed 12 September 2021
Bartrop PR, *The Evian Conference of 1938 and the Jewish Refugee Crisis* (Palgrave MacMillan 2018)
Batchelor CA, 'Statelessness and the Problem of Resolving Nationality Status' (1998) 10 International Journal of Refugee Law 156
Batchelor CA, 'Stateless Persons: Some Gaps in International Protection' (1995) 7 International Journal of Refugee Law 232
Bauböck R (ed), *Debating European Citizenship* (IMISCOE Research Series, SpringerOpen 2019)
Bauböck R (ed), *Debating Transformations of National Citizenship* (IMISCOE Research Series, SpringerOpen 2018)
Beco G de (ed), *Human Rights Monitoring Mechanisms of the Council of Europe* (Routledge Research in Human Rights Law, Routledge 2013)
Belavusau U & Henrard K, 'A Bird's Eye View on EU Anti-Discrimination Law: The Impact of the 2000 Equality Directives' (2019) 20 German Law Journal 614

Belton KA, *Statelessness in the Caribbean. The Paradox of Belonging in a Postnational World* (University of Pennsylvania Press 2017)

Berényi K, 'Addressing the Anomaly of Statelessness in Europe: An EU Law and Human Rights Perspective' (PhD thesis, Ludovika – University of Public Service 2018)

Berényi K, 'Statelessness and the Refugee Crisis in Europe' (2016) 53 Forced Migration Review 69

Bieber F, 'Is Nationalism on the Rise? Assessing Global Trends' (2018) 17 Ethnopolitics 519

Bisschop WR, 'Nationality in International Law' (1943) 37 American Journal of International Law 320

Blackman JL, 'State Succession and Statelessness: The Emerging Right to an Effective Nationality Under International Law' (1998) 19 Michigan Journal of International Law 1141

Bloom T & Kingston LN (eds), *Statelessness, Governance, and the Problem of Citizenship* (Manchester University Press 2021)

Bloom T, Tonkiss K & Cole P, *Understanding Statelessness* (Routledge 2017)

Boll AM, *Multiple Nationality and International Law* (Martinus Nijhoff Publishers 2007)

Bosniak L, *The Citizen and the Alien. Dilemmas of Contemporary Membership* (Princeton University Press 2006)

Bradburn D, 'Nation, Nationhood, and Nationalism' in Trevor Burnard (ed) *Oxford Bibliographies in Atlantic History* (Oxford University Press) last modified: 29 June 2011 <www.oxfordbibliographies.com/view/document/obo-9780199730414/obo-9780199730414-0070.xml> accessed 12 September 2021

Bradshaw J, 'Stateless in Europe. The Unbearable Lightness of Being an Unperson in the EU' in Nuno Ferreira & Dora Kostakopoulou (eds), *The Human Face of the European Union. Are EU Law and Policy Humane Enough?* (Cambridge University Press 2016) 260–292

Bradshaw J, 'Emerging From the Chrysalis: Union Citizenship Must Escape Its Nationality-Based Shortcomings' (2013) 34 Liverpool Law Review 195

Brekoo A, 'Statelessness and the European Union: Exploring the Potential Value of Union Citizenship (2020) 2 Statelessness & Citizenship Review 24

Brekoo A, 'A Role for the European Union in Addressing Statelessness? Assessing Obligations and Possibilities for Action' (BA Thesis, Tilburg University 2019)

Brouwer E & Vries K de, 'Third-country Nationals and Discrimination on the Ground of Nationality: Article 18 TFEU in the Context of Article 14 ECHR and EU Migration Law: Time of a New Approach' in Marjolein van den Brink, Susanne Burri & Jenny Goldschmidt (eds) *Equality and Human Rights: Nothing but Trouble? Liber Amicorum Titia Loenen* (SIM Special 38, SIM/UU 2015) 123–146

Brownlie I, 'The Relations of Nationality in Public International Law' (1963) 39 British Yearbook of International Law 284

Brubaker R, *Citizenship and Nationhood in France and Germany* (Harvard University Press 1992)

Brunet L, Carruthers J, Davaki K, King D, Marzo C & McCandless J, 'A Comparative Study on the Regime of Surrogacy in EU Member States. Study Requested by the European Parliament's Committee on Legal Affairs' (2013) <https://www.europarl.europa.eu/RegData/etudes/STUD/2013/474403/IPOL-JURI_ET(2013)474403_EN.pdf> accessed 17 October 2021

Busser A & Rodrigues P, 'Staatloze Roma in Nederland' [Stateless Roma in the Netherlands] (2010) 8 Asiel & Migrantenrecht 384

Cabral P, 'Case Note: *Sudita Keita v Hungary* – European Court of Human Rights Decision on the Right to Private Life of Stateless Persons' (2020) 2 Statelessness and Citizenship Review 324

Cahn C, 'Minorities, Statelessness and Citizenship in Europe' (2012) 14 European Journal of Migration and Law 297

Calic MJ, *Südosteuropa. Weltgeschichte einer Region* (CH Beck 2016)

Cambien N, Kochenov D & Muir E (eds), *European Citizenship under Stress. Social Justice, Brexit and Other Challenges* (Nijhoff Studies in European Union Law Vol 16, Brill Nijhoff 2020)

Caplan J & Torpey J (eds), *Documenting Individual Identity. The Development of State Practices in the Modern World* (Princeton University Press 2001)

Carrera S & Groot GR de, 'European Citizenship at a Crossroads. Enhancing European Cooperation on Acquisition and Loss of Nationality' (2014) CEPS Paper in Liberty and Security in Europe No. 72 <https://www.ceps.eu/wp-content/uploads/2015/01/No%2072%20European%20Citizenship%20at%20Crossroads.pdf> accessed 17 October 2021

Carter Wood J, '"Blessed is the Nation"? Christianity and National Identity in Twentieth-Century Europe' in John Carter Wood (ed), *Christianity and National Identity in Twentieth-Century Europe. Conflict, Community, and the Social Order* (Vandenhoeck & Ruprecht 2016) 11–31

Chan JMM, 'The Right to a Nationality as a Human Right. The Current Trend Towards Recognition' (1980) 12 Human Rights Law Journal 1

Checkel JT, 'Norms, Institutions, and National Identity in Contemporary Europe' (1999) 43 International Studies Quarterly 83

CoE, *Human Rights of Roma and Travellers in Europe* (Council of Europe Publishing 2012), available online <https://www.coe.int/t/commissioner/source/prems/prems79611_GBR_CouvHumanRightsOfRoma_WEB.pdf> accessed 3 January 2022

Cohen GD, 'The "Human Rights Revolution" at Work. Displaced Persons in Postwar Europe' in Stefan-Ludwig Hoffmann (ed), *Human Rights in the Twentieth Century* (Cambridge University Press 2011) 45–61

Congleton RD, 'Economic Development and Democracy: Does Industrialization lead to Universal Suffrage?' (2004) 21 Homo Oeconomicus 283

Conklin WE, *Statelessness. The Enigma of the International Community* (Hart Publishing 2014)

Craig P & Búrca G de, *EU Law: Text, Cases, and Materials* (7th edn, Oxford University Press 2020)

Craig P & Búrca G de, *EU Law. Text, Cases and Materials* (5th edn, Oxford University Press 2011)

Crawford J & Koskenniemi M (eds), *The Cambridge Companion to International Law* (Cambridge University Press 2012)

Crawford J, 'The Right of Self-Determination in International Law: Its Development and Future' in Philip Alston (ed), *Peoples' Rights* (Oxford University Press 2001) 7–67

Davies GT, 'The Entirely Conventional Supremacy of Union Citizenship and Rights' in Jo Shaw (eds), *Has the European Court of Justice Challenged Member State Sovereignty in Nationality Law?* (EUI Working Paper RSCAS 2011/62, European University Institute 2011) 5–10

Dermine P, 'Succession and EU Treaty Obligations' in Catherine Brölmann & Thomas Vandamme (eds), *Secession within the Union. Collected Think Pieces* (Amsterdam University 2014)

Dinan D, *Ever Closer Union. An Introduction to European Integration* (4th ed, Palgrave Macmillan 2010)

Donner R, *The Regulation of Nationality in International Law* (2nd ed, Transnational Publishers, Inc 1994)
Dorpalen A, *Europe in the 20th Century. A History* (Macmillan 1968)
Dugard J, 'The Influence of the Universal Declaration as Law' (2009) 24 Maryland Journal of International Law 85
Džankić J, *The Global Market for Investor Citizenship* (Palgrave McMillan 2019)
Eco U, 'The language of Europe is translation', lecture given at the Dixièmes Assises de la traduction littéraire (Arles 1993)
Edwards A & Waas L van (eds), *Nationality and Statelessness under International Law* (Cambridge University Press 2014)
Eijken H van, *European Citizenship and the Constitutionalisation of the European Union* (Europa Law Publishing 2015)
Einarsen T, 'Drafting History of the 1951 Convention and the 1967 Protocol' in Andreas Zimmerman (ed), *The 1951 Convention Relating to the Status of Refugees and Its 1967 Protocol. A Commentary* (Oxford University Press 2011) 37–73
Ersbøll E, 'Biao v. Denmark – Discrimination Among Citizens?' (2014) EUI Working Papers RSCAS 2014/79 <http://cadmus.eui.eu/bitstream/handle/1814/32015/RSCAS_ERS%20_2014_79.pdf?sequence=1> accessed 10 July 2021
Ferri D & Martinico G, 'Revisiting the Ruiz Zambrano Doctrine and Exploring the Potential for its Extensive Application' (2021) 27 European Public Law 685
Fitzmaurice P, 'Between the wars – The Refugee Convention of 1933: A Contemporary Analysis' in David Keane & Yvonne McDermott (eds), *The Challenge of Human Rights. Past, Present and Future* (Edward Elgar 2012) 236–255
Forlati S & Annoni A, *The Changing Role of Nationality in International Law* (Routledge 2013)
Foster M & Lambert H, *International Refugee Law and the Protection of Stateless Persons* (Oxford University Press 2019)
Fraser D & Caestecker F, 'Jews or Germans? Nationality Legislation and the Restoration of Liberal Democracy in Western Europe after the Holocaust' (2013) 31 Law and History Review 391
Fripp E, *Nationality and Statelessness in the International Law of Refugee Status* (Hart Publishing 2016)
Fullbrook M, *Short Oxford History of Europe. Europe Since 1945* (Oxford University Press 2001)
Ganczer M, 'The Right to a Nationality as a Human Right?' in Marcel Szabó, Petra Lea Láncos, Réka Varga & Tamás Molnár (eds), *Hungarian Yearbook of International Law 2014* (Eleven International Publishing 2015) 15–33
Gerards J, Waele H de & Zwaan K (eds), *Vijf jaar bindend EU-Grondrechtenhandvest* [Five Years of a Binding EU Charter] (Wolters Kluwer 2015)
Gilbert G, 'The Council of Europe and Minority Rights' (1996) 18 Human Rights Quarterly 160
Goodwin-Gill GS & McAdam J, *The Refugee in International Law* (3rd ed, Oxford University Press 2007)
Goodwin-Gill GS, 'The Rights of Refugees and Stateless Persons' in K P Saksena (ed), *Human Rights Perspective & Challenges (in 1990 and Beyond)* (World Congress on Human Rights, Lancers Books 1994) 378–401
Grant AJ & Temperley H, revised and edited by Penson LM, *Europe in the Nineteenth and Twentieth Centuries (1789–1950)* (Longmans, Green and Co Ltd 1961)

Grizo M, 'The Versailles System of Peace Treaties and the Minority Protection in Southeast Europe. The Bulgarian-Greek Convention for the Exchange of Population of 1919' (2010) 3 Belgrade Law Review 67

Groenendijk K, 'Nationality, Minorities and Statelessness. The Case of the Baltic States' (1993) 4 Helsinki Monitor 13

Groot D de, 'EU Law and the Mutual Recognition of Parenthood Between Member States: The Case of V.M.A. v Stolichna Obshtina' (2021) RSCAS/GLOBALCIT Special Report <https://cadmus.eui.eu/handle/1814/69731> accessed 17 October 2021

Groot GR de & Luk NC, 'Twenty Years of CJEU Jurisprudence on Citizenship' (2014) 15 German Law Journal 821

Groot GR de & Seling A, 'The Consequences of the *Rottmann* Judgment on Member State Autonomy – The European Court of Justice's Avant-Gardism in Nationality Matters' (2011) 7 European Constitutional Law Review 150

Groot GR de & Vonk OW, 'Nationality, Statelessness and ECHR's Article 8: Comments on Genovese v. Malta (2012) 14 European Journal of Migration and Law 317

Groot GR de & Vonk OW, *International Standards on Nationality Law. Text, Cases and Materials* (Wolf Legal Publishers 2015)

Groot GR de, 'The European Convention on Nationality: A Step towards a *Ius Commune* in the Field of Nationality Law' (2007) 7 Maastricht Journal of European and Comparative Law 117

Groot GR de, Swider K & Vonk OW, 'Practices and Approaches in the EU Member States to Prevent and End Statelessness. Study for the LIBE Committee' (2015) <https://www.europarl.europa.eu/RegData/etudes/STUD/2015/536476/IPOL_STU(2015)536476_EN.pdf> accessed 17 October 2021

Guild E, 'The UN Compact for Safe, Orderly and Regular Migration: What Place for Human Rights' (2018) 30 International Journal of Refugee Law 661

Guild E, Carrera S & Eggenschwiler A (eds), *The Area of Freedom, Security and Justice Ten Years On. Successes and Future Challenges under the Stockholm Programme* (Centre for European Policy Studies 2010)

Gyulai G, 'Statelessness in the EU Framework for International Protection' (2012) 14 European Journal of Migration and Law 279

Hailbronner K, 'Nationality in Public International Law and European Law', in Rainer Bauböck, Eva Ersbøll, Kees Groenendijk & Harald Waldrauch (eds), *Acquisition and Loss of Nationality. Policies and Trends in 15 European States. Vol. 1: Comparative Analyses* (Amsterdam University Press 2006) 35–104

Hall S, 'The European Convention on Nationality and the Right to Have Rights' (1999) 24 European Law Review 586

Harvey A, 'Statelessness: the "de facto" Statelessness Debate' (2010) 24 Journal of Immigration Asylum and Nationality Law 257

Henard K, 'The Shifting Parameters of Nationality' (2018) 65 Netherlands International Law Review 269

Hendriks K, Klaas J & Dael M van, 'Juridische spoken verdwijnen nog niet' [Legal ghosts are not disappearing yet] (2017) 2 Asiel & Migrantenrecht 75

Hirsch Ballin E & Leenknegt GJ (eds), *Artikelsgewijs Commentaar op de Grondwet* [Commentary on the Constitution] (Nederlandrechtsstaat.nl 2021) <https://www.nederlandrechtsstaat.nl/grondwet/> accessed 26 May 2021

Hirsch Ballin E, Ćerimović E, Dijstelbloem H & Segers M, *European Variations as a Key to Cooperation* (Research for Policy, WRR/Springer Open 2020)

Hirsch Ballin E, *Advanced Introduction to Legal Research Methods* (Elgar Advanced Introductions, Edward Elgar 2020)

Hirsch Ballin E, *Citizens' Rights and the Right to Be a Citizen* (Developments in International Law Vol 66, Brill Nijhoff 2014)

Hirschman AO, 'The On-and-Off Connection Between Political and Economic Progress' (1994) 84 The American Economic Review, Papers and Proceedings of the Hundred and Sixth Annual Meeting of the American Economic Association 343

Hobsbawm EJ, *Nations and Nationalism since 1780* (2nd edn, Cambridge University Press 1990)

Hoffmann-Riem W, 'The Venice Commission of the Council of Europe – Standards and Impact' (2014) 25 European Journal of International Law 579

Holborn LW, 'The Legal Status of Political Refugees, 1920–1938' (1938) 32 The American Journal of International Law 680

Hondius F, 'The New Architecture of Europe and Ius Commune Europeum' in Bruno de Witte & Caroline Forder (eds), *The Common Law of Europe and the Future of Legal Education* (Metro/Kluwer 1992) 213–222

Hoornick M, 'Addressing Statelessness through the International Convention on the Elimination of All Forms of Racial Discrimination (ICERD)' (2020) 2 Statelessness and Citizenship Review 222

Howard-Hassmann RE & Walton-Roberts M (eds) *The Human Right to Citizenship. A Slippery Concept* (University of Pennsylvania Press 2015)

Hunter W, *Undocumented Nationals* (Cambridge Elements in the Politics of Development, Cambridge University Press 2019)

Irving H, *Citizenship, Alienage, and the Modern Constitutional State. A Gendered History* (Cambridge University Press 2017)

ISI, *The World's Stateless: Deprivation of Nationality* (ISI 2020)

ISI, *World's Stateless: Children* (Wolf Legal Publishers 2017)

ISI, *The World's Stateless* (Wolf Legal Publishers 2014)

Jaghai S & Waas L van, 'Stripped of Citizenship, Stripped of Dignity? A Critical Exploration of Nationality Deprivation as a Counter-Terrorism Measure' in Christophe Paulussen & Martin Scheinin (eds), *Human Dignity and Human Security in Times of Terrorism* (T.M.C. Asser Press 2020) Ch 8

Jessurun d'Oliveira HU (ed), *Trends in het nationaliteitsrecht. Nationaal en Internationaal [Trends in Nationality Law. National and International]* (Sdu Uitgevers 1998)

Jessurun d'Oliveira HU, 'Decoupling Nationality and Union Citizenship?' (2011) 7 European Constitutional Law Review 138

Joppke C, 'Transformation of Citizenship: Status, Rights, Identity' (2007) 11 Citizenship Studies 37

Kadioglu A, 'Denationalization of Citizenship? The Turkish Experience' (2007) 11 Citizenship Studies 283

Kanics J, 'Preventing and Addressing Statelessness in the Context of International Surrogacy Arrangements' (2014) 19 Tilburg Law Review 117

Kaya B, *The Changing Face of Europe – Population Flows in the 20th Century* (Council of Europe Publishing 2002)

Keller H & Ulfstein G, *UN Human Rights Treaty Bodies. Law and Legitimacy* (Cambridge University Press 2012)

Kingston LN, '"A Forgotten Human Rights Crisis": Statelessness and Issue (Non)Emergence' (2012) 14 Human Rights Review 73

Kleinsorge TEJ, *The Council of Europe* (Kluwer International 2019)

Kochenov D & Dimitrovs A, 'EU Citizenship for Latvian "Non-Citizens": A Concrete Proposal' (2016) 38 Houston Journal of International Law 55

Kochenov D, 'The *Tjebbes* Fail' (2019) 4 European Papers 319

Kochenov D, 'The Ius Tractum of Many Faces: European Citizenship and the Difficult Relationship Between Status and Rights' (2009) 15 Colombia Journal of European Law 169

Kochovski I, 'Statelessness and Discriminatory Nationality Laws: The Case of the Roma in Bosnia and Serbia' (LLM thesis, Tilburg University 2013)

Konstadinides T, 'Drawing the Line Between Circumvention and Gap-Filling: An Exploration of the Conceptual Limits of the Treaty's Flexibility Clause' (2012) 31 Yearbook of European Law 227

Kruiniger P (ed), *Recht van de Islam 30:* 'Jihad, islam en recht: jihadisme en reacties vanuit het Nederlandse en Belgische recht [Law of Islam 30: 'Jihad, Islam and Law: Jihadism and Reactions from Dutch and Belgian law]' (Boom juridische uitgevers 2017)

Lawrance BN & Stevens J (eds), *Citizenship in Question. Evidentiary Birthright and Statelessness* (Duke University Press 2017)

Leerssen J, *National Thought in Europe. A Cultural History* (Amsterdam University Press 2006)

Lenaerts K, 'The Role of the EU Charter in the Member States' in Michal Bobek & Jeremias Adams-Prassl (eds), *The EU Charter of Fundamental Rights in the Member States* (EU law in the Member States Vol 7, Hart Publishing 2020) 19–36

Lesaffer R, 'The Westphalia Peace Treaties and the Development of the Tradition of Great European Peace Settlements prior to 1648' (1997) 18 Grotiana 71

Lynch M & Teff M, 'Childhood Statelessness' (2009) 32 Forced Migration Review 31

Maldonado Castillo C, 'The Cartagena Process: 30 Years of Innovation and Solidarity' (2015) 49 Forced Migration Review 89

Manby B, '"Legal Identity for All" and Statelessness: Opportunity and Threat at the Junction of Public and Private International Law' (2020) 2 Statelessness and Citizenship Review 248

Manby B, *Citizenship in Africa. The Law of Belonging* (Wolf Legal Publishers 2015)

Manly M & Persaud S, 'UNHCR and Responses to Statelessness' (2009) 32 Forced Migration Review 7

Manly M, 'UNHCR's Mandate and Activities to Address Statelessness in Europe' (2012) 14 *European Journal of Migration and Law* 261

Mantu S, 'Terrorist citizens and the human right to a nationality' (2018) 26 Journal of Contemporary European Studies 28

Mantu S, *Contingent Citizenship. The Law and Practice of Citizenship Deprivation in International, European and National Perspectives* (Ipskamp Drukkers 2014)

Mantu S, Minderhoud P & Guild E (eds), *EU Citizenship and Free Movement Rights: Taking Supranational Citizenship Seriously* (Immigration and Asylum Law and Policy in Europe, Vol. 47, Brill Nijhoff 2020)

Marcus J, *Social and Political History of the Jews in Poland 1919–1939* (De Gruyter Mouton 1983)

Marrero González G, *Civis Europaeus Sum? Consequences with Regard to Nationality Law and EU Citizenship Status of the Independence of a Devolved Part of an EU Member State* (Wolf Legal Publishers 2017)

Martini M & Damm M, 'Succession of States in the EU' (2014) Ancilla Iuris 159
McAdam J, 'The Global Compacts on Refugees and Migration: A New Era for International Protection' (2018) 30 International Journal of Refugee Law 571
McDougall G, 'Minorities and the Discriminatory Denial or Deprivation of Citizenship. Report of the Independent Expert on Minority Issues (15 and 16 December 2008)' in Gay McDougall, *The First United Nations Mandate on Minority Issues* (Brill Nijhoff 2016)
McGee T, 'Statelessness Displaced: Update on Syria's Stateless Kurds' (2016) Statelessness Working Paper Series No. 2016/02 <www.institutesi.org/WP2016_02.pdf> accessed 26 September 2021
Mestmäcker EJ, 'On the Legitimacy of European Law' (1994) 58 Rabels Zeitschrift für ausländisches und internationales Privatrecht 615
Milton S, 'The Expulsion of the Polish Jews from Germany October 1938 to July 1939 (1984) 29 Leo Baeck Institute Yearbook 169
Mindus P, *European Citizenship after Brexit. Freedom of Movement and Rights of Residence* (Palgrave Studies in European Union Politics, Palgrave Macmillan 2017)
Modood T, 'Multiculturalism, Liberal Citizenship and National Identity: On British Muslims' in Montserrat Guibernau & John Rex (eds), *The Ethnicity Reader: Nationalism, Multiculturalism and Migration* (2nd edn, Polity Press 2010) 243–250
Moeyes P, *Buiten Schot. Nederland tijdens de Eerste Wereldoorlog 1914–1918* (digital ed, Uitgeverij De Arbeiderspers 2011)
Molnár T, 'Remembering the Forgotten: International Legal Regime on Protecting the Stateless Persons – Stocktaking and New Tendencies' (2014) 11 US-China Law Review 822
Molnár T, 'Moving Statelessness Forward on the International Agenda' (2014) 19 Tilburg Law Review 194
Molnár T, 'Stateless Persons under International Law and EU Law: A Comparative Analysis concerning Their Legal Status, with Particular Attention to the Added Value of the EU Legal Order' (2010) 51 Acta Juridica Hungarica 293
Müller JW, *Contesting Democracy. Political Ideas in Twentieth-Century Europe* (Yale University Press 2011)
Niessen J, 'The Participation of Immigrants in Political Processes and Institutions' in Kristen Jeffers (ed), Inclusive Democracy in Europe (EUDO/European University Institute 2012) <https://cadmus.eui.eu/bitstream/handle/1814/24334/eBook_InclusiveDemocracyInEurope2012.pdf?sequence=1&isAllowed=y> accessed 28 October 2021
O'Leary S & Tiilikainen T (eds), *Citizenship and Nationality Status in the New Europe* (Sweet & Maxwell 1998)
Oosterom-Staples H, 'The Triangular Relationship Between Nationality, EU Citizenship and Migration in EU Law: A Tale of Competing Competences' (2018) 65 Netherlands International Law Review 431
Oppenheim L, *International Law. A Treatise* (Vol 1: Peace; Longmans, Green and Co. 1905)
Orgard L & Lepoutre J (eds), 'Should EU Citizenship Be Disentangled from Member State Nationality?' (2019) EUI Working Paper RSCAS 2019/24 <https://cadmus.eui.eu/bitstream/handle/1814/62229RSCAS%202019_24rev2.pdf> accessed 17 October 2021
Osterhammel J, *The Transformation of the World: Global History of the Nineteenth Century* (transl Patrick Camiller, Princeton University Press 2014)
Owen D, 'On the Right to Have Nationality Rights: Statelessness, Citizenship and Human Rights' (2018) 65 Netherlands International Law Review 299
Panhuys HF van, *The Role of Nationality in International Law. An Outline* (PhD Thesis Leiden University, AW Sijthoff's Uitgeversmaatschappij 1959)

Parra J, 'Stateless Roma in the European Union: Reconciling the Doctrine of Sovereignty concerning Nationality Laws with International Agreements to Reduce and Avoid Statelessness' (2011) 34 Fordham International Law Journal 1666

Perry Clark Carey J, 'Some Aspects of Statelessness Since World War I' (1946) 40 The American Political Science Review 113

Pilgram L, *International Law and European Nationality Laws* (EUDO Citizenship Observatory 2011)

Polakiewicz J, 'Alternatives to Treaty-Making and Law-Making by Treaty and Expert Bodies in the Council of Europe' in Rüdiger Wolfrum & Volker Röbin (eds), *Developments of International Law in Treaty Making* (Springer 2005) 245–290

Polakiewicz J, *Treaty-making in the Council of Europe* (Council of Europe Publishing 1999)

Poulain M & Herm A, 'Central Population Registers as a Source of Demographic Statistics in Europe' (2013) 68 Population 183

Preuss L, 'International Law and Deprivation of Nationality' (1935) 23 Georgetown Law Journal 250

Raucea C, 'Citizenship Inverted: From Rights to Status?' (PhD, Tilburg University 2017)

Recalde Vela MJ, 'How Far has the Protection of the Right to Nationality under International Human Rights Law Progressed from 1923 until the Present Day?' (Master, Tilburg University 2014)

Recalde Vela MJ, Jaghai-Bajulaiye S & Vlieks C, 'The State of Statelessness Research: 5 Years Later (2019) 24 Tilburg Law Review 139

Rees L, *The Holocaust: A New History* (Viking / Penguin 2017)

Reinecke C, 'Staatliche Macht im Aufbau: Infrastrukturen der Kontrolle und die Ordnung der Migrationsverhältnisse im Kaiserreich' in Jochen Oltmer (ed), *Handbuch Staat und Migration in Deutschland seit dem 17. Jahrhundert* (De Gruyter 2015) 341–384

Rijken C, Waas L van, Gramatikov M & Brennan D, *The Nexus between Statelessness and Human Trafficking in Thailand* (Wolf Legal Publishers 2015)

Ringelheim J, 'Minority Rights in a Time of Multiculturalism – The Evolving Scope of the Framework Convention on the Protection of National Minorities (2010) 10 Human Rights Law Review 99

Roberts JM, *A General History of Europe. Europe 1880–1945* (ed Denys Hay, 2nd ed, Longman 1977)

Roberts JM, *A General History of Europe. Europe 1880–1945* (Longman 1970)

Rodrigues P, '*De facto* Staatloosheid of de Uitdaging van Onuitzetbaren' [*De facto* Statelessness or the Challenge of Undeportable Persons] (2013) 5/6 *Asiel & Migrantenrecht* 281

Royer A, *The Council of Europe* (Council of Europe Publishing 2010)

Rürup M, 'Lives in Limbo. Statelessness after Two World Wars' (2011) 49 Bulletin of the German Historical Institute 113

Rütte B von, 'Social Identity and the Right to Belong – The ECtHR's Judgment in *Hoti v. Croatia*' (2019) 14 Tilburg Law Review 147

Salwin LN, 'Uncertain Nationality Status of German Refugees' (1946) Minnesota Law Review 372

Sands P & Klein P, *Bowett's Law of International Institutions* (6th ed, Sweet & Maxwell 2009)

Sardelic J, 'Romani Minorities on the Margins of Post-Yugoslav Citizenship Regimes' (2013) Citsee Working Paper 2013/31 <http://papers.ssrn.com/sol3/papers.cfm?abstract_id=2388859> accessed 26 September 2021

Sawyer C & Blitz BK, *Statelessness in the European Union. Displaced, Undocumented, Unwanted* (Cambridge University Press 2011)
Schade H, 'The Draft European Convention on Nationality' (1995) 49 Austrian Journal of Public International Law 100
Schärer R, 'The Council of Europe and the Reduction of Statelessness' (2006) 25 Refugee Survey Quarterly 33
Schärer R, 'Statelessness in relation to State Succession: The Necessity of an Additional Instrument to the European Convention on Nationality' in CoE, *2nd European Conference on Nationality "Challenges to National and International Law on Nationality at the Beginning of the New Millennium" (Strasbourg, 8 and 9 October 2001): Proceedings* (CoE 2001) CONF/NAT (2001) PRO, 173–188
Schärer R, 'The European Convention on Nationality' (1997) 40 German Yearbook of International Law 438
Schütze R, 'EU Competences: Existence and Exercise' in Anthony Arnull & Damian Chalmers (eds), *The Oxford Handbook of European Union Law* (Oxford University Press 2015) 75–102
Schütze R, *Foreign Affairs and the EU Constitution: Selected Essays* (Cambridge University Press 2014)
Scott JB, 'Nationality: Jus Soli or Jus Sanguinis' (1930) 24 The American Journal of International Law 58
Scott JC, *Seeing Like a State. How Certain Schemes to Improve the Human Condition Have Failed* (Yale University Press 1998)
Seet M, 'The Origins of UNHCR's Global Mandate on Statelessness' (2016) 28 International Journal of Refugee Law 7
Selm J van, 'Stateless Roma in Macedonia' (2014) 32 Forced Migration Review 46
Shachar A, 'Earned Citizenship: Property Lessons for Immigration Reform' (2011) 23 Yale Journal of Law & the Humanities 110
Shachar A, Bauböck R, Bloemraad I & Vink M (eds), *The Oxford Handbook of Citizenship* (Oxford University Press 2017)
Shachar A, *The Birthright Lottery. Citizenship and Global Inequality* (Harvard University Press 2009)
Shaw J, 'The Constitutional Mosaic Across the Boundaries of the European Union: Citizenship Regimes in the New States of South Eastern Europe' in Neil Walker, Jo Shaw & Stephen Tierney (eds), *Europe's Constitutional Mosaic* (Hart Publishing 2011) 137–170
Shaw J, *The Transformation of Citizenship in the European Union. Electoral Rights and the Restructuring of Political Space* (Cambridge University Press 2007)
Siegelberg ML, *Statelessness. A Modern History* (Harvard University Press 2020)
Skran CM, *Refugees in Inter-War Europe. The Emergence of a Regime* (Clarendon Press 1995)
Skran CM, 'Profiles of the First Two High Commissioners' (1988) 1 Journal of Refugee Studies 277
Snel M, *Meester(s) over bronnen. Een empirische studie naar kwaliteitseisen, gevaren en onderzoekstechnieken die betrekking hebben op het brongebruik in academisch juridisch-dogmatisch onderzoek [Master(s on) resources]* (Boom juridisch 2016)
Spiro PJ, 'A New International Law of Citizenship' (2011) 105 American Journal of International Law 694
Stearms PN, *Human Rights in World History* (Routledge 2012)
Štiks I, *Nations and Citizens in Yugoslavia and the Post-Yugoslav States: One Hundred Years of Citizenship* (Bloomsbury 2015)

Strachan H, 'Introduction' in Hew Strachan (ed), *The Oxford Illustrated History of the First World War* (new ed, Oxford University Press 2014) 1–10

Swider K & Heijer M den, 'Why Union Law Can and Should Protect Stateless Persons' (2017) 19 European Journal of Migration and Law 101

Swider K & Vlieks C, 'Discriminatie van staatloze kinderen zonder wettig verblijf [Discrimination of Children without Legal Residence]' (2016) 4 Asiel & Migrantenrecht 168

Swider K, 'A Rights-Based Approach to Statelessness' (PhD, University of Amsterdam 2018)

Swider K, 'Protection and Identification of Stateless Persons through EU Law' (2014) ACELG Working Paper Series 2014–05

Swider K, 'Pre-Accession Changes to Residence-Based Naturalisation Requirements in Ten New EU Member States' (2011) EUI Working Papers RSCAS 2011/18 <https://cadmus.eui.eu/bitstream/handle/1814/16195/RSCAS_2011_18.corr.pdf?sequence=3&isAllowed=y> accessed 17 October 2021

Szreter S & Breckenridge K, *Registration and Recognition. Documenting the Person in World History* (Oxford University Press/British Academy 2012)

Torpey J, *The Invention of the Passport. Surveillance, Citizenship and the State* (Cambridge Studies in Law and Society, Cambridge University Press 2000)

Tucker J, 'Questioning *de facto* Statelessness by Looking at *de facto* Citizenship' (2014) 19 *Tilburg Law Review* 276

UNCHR, *The State of the World's Refugees 2000. Fifty Years of Humanitarian Action* (UNHCR/Oxford University Press 2000)

Verneuil M de, 'Nationality: Romani; Citizenship: European' (2016) Statelessness Working Paper Series No. 2016/03

Vink M & Groot GR de, 'Loss of Citizenship: Trends and Regulations in Europe' (EUDO Citizenship Report 2010) RSCAS/EUDO-CIT-Comp. 2010/4 <https://cadmus.eui.eu/handle/1814/19575> accessed 22 August 2021

Vink M, Schakel A, Reichely D, Chun Luk N & Groot GR de, 'The International Diffusion of Expatriate Dual Citizenship' (2019) 7 Migration Studies 362

Vishniak M, 'The Legal Status of Stateless Persons' in AG Duker (ed), *Pamphlet Series: Jews and the Post-War World* (No. 6, American Jewish Committee 1945)

Vlieks C, '*Tjebbes and Others v Minister van Buitenlandse Zaken*: A Next Step in European Union Case Law on Nationality Matters?' (2019) 24 Tilburg Law Review 142

Vlieks C, Hirsch Ballin E & Recalde Vela MJ, 'Solving Statelessness: Interpreting the Right to Nationality' (2017) 35 Netherlands Quarterly of Human Rights 158

Vonk OW & Vink M, 'Global Protection Against Statelessness Database' (EUI Research Data 2015) <https://cadmus.eui.eu/handle/1814/64601> accessed 3 October 2021

Vonk OW, Vink M & Groot GR de, 'Protection Against Statelessness: Trends and Regulations in Europe' (GLOBALCIT, EUDO Citizenship Observatory, Country Reports, 2013/01) <http://cadmus.eui.eu//handle/1814/30201> accessed 22 August 2021

Vonk OW, *Dual Nationality in the European Union. A Study on Changing Norms in Public and Private International Law and in the Municipal Laws of Four EU Member States* (Immigration and Asylum Law and Policy in Europe, Brill/Martinus Nijhoff Publishers 2012)

Vos M de, 'The European Court of Justice and the March towards Substantive Equality in European Union Anti-discrimination Law' (2020) 20 International Journal of Discrimination and the Law 62

Vries K de & Groenendijk K, 'Annotatie [Case Note] Ghoumid e.a. t. Frankrijk (EHRM, nr. 52273/16 e.v.)' (*European Human Rights Cases – Updates* 17 September 2020) https://www.ehrc-updates.nl/commentaar/210803?skip_boomportal_auth=1 accessed 4 July 2021

Waal T de, 'Conditional Belonging: A Legal-Philosophical Inquiry into Integration Requirements for Immigrants in Europe' (PhD, University of Amsterdam 2017)

Waas L van & Albarazi Z, 'Towards the Abolition of Gender Discrimination in Nationality Laws' (2014) 46 Forced Migration Review 49

Waas L van & Khanna M, *Solving Statelessness* (Wolf Legal Publishers 2016)

Waas L van, 'Stateless Children' in Jacqueline Bhabha, Jyothi Kanics & Daniel Senovila Hernández, *Research Handbook on Child Migration* (Edward Elgar Publishing 2018) 213–228

Waas L van, 'Study: Addressing the Human Rights Impact of Statelessness in the EU's External Action' (2014) EXPO/B/2014/2014/07 <https://www.europarl.europa.eu/RegData/etudes/STUD/2014/534983/IPOL_STU%282014%29534983_EN.pdf> accessed 17 October 2021

Waas L van, "Are We There Yet?' Emergence of Statelessness on the International Human Rights Agenda' (2014) 32 Netherlands Quarterly of Human Rights 342

Waas L van, 'Fighting Statelessness and Discriminatory Nationality Laws in Europe' (2012) 14 European Journal on Migration and Law 243

Waas L van, 'Statelessness: A 21st Century Challenge for Europe' (2009) 20 Security and Human Rights 133

Waas L van, Waas, *Nationality Matters. Statelessness under International Law* (School of Human Rights Research Series vol 29, Intersentia 2008)

Walle E van de, 'Historical Development of Civil Registration Systems: A European Perspective' (2018) UN Department of Economic and Social Affairs Population Division Technical Paper No. 2018/1 <https://www.un.org/en/development/desa/population/publications/pdf/technical/TP2018-1.pdf> accessed 22 August 2021

Wassenberg B, *History of the Council of Europe* (Council of Europe Publishing 2013)

Weinberg GL, *World War II. A Very Short Introduction* (Oxford University Press 2014)

Weis P, *Nationality and Statelessness in International Law* (2nd ed, Sijthoff & Noordhoff 1979)

Weiss A, 'Case Note: Mennesson v France and Advisory Opinion concerning the Recognition in Domestic Law of a Legal Parent–Child Relationship between a Child Born through a Gestational Surrogacy Arrangement Abroad and the Intended Mother' (2019) 1 Statelessness and Citizenship Review 343

Weissbrodt DS, *The Human Rights of Non-Citizens* (Oxford University Press 2008)

Worster WT, 'The Obligation to Grant Nationality to Stateless Children under Treaty Law' (2019) 24 Tilburg Law Review 204

Worster WT, 'The Obligation to Grant Nationality to Stateless Children under Customary International Law' (2019) 27 Michigan State International Law Review 441

Ziemele I & Schram GG, 'Article 15' in Gudmundur Alfredsson & Asbjørn Eide, *The Universal Declaration of Human Rights. A Common Standard of Achievement* (Martinus Nijhoff Publishers 1999) 297–323

Ziemele I, *State Continuity and Nationality: The Baltic States and Russia. Past, Present and Future as Defined by International Law* (Martinus Nijhoff Publishers 2005)

Zweig S, *Die Welt von Gestern. Erinnerungen eines Europäers* (Deutscher Bücherbund 1981) <https://www.projekt-gutenberg.org/zweig/weltgest/titlepage.html> accessed 12 September 2021

OTHER SOURCES (REPORTS, BLOG ARTICLES, WEBSITES AND OTHER SOURCES)

'Joint Position Paper on a Comprehensive Child Rights Strategy' (2020) <https://reliefweb.int/sites/reliefweb.int/files/resources/Joint-Position-Paper-in-the-Upcoming-Childs-Rights-Strategy.pdf> accessed 12 March 2021

Achmad C, 'European Court of Human Rights: France Violated Child Rights in International Surrogacy Cases' (*Leiden Law Blog*, 28 July 2014) <http://leidenlawblog.nl/articles/european-court-of-human-rights-france-violated-child-rights-in-internationa> accessed 3 July 2021

AU, 'Member States Experts Meeting on the Draft Protocol to the African Charter on Human and Peoples Rights on the Specific Aspects on the Right to a Nationality and the Eradication of Statelessness in Africa' (*African Union*, 7–11 May 2018) <https://au.int/en/newsevents/20180507/member-states-experts-meeting-draft-protocol-african-charter-human-and-peoples> accessed 5 September 2021

Badri K, 'EU Strategy on the Rights of the Child Marks an Important Step towards Addressing Childhood Statelessness' (*ENS Blog*, 8 April 2021) <https://www.statelessness.eu/updates/editorial/eu-strategy-rights-child-marks-important-step-towards-addressing-childhood> accessed 17 October 2021

Bakonyi A & Gyulai G, 'Awaiting – Stateless Lives in Hungary' (*ENS Blog*, 11 March 2021) <https://www.statelessness.eu/updates/blog/awaiting-stateless-lives-hungary> accessed 10 July 2021

Bible, Luk. 2:1–3

Bloom T, 'Statelessness and the Global Compact for Safe, Orderly and Regular Migration. Policy Brief' (ENS/OU 2018) <https://www.statelessness.eu/sites/default/files/2020–09/ENS_Statelessness_Global_Compact_Migration_policy-brief.pdf> accessed 5 September 2021

Brett R, 'Using the UN Human Rights Special Procedures to address statelessness' (*ENS Blog*, 1 October 2015) <https://www.statelessness.eu/blog/using-un-human-rights-special-procedures-address-statelessness> accessed 4 September 2021

Bundesarchiv, *Memorial Book: Victims of the Persecution of Jews under the National Socialist Tyranny in Germany 1933 – 1945*, The Expulsion of Polish Jews from the German Reich 1938/1939 and their records <https://www.bundesarchiv.de/gedenkbuch/zwangsausweisung.html.en?page=1> accessed 12 September 2021

Cabral P, Protecting the right to a nationality for children of same-sex couples in the EU – A key issue before the CJEU in V.M.A. v Stolichna Obshtina (C-490/20)' (*ENS Blog*, 3 February 2021) <https://www.statelessness.eu/updates/blog/protecting-right-nationality-children-same-sex-couples-eu-key-issue-cjeu-vma-v> accessed 17 October 2021

Carozza P, 'European Law' in *Encyclopedia Britannica* <https://www.britannica.com/topic/European-law#ref992078> accessed 22 August 2021

Carter Center & OHCHR, 'Human Rights and Election Standards: A Plan of Action' (December 2017) <https://www.ohchr.org/Documents/Issues/Democracy/Elections/POA_EN.pdf> accessed 5 September 2021

CDCJ, 'Nationality' <https://www.coe.int/en/web/cdcj/completed-work/standard-setting/nationality> accessed 26 May 2021

CDCJ, 'Standard Setting – Completed Activities' <https://www.coe.int/en/web/cdcj/standard-setting-completed-activities> accessed 26 May 2021

CDCJ, 'Statelessness' <https://www.coe.int/en/web/cdcj/statelessness> accessed 26 May 2021

CoE & FRA, 'Handbook on European Non-discrimination Law' (2010) <https://fra.europa.eu/sites/default/files/fra_uploads/1510-fra-case-law-handbook_en.pdf> accessed 21 October 2021

CoE website <https://www.coe.int/en/web/portal/home> accessed 24 May 2021

CoE, 'About Conventions in the Council of Europe Treaty Series (CETS)' <www.coe.int/en/web/conventions/about-treaties> accessed 24 May 2021

CoE, 'Adopted Texts (Roma and Travellers)' <https://www.coe.int/en/web/roma-and-travellers/adopted-texts> accessed 7 October 2021

CoE, 'Advisory Committee on the Framework Convention for the Protection of National Minorities' <https://www.coe.int/en/web/minorities/advisory-committee> accessed 28 May 2021

CoE, 'CoE Strategic Action Plan for Roma and Traveller Inclusion (2020–2025)' (2020) <https://rm.coe.int/coe-strategic-action-plan-for-roma-and-traveller-inclusion-en/16809fe0d0> accessed 7 October 2021

CoE, 'Committee of Ministers – Documents' <www.coe.int/en/web/cm/documents> accessed 24 May 2021

CoE, 'ECRI – European Commission against Racism and Intolerance' (2019) <https://rm.coe.int/leaflet-ecri-2019/168094b101> accessed 28 May 2021

CoE, 'European Committee on Legal Co-operation' <https://www.coe.int/en/web/cdcj/home> accessed 24 May 2021

CoE, 'Ministerial Conferences' <https://www.coe.int/en/web/human-rights-rule-of-law/ministerial-conferences> accessed 1 July 2021

CoE, 'Parliamentary Assembly – Documents' <https://pace.coe.int/en/pages/official-documents> accessed 24 May 2021

CoE, 'Structure' <https://www.coe.int/en/web/about-us/structure> accessed 24 May 2021

CoE, 'The Venice Commission of the Council of Europe' <https://www.venice.coe.int/WebForms/pages/?p=01_Presentation&lang=EN> accessed 24 May 2021

CoE, 'Treaty Office' <www.coe.int/en/web/dlapil/treaty-office> accessed 24 May 2021

Council of the EU, 'Press Release: Council Adopts Conclusions on Statelessness' (2015) <https://www.consilium.europa.eu/en/press/press-releases/2015/12/04/council-adopts-conclusions-on-statelessness/> accessed 29 October 2021

Delegation of the EU to the UN, 'High-level Meeting on the Rule of Law at the National and International Levels. Pledge Registration Form' (19 September 2012) A.4 <https://www.un.org/ruleoflaw/files/Pledges%20by%20the%20European%20Union.pdf> accessed 17 October 2021

Dembour MB, 'Ramadan v. Malta: When Will the Strasbourg Court Understand that Nationality is a Core Human Rights Issue?' (*Strasbourg Observers*, 22 July 2016) <https://strasbourgobservers.com/2016/07/22/ramadan-v-malta-when-will-the-strasbourg-court-understand-that-nationality-is-a-core-human-rights-issue/> accessed 4 July 2021

EC, 'The EU Strategy on the Rights of the Child and the European Child Guarantee' (2021) <https://ec.europa.eu/info/policies/justice-and-fundamental-rights/rights-child/eu-strategy-rights-child-and-european-child-guarantee_en#the-eu-strategy-on-the-rights-of-the-child> accessed 17 October 2021

EC, 'Investor citizenship schemes: European Commission opens infringements against Cyprus and Malta for "selling" EU citizenship' (2020) <https://ec.europa.eu/commission/presscorner/detail/en/ip_20_1925> accessed 3 January 2022

ECRE/Gábor Gyulai, 'The Right to a Nationality of Refugee Children Born in the EU and the Relevance of the EU Charter of Fundamental Rights' (2017) <https://www.ecre.org/wp-content/uploads/2016/12/refugee-children-nationality-LEAP-leaflet.pdf> accessed 17 October 2021

EMN <https://ec.europa.eu/home-affairs/what-we-do/networks/european_migration_network_en> accessed 17 October 2021

EMN, 'Statelessness in the European Union' (2020) EMN Inform <https://ec.europa.eu/home-affairs/system/files/2020-01/00_eu_inform_statelessness_en.pdf> accessed 17 October 2021

EMN, 'Pathways to Citizenship for Third-Country Nationals in the EU. EMN Synthesis Report for the EMN Study 2019' (2020) <https://emn.ie/wp-content/uploads/2020/07/2020_eu_emn_study_synthesis_report_citizenship_final_en_0.pdf> accessed 17 October 2021

EMN, 'EMN Platform on Statelessness: A Progress Report' (2017) <https://emn.ie/files/p_20180124121544EMN%20Platform%20on%20Statelessness_Progress%20Report_final_2018.pdf> accessed 17 October 2021

EMN, 'Statelessness in the EU' (2016) EMN Inform <https://emn.ie/files/p_201702100930222016_emn_inform_on_statelessness.pdf> accessed 17 October 2021

EMN/EU Platform on Statelessness <https://ec.europa.eu/home-affairs/pages/page/platform-statelessness_en> accessed 17 October 2021

ENS, 'Statelessness Index' (2021) <https://index.statelessness.eu/> accessed 3 October 2021

ENS, 'Statelessness Index Thematic Briefing: Statelessness Determination and Protection in Europe: Good Practice, Challenges and Risks' (ENS 2021) <https://www.statelessness.eu/sites/default/files/2021-09/ENS-Statelessness_determination_and_protection_in_Europe-Sep_2021.pdf> accessed 26 September 2021

ENS, 'Statelessness and the EU Pact on Asylum and Migration: Analysis and Recommendations' (2021) <https://www.statelessness.eu/sites/default/files/2021-01/ENS-Statelessness_and_the_EU_Pact_on_Asylum_and_Migration-Jan_2021_1.pdf> accessed 17 October 2021

ENS, 'Position Paper: "Even before the pandemic, statelessness has been invisible" – Involving stateless people in Europe's COVID-19 response' (ENS 2020) <https://www.statelessness.eu/resources/even-pandemic-statelessness-has-been-invisible-involving-stateless-people-europe-s-covid> accessed 26 September 2021

ENS, 'Protecting Stateless Persons from Arbitrary Detention: An Agenda for Change' (ENS 2017) <https://www.statelessness.eu/sites/www.statelessness.eu/files/attachments/resources/ENS_LockeInLimbo_Detention_Agenda_online.pdf> accessed 3 January 2022

ENS, 'Protecting Stateless Persons from Arbitrary Detention in the United Kingdom' (ENS 2016) 8 <https://www.statelessness.eu/sites/www.statelessness.eu/files/ENS_Detention_Reports_UK.pdf> accessed 22 August 2021

ENS, 'No Child Should Be Stateless' (ENS 2015) <https://www.statelessness.eu/sites/www.statelessness.eu/files/ENS_NoChildStateless_final.pdf> accessed 22 August 2021

ENS, 'Preventing Childhood Statelessness in Europe: Gaps, Issues and Good Practices' (ENS 2014) <https://www.statelessness.eu/updates/publication/preventing-childhood-statelessness-europe-issues-gaps-and-good-practices> accessed 3 July 2021

ENS, 'Still Stateless, Still Suffering. Why Europe Must Act Now to Protect Stateless Persons' (ENS 2014) <www.statelessness.eu/sites/www.statelessness.eu/files/ENS_Still_Stateless_Still_Suffering_online%20version_2.pdf> accessed 22 August 2021

ENS, 'Strategic Litigation: An Obligation for Statelessness Determination under the European Convention on Human Rights?' (2014) ENS Discussion Paper 09/14 <https://www.statelessness.eu/updates/publication/obligation-statelessness-determination-under-european-convention-human-rights> accessed 17 October 2021

ENS, 'Mr. Nils Muižnieks, the Council of Europe's Commissioner for Human Rights, speaks exclusively to ENS' (*ENS Blog*, 15 January 2014) <https://www.statelessness.eu/updates/

news/mr-nils-muiznieks-council-europes-commissioner-human-rights-speaks-exclusively-ens> accessed 26 May 2021

ENS, 'Statelessness Determination and the Protection Status of Stateless Persons. A Summary Guide of Good Practices and Factors to Consider When Designing National Determination and Protection Mechanisms' (ENS 2013) <www.statelessness.eu/sites/www.statelessness.eu/files/attachments/resources/Statelessness%20determination%20and%20the%20protection%20status%20of%20stateless%20persons%20ENG.pdf> accessed 10 July 2021.

ERRC, 'Roma Belong – Discrimination, Statelessness and Marginalisation of Roma in the Western Balkans and Ukraine' (*errc.org*, 26 October 2017) <www.errc.org/uploads/upload_en/file/roma-belong.pdf> accessed 22 August 2021

ERT & Institute of Human Rights and Peace Studies, Mahidol University, 'The Human Rights of Stateless Rohingya in Thailand' (February 2014) <www.equalrightstrust.org/ertdocumentbank/The%20Human%20Rights%20of%20Stateless%20Rohingya%20in%20Thailand(small).pdf> accessed 26 September 2021

ERT, 'Guidelines to Protect Stateless Persons from Arbitrary Detention' (2021) <https://www.equalrightstrust.org/ertdocumentbank/guidelines%20complete.pdf> accessed 17 October 2021

ERT, 'Burning Homes, Sinking Lives. A Situation Report on Violence Against Stateless Rohingya in Myanmar and their *Refoulement* from Bangladesh' (June 2012) <www.equalrightstrust.org/ertdocumentbank/The%20Equal%20Rights%20Trust%20-%20Burning%20Homes%20Sinking%20Lives.pdf> accessed 26 September 2021

ERT, 'Unravelling Anomaly. Detention, Discrimination and the Protection Needs of Stateless Persons' (July 2010) <www.equalrightstrust.org/ertdocumentbank/UNRAVELLING%20ANOMALY%20small%20file.pdf> accessed 22 August 2021.

Ferschtman M, 'Litigating for the stateless – a bumpy, but steady road upwards (*ENS Blog*, 13 July 2013) <https://www.statelessness.eu/updates/blog/litigating-stateless-bumpy-steady-road-upwards> accessed 4 July 2021

FRA, 'Detention of Third-Country Nationals in Return Procedures' (2010) 25 <https://fra.europa.eu/sites/default/files/fra_uploads/1306-FRA-report-detention-december-2010_EN.pdf> accessed 17 October 2021

GLOBALCIT Global Database on Modes of Acquisition of Citizenship (2017) <https://globalcit.eu/acquisition-citizenship/> accessed 17 October 2021

Gov.uk, 'Types of British nationality' <https://www.gov.uk/types-of-british-nationality/british-citizenship> accessed 22 August 2021

Guterres A, 'Secretary-General's Remarks at Intergovernmental Conference to Adopt the Global Compact for Migration' (10 December 2018) <https://www.un.org/sg/en/content/sg/statement/2018–12–10/secretary-generals-remarks-intergovernmental-conference-adopt-the-global-compact-for-migration-delivered> accessed 5 September 2021

Institut de Droit International <https://www.idi-iil.org/en/> accessed 19 September 2021

ISI & Norwegian Refugee Council, 'Understanding Statelessness in the Syria Refugee Context. Research Report' (2016) <https://www.nrc.no/globalassets/pdf/reports/understanding-statelessness-in-the-syria-refugee-context.pdf> accessed 26 September 2021

ISI, 'Together We Can: The COVID-19 Impact on Stateless People & a Roadmap for Change' (ISI 2021) <https://files.institutesi.org/together_we_can_report_2021.pdf> accessed 26 September 2021

ISI, 'Sustainable Development Goal 16.9. Legal Identity, Nationality & Statelessness' (2018) Statelessness Essentials No. 9 <https://files.institutesi.org/Legal-identity.pdf> accessed 5 September 2021

ISI, 'Statelessness & Human Rights: The Convention on the Elimination of All Forms of Discrimination against Women' (2018) Statelessness Essentials No. 7 <www.institutesi.org/statelessness_and_CEDAW.pdf> accessed 4 September 2021

ISI, 'Statelessness & Human Rights: The Convention on the Rights of the Child' (2018) Statelessness Essentials No. 6 <https://files.institutesi.org/statelessness-and-CRC.pdf> accessed 4 September 2021

ISI, 'Nationality and Statelessness in the UPR' (2017) <www.statelessnessandhumanrights.org/upr-universal-periodic-review/nationality-statelessness-in-the-upr> accessed 4 September 2021

ISI, 'Nationality and Statelessness under the CRC' (2017) <www.statelessnessandhumanrights.org/crc/nationality-statelessness-under-the-crc> accessed 4 September 2021

ISI, 'Policy Brief: Arbitrary Deprivation of Nationality and Denial of Consular Services to Turkish Citizens (July 2017) <https://files.institutesi.org/policy-brief-Turkey-arbitrary-deprivation-of-nationality_2017.pdf> accessed 26 September 2021

ISI, 'Statelessness, Human Rights and the Sustainable Development Agenda. A Working Paper' (2017) <www.institutesi.org/SDG_working-paper2017.pdf> accessed 4 September 2021

ISI, 'Counting the World's Stateless: Reflections on Statistical Reporting on Statelessness' in UNHCR, 'UNHCR Statistical Yearbook 2013' (2014) 41–47

ISI Database on Statelessness & Human Rights <https://database.institutesi.org> accessed 4 September 2021

Kostic I, 'Discrimination and Statelessness – the Roma in the Western Balkans' (*Statelessness.eu*, ENS Kick-Off Seminar 19–21 November 2012) <www.statelessness.eu/sites/www.statelessness.eu/files/attachments/resources/ENS%20kick-off%20seminar%202012%20-%20Discrimination%20and%20statelessness,%20the%20Roma%20in%20the%20Western%20Balkans.pdf> accessed 26 September 2021

Krüger HC (Deputy Secretary General of the CoE), 'Opening Speech' in CoE, *1st European Conference on Nationality: Trends and Developments in National and International Law on Nationality – Proceedings* (Strasbourg, 18–19 October 1999, CONF/NAT PRO 1)

Lepoutre J, 'Ghoumid and others v. France: The Grey Hole of Nationality Revocation' (*GLOBALCIT Blog*, 5 August 2020) <https://globalcit.eu/ghoumid-and-others-v-france-the-grey-hole-of-nationality-revocation/> accessed 4 July 2021

Lexico – powered by Oxford University Press <https://www.lexico.com/definition/nationality> accessed 22 August 2021

Meijers Committee, 'Policy Brief on Differential Treatment of Citizens with Dual or Multiple Nationality and the Prohibition of Discrimination' (2020) <https://www.commissie-meijers.nl/wp-content/uploads/2020/12/cm2016_policy_brief_on_differential_treatment_of_citizens_with_dual_or_multiple_nationality_and_the_prohibition_of_discrimination.pdf accessed 24 October 2021> accessed 24 October 2021

Meijers Committee, 'A Proposal for an EU Directive on the Identification and Protection of Stateless Persons' (2014) <https://www.commissie-meijers.com/sites/all/files/cm1410_proposal_for_an_eu_directive_on_the_identification_and_the_protection_of_stateless_persons.pdf> accessed 17 October 2021

Minority Safepack Initiative <www.minority-safepack.eu/> accessed 28 October 2021

Molnár T, 'The Charter of Fundamental Rights and the Protection of Stateless People in the EU: A Dormant Giant?' (*ENS Blog*, 28 September 2017) <https://www.statelessness.eu/updates/blog/charter-fundamental-rights-and-protection-stateless-people-eu-dormant-giant> accessed 17 October 2021

Muižnieks N, 'Stateless but Not Rightless: Improving the Protection of Stateless Persons in Europe', Keynote Speech at the Conference organized by UNHCR and ENS in Strasbourg, 8 April 2014, CommDH/Speech(2014)6

OHCHR, IOM, UNHCR & WHO, 'The Rights and Health of Refugees, Migrants and Stateless Must Be Protected in COVID-19 Response' (*UNHCR*, 31 March 2020) <https://www.unhcr.org/news/press/2020/3/5e836f164/rights-health-refugees-migrants-stateless-must-protected-covid-19-response.html> accessed 26 September 2021

Open Society Foundations, 'Litigation: Zhao v Netherlands' (2017) <https://www.opensocietyfoundations.org/litigation/zhao-v-netherlands> accessed 3 January 2022

Pluym L, 'Mennesson v. France and Labassee v. France: Surrogate Motherhood Across Borders' (*Strasbourg Observers*, 16 July 2014) <https://strasbourgobservers.com/2014/07/16/mennesson-v-france-and-labassee-v-france-surrogate-motherhood-across-borders/> accessed 3 July 2021

Puppinck G, 'Status of the Recommendations of the Committee of Ministers in the Legal Field of Council of Europe – Synthesis' (European Centre for Law and Justice, March 27, 2012) <http://eclj.org/PDF/status-of-the-recommendations-of-the-committee-of-ministers-in-the-legal-field-of-the-council-of-europe%E2%80%93synthesis-english.pdf> accessed 26 May 2021

Schlüter A, 'Biao v. Denmark: Grand Chamber Ruling on Ethnic Discrimination Might Leave Couples Seeking Family Reunification Worse Off' (*Strasbourg Observers* 13 June 2016) <https://strasbourgobservers.com/2016/06/13/biao-v-denmark-grand-chamber-ruling-on-ethnic-discrimination-might-leave-couples-seeking-family-reunification-worse-off/> accessed 10 July 2021

Swider K, 'Hoti v. Croatia – A Landmark Decision by the European Court of Human Rights on the Residence Rights of a Stateless Person' (*ENS Blog*, 3 May 2018) <https://www.statelessness.eu/updates/blog/hoti-v-croatia-landmark-decision-european-court-human-rights-residence-rights> accessed 10 July 2021

Tryfonidou A, 'The Cross-Border Recognition of the Parent-Child Relationship in Rainbow Families under EU Law: A Critical View of the ECJ's V.M.A. ruling' (*European Law Blog*, 21 December 2021) <https://europeanlawblog.eu/2021/12/21/the-cross-border-recognition-of-the-parent-child-relationship-in-rainbow-families-under-eu-law-a-critical-view-of-the-ecjs-v-m-a-ruling/> accessed 3 January 2022

UN Special Procedures <https://www.ohchr.org/EN/HRBodies/SP/Pages/Welcomepage.aspx> accessed 4 September 2021

UN Treaty Collection <https://treaties.un.org/Pages/Home.aspx?clang=_en> accessed 3 January 2022

UNHCR (Hugh Massey), 'UNHCR and de facto Statelessness' (April 2010) LPPR/2010/01 <www.refworld.org/docid/4bbf387d2.html> accessed 22 August 2021

UNHCR & CoE, 'Identifying and Protecting Stateless Persons in Europe – Technical Meeting of Experts Issue Paper' (2021) <https://rm.coe.int/briefing-paper-session-1-with-coverpage-en-unhcr/1680a3e6a5> accessed 27 September 2021

UNHCR & CoE, 'Realising the Right of Every Child to a Nationality in Europe – Technical Meeting of Experts Issue Paper' (2021) <https://rm.coe.int/session-2-thematic-paper-coverpage-en-final/1680a3e6a1> accessed 27 September 2021

UNHCR & IPU, *Nationality and Statelessness. Handbook for Parliamentarians No. 22* (2nd ed, UNHCR 2014)

UNHCR, 'Global Trends. Forced Displacement in 2020' (UNHCR 2021) <https://www.unhcr.org/60b638e37/unhcr-global-trends-2020> accessed 22 August 2021

UNHCR, 'Good Practice Papers – Action 6: Establishing Statelessness Determination Procedures for the Protection of Stateless Persons' (2020) <https://www.refworld.org/docid/5f203d0e4.html> accessed 10 July 2021

UNHCR, 'UNHCR Statistical Reporting on Statelessness' (UNHCR Statistics Technical Series 2019/1) <https://www.unhcr.org/statistics/unhcrstats/5d9e182e7/unhcr-statistical-reporting-statelessness.html> accessed 22 August 2021

UNHCR, 'Stateless in Europe. Ordinary People in Extraordinary Circumstances' (2018) <https://www.refworld.org/docid/5aa79f9d4.html> accessed 17 October 2021

UNHCR, 'Stateless Persons in Detention: A Tool for Their Identification and Enhanced Protection' (UNHCR 2017) <https://www.refworld.org/docid/598adacd4.html> accessed 3 January 2022

UNHCR, 'Good Practices Paper – Action 7: Ensuring Birth Registration for the Prevention of Statelessness' (2017) <https://www.refworld.org/docid/5a0ac8f94.html> accessed 4 September 2021

UNHCR, 'The Sustainable Development Goals and Addressing Statelessness. Briefing Note' (2017) <https://www.refworld.org/pdfid/58b6e3364.pdf> accessed 5 September 2021

UNHCR, 'Identifying Stateless Persons in the European Union. Intervention by Vincent Cochetel, UNHCR Director of the Bureau for Europe, on the occasion of the meeting of the Strategic Committee on Immigration, Frontiers and Asylum in Brussels, 25 April 2017' (2017) <https://www.refworld.org/pdfid/5911d8c34.pdf> accessed 17 October 2021

UNHCR, 'I Am Here, I Belong. The Urgent Need to End Childhood Statelessness' (UNHCR 2015) <www.unhcr.org/ibelong/wp-content/uploads/2015-10-StatelessReport_ENG15-web.pdf> accessed 3 July 2021

UNHCR, 'Global Action Plan to End Statelessness' (4 November 2014) <www.unhcr.org/statelesscampaign2014/Global-Action-Plan-eng.pdf> accessed 4 September 2021

UNHCR, 'Storytelling: Railya' (2011) <www.youtube.com/watch?v=GUEfwLtBcUY> accessed 17 October 2021

UNHCR, 'Mapping Statelessness in the Netherlands' (2011) 16 <https://www.refworld.org/docid/4eef65da2.html> accessed 26 September 2021

UNHCR, 'Statelessness: An Analytical Framework for Prevention, Reduction and Protection' (2008) <www.refworld.org/docid/49a28afb2.html> accessed 22 August 2021

UNHCR, '#IBelong Campaign', <https://www.unhcr.org/ibelong/> accessed 4 September 2021

UNTC <https://treaties.un.org/pages/Home.aspx?clang=_en> accessed 3 January 2022

Vlieks C & Swider K, 'The *Jus Sanguinis* Bias of Europe and What It Means for Childhood Statelessness' (*ENS Blog*, 17 June 2015) <www.statelessness.eu/blog/jus-sanguinis-bias-europe-and-what-it-means-childhood-statelessness> accessed 22 August 2021

Waas L van, 'A 100-year (Hi)Story of Statelessness' (*Peace Palace Library Blog*, 25 August 2016) <https://peacepalacelibrary.nl/blog/2016/100-year-history-statelessness> accessed 4 September 2021

Women's Refugee Commission & Tilburg University, 'Our Motherland, Our Country. Gender Discrimination and Statelessness in the Middle East and North Africa (June 2013) <www.refworld.org/docid/51c02a084.html> accessed 26 September 2021

Human Rights Research Series

The Human Rights Research Series' central research theme is the nature and meaning of international standards in the field of human rights, their application and promotion in the national legal order, their interplay with national standards, and the international supervision of such application. Anyone directly involved in the definition, study, implementation, monitoring, or enforcement of human rights will find this series an indispensable reference tool.
The Series is published together with the world famous Netherlands Network for Human Rights Research (formerly School of Human Rights Research), a joint effort by human rights researchers in the Netherlands.

 For previous volumes in the series, please visit http://shr.intersentia.com.

Published titles within the Series:

87. Kasim Balarabe, *Realising the Right to Water and Sanitation in Nigeria*
    ISBN 978-1-78068-901-2
88. Leonie Huijbers, *Process-based Fundamental Rights Review*
    ISBN 978-1-78068-887-9
89. Vincent Willem Vleugel, *Culture in the State Reporting Procedure of the UN Human Rights Treaty Bodies. How the HRC, the CESCR and the CEDAWCee use human rights as a sword to protect and promote culture, and as a shield to protect against harmful culture*
    ISBN 978-1-83970-006-4
90. Laura Íñigo Álvarez, *Towards a Regime of Responsibility of Armed Groups in International Law*
    ISBN 978-1-83970-004-0
91. Getahun A. Mosissa, *A Re-examination of Economic, Social and Cultural Rights in a Political Society in the Light of the Principle of Human Dignity*
    ISBN 978-1-78068-987-6
92. Veronika Flegar, *The Transformative Potential of a Vulnerability Focus in Basic Assistance Policies*
    ISBN 978-1-83970-039-2
93. Marieke J. Hopman, *Looking at Law through Children's Eyes*
    ISBN 978-1-83970-101-6
94. Daniela Heerdt, *Blurred Lines of Responsibility and Accountability. Human Rights Abuses at Mega-Sporting Events*
    ISBN 978-1-83970-117-7
95. Annick Pijnenburg, *At the Frontiers of State Responsibility. Socio-economic Rights and Cooperation on Migration*
    ISBN 978-1-83970-148-1
96. Amy Weatherburn, *Labour Exploitation in Human Trafficking Law*
    ISBN 978-1-83970-154-2

www.ingramcontent.com/pod-product-compliance
Ingram Content Group UK Ltd.
Pitfield, Milton Keynes, MK11 3LW, UK
UKHW051921100926
8556IPUK00021B/1299